HORIZON
IS WHERE
HEAVEN AND EARTH
MEET

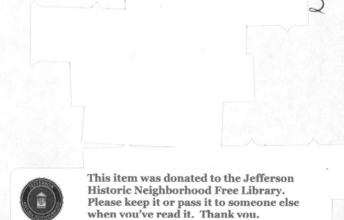

HORIZON IS WHERE HEAVEN AND EARTH MEET

A LOVE STORY THAT CROSSED BOUNDARIES

DIANA WILLIAMS

BANTAM BOOKS
SYDNEY • AUCKLAND • TORONTO • NEW YORK • LONDON

Horizon is Where Heaven and Earth Meet
A Bantam Book

First published in Australia and New Zealand
in 2001 by Bantam

National Library of Australia
Cataloguing-in-Publication Entry

Williams, Diana 1946– .
Horizon is where heaven and earth meet: a love story that crossed boundaries.
ISBN 1 86325 2118

1. Williams, Diana, 1946– . 2. Williams, Ron.
3. Aborigines, Australian—Biography. 4. Missionaries—
Australia—Biography. 5. Interethnic marriage—Australia.
I. Title
306.8450994

Transworld Publishers,
a division of Random House Australia Pty Ltd
20 Alfred Street, Milsons Point, NSW 2061
http://www.randomhouse.com.au

Random House New Zealand Limited
18 Poland Road, Glenfield, Auckland

Transworld Publishers
a division of The Random House Group Ltd
61-63 Uxbridge Road, London W5 5SA

Random House Inc
1540 Broadway, New York, New York 10036

Edited by Jude McGee
Front cover photograph by Louise Lister Photography Pty Ltd
Back cover photograph by Claver Carroll/Austral
Typeset by Midland Typesetters, Maryborough, Victoria
Printed by Griffin Press, Netley, South Australia

10 9 8 7 6 5 4 3 2 1

I dedicate this book to the people of Australia
on whose soil and in whose faces I have learned so much.

The pain of the earth and the joy of the heavens meet at the horizon of life. It is at the horizon that there is balance.

'There are heavenly bodies and there are earthly bodies; but the splendour of the heavenly bodies is one kind, and the splendour of the earthly bodies is another. The sun has one kind of splendour, the moon another and the stars another; and star differs from star in splendour.'

1 Corinthians 15: 40–41

CONTENTS

✺

ACKNOWLEDGMENTS

Perfect timing is like a flash of light that zips across the night sky and is swiftly captured by the upward gaze. The conception of this book is due to perfect timing. My friend, publisher Kevin Weldon, gazed for a moment along the shelves of a newly-opened bookstore in Sydney and caught the eye of a publishing-world colleague and literary agent, Selwa Anthony. 'Have I got a story for you,' he said, as he held two of her recently nurtured titles in his hands.

A few days later, during one of my rare visits to Sydney, I received a phone call that would change the course of my days for the next two years. 'How would you like to write a book?' asked Selwa. After recovering from the shock, then chatting together over lunch at her home while we watched the sparrows and finches play through the trees that sheltered the back verandah, I was launched into a long-awaited dream of writing my story.

I want to thank Selwa for her genuine care, support and honesty throughout the writing process. Not only have you been my guide through the incredible world of publishing, but you have also become my friend. I have never found another woman who has cared for her dogs as much as I have cared for mine, either. We were meant to meet.

My husband Ron had urged me to write a book in one of his many letters during our courtship. What on earth would I have written about back then? I thank you, Ron, for urging me to keep climbing mountains with you for almost two decades and for being there when I wanted to give up. This is your story too.

I especially thank all of my Aboriginal family and friends who have been my teachers, have chuckled at my mistakes but still loved me, and who have drawn me in to share their lives. Gabrielle, thanks for your stories. Emily, your love for me never stopped and now you are singing with the angels in heaven. Rosie, I am proud to have you as my sister. You must have shaken your head at this 'whitefella' relative of yours many times. Noelene, thanks for giving me your confidence and Michelle, thanks for your trust. Tim and Mary, you have been honest with me, shared some of your secrets and I appreciate your gift of friendship. To Richard and

Sandra, my very close mates, who cried with me when my mother died—I'll never forget that. Geoffrey, you've always remembered to bring us a goanna and kept us laughing. Greg, what can I say? You've been a friend through all the rough roads and I thank you for stepping into Uncle Ben's place as a brother for Ron. God bless you and Carol for all that you have done for us.

We have had many special friends along the Australian roads who have given us their time, their tears and their prayers: Noel and Olive, Wilf and Beth, Denzil and Shirley, Ray and Sharon, Roger and Helen, Kevin and Ann, Courtney and Pat, Gary and Elaine, Keith and Margaret, and, more recently, all our friends in Canberra.

To my heart-sister, Glenda Weldon, who has provided me with gallons of 'real' coffee, views of Sydney Harbour Bridge, and bagels and cream cheese sprinkled with memories of New York City—thank you for listening to my urges to break away from mediocrity.

I have found that writing a book is not a singular task, but a collective act of love. To Arleen, thank you for your many hours of reading and 'push' when I thought no one would want to read about my crazy life. You are special.

To everyone at Random House—you are a wonderful bunch of midwives, nurturing the birth of this 'baby'. Fiona, you are tops. You have stood by me from the beginning when Ron and I first sat around the oval table at your offices. We must have looked like we just crawled out of the bush. Alex, your enthusiasm has been contagious from the very beginning. Jo, thanks so much for your gentle touch and willingness to sit with us for hours on the side of sand dunes at Kurnell, waiting for the 'right' light.

To my editor Jude McGee—without you I couldn't have found my way around the 'waterholes'. Thanks for your sensitivity toward my life experiences, for your structural eye and encouraging me to dig deeper for what was really important to share with others. You've given me a lifetime of learning and precious gems for the future.

I especially want to thank my daughter, Lydia, for patiently watching her mother spend hours at the computer, sometimes not even hearing her questions. You have been my greatest teacher, Lydia, and I thank you for the privilege of being your mother.

And finally, I thank God for the journey I have taken throughout Australia, for the incredible gift of His people everywhere and for the opportunity to share the road with them.

CHAPTER 1

A Wedding at Skull Creek

There was going to be a wedding at Skull Creek.

On the morning of 28 May 1984, I walked along the edges of the dry creek bed as I did every day to greet the creek dwellers before the heat of the sun began to warm the dusty red earth. Today, as I edged my way through mounds of sand, rocky terrain and dry mulga bushes, I was reading a letter from my father, which had arrived on the weekly mail plane the day before.

'I want to extend my love and prayers to you and Ron for a marriage made in heaven. Surely the most imaginative fiction writer would not come up with a plot involving my dear daughter from New York City and a bush Aborigine becoming husband and wife among the flora and fauna of Western Australia. You have my blessing,' he wrote.

'Yes,' I mused. 'Maybe it is fiction, stranger than truth.'

But truth it was. My wedding was going to take place at Skull Creek, on the outskirts of the small mining town of Laverton, which is poised at the end of the bitumen road that runs through the area of Western Australia known as the goldfields.

The edge of this creek bed had been my home for almost a year and a half. I had left the United States with a small group of missionaries.

We had been showered with prayers, gifts and hopes that we would be able to do something useful for the tribal people of Australia. With packs on our back, a few changes of clothes, guitars and books, we had come with a desire to make a positive difference to people's lives. We were what *Time* Magazine once called the 'new missionary', intent on learning the culture and the language, careful not to propagate western ways and with a willingness to become absorbed into a simple lifestyle.

When we had arrived in Kalgoorlie and met some of the seasoned workers among the Aboriginal missions, a gracious couple had offered their small desert block, complete with a fresh-water well around which we could construct our camp. During the summer months we had struggled to set up a few tents along the creek bed, had laboriously cleaned the well of dead snakes and broken bottles and had erected a hot water system from a variety of pipes and a 44-gallon drum precariously perched over a fire. It was around that fire and many others like it that we began to meet our fellow creek dwellers.

Everyone whom I had grown to love in Australia was associated with Laverton and Skull Creek. The Aboriginal families who lived in town and worked in the various mines which dotted the landscape had grown up in that region, and had family histories that spanned generations upon generations. Traditional Aborigines who lived in the outlying desert communities had long used Laverton as a social meeting place.

Then there were the creek dwellers. These were the families living, loving, laughing and weeping on the fringe of town. Over the years they had drifted into the populated centres looking for work, following relatives or trying to 'fit in' to the whitefella style of life. When some of the men and women found that western society didn't want to absorb their culture, but kept them at arm's-length via evening curfews that forced them out of town, or they couldn't or didn't want to change their nomadic life style, there was no place left to live except along the edges of the creek at the fringe of town, under the mulga trees and makeshift canvas tarps. It was along these edges where I first encountered the joys and the sorrows of Aboriginal fringe dweller life.

Daily I swept out my tent, relieving it of its film of red dust. It was impossible to keep the red dirt out of my clothes, my bedding, or from under my nails. Grit had become a permanent part of my body, the small grains nestling themselves into my ears, nostrils and between my teeth.

After sweeping out the tent I would boil water for my morning coffee over an outdoor cooking pit. In my canvas dilly bag, originally purchased from L L Bean, an upmarket outdoor supplier in the United States, I would pack a notebook, a small copy of Bible portions translated into the local language and an all-important bottle of water. Then, with my dilly bag and guitar slung over my shoulder, I would set out along the dry, sandy bed of Skull Creek. Its imaginary banks were dotted with a variety of Aboriginal camps that sprouted up and then disappeared during the cycles of nomadic life. Some of them were constructed of boughs from trees and bushes, which were then covered by well-worn canvas tarps, the marks and stains on which told a family history of bush camps, walkabouts and gutted kangaroos. Other camps were made of iron and tin, which glistened in the early sunrise and pretended to provide shelter from the heat.

The camps along Skull Creek came to life every morning with the barking of dogs, the stirring of coals from the previous night's fire and the squeals of little children playing chasey between the tents and across the mattresses that lay sprawled in plain view. By the time I arrived in the morning, the billy cans were boiling and chunks of kangaroo flesh were sizzling in the camp oven or smoking on top of flat mesh covering a small mound of coals. Men and women would be sitting cross-legged on their mattresses and blankets, which formed a circular pattern around the fire.

'Yuwo-o-o,' one of the older women would call out, and she would motion with her upturned hand for me to come and join them, then pat an empty space beside her on the mattress. So the day would begin, all of us singing Aboriginal language songs, the grandmothers tapping with sticks to keep the rhythm and this American creek dweller reading a verse from the Bible portion while all heads turned to one another, nodding approval and having a good laugh hearing an American accent trying to pronounce desert lingo.

Every day there would be reminders of the fast-approaching wedding day. 'When a'ya marryin' Kurta Ron?'

'We'll be there.'

'Skull Creek, huh? You'd never think ya'd really get married here.' A dark hand pointed to the sand beneath our feet.

Certainly, Skull Creek has had a colourful and rather infamous past.

Toward the end of the 1800s, maybe around 1880, the wars between Aboriginal tribes had increased. A number of Darlot warriors had moved into the Laverton tribal area and speared some of the Laverton Walgen mob while they were sleeping peacefully by their camp fires. The police came shortly afterward and found them tragically lying in tangled array, a look of fear, agony and surprise on their faces. The creek bed on the outskirts of Laverton ran with tears and sorrow.

A few years later Irish prospectors who were digging for gold in the area had an altercation with some of the Aborigines. After a brief skirmish, one prospector received a spear wound to the arm. There was commotion everywhere, yelling, running, pots and pans scattered among the rocks. A shot was fired and the Aborigines disappeared into the squat, mushroom-shaped bushes of the desert. In those days, there was always retaliation. The miners and prospectors joined together and decided to put a stop to the wandering bands of Aborigines who, in the process of looking for food and spying out what was happening to their land, sometimes spooked the horses and harassed the men. The result was another shooting of a number of Aborigines as they camped along the creek bed. Their bodies were left to be covered with flies and sand. When the rains came a few years later and flooded the creek, a human skull emerged at the place of the massacre. From that time on, that dusty, shallow, meandering trench was known as Skull Creek. The year was 1898.

Almost a century later, on 21 September 1969, the headlines of *The Kalgoorlie Miner* sang out that there had been a 'wild brawl' at Laverton. Two policemen were injured and flown out of the town to Kalgoorlie by the Royal Flying Doctor Service. A native man was shot dead—the official cause was air embolism, air entering the wounds made by a shotgun blast. He died in an ambulance going to Leonora. The native man had been forbidden to go on the plane with the policemen, so he took his last breath in the arms of an elderly missionary who had looked after him as he had grown to manhood. All the Aboriginal people who lived by the creek or on the reserve packed up their meagre belongings and moved away, leaving behind only the skeletal remains of once inhabited campsites. Skull Creek again had flowed with blood.

Traditionally, Aboriginal people leave a community or a town when there are deaths. Since most of the families around Laverton were related, the tragedy affected everyone. Laverton became like a ghost town to them and only after a year or so did they drift back into the area when the sorrow had abated and they felt able to pick up their lives again.

Why would anyone get married at such a place of sorrow? Would any Aboriginal people come to such a place, while grappling with past memories? Ron, the man I would soon be marrying, had chosen Skull Creek because he believed that something good could overshadow the repetitive sorrow of days long ago. He believed that our wedding would help to take away the pain of the history of Skull Creek. Ron had an amazing love of history and the symbolic. To have a ceremony at a place where there was a history of bloodshed and shame would be a statement to the world that the past had been turned around, that everything and everyone could be transformed from dark to light, from sorrow to happiness. It would mean that people who lived near the creek could laugh again, and when the old people would gather around the campfire at night, the stories would not always be of death and policemen, but of life and reconciliation. 'Do you remember when Ron married that lady from New York in our creek?' And another would say, 'Yeah, I was there ... there ... at that wedding.'

Years later as we travelled, Ron and I met many people who said to us, 'Yeah, I was there ... at the creek. You know, when you fellas got married.'

There were others who agreed that a wedding at Skull Creek would be a rather unique event. One of the reporters of the *Daily News* in Perth, who had written a few stories about Ron in the past, found out about the scene of our wedding and wanted to write a story about it. It eventually made its way to the front page of the paper in Adelaide and on to Melbourne as well.

I had first met Ron on New Year's Eve, 1983, after travelling to Kalgoorlie for the Christmas season in search of a bit of respite from the dust and flies of the bush. New Year's Eve in Kalgoorlie was a riotous affair with the pubs 'on every corner' full to overflowing, music filling the wide streets of the town and no one going home until the sun started to peer over the upper end of Hannan Street, the main thoroughfare that ran through the centre of town and eventually became the Great Eastern Highway that headed toward Perth. Ron Williams, a well-known Aboriginal pastor and evangelist, who had roamed Australia for twenty-five years, 'making this world a better place', as he often would say, singing, preaching, praying and helping people to laugh and smile, had decided to conduct a singalong at the rotunda at Victoria Gardens.

The gardens were tended by the Little Sisters of the Poor, a Catholic order that devoted itself to caring for the elderly. Victoria Gardens are a Kalgoorlie landmark, built by the Afghan water carters who were the mining region's lifeline years before the famous 600-kilometre-long pipeline that snakes its way from Perth through the wheat fields to the Kalgoorlie Goldfields was built. The rotunda had been a backdrop for many celebrations of the past, complete with camels and wagons. Weddings had adorned the gardens and no doubt many proposals of marriage had taken place there. On that New Year's Eve, I sat cross-legged on the ground with some of the tribal women and Kalgoorlie fringe dwellers (yes, almost every town or city with an Aboriginal population has them) who had come to hear the music and see one of their favourite preachers. The nuns from the Little Sisters were serving cups of tea and special holiday biscuits and cakes all around.

I keenly observed the man who had brought us here, starting with the thongs on his feet and working my way up to his slightly flattened Akubra hat. He wore a nylon cowboy shirt in two shades of blue, its tail hanging slouched over his belt, which he intermittently hiked up when his polyester brown trousers began to slide down over his slim hips. Once when he reached under his hat to scratch his head, I noticed that his black, curly hair formed a ring around the balding spot in the middle. From time to time an appealing smile would flash across his wide, dark face as he sang country and western gospel songs while strumming on an oversize red acoustic guitar. In between songs he would encourage the stoop-shouldered spectators with words of hope from the Bible, lightly touch the arm of an elderly woman lying on a blanket, or spin a few stories of his latest trip around Australia, complete with his doctor's orders to slow down or his heart might give out.

'Hullo,' he said with his hand stretched out to shake mine. My eyes moved past the smile to his dark eyes, which almost seemed lost under his even darker bushy eyebrows. Out of them I noticed not just a twinkle but a cunning gaze that seemed to say that he knew all about me. 'I hear you come from New York City. What did you do before coming to Australia?'

I took his hand and he seemed to hang on a bit longer than I expected.

Little did I know that Ron had already been given my complete biography by a missionary friend of his who had been teaching me the desert language.

'Oh, I was a teacher,' I replied.

'And what's your name?' he asked, still with that smile on his face. When I said that my name was Diana, he chuckled and said, 'Oh. I'll remember that. That's the name of the Phantom's sweetheart.' Then he turned away to sing 'What a Friend' and greet other people who were starting to drift into the rotunda.

I sat watching him and wondering what sort of man he was. I had heard a bit about him from a few people, both black and white. One man had described him as the most 'humble' man he had ever met. Another missionary had said that Ron was very special, there was no one like him, and that even the tribal people in the desert called him 'Kurta Kurta', which meant 'everybody's brother'. Someone else commented that no one could tie him down. 'Ron Williams goes wherever he pleases and whenever he pleases.'

While I chatted away to the women sitting around me, I was pondering this brief interchange of words and imagining who the Phantom was. Being one who was not an avid reader of comic books, it wasn't until later that I found out that the Phantom was a man of daring who saved many in distress and who indeed had a girlfriend named Diana along with a black dog named Devil that followed him everywhere.

As I continued to contemplate this tall, big-chested, slim-legged Aboriginal man, I heard a distinct voice speaking to my inner spirit. It was one of those times when your conscience speaks, but this time it was louder, more emphatic. It was so loud in fact, that I looked around quickly, in all directions, to see if someone was speaking behind me. 'That's the man you're going to marry,' the voice said. I was never a person given to crazy hallucinations or wild flights of fancy. I had earned two university degrees, had lectured in colleges, high schools and in the corporate world for over fifteen years. That was why this moment was so unusual; one of those moments that causes one to sit up and take notice. Plus this voice made sense.

My previous romantic life had been a tangled mess. I had come from a family that carried deep wounds resulting from a hostile divorce. During my university days, I had sought comfort by marrying 'the boy next door' from high school. That marriage promptly broke down during the aftermath of the Vietnam War. Since that time I had had several flings, but they had all been less than I desired. During the previous seven years before coming to Australia I had dedicated myself to serving humanity by counselling heroin addicts in New York, giving relief to the homeless, starting an alternative school for emotionally disturbed primary school children and then committing myself to missionary work in Australia. The thought of any romantic relationship had faded into the hidden recesses of my heart. I didn't want to be hurt again.

However, a day had come, only a few weeks before New Year's Eve, 1983, in the bush not far out from Laverton. This lonely, 37-year-old woman, who had dedicated her life almost exclusively to serving others, cutting off any thought of marrying again, had sat on a rock in the desert and cried. I spoke out loud to whoever would listen, hoping it would be God. I suddenly realised my desire to have a life-long companion, someone to share with, to cry with and to be happy with. That prayer escaped from deep within my soul. But I didn't trust myself. I didn't trust my own emotions or ability to choose someone who would not hurt me in the end. The words that overflowed to heaven were, 'Just point him out to me, God. I'll trust your choice.' After that, I got up from the rock, wiped my hands together as if to say it was finished, walked back to camp and promptly forgot what I had prayed. That is, I forgot until that New Year's Eve, at the rotunda. Now the hand of God was pointing him out. That's why it made sense.

During our brief conversation that night Ron had offered to give me some cassette tapes of Aboriginal singing, preaching and storytelling that would help me to grasp better the heartbeat of his people. I was keen to learn all I could so the next day I rang the number of the missionary's home where he was staying. When I asked if I could speak to Ron Williams, the man replied, 'Oh, he left earlier this morning on the train to Port Augusta.' For a few seconds, I was stunned. What was the voice that I had heard? What was I supposed to do now?

From the other end of the phone, the voice of Wilf Douglas, Bible translator, cultural companion to many Warburton tribal men, and long-time friend of Ron's, was offering me Ron's address. I didn't know what to do. Maybe God needs a little nudge, I thought, as I wrote down the address, since Ron seemed to have disappeared from view. Later, I wrote a small note; just a little card, with a scene on the front of a sad, tired dog lying down and a twittering bluebird perched on a branch above him. Inside I reminded Ron about the tapes and mentioned that I would like to get to know him better and hear more about his life travelling among Aboriginal communities.

But as soon as I pushed the letter through the slot in the letterbox, a wave of regret and panic swept over me. I wanted to reach in and pull the letter back out. There I go, I thought. A pushy American. No wonder everyone thinks we're too bold and brash. Here I go proving it.

I walked away silently, wishing the post office would lose the letter. However, not only did the letter arrive at its appointed destination in Port Augusta, but, two weeks later, I received a reply of sixteen pages folded inside a wistfully beautiful friendship card. That was the beginning of our courtship.

After spending two weeks in Port Augusta, Ron had been asked to fill in as principal of the Aboriginal Bible College in Cootamundra, New South Wales. I was still living in my tent in remote Western Australia. Our letters crisscrossed the country, fast and furious, with much reading (and writing) between the lines. Ron loved to compose poetry, which unleashed my creative juices as well. I sang songs onto tape and sent them through the post, wrote short verses of rhyme and mailed photographs taken of the bush around Laverton.

In letters we were both free to express ourselves in an unfettered way, sharing our dreams for the future and our needs for a close companion. He shared his desire to have someone who would be able to cope with his difficult lifestyle, travelling constantly, caring little for one's own comforts, living on the 'smell of an oily rag', as he explained. Since I was living in a tent at that time, anything seemed an improvement, so the prospect of life as a nomad didn't present any barriers. Ron's vision of his future was global in nature, far beyond the self-imposed boundaries of the Aboriginal people I had met. As the letters continued, I learned that this man was unique. He seemed to hear a different tune from most people I knew. More and more I wanted to hitch my wagon to this shooting star.

Underneath all the dreams, though, I was searching for the man, the companion I needed and the heartbeat of love. I sensed that he was searching for that as well. We were almost brutally honest when we told each other of our previous marriages, our moments of coping with divorce and death, the lonely times without a mate, and our desire to love another as deeply as we wanted to be loved in return.

Three months after the five-minute introduction at Victoria Gardens, Ron asked me in a letter to marry him. 'I can't really go on like this any more,' he wrote. 'I fell in love with you, honey, the first night I met you, but I had to wait and see if you cared for me. We're both old enough to know what we are doing. Let's not beat around the bush, or tug on each other's heartstrings. I want to know if you will be my wife. By the way, here is a little verse to help you decide. If you can accept this, then we'll make it.'

I might have thought that the little verse from the Bible would be one about love, maybe the famous passage from I Corinthians 13, about 'how patient and kind love is'. Or maybe a verse out of Song of Solomon, from the pen of a man who seemed to think he knew all about women. Or maybe even something from the Psalms, perhaps 'The Lord is my Shepherd'. Everyone knows that one. But what did I read? The words were written in bold letters at the end of his proposal of marriage: 'Endure hardship as a good soldier of Jesus Christ.' I had no idea then how true those words were to become, but, at that moment, I began walking the three kilometres to the phone box reading his words over and over again: 'My feet have been guided out of the wilderness, Diana. I love you very much. I want to marry you, care for you and help you fulfill your life's dreams.'

Separated by three thousand kilometres, I cried into the phone, 'I will! I will!' I trusted that Ron was the one I had been waiting for, eleven years after my first marriage had crumbled. Every letter had brought us closer together—at least on paper—close enough to take this life-changing step of faith.

Excitement began to mount as we made plans for our bush wedding. We chose 15 December, which allowed Ron time to get back to the west after his stint as principal had come to an end in September. That gave us only three months, not only to pull together the details, but also to get to know each other more in the process. Ron spent a lot of time on the road travelling back and forth over a thousand kilometres from the south-west to Laverton. We had virtually no money for a wedding but friends from all over the state who knew Ron and had met me began to offer to help. There were promises of kangaroo meat, guitar players, a wedding cake, and even a wedding dress. Wherever I met my Aboriginal friends throughout the desert communities, they would throw their arms around me, cry into my shoulder, or pat my hand and whisper Ron's name. My creek-dweller mates began to move camps and clean up the banks of Skull Creek.

Ron came to Laverton a week before the wedding to make the final preparations. We walked along the creek bed digging our boots into the sand and unearthed a number of rusty horseshoes, perhaps from the horses that the policemen rode as they patrolled the creek many years before. Ron began to collect the horseshoes, slinging them over his arm, one by one. He grinned at me. 'You need an aisle to walk down, don't you?'

When the spot was finally chosen, not far from where my tent home was, Ron unpacked his panel van of all sorts of trimmings for a bush wedding. Bunches of dried wildflowers from the south-west, and a huge banner that he tied between two trees for a backdrop. The banner was special to Ron, painted years earlier by his missionary friend, Wilf Douglas, and had once decorated the Perth Concert Hall as Aboriginal people from all over Western Australia sang gospel songs.

I ran my hand over the large canvas following the outline of an Aboriginal man with a spear by his side, pointing to the sunrise coming up over a hill in the distance. His wife sat at his feet near a campfire watching the scene before her. For a moment I sensed my life becoming like hers as I watched Ron bringing symbols from all over Western Australia into the creek bed at Laverton in preparation for a day to celebrate a union, of man and woman, black and white, in a place where years before there had been killing.

✪ ✪ ✪

'I'm prayin' for a goanna,' said Ron, turning to me from behind the wheel of his car.

It was the day before our wedding and we had driven to Leonora one hundred kilometres away, for some supplies. I quietly couldn't believe that someone would pray for a goanna. But once you know just how much a black fella raised in the bush loves his goanna, you come to understand why he would even pray for one.

'We need one for our wedding, just special for us, y'know.'

All of a sudden the car came to a halt and began to swerve. 'There it is,' Ron said with confidence. He pushed on the accelerator and turned back. There was a recently killed goanna on the side of the road. Ron jumped out of the car and, holding it up proudly with a grin on his face, said, 'I just knew we'd get one. This one is special, for our wedding breakfast.' He broke off a small twig and proceeded to gut the lizard and then wrapped it in a plastic bag. This was to be the first of many times that we would stop alongside the road to 'bag' our dinner, or else to provide dinner for a myriad of other travellers along the bush tracks of the Australian outback.

❂ ❂ ❂

I dressed for the wedding at Judy Murray's house. Judy was a great friend, had known Ron for many years and came from a prominent Aboriginal family in the goldfields. We laughed and joked as I squeezed into my borrowed lace dress. Shirma, another Aboriginal friend, hearing of my need, had gingerly brought one of her bridesmaid's dresses to me a few weeks earlier. She had laid it in my lap, and whispered, 'For you. For Skull Creek.'

Judy drove me through the bush behind the state battery to the edge of the clearing, ringed by a few trees, where the wedding party and guests had assembled. She parked behind a tree so I could wait unseen until the music began. I stood for those moments composing myself and surveying the scene before me. Three pastors were waiting to perform the cere-mony, to well and truly tie the knot.

Ray Minniecon, the Aboriginal pastor (who now coordinates Aborig-inal programs with World Vision) dressed smartly in a suit on this hot day in December and sporting a bushy Afro, was speaking into the micro-phone, welcoming people from Kalgoorlie, Laverton, Geraldton, Warburton, Mount Margaret, Cundeelee, the south-west, Esperance, Perth, Wiluna, missionaries and family. One specially invited guest was Harry Lupton, who had been one of the first missionaries to go out to the Warburton Ranges on a camel in the 1930s with William Wade. Mr Wade, who eventually established the mission there had worked together with R.M. Williams, the now renowned boot maker and bushwear supplier. They went across the desert from Oodnadatta together on camels in 1926. Will Wade's story is wistfully told by R.M. in his book, *Song in the Desert.*

Groups of people huddled on blue plastic tarps under the scrub trees trying to find some shade, a few on folding chairs. Earlier that day, Ron had hung buckets and containers of water in the small trees to help quench the thirst of the guests in the 40-degree temperature. The two reporters were wandering through the groups, taking photographs and writing in small notebooks. Four-wheel drives and panel vans dotted the scene, forming a protective shield around this 'sacred site'.

I couldn't believe I was actually standing in this spot, ready to walk through horseshoes, to come face to face with a man I really didn't know but somehow felt safe with, to unite with a society of people whom I had come to love, but hadn't yet fully understood. My silent meditation was interrupted by the twanging of guitars being tuned and I saw two bushy-haired, smartly dressed tribal men, Donny and Rhys, the desert's best guitar pickers, nodding to Ron that they were ready.

As the twang of the melody of 'We Are One Big Happy Family' began, I stepped out of the shade of the gum tree and slowly began my walk down the 'aisle'. Oblivious to the crowds of people sitting, standing, singing, I walked past the trees with water bottles hanging from their branches, my gaze fixed to the front. Ron calmly turned around to catch my eye. At the altar, which consisted of the banner, wildflowers and a small table for signing the register, I took Ron's hand. The guests sang in English and tribal language. Competing for the shade, dogs wandered around and people brushed away the flies that continued to keep them company. As Ron and I faced each other I thought to myself, 'My family would never believe this.'

Ron and I sang a song together, 'Your People Shall Be My People'. Little did we know the full import of those words and what they would mean as we started our life together. Others also sang songs for us. The second pastor, a dear missionary friend of ours, Noel Blyth, the owner of the Laverton block where I had pitched my tent, performed the ceremony and pronounced us man and wife. The third pastor from Kalgoorlie prayed for us as we knelt together on the red dirt and imparted a special blessing upon us. As I look back upon that moment, I recognise the significance of these three men from three different spiritual and cultural backgrounds putting their hands together to pray for us, for the life ahead would have unravelled with anything less than full commitment to one another and to the life we had chosen to live.

America couldn't come to me, so I brought some of America to the reception. Tradition dictates that when the bride and groom cut the cake, they must each take a piece and feed each other as a symbol of their love and care for one another. I had just finished explaining this and we each took a piece of cake in our hands. Ron, smiling and waving to the crowd, forgot all about feeding me but put the cake into his own mouth. Everyone broke out in laughter. Ron grabbed another piece of cake and shoved it into my mouth.

He then jumped up on the bonnet of his panel van to call everyone to attention to say grace before proceeding to hand out chunks of kangaroo meat, which our tribal friends from Warburton had cooked in the traditional way, steamed whole in an underground oven. Still clothed in my wedding dress, I sat on a blanket beside one of my desert friends while she turned a hunk of meat on the fire. Through the smoke curling across the lawn I saw a slow-moving collage of bare feet, white shirts and ties, singlets, Akubra hats and cowboy boots, dogs looking for scraps and children, black and white, squealing and running between the small fires. Inside the small community hall, there were endless tables covered with decorated cakes, biscuits, sandwiches and other delicacies, whitefella style. The three-tiered wedding cake with pink everlastings on the top had arrived intact after travelling a 500-kilometre stretch of corrugated road on an old school bus through the back track from Wiluna. The usual wedding trappings, placed alongside the damper cooked in the ashes and kangaroo and goat meat served on tarps, were part of an interesting mixture of cultural traditions. If food could join two cultures, we would all be friends around the world and the fragrance of reconciliation would seep through our oven doors.

It soon came time to leave. For weeks we had discussed where we would spend our honeymoon night. Laverton was quite remote, with not much of a hotel for such a special night, and to drive the four hours to Kalgoorlie after dark and a long day would be too tiring. True to his nature, Ron had suggested something unique. 'How about climbing the hill with me? It's a very scenic spot.'

At this point in our relationship I didn't speak up much. I didn't know how to respond to some of these suggestions.

The spot he was referring to was a cave on top of Mount Margaret Hill. Another place of history. When John Forrest had first explored the area, he had climbed to the top of this hill, placed a marker of stones and named it after his wife, Margaret. Eventually the whole area was called the Mount Margaret goldfields. The hill stood as a lookout over the mission community of Mount Margaret, which was started in the 1920s by Rod Schenk. The day before the wedding Ron had climbed the hill, swept out the cave and sprayed disinfectant to keep out the kangaroos and other slithery creatures.

The sun had already begun its plunge towards the hills in the west when we changed our wedding clothes and waved goodbye to our friends. As we sped off down the dirt track, car loaded with swags, a Bible, the remains of a goanna, a radio, and our two beloved travelling companions—a blue heeler named Maru (blackie) and Toby, a labrador-blue terrier cross—we were followed by the reporters.

It took twenty minutes to climb Mount Margaret. Ron went ahead, carrying the swag, which he laid on the brush mattress that he had prepared. The reporters kept up with him, yarning all the way and snapping photographs. I followed gingerly behind, thinking, 'What woman in her right mind would do this? I'll bet no one else, black or white, would be climbing up this stupid mountain on her wedding day.' I couldn't understand why the climb seemed so frightening, because I had always thought of myself as being quite brave and strong, with a sporting background in basketball and having run—and finished—the 1978 New York City marathon. But now, all that courage seemed to have left me and I stood frozen on a mound of rocks, a mere three giant steps from the entrance to the cave. I couldn't move, backward or forward. As I stood there, thinking whether or not I should call out to Ron, he noticed that I had stopped still. He reached out his hand for me. Those last three steps we walked together.

When the photos were snapped and the two Perth reporters said their farewells and drove off, it was suddenly silent. The dogs roamed over the top of the hill, noses sniffing the air for the scent of kangaroo, and we walked to the marker that John Forrest had built. Later Ron started a small fire in the mouth of the cave, trying to be romantic, but when the wind shifted, the cave filled with smoke and I couldn't breathe. Coughing and spluttering, I had to climb back up to the top of the hill and Ron knocked the fire down the hill.

While Ron explored the back of the hill with the dogs, I sat by myself at the opening of the cave, looking out over the wide desert land. The setting sun glimmered from the horizon and the sky slowly turned a darker blue. The moon seemed to float along on a cradle of dusky clouds. I could see no sign of modern civilisation. For a few minutes, I sensed a time generations ago when no white man walked this territory, when there was no noise except that of nature and no time except that of the seasons. Those minutes seemed suspended in eternity as if I was there with the Aboriginal people of that time and place, of that sacred site. I had begun my journey with the people of this land by sitting on the ground, by learning from the heart of the tribal people. What a privilege to have such a beginning! Where would this journey now take me, with a man who belonged to an ancient culture, to a people so different from mine? A life that seems so exotic in one moment can carry incredible pain in the next. I sat there, alone with my vision. The heavens seemed to reach down to meet the earth, and what held my gaze was the horizon, the place of balance.

CHAPTER 2

Born in America

I n 1942 when my dad had announced to his mother and father that he had enlisted in the air force, some of the family were concerned that he might be sent to fight the Germans. They were his people. My dad's family had migrated from Germany two generations before, and had settled around York Street and the East 80s in Manhattan, New York City, which had come to be known as little Germantown.

Dad, an only child, was born in New York City, played stick-ball and shopped at Macy's, the world's largest department store, for Christmas. His mother, who sometimes sang on radio, had dreamed of becoming an opera diva, and practised day and night her repertoire of arias. When my father was born, her career hopes seemed to vanish, but she continued to carry the dream in her heart.

As the war had approached and America's relationship with Germany became more tenuous, some German American families had changed their names to try to escape rejection, detention camps, even persecution. John, my dad's father, never dreamed of changing the Mehring name. In German, it meant 'my ring', or better translated 'my own mob' or organisation, possibly designating a political, or craft guild. *Time* magazine once carried a story during the Cold War about an escape route from East to West Germany, describing a man who had carefully made his way through a maze of streets in Berlin, one of which was Mehring Strasse.

As a young man, John Mehring, my grandfather, had enlisted in the

United States Navy during World War I as a helmsman. He was assigned to a troop ship, the *USS President Lincoln*. After docking in France and taking aboard their load of wounded soldiers, they were two days out of port, heading for America, when the ship was torpedoed by a German submarine. A number of men, including John, abandoned ship before it sank and clung to life rafts for two days before they were rescued.

After the war, John had roamed the country, out west to Wyoming, tried his hand as a sheepherder and then as a labourer in the oil fields of the west before returning to New York City to finally become a certified public accountant. It was at an East Side neighbourhood block dance that he had met Blanche, my grandmother. In those days, the block parties were the places to go to meet eligible young men or women. His subsequent position as treasurer of Ethel Oil Company had kept him in New York City. He commuted back and forth, even after he finally moved his family out to Long Island and then to Statsburg in upstate New York.

My dad loved his father, and together they spent days on end hunting pheasants and quail, taking the retrievers out for a run, and fishing in the streams. They shopped together at Abercrombie & Fitch, where my grandfather would outfit his only son with English waders, fly fishing equipment and other sporting supplies.

When they moved to Long Island, Grandfather had ordered a boat to be built by a Norwegian builder, and he took my dad every week to see it take shape. Eventually there were other boats: a cabin boat where they spent weekends and a dinghy where Dad took his little German schnauzer friend catching eels and crabs in the bays along Long Island Sound.

During Dad's high school days, his father bought a property of 176 acres in Statsburg, near Hyde Park and the Roosevelt home, nestled in the Hudson Valley. The estate, which included a three-storey home, numerous outbuildings, a machine shop and a six-room manager's cottage, had once belonged to a former treasurer of the United States. My dad roamed the orchards and spent weekends trapping, hunting and fishing.

When Dad had wanted to leave his studies at Rensselaer Polytechnic Institute (RPI) to enlist, my grandfather, who had been pushing for him to study chemical engineering, reluctantly let his only son go. As the war extended and stories filtered back of the atrocities, the pro-Hitler feelings among many of the Germans started slowly to change. An old wood-carver who lived near Dad's family had been in the German army under the last Kaiser. Dad used to visit him and play adolescent war games with a spiked German helmet that dated back to the 1860s and an old German Mauser. But my grandfather would tolerate none of that 'German pride' attitude because he had been born a United States citizen and had become a serviceman, willing to give his life for America. When the father of one of Dad's boyhood friends joined the Brownshirts, an organisation of Nazi sympathisers and asked Grandfather to come to a meeting, their friendship abruptly ended.

After enlistment, Dad was sent to Houston, Texas, for aviation cadet training and then to bombardier and navigator schools. Texas was a rather bleak, dry, barren place after the lushness of the eastern seaboard and the forests of upstate New York, but Dad had his mind on other things. When he left the base on weekends, like the other young fellows, he would frequent the local soda fountains. His slim build, bright smile, straight Roman nose and dark wavy hair attracted many women. But he kept watching one in particular, as he drank his usual order of orange juice with a straw. A young woman with tiny feet suited for modelling shoes and just out of high school had moved to Houston from Oklahoma City with her family and had taken a job at the soda fountain where she often served an orange juice to a young soldier from New York.

My mother, Jean Greer, was a Midwestern girl, born in the small town of Pittsburgh, Oklahoma. Her dad had worked on drilling rigs in many of the oil fields, occasionally having brief encounters with the Bureau of Indian Affairs, since Oklahoma was home to much tribal land. He wore cowboy boots and a stetson hat and sported a wonderful collection of silver belt buckles. Along with his wife, my mother and her elder sister, they were a gentle, easygoing, close family. My mother was pretty and soft-spoken. She also had a boyfriend, the son of a local doctor.

But the excitement and pace of war-time life moved my mother and father rapidly toward marriage, and after knowing each other for only six weeks, they stood together in the Greers' living room and said 'I do'. My dad's parents were also in attendance, since they had sold their New York property when Ethel Oil had transferred my grandfather to Baton Rouge, Louisiana, during the height of the war.

During those unpredictable years of world war, young men did not dare to speculate that they might not come back from their tour of duty, yet somewhere in their hearts was a shadowy fear of a life cut short. Most of the men had the desire, unspoken in words, to leave behind a future, a child for posterity. 'If I didn't come back, I wanted to leave a child to carry on something of me,' explained my dad, years later. 'Two years went by and nothing happened. We even went to a physician. It took a lot for a man to do that in those days. But the doc said maybe it was all the high-altitude flying that I did.'

Dad flew thirty missions to Japan from bases on Johnson Island and Saipan in the Pacific Ocean. His first mission, to take photographs and drop bombs, was on Christmas Eve in 1944.

He came back home to Texas in June 1945. Wartime policy was that after thirty missions a soldier was entitled to get out of the military. Dad decided to leave active duty, but remained in the Army Reserves until retirement many years later.

It was April 1946. The bombs had ceased. The word 'victory' was still on people's lips everywhere. Ex-soldiers were going back to university and looking for jobs. The era of the yet-to-be-named 'baby boomers' had begun. I was born in Our Lady of the Lake hospital, Baton Rouge, Louisiana, ten months after Dad left active duty.

'I named you,' he told me. 'Your mother said it was okay. She didn't know what to call you, but something about mythology came to my mind. The stories I used to read about Diana, the Roman goddess of the hunt. Y'know I liked to hunt and, I guess, well, that's why I named you that.'

After the war, the government instituted what was called the '52/20 Club', which meant that each soldier was paid twenty dollars a week for fifty-two weeks while they looked for jobs. Dad worked as a carpenter's apprentice until my grandfather took him on a trip to the east to search out a place for them to live. It turned out to be a house on a hill in Vermont. When I was six months old, my parents left Louisiana and took a train several thousand miles through the eastern half of the United States to Vermont. It was a difficult trip, rattling along the tracks for days, Dad having to warm my bottle under his arm or on the radiator of the railway carriage. My grandfather had bought Sugar Bush Farm in the Vermont hills, with the dream of farming dairy cattle and raising chickens with his only son and his family. It was a confusing time for my parents. Men who had fought in the war were returning home and facing many decisions for their future, and many found themselves at loose ends. My grandfather thought to create for my dad something of his childhood—hunting, walking in the woods, working together. But a dairy or a chicken farm was not Dad's idea of a fulfilling life. He didn't relish milking cows twice a day and my mother couldn't stand the flies or the smell.

Eventually my parents made their way to the oil fields of Oklahoma, where Dad worked as a project engineer with Conoco Oil until he retired. Oklahoma was originally the Indian Territory and a land of red dirt, settled by a gunshot at noon on 22 April 1889, then nicknamed the Sooner State because of those who sneaked across the border the night before in hope of claiming the choice tracts of land 'sooner' than everyone else. It gradually became the dustbowl of the 1930s, which was later transformed to a place where 'the wind comes sweepin' down the plain'. There were times when Dad hated the place, especially when the skies turned brown and the dust seemed to roll into town in huge billows, seeping under the doors and along the window sills, covering the kitchen table with sandy grit. But there we stayed because the work was good.

Dad began to take me hunting when I was just a bit taller than a shotgun. We looked for rabbits in their holes, flushed out quail and pheasants and even shot squirrels. When I turned twelve, he took me to rifle-safety classes and I joined a target shooting team, winning medals for Oklahoma in the state championships. I think Dad had wanted a boy so he taught me all the things he had enjoyed in childhood. I loved him and I knew he loved me because he even said so, once, that I can remember as a child. But in the midst of the closeness that I felt toward him, a dark cloud began to rise over the family, threatening to engulf us completely. Dad began to drink, more and more often. Sometimes he fell over and couldn't get back up and my mother had to call in someone to help.

One night, after Dad had been put into bed, the doctor had visited and the house was quiet again, I peered through the doorway into their bedroom. I could just barely see the outline of my dad lying on the bed with the light from the closet reflecting over him. I remember feeling very frightened of that room at night because there would be usually a lot of arguing coming from within its walls. I noticed my mother was sitting slouched over in a chair in the corner and a funny smell of what seemed like medicine permeated the room. I didn't know what to expect as I tip-toed toward him. I thought that perhaps he was asleep, but he stretched his arm out, touching my shoulder as I stood just slightly taller than the edge of the bed. 'Diana,' he mumbled. 'No matter what happens, never forget that I love you.'

Those words seemed to vanish over the years, getting lost somewhere along the track of growing up. My sister, Pat, came along and then a brother, John, and it seemed that the tension in the family increased year by year. After Pat was born, my mother had a breakdown, but I didn't know it at the time. All I knew was that she went away for a while and my grandparents came to help look after us. The arguments between my parents grew worse and so did Dad's drinking. The routine at the meal table usually began with an empty beer bottle or vodka glass, the food being passed around, then escalate to a glass of milk or juice being spilled, a hand coming out to hit one of us for the misdemeanour and then getting up to leave the table. I would go into my bedroom, sit on the edge of the bed and hold my breath, hoping that I would pass out. My child's mind reasoned that if I could just pass out on the floor, Dad or Mum would find me and rush me to the hospital, and when I woke up, they would be so happy to have me alive that their marriage would change and we would finally be a happy family. But I never did pass out.

Years later I would listen to young high school students who had already run away from home or who wanted to run away from home. They would look at me with faraway eyes and a tear or two, expressing the same thought: 'I just wanted my parents to love each other.' Why do so many children think they can save their parents' marriage by their own sacrifice?

❂ ❂ ❂

It seemed like Dad wore an army uniform all the time. Every other weekend he dressed up in his starched and ironed military garb, complete with spit-shined shoes, before attending army reserve duties. Then during the summer he went to reserve camp in Louisiana. But he could have worn the uniform all the time, because we were on duty twenty-four hours a day. He commanded his family like an army platoon and expected perfection. I tried hard to do the right thing, but never seemed to hit the mark. Never good enough.

'You have to learn to take care of yourself, Diana, because no one else will do it for you. If you are going to survive in this world, you have to learn to take care of yourself.' That was his advice to me. Take care of myself. I learned not to trust, not to let anyone into the secrets of my heart.

I was a good student. I felt I had to be or risk never measuring up to what he wanted. His presence loomed larger than life to me and I lived every day to please him. He pushed me all the time and I ran. In the midst of the running, I wanted to hear those words again, 'Don't forget that I love you,' but they never came. I was hurting and slowly I grew bitter and angry.

'Why don't you leave each other? Why don't you just get a divorce?' I asked Mum one day as she ironed our school clothes. It was winter and I was standing on the grating that covered the oil furnace. Every morning I would get dressed for school on this only warm spot in the house. It was the time of day when Mum and I had most of our conversations, but she never seemed to answer my questions satisfactorily. Mum never seemed to enjoy life except when she was with her parents or her sister. My picture of her was always one of cleaning the house or ironing the clothes. She never talked about the problems of the world, the big questions of one's future, nor did she read very much. As I grew up, I thought of her as being 'stuck' in a way I never wanted to be.

Perhaps it was during my early teen years that an unspoken vow first entered my mind: 'I never want to grow up to be like my mother and let a man walk over me.' It was a fight for survival behind the closed doors of Third Street in Ponca City, Oklahoma. My own identity seemed at stake: how to balance my love–hate feelings toward a father who was strong and intelligent but distant and tough, with my desire to know but also withdraw from a mother who seemed breakable and somehow unreal.

Our Midwest town seemed to be just the same. Reality locked behind closed doors, while faces were always smiling, as if to say, 'If you pretend long enough, it will all go away.' As long as everyone dressed well, achieved scholastically and attended all the right social events, then we must have been doing all right. It was a town of wealthy oil barons striving to be a cultural oasis in the midst of the dusty wheatfields, cranking drilling rigs and annual rodeos. I sang in the choir at the Methodist Church every Sunday, clothed in a long black robe, standing in the choir loft situated behind the minister and facing the congregation. I never saw the minister's face as he preached every week, but I did see the owner of a shoe store, a high school teacher and the father of one of my best friends having their Sunday morning naps during the sermon. I used to wonder if this is what religion was all about, and if it was, I wasn't interested. My mother would dress us neatly and make sure that we sat all together along one of the middle rows of wooden pews. She was always concerned about appearances, to the point of being superficial. I felt like we were always on show, particularly to my mother's family.

I looked for a way to escape my troubled childhood and I found it, in the world of books. It was Grandfather Mehring who opened the door to the escape route, although he never knew it. He cast a tall shadow in my life which somehow linked me to the east, to New York, to a cosmopolitan culture, to Germany, and to books. Periodically a package would arrive in the post from him that contained beautiful, old books. Stories from Hans Christian Anderson, Herman Melville, Hans Brinker. I devoured them. These books were my life line and I associated them all with my grandfather. Then one day, I received a paperback edition of *Jane Eyre*. That's when the obsession struck, that's when books became my companions. When relationships in the home got too difficult, I no longer held my breath. I had something to live for, a world of promise held captive between the pages of a book.

I would often curl up in a chair that sat next to an old desk in the corner of our living room. Its light green paint had started to peel, uncovering a deep, warm grain of oak underneath. It stood almost five feet tall, with a pull-down desk top, behind which were hidden all sorts of cubbyholes and drawers. Underneath the desk top were three drawers with brass ring pulls. Something always drew me to that desk. I wanted to open the drawers and rummage through the cubbyholes. For what? Perhaps a clue to some family secret.

At home one day by myself, I decided to begin the search. My hands slowly ran over the outside of the desk, carefully pulling on the brass rings as the heavy bottom drawer slid toward me. I found papers from the army, books on military manoeuvres and then, at the bottom of everything, some old World War II cartoon books. I sat for an hour looking at the caricatures and reading the captions, some of which I didn't understand. As I leafed through the rest of the books, trying to make sense of what happened in World War II, and searching for clues to my dad's cynicism and rigidness, out fell two black and white photo-graphs. One was a front view of a stately, almost mansion-like house, set in a grove of trees. The other was an aerial view of what appeared to be the same house. I could sense the importance of this find, to me anyway. For days I kept going back to the drawer whenever I was alone, gazing again at the photographs, wanting to know their meaning. I finally summoned up the courage to ask my mother what these photos were.

'That's the house in Vermont,' she said matter-of-factly.

I wanted to know more. Somehow I was connected to this place and I wanted to know why. She would never tell me much about it, only that the place was dark and no one was happy there. She told me how Grandfather Mehring had bought the place for all of us, but it didn't work out. We left, but my grandparents continued to live there until they retired to Florida. She showed me some items that she brought from that house in Vermont: an oil painting, a brass kerosene lamp, a cherry oak chair with a needlepoint seat, and the oak desk. They stood as silent reminders of what could have been. They were a connection to a past time and place that somehow belonged to me, but was just out of reach. It would be years before that place called to me again.

⊙ ⊙ ⊙

'Where were you when President Kennedy was shot?' All over the world, people have been asked that question when the conversation turns to memorable moments of the past decades. That single event altered the lives of every American who lived during the 1960s. It was a trauma that seemed to change America forever. No longer were the baby boomers saluting the American flag as before. No longer did we believe that America had all the answers, or was the safest place on earth to live. I knew where I was that day. Standing in the front office of Ponca City High School waiting for some files to take to the library when the announcement came over the loudspeaker. That was my graduation year. Studies had competed with the latest Beatles records, the Friday night dance in the high school gym, Dairy Queen sundaes and the Root Beer Drive-in, and now our President was dead by an assassin's bullet. All the ingredients of the movie *Forrest Gump*.

Graduation day arrived along with the senior prom, a heralded tradition in American high schools. Before the actual prom dance, parents would attend the senior parade of the young beauties and their beaux in the school auditorium so we could flaunt our maturity and celebrate reaching the launch pad into adulthood. My heart sank when I saw Dad in the front row, nose slightly red from drinking and talking animatedly to others around him. I was sure he would embarrass me. I tried not to look at him as I walked across the stage and down the steps at the other end. But out of the stillness of the moment, the slurred voice echoed for all to hear, 'There's my Diana. Isn't she beautiful!' It wasn't until thirty years later, when I had taken my own journey through the twists and turns of life and had a daughter of my own, that I could even begin to understand what Dad's real feelings were towards me.

I left home in August 1964 to start my freshman year at Oklahoma State University. Biology was my first love and, since childhood, I had dreamt of becoming a research scientist, but I was equally enamoured with journalism, literature and the social sciences. After my first year, I decided to leave the research, chemistry and higher maths behind and I changed my major to include English, social sciences and education. I started to observe people rather than bacteria on a petri dish. University life was full and I took a double load of classes so I could graduate with a four-year degree in three years, working three jobs to pay my way. At the end of my second year, John, my childhood sweetheart, asked me to marry him, the same month that my parents announced their divorce. Even though I had once mentioned divorce to my mother, I never really expected that it would happen. It's similar to the feeling you have when you have known for a long time that someone you care about is dying, but at the moment when it finally happens, you can't believe it or accept it and denial sets in.

'But it's like you're leaving us, too,' I cried to my dad when I visited him in the dark motel room where he retreated after leaving our house. It didn't matter that I no longer lived at home, or that I was contemplating getting married and starting my own independent life. I still felt that he was walking out on me, too, not just my mother. For years I had known that my parents no longer loved each other, but I had also struggled with the desire that I *wanted* them to love each other. There was no hope now. He was leaving to live with another woman.

During our last drive together back to university, our last drive with my mother and father together, I made some hurtful, sneering remark about the situation. Dad backhanded me across the front seat of the car. As my lip began to swell, I made a vow in my heart that I never wanted to see him again. It's not always the circumstances and events that happen *to* us that change our lives, but, even more so, it's our reactions to those events. And I certainly reacted.

I married John in 1966. When Dad walked me down the aisle it was the last time I was to see him for the next ten years. My face was white with strain behind my wedding veil. My father had chosen a new life to live and his mind seemed elsewhere. My mother was consumed by her grief and anger in the wake of the divorce and had my brother and sister to care for. What was to have been one of the happiest days of my life was, instead, full of sadness.

John and I lived in a mobile home while I finished university. I graduated in 1967 with a double major and had started to study for a master's degree when the military call-up began for the Vietnam War. John knew that he would be on the list, so he signed up. The world around us was in turmoil: students were beginning to demonstrate on campuses, young men were dying in Vietnam, I had just finished three years of painstaking study to complete my long-cherished dream of a college degree, my brother and sister felt they had lost their father, my mother was bitter, and I was in desperate need of love and attention. John got orders for Massachusetts. Three months later, I left university and followed, driving halfway across the United States, car packed with as much as I could take and our faithful dachshund by my side, to begin a four-year stint as an army wife.

It was depressing. The whole country was against the military and the war. I didn't want to admit to people that I was connected to the armed forces. John was to be stationed in Turkey at a radar listening post. I watched the television as anti-war demonstrators were tear-gassed, and listened to army lieutenants cursing the long-haired hippies. I lived in two worlds: one that existed in my own thoughts and dreams, and the other that consisted of the actual motions of everyday life. I took a job teaching high school in Groton, Massachusetts, and completed a master's degree in education when John went overseas for a year. I drowned myself in the job, preparing lessons late into the night, studying, coaching basketball, running the drama group and counselling students.

When John returned after a year away, we were strangers. I had become independent, taking care of car repairs, financial matters and job security. He, on the other hand, was used to the army providing for him. After his discharge, he worked in the computer industry. We bought a little house on the hill in Massachusetts, a Ford truck, a Honda motor-cycle, and a house full of furniture, but nothing helped to bring us together. We began to drift even further apart, and separated for a time. Then one day I came back to our home to find another woman's clothes in the bedroom. In 1973, seven years after I had married and seven years after my own parents' divorce, my marriage ended.

I felt adrift, with no family ties. I had never met my dad's new wife and I hadn't met my mother's new husband. My sister had married her childhood sweetheart, and eventually had three children, and my brother had gone to Denver University and, later, to Princeton to study law. I sought to escape the emotional pain I felt by doing exactly what I had hated my father for doing. I turned to alcohol—straight Southern Comfort with two ice cubes. Every Friday afternoon during the 'Thank God It's Friday' happy hour at the local bar, I met with some of my fellow teachers to drink away the tensions of teaching classes of hormonal high schoolers and the frustrations of living in unhappy marriages.

The change I thought I needed came with a man named Jesse. A tall, Afro-American who loved jazz, had a sensitive heart, and smoked dope every day fell in love with me. One night he happened by the club near Boston where I was playing keyboard with a local rock and roll band, part of my self-improvement program to forget the marriage break-up. We needed a singer and he got the job. When the group split up because of personality differences, we hopped into my van and drove into New York City, his home town. It was during the closing months of 1973.

I looked up at the tall buildings and the grey sky, what I could see of it, and said to myself, 'I'm not going to let this metropolis change me.' Over my lifetime, I have been determined about a lot of things and I've made many strong statements, including this one. But New York did change me, for the better and for the worse. When I approached the education department to find a job and learned that the city schools were beginning to install metal detectors at the front doors, I decided to try to make my living elsewhere. I wasn't an actress or a performing musi-cian, so the choice remaining was in the business world. But would they employ a woman with a teaching background?

A commodities stock broker decided to hire me as his assistant, provided I would study for the exam to become a licensed commodities broker. The excitement was titillating, standing in the brokers' ticker room with numbers changing every few seconds and the machines spitting out reports of incidents in Brazil affecting coffee prices and fighting in South Africa bringing the gold prices down. The brokers would pace back and forth, grabbing the telephone every few minutes to advise their clients, who were mostly men with millions gambling their thousands on the roller-coaster futures market.

But I didn't live in this world of money where the gain or loss of it was the sole purpose of existence. In the evening I was listening to jazz music in apartments in Harlem, wearing tracksuits and smoking dope. Most of the time I was the only white face in a smoke-filled room crowded with Afro-Americans, Puerto Ricans and Colombians, spending hours talking about prejudice, dope, jazz and justice. Jesse wanted to marry me, but I kept resisting, even when his mother took up the plea. I was still hurting from the divorce and I wasn't about to make myself so vulnerable again.

After a few months I left Wall Street and took a position in organisational development with one of the commercial lending departments of Chase Manhattan Bank. This department financed the fashion industry of Seventh Avenue. I rubbed shoulders with executives of such fashion houses as Chanel and Gucci. I lunched with the managers, gave advice on people skills, scanned five-year business plans, and promoted the rights of women in the business world. Every day I played the part, wearing a business suit, carrying my briefcase, pushing and shoving to get on the overcrowded subways or buses that made their way through Manhattan, delivering their live cargo every few streets. Chase Manhattan had lost a lawsuit to the Women's Affirmative Action Lobby and was ordered to promote training and provide promotion opportunities for women into executive positions over the next five years. I had been hired as part of that scheme. Otherwise a corporation like Chase would not have even considered someone who did not have an MBA.

Not long after moving into New York and taking an apartment on East 74th Street in Manhattan, I realised that I was living quite near the area where my father had been born and his aunt, my grandfather's sister, still lived. I decided to pay a visit to my aunt. I found her after climbing four flights of narrow stairs in the red brick tenement where she had lived most of her eighty-five years. Here was the woman of Macy's, who had been a seamstress for women 'of means' in New York and who had sent us chocolate biscuits every Christmas since I was a small child. Aunt Carrie was slightly hunched in her shoulders from years of sewing. Looking up at me over her spectacles she said, 'My goodness, you do look like your father!'

I began to visit Aunt Carrie regularly. She loved to spend hours telling me about my grandfather and the early years of my father's life. One story that was repeated a number of times was about the fire on the *General Slocum*, and the children who died on a Sunday School picnic.

The *General Slocum* was a huge floating barge with paddle wheels that circumnavigated the East River and could hold over a thousand people. One weekend in June 1904, groups of children and families from a number of churches in the Lower East Side of Manhattan thronged onto the barge for a sailing picnic. Women were dressed in their Sunday best and held hands with the children as they walked up the wooden plank from the shore, while the men jostled the heavy picnic baskets loaded with German cuisine. As the slowly moving hulk entered the Hell's Gate area of the East River, it caught fire and the *General Slocum* became a death trap, sinking and taking hundreds of children and adults with it. Some of the victims were later found clinging to one another, wrapped in each other's arms, barely an hour after they had waved goodbye to family and friends at the dock.

Among them were some of our relatives, people I was never to meet. It was one of the great marine tragedies of that time and it sent shock waves throughout the German community. In the aftermath some survivors committed suicide and those who remained moved into other areas of Manhattan, particularly the Upper East Side or Yorkville. The entire community in the Lower East Side disappeared forever.

It was an event that was engraved on the American-German psyche of New York, and even seventy years later, my elderly Aunt Carrie, with thick glasses and white hair pulled back into a bun, hunched in her chrome kitchen chair, retold the story with tears brimming in her eyes, still reliving those very moments. 'They were your people, Diana. They were young, simple and innocent. A shameful, needless thing . . . your grandfather was supposed to go . . . Thank the Lord, at the last moment . . .' Carrie bowed her head, her voice trailing off into a whisper. Today a small monument in

Tompkins Square, Lower East Side states simply: *They Were Earth's Purest Children, Young and Fair.*

My relationship with Aunt Carrie began to create a chink in the hard exterior I showed toward my family. The more photographs she showed me of German relatives, the more I wanted to know, but I still wasn't talking to my dad. In 1976 my brother made a surprise visit to New York and ended up staying for a while. He was impressed with my work with the women's movement, particularly in relation to the business world, but he was caught up with another kind of movement, that of championing the cause of gay rights. Johnny had always been sensitive to the underdog, had helped with political campaigns for the Democrats and had led rallies for protest groups. He and I were very much alike—idealistic, with dreams for a better world. He saw me as an ally and we spent some time together, talking at length as I tagged along with him to gay bars along Christopher Street, seeing a part of life that most people wanted to hide from. Later we drifted apart, the pain that still remained from the early part of our childhood creating a barrier that we could not cross together.

❂ ❂ ❂

Almost ten years had gone by since I had spoken to Dad. I had heard that he and his wife had gone to live in England on an assignment with Conoco Oil Company. Every week, as I visited Aunt Carrie, more of his background, his family, my family, was emerging from the dark shadows. Something was stirring within me. I decided to hire a car and drive to Vermont. I wanted to find that house on the hill, where I had lived when I was six months old, where my grandparents had lived and which perhaps my father would have still owned had he stayed there. I wanted to find that house in the photograph that was hidden in the drawer of the old oak desk.

My car handled the Vermont roads with ease. I began to slow down at the sign that read 'Grafton', then continued over the covered bridge. After parking on the short main street and looking around at the quaint New England buildings, which probably hadn't changed in two hundred years, I walked into the post office–general store, the tinkling bell announcing my entrance. I enquired about a house on the hill and mentioned the name of Mehring.

'Mehring?' an old fellow popped his head up from behind the counter. 'I remember that name. Your grandfather, eh? Well, he was a nice old man. Served on our school board for a number of years. Their house . . .? Oh, that's up the hill, just out of town. Sugar Bush, it is. Easy to find.'

I began to feel the connection as I drove up the hill and, standing at the gate, I could almost touch the past, that part of me that had belonged there. I didn't want to knock at the door. I just said a prayer of thanks into the wind and drove back over the bridge.

On the way out of town I saw a quaint weatherboard house where second-hand books were sold. I stopped and went in, and browsed through the shelves, touching the decades-old copies of the classics. It must have been the shop where my grandfather had bought books for me.

Something was complete in my life now with this journey into the past. I had picked up some of the pieces that had always seemed out of reach. It was all a preparation to reconnect with my dad.

❂ ❂ ❂

Everyone either loves New York or they hate it. There is no in between. Out of ten years that I lived there, there were only six months that I hated it. During that time I wanted to get out in the worst way. The harsh realities of city living were closing in on me at a very fast pace. I daydreamed constantly of leaving the city and seeking refuge in a cottage in upstate New York, nestled by the side of a river, with no running water or electricity. I wanted to talk to the animals, touch nature once again, every cell of my body reacting to the hardness of the city and lack of contact with the soil. I read the book *Pilgrim at Tinker Creek* by Annie Dillard over and over and dreamed of waking one day to find myself lying prone in the tall grass listening to the music of the insects.

In New York, Jesse and I lived mostly in the lounge room–kitchen combination of our one-bedroom apartment. The apartment was rather dark already, being one of thirty or so studio or one-bedroom apartments in a building that was sandwiched between two other high-rise structures. The apartment's one window faced the fire escape and had bars on it. There were three locks on the only door. Those three locks always amused me as I would never be able to unlock them in time if someone with evil intentions was following close behind.

No one in the building seemed to want to know their neighbours. On the corner of one city block there could be over a hundred people living virtually on top of one another and yet no one spoke. The code of silence, born of fear mixed with survival, was strictly adhered to. I could almost brush shoulders with the couple living across the hall, their door only one and a half metres from mine, and not know them beyond a smile and a hello. Life in New York was a lesson on how to be lonely in the midst of eight million people.

One of my hobbies was photography, and I set up a small dark room in a corner of the apartment. It was photography that kept me in the Big Apple. One day I took my Nikon camera and walked the paths of Central Park. Through the lens, I focused on a young girl sitting alone on the edge of the duck pond. Via the eye of the camera I spied on other lonely people dotted here and there: a man feeding pigeons from a paper bag, an obviously homeless man wearing threadbare jeans sleeping on a park bench, a bag lady adjusting all three coats that she wore on her back. I suddenly knew that this was my home. Perhaps it was that I identified with the loneliness or that I had made my peace with New York City, the birthplace of my dad.

As Father's Day in 1977 approached, I began to think about Dad more and more. As I walked back and forth from my work, everywhere I turned I noticed the posters portraying gifts and cards for fathers. 'I'll just look,' I thought, as I entered a shop. 'But what if he died and I hadn't spoken to him and straightened things out. After all, I do love him,' I kept thinking as I fingered one card after another. In the end, I bought one. I spilled out the pain I felt toward him in a separate note. The final words at the bottom were, 'But I do love you, Dad.' I closed the envelope and let it go.

Two weeks later a reply came. A small card. My eyes quickly scanned the familiar handwriting on the inside. 'I want you to know that I have always loved you and I ask your forgiveness. I have learned over the years that true forgiveness comes from God through Jesus Christ. You were always the apple of my eye.' My breath caught in my throat and I couldn't believe that in one moment, holding this card in my hand, my view of my dad, my view of God and even my view of pain could change so radically. At thirty-one years old I had taken the first step toward a long journey home.

My first meeting with Dad after ten long years took place across a white cloth-covered table at an Upper West Side restaurant in New York. A business trip had brought him to me. My stomach had churned with nervousness as I walked the three blocks from the subway toward the appointed spot. We chatted over a few mundane bits of information: his time in England, his wife Ellie, his job now, his fishing holidays. The fear slowly melted away and I was finally able to see him as he really was—my father, a man with faults and weaknesses, but a man whom I resembled, a man who gave me gifts of intellect, wisdom, a love of nature, strength to survive hard knocks. I was able to make small steps toward honesty with him, explaining my hurt and, at the same time, my love for him and need for his approval. We hugged briefly before I turned back toward the subway to my apartment.

This was the beginning of opening up the stories of both my father and my mother, stories I had never seen or heard before. I was seeing their relationship now through the eyes of an adult, rather than through the eyes of a child. The view was very different. The yearning within me, as well as within my brother and sister, had been for family. None of us understood the hurts inside both our parents that led to the divorce. We didn't know our parents, really. They were both closed with their feelings, maybe even to each other.

It wasn't until many years later, as I walked along the edges of a dry creek bed in Oklahoma with my father, at a place where we used to hunt for Indian arrowheads, that I learned what he felt long ago when we all lived together in the same house. It wasn't until then that I learned of incidents during the war that led to some of my father's frustrations. It wasn't until then that I learned how hard it was for him to cope with my mother's family, feeling smothered and manipulated, because she always seemed to turn to them to make decisions. It wasn't until then that he told me that his own mother had never said the words 'I love you' to him until a few years before she died, at the age of ninety-eight.

It also wasn't until many years later, sitting on the edge of my mother's bed talking about her mastectomy a few years before and her battle with cancer that I heard about her other struggle with loneliness and pain from the events leading up to the divorce. I heard how she continued to love and support my sister through two subsequent divorces and a devastating mental illness. How my mother could never abandon her even when it meant the sacrifice of her own health. It wasn't until then that I could love my mother more than I ever had as a child, because now I had grown up, had experienced many disappointments as well from broken relationships and smashed dreams in my own heart.

❂ ❂ ❂

My search for spiritual answers to life began in psychotherapy. For two years I lay on a couch once a week and told my story to a therapist, bit by bit, alternating between self-hate and tears of compassion. At the same time I explored a number of pathways to meaning, in books on eastern religion, meditation and pop psychology. Everyone seemed to have THE answer. It seemed as though I was in a frantic search to find the right track to run on, discussing morality with members of the New York Human Ethics Society, enrolling in PhD subjects in clinical psychology at New York University and joining a women's therapy group. As I walked home day after day from my office at Chase Manhattan, I was drawn to the famous St Patrick's Cathedral along Fifth Avenue, and I often slipped in to sit in the back row, trying to think clearly and bring together the jumbled jigsaw pieces of my life.

Jesse was still pressuring me to get married, my position at work was no longer satisfying, my mind was constantly being drawn back to my own family, and my grasp on my future was slipping. As I leafed through the pages of William James's book, *The Varieties of Religious Experience*, I found someone I could identify with. It was on a vacation climb in the Adirondack Mountains in New York State that James had had a religious experience, as if there was 'an indescribable meeting of the gods in [his] breast'. That was exactly what I felt was happening within me. In one of my journals I asked myself a question: 'Could it really be true that the Jesus of my childhood has the answer to my life now? Does he embody the truth of human personality and if he does, I want to know it.' I never wanted the religion of man, but to meet God himself.

For the first time in many years I decided to visit my family in Oklahoma for the holiday season. It was to be a meeting of crisis. My mother and I had an argument because she couldn't understand my relationship with a person 'of colour'. She told me of other parents who had disowned their children when they married cross-racially, even going so far as to not acknowledge their grandchildren. I had never dared to suggest to Jesse that he accompany me on this trip, knowing deep down what my mother thought. I flew back at her with cutting remarks, asking how she could attend church every Sunday and still have such negative opinions toward other people of the human race.

I never told my dad about Jesse, fearing more of the same attitude, but I could tell that his opinionated personality had now changed somewhat, probably due to the persevering strength of his wife, Ellie, whom I had met for the first time on this trip. On Christmas Eve day of 1977, after a week of agony, I boarded the plane back to New York, relieved to be turning my back on the bickering, the obvious pain that was still there in my mother's heart, and the lingering bitterness of divorce. Ellie had thrust a Bible into my hands as a last-minute gift before I left and it lay closed on my lap as the flight headed toward New York. My mind was jumbled with questions and my heart was tired of trying to please my parents. I glanced out at the clouds and the words jumbled out: 'Well, God, where is the truth of all this, anyway? I'm tired of looking.'

A quiet voice spoke deep into my spirit, a voice of peace and truth. 'You've come home, Diana. I am the truth and I've placed it there in your heart.' The Christian values I had learned as a child suddenly began to make sense. They were no longer just part of a church system or organisation but they were living, transforming, and connected to a spiritual world which I had denied for so many years. When the flight attendant announced our arrival at Kennedy Airport and I walked through the terminal and caught a taxi to my 74th Street apartment, I was seeing my future in a totally different way.

Jesse and I eventually parted. I couldn't commit myself anymore to a life of smoking dope, feeling angry at the past, or climbing up the corporate ladder. My search for spiritual direction led me from a friendship with a Catholic nun at a charismatic worship group to some prayer with a Franciscan brother who held retreats in the countryside, and then to a small independent, non-denominational church called New York Christian Fellowship, which met in a room underneath a Chinese restaurant in Greenwich Village. It was positioned opposite Washington Square Park, which had been the scene of a 1960s movie called *Needle Park*, which documented the hippie drug scene of that area.

Greenwich Village was a marvellous place. Its narrow side streets were lined with four-storey apartment buildings and corner coffee house tables spilled out onto the sidewalks. There were more trees along its side lanes than many other places in Manhattan and most apartment windows were decorated with potted flowers. Walking down East 13th Street, one could hear buzzing, philosophical conversations filling the cafes, as customers sipped on French onion soup and small glasses of brandy. On a sunny afternoon, there were sidewalk art shows, young men doing handstands on skate boards, kids on roller skates swerving around the parking meters and groups of long-haired jazz musicians performing in the open squares. Life happened outdoors. No one seemed to care how others were dressed; in fact, the more of a statement one made through outlandish clothing, the better. Our church was in the middle of it all. It attracted men and women who were searching for spiritual meaning to their lives but at the same time did not want to be a part of mainstream Christian denominations. It was like no other church I had ever seen, as it strived to emulate the New Testament lifestyle, complete with semi-communal living, a non-hierarchical structure, and open to one and all. Set in the middle of the zany, the weird and the wonderful slices of Village life, the clientele that wandered in proved to be a challenge. I was captivated by a panoply of street people and I soon resigned from Chase Manhattan and embarked on a career in serving my fellow man.

It started with the Salvation Army. In the Village area, the Salvos supported a house for women who had come out of prison on drug-related charges and who were interested in staying 'clean' and changing their lives. There I met a young woman named Magdalena who was recovering from an operation on her feet. She had been a heroin addict for a number of years and had eventually exhausted the most obvious places on her body to inject the drug. The last spot had been between her toes, resulting in both her feet becoming terribly infected. For six weeks she couldn't walk and had to sit with her bandaged feet propped up on cushions. We spent long hours talking about her life and what events had brought her to such a place. 'My mother named me after the woman in the Bible. Said I was special. But then she left me . . . I never saw her again.' Magdalena described a string of foster homes and eventually her days and nights on the streets around Times Square, being taken care of by the pimps. 'I don't wanna go back out there,' she used to cry to me.

So many people who were born and raised in New York City often dreamed of leaving, of getting out of the concrete jungle to see something more of the world and to touch the reality of life outside. There was a constant desire to feel the earth, connect with nature and travel the countryside, but not many were able to make it out of the boundaries of their own 'hoods. I knew Magdalena had such a dream.

Some weeks later, close to midnight, I was visiting the street walkers around the Times Square district, helping to serve coffee from the van donated by one of the other churches. The regulars along the street had come to know us and, somehow, I always felt protected by them. That night, as I rounded the corner and approached a young lady cuddled up to a guy, I asked if she had seen Magdalena. Her hand motioned toward the door of a dark hotel and out from its shadow stepped my friend. We hugged, laughed and talked. 'I really wanna get out of here. I have a card here.' She dug into her tiny handbag. 'I'm going upstate to get cleaned up.' With those words, she was led away by a customer. I never saw her again.

In the midst of experiencing a part of society that, on the outside at least, had been so different from my own world, I heard that my sister had left her husband after having three children, an ectopic pregnancy, and post-natal depression. All I could say to her on the phone was not to do anything in a hurry, but within six months she had secured a divorce and had married a young man who had escaped from Romania two years before. She didn't really know him, and three months later, she was forced to take out a restraining order against him for violence. The marriage ended up in a divorce. My mother became the primary caretaker of the children when Pat's emotions took a plunge.

By 1982 I had worked full-time in a variety of church-sponsored activities, organising a one-room school for emotionally disturbed children who needed individual help, continuing to counsel heroin addicts at Odyssey House, sharing an old weatherboard house on Staten Island with women who were homeless, and collecting books and clothing for the street beggars in Colombia, South America. My salary consisted of fifty dollars a week, room and board, plus donated clothes. What a change from shopping at Sax Fifth Avenue!

A missionary, that's what I wanted to be. Remembering back to the 1960s during the Kennedy era, I had been fascinated by the American

Field Service, a group that sent young people all over the world to give
their time and talents to developing countries and small villages. The
main reward was a sense of satisfaction and service to the global community. Ever since the voice of God spoke to me on the plane, my values
had been changing. Material possessions were no longer important.
Career advancement no longer brought delight or challenge.

If the church sent a team to Colombia, I wanted to go. I could speak
a little Spanish and I felt ready for a change. But the pastor and his wife
had told me about plans to take a small group to Australia, to live among
tribal Aboriginal people. Would I consider going with them? I went for
a walk along the East River Boulevard not far from the United Nations
complex, where I used to talk things over with God, myself and the
seagulls that pecked at scraps lying around the wooden benches. Couples
would stroll along the wide concrete pathway, sometimes throwing bits
of bread to the pigeons that were permanent fixtures of New York life.
Men and women would take their daily jog along the path, huffing and
puffing, wearing the latest Adidas gear and water bottles strapped to their
waist.

As the cosmopolitan world swirled around me, the most important
question for me was this: 'Was I ready to leave America?' There were
ten churches who had never been involved in missions before but now
were prepared to support a team of five or six to live in the desert regions
of Australia, a team that would encourage the Aboriginal leadership to
take its place in the church. The spot was not definite, but research and
contacts pointed to the Western Desert region outside a place called
Kalgoorlie. We didn't really have a clear pathway, but just as Abraham
had left his country not knowing where he was going, so too were we
ready to leave.

It seemed that all my paths had merged at this point. The hurts of
rejection in my childhood, the journey of reconciliation with my dad,
the broken marriage relationship and the world of drugs to ease the pain,
the visits to Harlem and experiencing racism's many ugly contours, the
walks along the streets of Times Square's night life, all seemed to point
ahead to something much bigger and stranger than I could imagine.

For a year, our team prepared, studied, wrote letters, made Australian
contacts, prayed together, and even argued together. During my research
at libraries and at the Australian Consulate, on our destination, I found

a dictionary of Western Desert language, a portion of Scripture and an anecdotal account of a visit to the tribes in that area by anthropologist John Greenway. A common name kept cropping up throughout all these readings—Wilf Douglas—linguist and respected missionary. From New York City I wrote to the publisher of the book with a note to Wilf, never thinking it would find him. Much to my surprise, several months later I received an answer, and a personal connection to the future. Our team sold all our goods and bought one way tickets. It was 1983. I said my goodbyes: to my father, who thought I was going on an interesting journey; to my mother, who was sad to see me go so far; to my brother, who screamed at me, 'You'll just die over there in Australia. Aren't there enough people here in America to help?'; to my sister, who had just begun psychiatric treatment for manic-depression and showed me a shelf-full of prescription drugs; and also to Jesse, whom I hadn't seen in over three years. 'I wish I could be like you. The peace I see on your face,' Jesse said sadly, 'but I can't give up the reefer and the streets of New York.'

When the plane took off from Los Angeles Airport, I knew I was going for good. No one ever said it out loud, but somehow I knew. The bridges behind me were going up in smoke and I turned to face a new hope, a new life and a new challenge. I really didn't know what to expect, but two things I knew for sure: I was ready to live on the land, under a tree, if I had to; and I wanted to learn, not just about, but from, the remote tribal people of the desert in the sunburnt country of Australia.

CHAPTER 3

Old Mary

Ron's family history was characterised by many twists and turns, much of it the result of the pain of the settling of Australia and the dislocation of Aboriginal people. Sitting in the place of prominence at the kitchen table with the green formica top and chrome legs, Ron's Uncle Gerald would spin the yarns about the family's history, beginning with Old Mary, the Wongi matriarch from the gold-fields region of Western Australia.

Mary and her brother Charles were born in the Darlot region, out from Wiluna, probably in the 1880s, during a period of tribal wars in the area around Mulga Queen, Leonora and Menzies. Mary and Charles were dodging the spears as they ran into the bush when they couldn't see any of their family left standing. They escaped together into the night, finding bush food to eat. Eventually they reached Esperance. There, the Native Welfare scooped them up and sent them onto the south-west reserves, which were parcels of land on the edges of towns set aside for Aboriginal people. Eventually, Mary met Willie Kikar, a tribal lawman who was feared far and wide for his magic powers. Mary herself knew the skills of bush healing and would 'doctor' many children who were sick and chase away evil 'charnack' spirits by taking hot ashes in her hands and throwing them into the darkness in the direction of the spirit or talking special 'talk' so 'it' would go away. She taught the younger children to hunt for bardi and goanna eggs and how to cook them on the hot ashes. Old Mary was a tall, stately woman whose walk and posture never revealed the harsh life she lived or the years she spent running.

In most families who lived on the fringes, it was the women, especially the grandmothers, who held the clan together, delivering babies, chopping firewood, finding food for the children. The men were either getting work on the farms or stations, helping to clear the land, or away drinking with their mates. Young women went where the young men were and brought back more children for the grandmother to look after. In those days it was especially hard since there was no such thing as welfare benefits. Sometimes food was so scarce that all that was left was sugar in a bag to suck on, or some bread dipped in tea, known as 'chalkbread' to Gerald and his cousins.

When Mary travelled with her husband, Willie, through the south coastal areas, and they were camped around the fires at night, Willie would tell his people that change was coming. 'We gotta be peaceful,' he'd say. 'That's the only way we can survive.' Farmers in the area trusted him with their donkey teams and he would often be seen carting wool from Jerramungup to Albany. Mary worked on the farms right alongside Willie, doing as much heavy lifting of hay bales and clearing of stumps as the men did. Willie seemed to have a way with horses, roaming the Stirling Ranges with the wild brumbies, making them quiet and training them for the light horsemen during World War I.

The bush was their home and so were the rolling hills and the sharp craggy peaks of the Stirlings and the Porongurups. They could often be seen shepherding the sheep, both of them tall and dark, with Mary wearing her distinctive long coat and hat. Mary, a full-blood Wongi from the goldfields and Willie, a full-blood Noongar tribal warrior from the south-west—even in those times theirs was considered a cross-cultural marriage. The Noongars were always slightly afraid of the Wongis because of their ceremonial initiations, their featherfoot warriors, who wore boots from emu feathers so they couldn't be tracked when they performed a tribal killing, and their system of payback. But the Wongis always found a welcome with Mary and Willie when they came down south, and they never forgot the acts of friendship from the Kikars.

Willie and Mary had four children: three sons and a daughter. Joe, their eldest child, was Ron's grandfather and guardian. On one of the farms, the boss said to Willie, 'Can't call you Kikar. What sort of name

is that? We'll call you Willie, eh? Willie Williams.' That's why their son
Joe's surname was Williams, why their great grandson Ron is called
Williams and why I am a Williams.

Joe was born to Mary and Willie when they were working on the
farms near Mount Barker. He grew up moving from farm to farm, gradually learning to clear the land, make harnesses for the horses and wooden
carts for them to pull. The bush was their life. Their home was a tent,
under a tree or in a shack at the back of properties owned by the
pioneering Hassell family. On any given night, dotted across the
paddocks, flickering among the tall native trees, there were camp fires
around which small family groups could be seen in silhouette, sitting in
a circle telling 'yarns', passing the billy tea and dipping bread into melted
sheep's fat. Little children would sit cross-legged on the ground and the
adults would perch on logs or wooden crates. Trills of laughter and
nostalgic singing would echo through the valleys and into the next field.

Ron's relatives recall those days in voices that are warm and smooth.
Their wrinkled faces soften as the stories are retold. It was a time of
struggle and coping with changing patterns of life, but it was also a time
of strength, when families lived for each other, could tell a good joke
and understood that sticking together meant survival. But even that was
about to change.

The year 1905 in Western Australia is etched into the memory of
every Aboriginal person in the state. This was the year of the The Act.
Called a 'Protection Act' by some strange twist of the bureaucratic mind,
it actually brought in rules and regulations regarding even the simplest
things of life. Permission was needed by Aboriginal men and women to
do anything: visit relatives, get married, have a job, travel, receive blankets and clothing, give away or sell blankets or clothing. The main result
of these laws, which affected Ron's family and many thousands of others
in Western Australia, was that the Commissioner was to become the legal
guardian of every native child until the age of twenty-one, even if they
had parents or relatives who were living.

Gracie Harris was, like so many other young children, taken away
from her mother, Emma, and raised in a mission home in Perth. Gracie
had been born in the Busselton area on the Ellensbrook property, near
the sea. Her grandfather had come from England during the early convict
days. He constantly stroked his long white beard, rode a big white stallion

and used to tell Gracie stories from a huge family Bible. It was this man's son who took a fancy to Emma, a woman of Aboriginal and Black American descent, and they had two daughters, Gracie and Ida. Eventually he left Emma with the two girls, moved to Perth and married a socialite.

Emma named her younger daughter after Gracie Bussell. One of their relatives, old Sam Isaacs, who lived on the Ellensbrook property, had taught young Grace Bussell to ride a horse. The Noongar story has it that they were riding along the river as it went out to sea and they saw that the ship, the *Georgette*, had run aground. Without so much as a thought, Sam rode straight into the water to help save the people who were drowning. Grace followed him into the water and pulled some of them ashore. The newspaper broadcast the whole story about the bravery of young Grace and called her the Darling of Australia. But they never mentioned Sam, strong Sam, whose horse pranced up and down the shore as he lifted people out of the water until he was exhausted. As Emma cuddled her new-born daughter, perhaps wishing for her to grow up strong in order to face the disappointments in life, she whispered her name: 'Grace'.

When Grace Harris turned four years old, a government worker took her away to Perth—because she was too white. Eventually Grace was moved to Carrolup Native Settlement, thirty kilometres outside of Katanning in the Great Southern. Her mother Emma had married an Aboriginal man named Colbung, who worked on farms around Gnowangerup and Tambellup, and together they made application to get Gracie out of Carrolup, but the police reported to the Protector that Colbung was not a desirable person to have control of the young girl. Eventually Emma was taken to Moore River Settlement with some of her other children. She always felt a prisoner, and even wrote a heart-wrenching letter in beautiful handwriting to the superintendent:

Dear Sir,
I want to know if I can go home to Busselton and take Mabel. She is a great worry hear. She is worrying all the time and say she wants to go back to Busselton. I don't know why I am made a presoner when I came hear on my own free will. Plenty of other people outside worser than I am and they can come in and out when they like . . . please, Mr. Coppen, have pity on me and let me go home to Busselton.

Emma remained at Moore River Settlement for many years. She died in Perth in 1932.

Grace was separated from her family, and cried for a mother she had not been able to know. She spent a number of years at Carrolup, a settlement that began in 1915 as a place where Aboriginal families could be taken, away from the sights and sounds of the south-west towns. Because Grace was fair in colour, she and other children like her were to be assimilated into white society, their Aboriginality to be gradually bred out. Even the families that voluntarily went there were separated from their children. The boys and girls were put into dormitories with beds lining each wall, locked in at night to prevent them from running away and given very little bedding even during the cold, harsh winter nights. Grace tried to run away a number of times, only to be caught and returned to face punishment, which ranged from solitary confinement to a shaved head. Children who wet their beds faced dire consequences, including having to sleep on their damp urine-drenched mattresses. The evening meal usually consisted of bread, jam and black tea. Disease was rampant, the VD clinic well-visited, and in the early 1920s there were outbreaks of TB and measles that caused a number of deaths. The adults' camps, which dotted the bush surrounding Carrolup, were often in an uproar over the deaths of members of their extended families.

When Joe Williams was visiting some Noongars at Carrolup, he met Grace and they ran away together, but she was caught a few days later and brought back to the settlement. Late in 1921, Joe made application to the superintendent concerning his desire to marry Grace. On 24 January 1922, the superintendent gave permission for the engagement and marriage, since Joe was an 'able-bodied, splendid example of an Aborigine'. Joe was handsome and strong, a hard worker who could clear a jump of six feet from a standing position. As an initiated tribal man, he was not afraid of anyone, not police, bosses on the farms or other tribal men. The wedding was held at Carrolup, complete with a white wedding dress, sent from Perth, which was standard issue from the Native Welfare Department.

Not long after the wedding, Carrolup was closed down by the government and remained closed for sixteen years until 1938, when the public began to cry out for the government to do something about the Aboriginal outcasts hanging around the towns. In 1934, the Moseley

Royal Commission in Perth heard arguments regarding the future of the Aboriginal race. One comment by a medical practitioner on the commission records (section 1032) states:

> The mating of half-castes with half-castes means nothing more than the perpetuation of the black and coloured element against which we are all of us so set . . . We will on the other hand do all in our power to displace the black strain by an infiltration of white blood. I am not advocating marriage of white with half-caste . . . but the mating of half-caste with a coloured person who has more white blood in him or her, with one who, as a quadroon or octoroon, is higher up on the white scale.

It was this report and the decisions that followed that have echoed down through the years into the unconscious collective mind of Aboriginal peoples, into Ron's family life, consequently into our life together and, undoubtedly, into the future of our daughter.

Soon after leaving Carrolup, Joe and Gracie went on a shepherding run down to the Cape Riche coast of Western Australia. On the way through the hills, Gracie walked off into the bush and gave birth to her first child, Cissie Carmen. She then quickly joined the flock again as they made their way south. Gracie eventually had six other children but lost two, one as an infant and one at three years of age. Cissie grew up helping to clear the farms, shepherd the sheep and break the horses. She never went to school, but worked like a man. She stood about six feet tall, and was dark, with muscular arms from swinging an axe. The little family usually pitched their own tents and Gracie would tan the hides of kangaroos or sew wheat bags together to keep them warm. When the water ran low, Cissie and her sister would take the billy can and shake the leaves on the bushes so that the drops of water could be collected.

At times, survival was critical and the food supplies ran very low. Kangaroos were not plentiful, other bush game had long since been eaten out or moved on because of the clearing of the land, and rations depots operated only once a week. At the beginning of World War II, young Aboriginal women were drawn to the docks of Fremantle or Albany, exchanging sex with the American soldiers for a bit of money, which they used to buy tea, flour, sugar or a bottle of wine to liven up a meagre existence and to keep warm at night.

In 1939, at the age of sixteen, Cissie found herself pregnant. She continued to work with her parents on the farms, doing the same heavy work that she had always done. They eventually camped at the edge of Deadman's Lake in Albany in a small two-room hut. The weather was damp and cold. Cissie found it increasingly awkward to move around and then, one day, after chopping and stacking wood for the evening fire, the pains became severe. For a couple of days, she groaned and cried inside the little hut. Old Mary, alerted by Gracie, arrived late at night from the reserve. There, inside the thin-walled hut, on a bush mattress, Ron was born two months premature on 19 June 1940, to the background music of croaking frogs on the shores of the lake. Granny Grace called him Ron, another old auntie called him Amos and his Uncle Barney gave him the tribal name Parndang, which means wandering crow, always watching and calling out in warning. Ron was his official name, but it was Parndang that described his character.

Joe and Gracie immediately became Ron's parents. They had lost a baby themselves just a short time before and Cissie gladly handed Ron to her parents and went away with other girls, finding men or travelling around Perth. When she was back at camp, Ron remembers her sitting by the fire, heating up rubber-coated copper wire and then wrapping her hair in ringlets around the wire and letting it dry.

'My mother was a beautiful woman,' Ron explained. 'She always fixed herself up, wore high-heeled shoes and liked to sing American love songs like "All the Nice Girls Love a Sailor" around the camp fire at night.' But she was a fighter, too, and Ron was afraid of her, especially when she would drink.

He never called her 'Mum' because he was too ashamed of her. 'She couldn't read or write. She was darker than me and when she would come to my school I would try to pretend I didn't know her. I told her not to talk to me because the other kids would call me "nigger". She just walked away after that. It wasn't until I had grown up that I realised I really did love her.'

There were a few times that Ron remembered his mother with fondness. Like the time she saved him from a wild bull. Her strength came in handy when she and her sister took Ron, about six years old, hunting for birds. A wild red bull spotted them, broke through the fence and made his way directly towards them, pawing the ground. Cissie grabbed Ron by the arm, lifted him into a tree and then shot the bull with a double-barrelled shotgun, stunning it long enough to grab her little son, run through the paddock and jump the fence to safety.

Ron never knew who his own father was. No one in the family seemed to know either, and if Cissie knew, she wasn't telling. Many times Ron wanted to ask his mother, but he was afraid to. Some said that his father was a white sailor in Perth whom Cissie used to flirt with; others said he was a German spy who grew vegetables around Albany. Ron had seen his mother with him once and then later he heard that two soldiers had come and shot him because he was a spy.

It was Grandfather Joe who was Ron's mentor. He loved Ron like his own son, going out of his way to look after him. 'My grandfather must have loved me,' said Ron, 'because when I was a little tacker, there was this spread of the whooping cough and meningitis. Lots of us died and some even got crippled. But my grandfather, he bundled me up and took me into the hospital when I started coughing. He picked me up in his strong arms, wrapped me up in a blanket and wedged me between two flour bags in the cart, bridled the horse and went over a hundred kilometres, with me bumpin' around in the back. He didn't have to do that. He hated hospitals.' Noongars didn't like going into the hospitals. They were afraid that they might never come out again and most of them ran away, still clad in hospital greens, before the full treatment could be given.

Aboriginal families who camped around the farms and towns in the south-west were beginning to experience more visits from workers at Native Welfare, who were reporting on their living conditions. From time to time, these families would disappear, taken to native settlements a long way from their homelands. The police often stopped by the farms where Joe worked, making inspections and intimating that if he didn't build a proper house, they would all be taken away. Gracie had been put into mission homes and settlements too many times and was desperate to stay free. Joe made their camp deep in the bush away from the other farms. The best he could do was to erect an eight-by-ten tent and a small bough shed while he tried to gather enough iron and timber to build a more waterproof house, but on a sporadic wage of three pounds a week, it was almost impossible.

One night, as the family gathered together outside the bough shed and the children were playing chasey around the fire, a large billy can, boiling furiously, was tipped over onto Ron. He was badly burnt on his legs and bottom and was taken to hospital. He was screaming in pain and the matron said he would have to stay in hospital for a month. That was devastating news for Joe because it meant that again they would come under the scrutiny of the Native Welfare Department. The moment that Ron was released from the hospital a warrant was issued for the apprehension and removal of the Williams family to Carrolup, stating that 'this family requires a period of supervision at a native reserve'.

The Noongars could 'smell' trouble on the wind and news travelled fast on the grapevine. Joe and Gracie heard that the police were searching for them. They made a new camp five miles into thick bush down a swampy track near Albany. From the top of the ridge behind them Joe could see the police car wandering around some of the back tracks looking for them. The first day, the police searched for a total of seventy-two miles and couldn't find any sign of them. The second day, they came quite close, but couldn't navigate the swampy track, although they had driven in circles for over sixty miles. Every time the police got close, Joe would give a bush call and his own children, along with Ron, would hike up the back of the tent flaps, fall to their stomachs, crawl underneath, run down the track and hide further in the bush.

'We were always on the run,' explained Ron. 'Grandfather didn't want to lose his family to any police or welfare.' Even today, when a knock sounds at the door of the family's house, the curtains are cautiously pulled back just enough to see who is there and the kids all run to the back of the house before the door is opened a crack. It takes a long time to bridge the gulf that years of official harassment, mistrust and oppression have created.

The government finally caught up with the Williams family. Early on the third day of the search, the children heard the police car grinding its gears along the boggy path but the sound had faded away by lunchtime. As night began to fall, Gracie started to cook some flaps over a small mound of coals, wary of sending signals that might give them away, when one of the farmers Joe had worked for came riding through the thicket on his horse, calling out his name. 'It's just me, Joe, old Green.' He motioned breathlessly, begging Joe to give up. 'They won't stop coming, Joe. You know that.' The family couldn't stay there much longer without being found and he wanted to reassure Joe that all the farmers would try to help get them out of Carrolup.

Ron's burns were still not healed and Joe knew that he had to give in. Reluctantly, they all followed the man on the horse back to the farm the next morning. The police were waiting and rounded them up together, Gracie, Joe and the five children. They were piled into the police car and bounced along the bush roads into Katanning. Ron and his family were squeezed into a small cell with no roof, just a grating so no one could climb out. It started to drizzle with rain, dripping into the cell.

'All we had was one blanket for the lot, so we huddled together in the corner and wrapped it around us,' Ron whispered, as if it happened only yesterday. The next morning the family was taken to Carrolup in an old ex-army truck.

Joe only had to wait three weeks before a letter arrived at the superintendent's office in the form of a petition signed by ten farmers in the Mount Barker and Albany district asking for his release to be able to work. They also asked that his wife Gracie and the small boy, Ron, be released with him. They were willing to provide plenty of work in horse-breaking and land clearing and promised to help him build a suitable house.

On 30 October 1945, Joe was released from Carrolup, but Gracie had to stay behind. For several months he worked hard while trying to build a house. The farmers had not come good on their promise to help and when the medical inspector came in March, he filed this report: 'The dwelling is not satisfactory.' It went on to say that Joe was required to build two more rooms, a kitchen and a lavatory, all to be made of wood and iron and not with walls made from hessian bags, which Joe had painstakingly sewn together. He was also told to bring beds and bedding from Albany, even though he had no means to do that. At the bottom of the official report, a small note was added: 'There is one more difficulty, however, that the police reserve he is camping on is not for natives and he might have to pull the house down at any time.' As Joe listened to these words read to him by one of the farmers, he murmured something about 'what do we need beds for anyway, bales of hay work just as good' and screwed up the report in his strong, work-hardened hands and tossed it on the ground. A few weeks later, Gracie and her children ran away from Carrolup. With the help of the boss of Hay River Farm, old Bill Souness, never again was the Williams family removed by government officials.

In 1948, Ron went to school for the first time. Until that year, an Aboriginal child was not allowed to attend a government school, but then in 1948, the rules changed. Ron had just turned eight and Joe talked it over with Gracie. 'We're sendin' that boy to school. None of us ever went there, 'cept you. And Ron? Well, he's smart and he needs to learn to read, so he can make somethin' of himself. I've got a clever boy, you know.'

'I didn't know if I wanted to go to school, back then. I used to see my Grannie reading by the moonlight,' recalled Ron. 'She learned to read in the mission and we all loved to hear the stories about the Texas Rangers. No one would say a word while she read to us the adventures in the Wild West, and then all us kids would act out the stories and pretend to kill each other with sticks shaped like guns. When the moon wasn't out, we made a "fat light". A piece of rag stuck in wet sand with mutton fat around it. It used to smoke like a train, but we didn't care. At least Grannie could read us a story.

'From time to time my Uncle Allan would come down from Meekatharra and he would tell wonderful stories about a man named Ned Kelly. He was my hero and every night I would take a little hurricane lamp across the clearing to his camp and beg him to tell me the stories again about Ned Kelly's spirit. I would get so scared that he would have to walk me back to my camp. Those days were special, full of fun, yarns, jokes and tears. It kept us alive when there wasn't much else. We used to listen to the night birds calling and the sounds of the insects. These were signs for us. The bush spoke in many languages. It told us when things were happening, when people died, when strangers were coming, when life was changing. We could "read" the sky, the trees and the animals. It gave us comfort, it was our "school".'

Ron did go to school, sometimes with bare feet and most of the time with clothes that were too big. The other kids called him 'nigger' and 'stink' and sometimes he got into a fight. It was hard to face that walk to school everyday when he knew he wasn't wanted. Some of the teachers were kind and tried to help, but when Ron turned fourteen, he decided he had had enough. He had only finished fifth standard, but he never went back again. The only thing he had liked about school was reading, especially the history books. When he returned to his camp, he delighted in being able to read stories to his uncles and aunties and then to Rosie, his younger sister who had been born to Cissie after Ron had started school.

Her father wasn't around either, so the Williams clan kept growing.

Two years later, Cissie announced that she was getting married. Even though her new husband was a man of quick temper and had a history of domestic violence, Cissie was proud, he 'put a ring on my finger'. They had two children, even though he spent most of their marriage in and out of gaol. In a fit of rage one night, he took their young son and threw him in a fire bucket just to spite her. Ron's young brother went through many years of skin graft operations as a result and the pain continued into adulthood. Cissie suffered years of beatings, not being able to break free of her need of this man. When her health finally broke down, the two younger children were sent to a Catholic mission home in the south-west.

After Ron left school, he would hang around the older men on the edges of town, sit with them around the campfires and listen to their exploits in and out of gaol. In those days, the men referred to prison as 'high school'. Some of Ron's uncles would return from months 'inside' looking healthier than they had ever been. 'My Uncle Fred often used to tell me that gaol was where you could be fed and treated okay. It was where you could learn a trade, even learn to read and write. We were often discriminated against in schools, shops and on trains. But in the prison, everyone was equal.' Sometimes the men would even pretend to have fights when they were in town so they could get a good feed in gaol or spend a few days out of the cold, knowing that the police would come and arrest them.

When the food supplies dwindled and the government endowments were spent, the only means of filling an empty stomach was to steal. Ron and his Uncle Barney, only six years older, would climb over the farmers' fences and take a few watermelons, maybe a chook and some vegies. Sometimes at the back of the baker's shop there would be some bags of old bread leaning against the verandah. When they asked the boss if they could have some, they were told, 'No, son, that's for the race horses over at the stables.'

In 1955, Ron's family went to Perth to visit relatives, but the only place they could find to camp was near the rubbish tip. There was a bit of work at the vineyards in the Swan Valley, but the pay was not enough to go around. Many of the Noongars would spend hours sifting through the piles of rubbish and off-scourings of Perth families, finding stale bread,

clothes and scrap metal. One night, Joe got ready to go on a foray to
the tip and he called out to Ron. 'You comin', Ronnie boy, I'm walkin'
down to the tip.' But Ron was too busy with his mates, being fifteen at
the time, and told his grandfather he didn't want to go. He glanced up
to see Joe walking off in the direction of the rubbish tip, disappearing
into the fast-falling darkness. Gracie and some of the young children and
teenagers were laughing and joking around the small fire flickering in the
four-gallon drum.

About two in the morning, Old Bluey, a friend of Joe's came into the
camp and woke Gracie from her sleep on a mattress of blackboy tops
and grass, squeezed into the corner of an old hut made of tin. He
whispered words that would change her life in a devastating way. 'Gracie,
the old fella's not coming home anymore. There was a fight down at
the tip and they killed him. I found his body, no life left in him, hidden
away in the bush.'

Gracie let out a piercing wail. Everybody woke up with a start and
knew straight away that it was something bad. She cried and cried while
Ron sat with her, numb with disbelief. The only dad he had ever known
was dead and he blamed himself.

'If only I had gone with him,' Ron murmured over and over, his
shoulders shaking with grief. 'But I wanted to be with my mates . . . tired
of going to the tip.'

Joe was given a pauper's burial and, years later, some of those graves
were emptied and tipped into the sea to make room for more. Even at
the end, Joe had no place to rest.

For several years, Ron carried the guilt around with him and became his
family's biggest worry. He took to the drink and would sit around the
campfires at night, singing the old country and western songs in exchange
for a bottle. The tough Noongar men who had scars on their chests, their
arms and sometimes on their faces from the fights and struggles of living in
an unwelcoming society, would listen and sometimes sing along in voices
out of tune, with tears running down their cheeks.

'I couldn't understand it,' said Ron. 'These men were my heroes, for
they were strong in ways I couldn't be, but I wanted to be. I couldn't
understand why they would cry.' To Ron, these men had always seemed
tough, unafraid of the challenges that life brought them, not conforming
to what the white world wanted them to be. They were his heroes after

the death of his grandfather. But when their guard was down, he saw the loneliness, the pain and the sorrows of living that cast a long shadow across his path. His Uncle Barney used to yell at him when he drank too much, yanking the bottle away from him and giving him a punch. 'You stupid, kid,' he'd say, in a voice that indicated otherwise. 'You'll be the biggest boozer under the sun, just like your mother.'

Ron kept drifting, feeling that he didn't have anything left to live for. He would wander around with at least half a dozen dogs and wore clothes two sizes too big. His family called him 'Spook'. He wandered until the spring of 1958, when a young man named Frank, from Tasmania, took a liking to him and began to invite him to church. Ron couldn't bring himself to go because he felt ashamed—his clothes were dirty and he had no shoes. One weekend, Teresa, his five-year-old niece, kept asking him over and over again: 'I wanna go to Sunday School, Uncle, please take me.' Ron wasn't really interested. He'd heard all the Bible stories from his grandmother and his Uncle Fred had brought him gospel tracts from Fremantle prison. He thought all this talk about Jesus was for white people, but as he looked at his little niece crying to go to church, he thought he might as well go. If anyone teased him, he would just say that he had to take this little girl along.

The tall Methodist preacher, balding with a trace of grey hair, stood at the door and shook his hand warmly: 'We're glad to see you here, son.' No whitefella had ever called him 'son' before. He hadn't heard that word since his grandfather died. The preacher kept talking. Ron didn't understand most of it, but he did remember one thing: 'God wants you to have the best, my son. He wants to put the best robe on you, like the prodigal son.' Those words rang in his ears as he walked away from that little mission church. 'God wants you to have the best.'

Frank Cole had come to Western Australia to find work on an Aboriginal mission. After a short time in Carnarvon, he had eventually made his way to the United Aboriginal Mission in Gnowangerup. He had walked around the reserve camps, visiting the Noongars, sitting in the dirt with them. He was a happy, friendly character, joining in the jokes and fun. Ron used to watch this whitefella and wonder why he hadn't come like the others to flirt with the Noongar women or sell grog. He wondered why he was just sitting there, enjoying their friendship, and gradually Ron started to trust him.

Gnowangerup Show Day was approaching, the day that most Noongars looked forward to and Ron was no exception. But in October of 1958, Ron was less excited than usual. He was unhappy with his life, getting tired of the drink, the songs late at night, the despondency he still felt from his grandfather's death. He sat quietly alone under a gum tree near the boxing tent, watching the crowds of people passing by, shouting at one another over the beating of the bass drum in the band, and the children screaming on the rides that threatened to spill them out. Suddenly Frank caught his eye and walked toward him. Ron wondered why this man had singled him out in the midst of all these white fellas he could talk to.

When Frank sat down next to Ron, he handed him a Bible. 'This is for you, Ron.' Along with the Bible, Frank had brought him a small picture of Jesus, carrying a lamb in his arms. When Ron looked at the picture, he knew he felt just like that lamb, somewhat lost, discouraged, looking for hope. Was it this Jesus who could pick him up like that little sheep? It was that afternoon, under the gum tree, that two men, one whitefella from Tasmania and the other a bush native from the south-west, sat with their heads bent toward one another, praying together. Ron asked Jesus to change his life for the better and give him hope.

It marked a change that was so real and so deep that during the forty-one years that followed that day, Ron was never again a drunk or a spook. The pain of the earth had been touched by the heavens. The struggle of learning his identity, the questions and complexity of the threads of his life—white, full-blood, half-caste, black American, Wongi and Noongar—seemed to be forming, not a dark tapestry, but one of many colours and hues. He could then look up and see something on the horizon, something, someone who beckoned him to follow, to take a path that, 'if it were told to him, he would not believe it'. The horizon, where pathways eventually come together, where the gaze is fixed with hope for what lies beyond, was there waiting for him.

❂ ❂ ❂

'Mr Williams, your mother is very sick. She doesn't have long to live.' Ron got the message from a relative in Perth. He hitched a ride from Gnowangerup to see her. The bitterness he had felt toward Cissie had gone and he realised what a toll the alcohol had taken on her life and on their relationship. He wanted to find her to tell her that he loved her. But when he enquired at the desk, the nurse slowly shook her head. 'I'm sorry, sir, but your mother died yesterday.' The years of beatings had contributed to the growth of cancerous lumps in her chest and her head, her body eventually succumbing to the disease.

Ron quickly left the hospital because he didn't want anyone to see him crying. It was the first time he had ever cried for his mother. Why hadn't he ever told her those simple words 'I love you'? Why had he never called her 'Mum'? That moment has lived with him for forty years, driving his desire to say kind things to people because he knows he might never see them again.

CHAPTER 4

Deserts and Crowbars

R on and I journeyed to the deserts of Australia from different directions, and it was the desert that held important experiences for each of us at separate times and in diverse circumstances. The parallel lines of our lives were eventually to run through the red dirt, past the smiling faces of tribal desert people and over the contrasting contours of the land before meeting.

At first glance one might describe the centre of Australia as dry, barren, and covered with shrubs and squat, spindly trees which somehow forgot to grow. But the mood of the desert changes as often as one changes clothes. In the spring, the long-hidden varieties of wildflowers wave in the breeze, making their appearance for a few short weeks. In good seasons, a light carpet of white everlastings covers the desert floor, giving the appearance of a dusting of snow. Clumps of red kangaroo paws dot the sides of desert pathways. At night, the sky covers the bush traveller with a blanket of stars that seem never-ending. Tucked into a swag, one can see the sparks from the camp fire shoot towards the heavens, mingling for a moment, then disappearing into a time and space far beyond what the eye can see.

During the wet seasons, cyclones that violently swirl along the north-western coastline sometimes stretch their fingers inland toward the desert region, bringing dark skies and short torrents of rain. The red clay mixture of the paddocks turns to boggy mud, causing a vehicle to stay mired for weeks. Winter days are full of sunshine, while the nights can be bitterly cold, and the midsummer air reaching fifty degrees Celsius can be stifling when stepping out of an air-conditioned four-wheel-drive. The desert is a paradox of beauty and harshness. It is a place that beckons the visitor to find the glimpses of colour or the life-giving water hidden beneath the rocks. It is a place that gives a greeting of quiet peacefulness, but then just as quickly saps one's strength with the relentless rays of the sun and mocks the traveller with an endless terrain of nothingness.

After meeting his God, Ron spent two years in the first Aboriginal Bible College in Western Australia, which was established on farming property in Gnowangerup. He studied to be a pastor and missionary and then, in 1962, he was sent as a cross-tribal missionary by the United Aboriginal Mission (UAM) to the Warburton Ranges in the western desert region, approximately 1600 kilometres north-east from Perth. There the Aboriginal men called him 'whitefella' for eighteen months because his skin was a lighter colour. A tribal man had been speared just before Ron arrived. No matter what the missionaries or nurses tried to do they couldn't save him and the man bled to death in the arms of a missionary friend. This incident deeply affected Ron. One afternoon he penned a tribute to the dying man:

> In the outback of Australia, where our native people roam
> came this heart cry to God's servant:
> 'I'm lost and I'm not going home.
>
> 'For you can't help me now, no, you can't help me now,
> you can't help me now, you've come too late.
> My life is nearly past, I'm left out in the dark.
> You can't help me now, you've come too late.'

That song continued to cry from Ron's heart, driving his desire to connect with as many of his people as he could.

When he arrived at Warburton, one of Ron's jobs was to dig wells to find fresh water for the camp dwellers. The water holes were drying up and the food sources were being depleted as mining corporations began to take over tribal lands. The mission workers were trying to dig wells in order to provide water to the tribal families who travelled through the area. Ron would often be lowered down on ropes into the wells with sticks of explosives strapped to his back in order to blow open a deeper hole. The water that eventually came out tasted slightly salty with a hint of dynamite.

He went hunting with the tribal men and listened to their stories of creation, land and kinship. He learned their tribal language and slept on the ground after digging in the sand to make a 'hip hole' to sleep in. On one trip out from the camp, Ron accepted a cup of black muddy water drawn from a soak by a tribal woman who had walked two miles to find it. She had carried the precious contents back in a battered billy can balanced on top of her head. She gave Ron the first taste.

Huddled and sweating under a blanket in fifty-degree temperatures, Ron would try to hide from the flies that buzzed around the scores of boils on his legs. The boils recurred frequently due to the lack of fresh fruit and vegetables. He was never tribally initiated into the circle of men but they accepted him and loved him as their brother.

The traditional desert people were tall and dignified, confident in their skills of living with the land. The shapes of the hills, the rock holes and caves were their friends, their guides through a bush land that was inhospitable to all but them. Their approach to God's creation was not one of manipulation, domination or greed. Over many generations they had learned to live *with* it, to listen to it, to move with it and to appreciate it. Those who came after them were not of the same mind. Explorers and surveyors trekked across the tribal lands and then the dingo trappers and prospectors came shooting out the game and looking for deposits of gold and other minerals. Stories soon filtered back to the mining camps, that joked and boasted of the shooting and poisoning of the natives who were unlucky enough to be caught by surprise in their own homeland areas.

Bush storytellers described the chaining of Aboriginal women to trees until they were thirsty and then tracking them to a water hole. When muscular warriors with raised scars on their chests indicating initiated status were sighted, the explorers on camels would approach them, trying to promote friendship through gifts of salt beef. Then they would wait until the men fled into the bush to find water. Several generations later, the descendants of these same Aboriginal people retold the stories echoing the pain that was still alive in their collective memory.

It was the tribal warrior who led the white man to water in the early days, and when the Aboriginal warrior turned his back, his water, his land and his woman were taken away from him. Deep within his heart, Ron believes that Aboriginal people can again lead this nation to water, a new kind of water of understanding that gives life to our soul and our heart as we all drink from the same spring of hope and reconciliation. From the spiritual heart of Australia, from deep within the recesses of Uluru, flows the clear water of Maggie Springs, which the Aboriginal warrior knows is the symbol of life in an otherwise dry, harsh land.

There were no white women in the Warburton area until missionary couples came during the 1930s, so the explorers and prospectors often used Aboriginal women for sexual sport. Half-caste babies began to be born and the undermining of traditional society began.

From some six hundred kilometres away, at the mission compound at Mount Margaret, the superintendent sent William Wade along with Fred Jackson to go with camels and on foot to scout the ranges. They took a ten-week journey into uncharted territory through spinifex clumps and sand hills. Wade had been in the merchant navy and used the sextant and telescope to guide him by the stars through this unmapped bush land. During a second trip in 1934, the men erected huts and shelters from the red flat rocks of the desert along with mud mixed with spinifex. Some of those buildings are still standing. It was into this mission compound that the workers with the UAM were hoping to gather together the Aboriginal people of that region in order to protect them from dying out by the explorer's bullet or the dingo trapper's poison.

When the mission was established the children were housed in dormitories built around a church, a school and a hospital. Their parents stayed in native camps a few kilometres away and could have their children with them during the school holidays.

Ron loved the kids and they followed him like a Pied Piper. He would carry the little bush boys around on his shoulders, and would play his guitar late into the night, teaching them his favourite country and western songs. He teased them and made them laugh and they, in turn, took him into their confidence and taught him their desert lingo. Twenty years later, when I first went to Warburton for a convention at Easter, just after Ron and I had announced our engagement, these same kids, now adults, came and hugged me. Crying and laughing at the same time they murmured, 'Oh, Kurta Kurta, he's our family. He carry us all around when we was little. You one of us now.'

The Australian education system of the time did not concern itself with the study of Aboriginal languages. The unwritten rule was that every Aboriginal should learn English. The children had to change from using their own 'heart' language to trying to grasp a foreign one, English. Their very first experience of writing also had to be in a strange language. If Aboriginal students were caught speaking in their own lingo at most of the mission schools, they risked being rapped on the knuckles with a cane. Years later, one tall, broad-shouldered man from Warburton sat next to us, tears running down his cheeks, head in his hands, remembering those scenes from his childhood, unable to fully express himself in English. There were only a few missionaries living there who had a dream of translating and teaching in the desert vernacular and these ideas were not well-supported by the authorities in charge.

Ron spent seven years in the Warburton area, finding his identity there with the tribal people. Old Wally Porter, a white-haired elder, who had met the first white man on camel near what is now Giles weather station, adopted Ron as his tribal son. That meant reciprocal responsibilities as well as privileges. After one of Wally's hunting expeditions, he returned to camp with two roo legs straddled across his back. He stoked up a fire and began to prepare one of the legs for cooking, chuckling to Ron that he had stolen them from the dingoes. Then he handed Ron the other leg to take back to his camp. On the way, Ron saw one of the young mission girls who cleaned the school and worked as a domestic. He felt sorry for her and her family, knowing that they hadn't had kangaroo meat for a long time, so he gave her the leg to take to her camp. The next day, one of the missionary wives came frantically searching for Ron, asking him if he wanted this mission girl for his wife. Ron stared at her blankly and shook his head: 'No!' 'Well,' she said, 'that's what she's telling everyone. Giving a girl some kangaroo meat out here means a marriage proposal!' Old Wally laughed about it for weeks after. Such are the pitfalls of cross-cultural misunderstanding.

Not long after, Ron did fall in love. A nursing sister who was dedicated to the bush people caught his eye. He watched as she cleaned and bandaged wounds from spear fights and burns from the camp fires. Ron often made excuses to visit the hospital where they talked and shared the realisation that they were attracted to one another. He was afraid to tell anyone else about his feelings because he knew what the missionaries thought about black and white relationships. When the nurse was about to return to Victoria for a holiday, Ron arranged to visit her in order to ask her dad if he could marry her.

Several weeks later, he travelled day and night on the train to Shepparton, but when he arrived there was only a note waiting for him saying that her father didn't approve of the friendship. 'He doesn't want to see anymore half-caste babies come into this world,' the note said. Discouraged and with no place to go, that night Ron slept by the Goulburn River, wrapped in newspapers, which formed a shield against the mosquitoes.

In the morning, he drank coffee at the local deli while he told his story to the Italian owner. 'Now look, young fella,' said the friendly man behind the counter. 'People are like that. You'll always find someone who will give you a hard time. But you can't give up. You keep helping your people. They need you.' When Ron returned to Warburton he heard that his girlfriend had taken up a nursing post in another tribal community hundreds of kilometres away.

The UAM also managed Cosmo Newbery, a station property that had been a penal reserve, better known as a 'spirit breaker' for the radical, outspoken Noongars around the Perth–Fremantle area. When the mission took over, it restored the property to its original purpose as a cattle and sheep station and brought young Aboriginal boys from the desert communities to be trained. Ron was sent there by the mission to help round up cattle and work alongside the other men.

In October 1963, Ron had stayed behind at a Cosmo out-station when the work team left, so he could catch a few of the strays. Riding through the scrub, he realised he had lost his stock whip. He tracked himself back to the spot, picked up the whip and started to gallop back to his hut for lunch, but the hard-mouthed horse he was riding wouldn't obey the pull of the reins. The stubborn animal ran him right into the sharp branch of a mulga tree. He was knocked off his horse, which galloped away. Ron lay there in a pool of blood, kicking for awhile before he became unconscious.

When Ron finally woke up he was lying inside his little hut. He never knew how he got there, but he reckoned it must have been an angel.

His head was aching and when he put his hand up to feel the side of his head, he realised that his ear was torn and bleeding. He walked unsteadily out of the hut, saw the sun setting into the horizon and couldn't grasp what had happened. He spotted the patch of dirt that had been dug out by his heavy boots. It was dark with blood that had soaked into the ground. Oblivious to what he was feeling, he saddled another horse and rode out to track the one that got away. Then he fed the other horses, lit a hurricane lamp and ate a tin of spaghetti for tea.

His head began to throb with pain and his whole body burned like fire. Rummaging through the hut, the only medicine he could find was rubbing alcohol. He lay as still as he could on his swag, his face and upper body drenched in sweat and his mind entertaining delirious thoughts of death by poisoning. He prayed that God would take his life because he couldn't bear the pain any longer. In the midst of the screaming throb in his head, he heard a distinct voice say, 'You shall not die, but live and proclaim what the Lord has done for you.'

After a few hours sleep, he managed to ride into the main mission camp at Cosmo. The workers took one look at him and put him on a train to Perth. One side of his head was lopsided, his ear was torn and caked with blood and one eye was part closed. Everyone on the train thought he was drunk. When he opened his guitar case to play and sing songs during the entire eight-hour trip to Perth, the passengers were sure he must have been drunk and no one dared sit next to him.

Ron remained on the danger list for a week in Royal Perth Hospital after an operation on his ear and skull to repair a pinched nerve and a multiple fracture of the skull. The doctor sternly told him that he was lucky to be alive but he doubted that Ron would ever be able to drive a car or fly in an airplane. While Ron began to recuperate physically, he also suffered from depression that was to last for a few years. Resentment began to grow in his heart toward the rejection he felt from the white world around him. His first love had been thwarted because of racial prejudice, and the bleak announcement from the doctor caused him to lose heart.

Anger brewed inside Ron, at times like a sleeping lion, at other times loudly roaring. One evening, while enjoying a good Australian meat pie in a Leonora diner with a long-time resident of that mining town, Ron shared his hopes and dreams for his people and how he wanted to help them have a better future. To his astonishment, his dinner companion pushed his chair back, stumbled to his feet, and scoffed, 'Aboriginals today are no bloody good! Years ago you could belt 'em with a stock whip and they would do what you said. Now, I couldn't care less if an atomic bomb dropped on them, and blew all their dust away!' With that, he stormed out of the restaurant. Ron's head began to throb.

Some nights later, on a hot desert evening in the same town, Ron found an old Aboriginal friend asleep on top of some beer barrels. He knew that if the police saw this fellow lying there they would haul him into gaol. Ron heaved the sleeping weight up on his shoulders and carried the man towards home. A police car slowly followed him down the streets. As Ron turned to look, he heard the voice behind the steering wheel. 'You're trying to show the black bastards a bit of light, eh? Well, take him home or I'll put him in the lock-up.' The lion in Ron's heart roared again and his head began to throb even more.

These attitudes toward Aboriginal people were not confined to the western desert area, as Ron would find out. Some months later, he was in Sydney for a missions conference. Ron loved to walk around the city streets, talking to people, sitting with them on the park benches, hearing their stories. He glanced at a man walking toward him on the street, smiled and said, 'G'day, mate!' The man turned angrily to Ron and snarled in his face. 'You black bastard! I hate you . . . I wish to God that my forefathers had killed you all . . . You talk like us . . . You wear our clothes . . . oooooh, how I hate you!' Ron turned away, saddened. This time he felt sorry for the man, sorry for the whole human race. The angry lion roared with a tinge of pity.

In 1969, Ron decided that he would leave the goldfields area and travel Australia, expanding his missionary work with the UAM. In previous years, he had hitchhiked and jumped on the back of mail trucks when he went to the Aboriginal reserves and communities throughout the wheat belt and to the south-west of the state. At times he even pedalled a pushbike hundreds of kilometres over bumpy roads, just to visit small family groups hidden from the rest of mainstream society.

Part of Ron's reason for travelling was to try to find himself. The security of his younger days on the reserves and in the tents with his cousins, uncles and aunties was giving way to the uncertainty of facing the prejudice and anger of the world beyond. The depression still lingered. It was the kindness of Bruce Rowe, a Warburton truck driver, that changed the direction of Ron's heart. The Aboriginal men who worked beside Bruce loading the trucks would sometimes get sick and even die because there was no doctor in that part of the world. Bruce tried his first-aid but his good friends couldn't be saved without proper diagnosis and medication. He vowed to do something about it when his time at the mission was over. Some years later, Bruce Rowe returned to Leonora and the Warburton area as Dr Bruce Rowe, travelling in his Landrover around the communities to bring help to his Aboriginal friends.

Ron spent hours yarning with the doctor, and became his friend. A number of times they discussed Ron's accident and the apparent bleakness of any hope of getting a driver's licence. One afternoon, drinking tea together, Dr Rowe made an offer. 'I'll help you get your licence, Ron.' And he did. Not only did the doctor succeed in helping Ron get that licence, but he also gave him the Landrover. From that time, Ron never looked back. He took to the road, driving to every corner of Australia, especially taking those roads that seemed to lead to nowhere. At the end of the Nowhere Road, he would find a lonely miner who needed a smile, or a family whose hearts were broken because of racial prejudice, gaol sentences or broken relationships. No place was too far off the beaten track for him to go. Years later, as we travelled this road together, I was often challenged by Ron's commitment to the 'forgotten' person of this land. It was that moment, passing the test for his licence and taking possession of that Landrover, that gave Ron his life's direction.

After his journey around Australia, Ron married an Aboriginal woman whom he had met during his Bible college days. Marj James was from the Kimberley and shortly after the wedding they moved to Derby, where Ron pastored a small church. Never being a man to stay in one place day after day, he travelled extensively, visiting cattle stations and conducting church services and encouraging the stockmen and their families who camped on the homesteads in the vast territory of the north-west. Marj couldn't always go with him, having to battle the effects of a rheumatic heart condition that had steadily weakened her body since childhood. Having children would have most certainly meant her death, so her life was often a lonely one. One day in 1972, while Ron was circuit-riding the stations, a social worker contacted Marj with the news that a little two-year-old girl named Coral needed someone to look after her. Coral was the daughter of Marj's cousin Maisie.

Maisie was a tribal girl who had caught the eye and captured the heart of Bill Gunn, a tall Irishman who had worked on the stations around Hall's Creek. All the Aboriginal girls were crazy about this hot-témpered Irishman, but he only wanted young Maisie. He bought her presents with his pay: dresses, jewellery and bottles of wine. One night, when she had fallen asleep after drinking with him and a few of their mates, Bill put her in his car and drove to Hall's Creek, getting into town in the early hours of the morning. When she woke up, she demanded to know what was going on. 'I'm going to marry you, Maisie Street,' he announced and he took her into the police station where the sergeant married them that morning.

A few years later, Maisie got sick while they lived at Louisa Downs Station. Looking after three children in their hut was difficult and Bill was often away working. The health sister from the local clinic was concerned about the youngest of their three children, who was malnourished, so the little girl was taken to the hospital. At almost two years of age, Coral was unable to walk. Marj wanted to care for this little girl.

'I've got nobody,' Marj said to Ron. 'When you're away, I have nobody.' With Bill and Maisie's approval, they decided to raise Coral for as long as they could.

'Ron,' said Bill. 'I know there's nothin' for young girls up here. They just get themselves married to some ol' man, and then they have babies. So you do what you can, I won't hold it against you.' With that, Bill released Coral to their care. Each year for the next ten years, Coral visited her family in Hall's Creek, because Ron didn't want her to lose touch with them, but it was increasingly difficult for her to identify with two very different families as she grew toward adolescence.

Ron and his family left the north-west in 1973, and for the next eight years moved around from place to place while Ron attended further religious training in South Australia, pastored churches, conducted funerals and weddings and visited numerous people in hospitals and prisons. When Marj was too ill to go with him, Ron chopped and stacked the wood for the fire to keep her warm, arranged for other ladies to cook some meals for her and then he would circuit-ride the country for a few weeks at a time. Once in a while Coral would accompany him, sleeping in the back of the Landrover as he drove through the long nights from communities to camps and back again.

Ron was a man who had not finished high school, had no degrees and had written no books or articles, but he had a driving vision to give encouragement and love to people of all walks of life around Australia. He thought of the entire nation as his field of work and his love for Australia went deep into the soil. This was 'his' country and he wanted to welcome strangers to it, and see them become part of the Australian heritage that he was so proud of. Over the years he collected thousands of stories, becoming the custodian of the 'forgotten' man's dreams, all stored within his memory.

By 1977, Marj had grown much weaker and Ron decided to rent a small house by the sea in Geraldton and try to settle down. They were just about to make the move when a call came from the Bible college in Gnowangerup, asking him to be their principal—in fact, to become the first Aboriginal man in Australia to be the principal of a Bible college. Taking the position would mean a lot of work and it could shorten Marj's life, but Ron could not walk away from it. For four years he trained, encouraged, listened to, supported and guided Aboriginal men and women from all over Australia, who came to that little south-west town because they knew 'Kurta Kurta' or 'Uncle Ron' would look after them.

In 1981, he recognised that the pace of his life had to change. Marj was getting weaker and needed more care. Ron looked around for a place to go. For twenty years, since he graduated from the same college, Ron had only received small gifts of money, petrol, food and clothing for his job of 'tending the Aboriginal flock' all around Australia. There was no steady wage, superannuation, life insurance policies or bank accounts. Financial support only came in when generous Christians donated money to 'Aboriginal work'. Ron never took the dole, pension or other government support, preferring to live by faith in his God. There usually wasn't much, but there was always enough, and he always received it with thanks.

After eleven years of marriage, twenty-one years of travel and a life dedicated to serving his people, he had no house and no property. All he had was a huge collection of photographs stuffed into scores of boxes and in between the pages of magazines and folders, cassette tapes, Bibles, historical documents, and books and more books. These were treasured items that he carried around with him year after year, probably one of the only Aboriginal men born in the bush to have such a tangible collection of memories, voices and images of his people around Australia.

The only place that would take his family was the old Carrolup settlement with its new name, Marribank Family Centre. It was the place to which Ron had been taken in the back of a truck when he was but six years old. There was already a pastor there, but Ron would be able to have a house for his family, people around to help care for Marj and a base from which to continue to travel.

In 1982, less than a year after they moved, Marj passed away while riding in the bus that transported the community people in and out of Katanning, some thirty kilometres away. Ron was in Canberra at the time. Three weeks later, he took Marj's funeral in Halls Creek, and shortly after, Coral went to live with another family at Marribank for the next three and a half years.

Loneliness grew in Ron's heart. He knew he needed a mate, a partner to love and to walk alongside him. As he travelled, he wondered what to do, and considered all the available women he met. Many of the Aboriginal women did not want to leave their extended family, most of the younger women wanted more children, some of the older ones wanted to settle down. Most of the women he approached told him his life was too demanding or that he was too pushy and his life too unpredictable to cope with. In desperation, he even scanned the matchmaking advertisements. In late 1983, Ron travelled the circumference of Australia again, this time with five other men, visiting the missions, the churches, the outback stations and Aboriginal communities. It was at Christmas time of that year that he drove into Kalgoorlie, not suspecting what would happen on that New Year's Eve night at Victoria Gardens and the coming of the Phantom's sweetheart in an airmail package from New York City.

❂ ❂ ❂

I was struggling to keep my balance, trying to hold on to the centre pole with one hand and the heavy, faded army tarp with the other as the willy-willy gathered speed in my direction. It was one of those moments when I asked myself the question, 'What am I doing here?' Thoughts of New York City suddenly seemed rather appealing. Our American team had set to work putting up tents, cleaning out the well, and erecting a common eating area under the huge, donated army tarp on the spacious block outside Laverton along Skull Creek. The summer sun was taking its toll and I was trying to get used to smiling with my teeth closed to keep out the flies that kept me company, most of the time too close for comfort. Once I had taken a breath only to feel a fly buzzing in one of my nostrils, slowly making its way deeper into my nasal passage.

My bright, shiny billy can was now blackened by the fire and I often had to fish foreign objects out of it before pouring the tea to drink. Cooking over an open fire was a new experience and the charcoal-encrusted chops created an interesting sight on my dinner plate. But as the days and weeks went by, I found that none of these inconveniences seemed to bother me. I had come to Australia so wanting to live within the community life of the tribal people that I welcomed every challenge and every assault on my previous ideas and ways of thinking and living.

Once in a while as I attended to the duties in our outback camp, my thoughts would wander back to my childhood in Oklahoma and I would almost laugh out loud at the irony of my life here. When I fled Oklahoma in 1967, I was so glad to leave the dry, dusty country with red dirt that turned to red clay and mud when it rained, leaving indelible stains on my clothes, that I vowed I would never go back there to live. Sometimes, fate has a way of backfiring, because here I was again, in the middle of red dirt and dust storms, only this time it was halfway around the world. In the early morning desert haze, I would sit on a rock a few kilometres from our camp and think of the Pioneer Woman statue, which is a landmark in my hometown. As a young girl I had often sat at the foot of the statue of this woman, which towers seventeen feet into the sky. She was a gift given to our city by the wealthy oilman, E W Marland, who desired to honour the spirit of the women who had played such an important part in battling the elements of that dry, barren part of the United States. That statue symbolised the pioneering spirit within my own heart, to set out as she had with head held high, holding the hand of her little child, boldly facing whatever lay ahead.

The traditional people of Laverton were to become my teachers. I sat on the desert floor among the broken bottles, the rocks and the spinifex clumps, longing to hear their heartbeat while they shared their life with me. Sometimes when I joined the circle under one of the mulga trees along the bed of Skull Creek, the men and women would try to hide their wine flagons or stubbies, along with their shame, behind their backs.

'They don't want you to see that,' whispered one old lady under the tree. 'You a yinkata—a *real* Christian—and they shame for what they doin'.' When they realised that I had no disdainful attitudes toward them, the men and the women opened up their secret lives to me.

The women would often take me hunting for kangaroos. Whenever the time for an expedition was near, several women would appear at the outskirts of our camp, motion with their hands for me to follow, or point with their lower lip in the direction that they were going. A lean, spotted kangaroo dog usually led the way and a couple of the women would carry crowbars. The crowbar was an essential tool for every Aboriginal woman who lived in a traditional manner. It was actually a metal version of the digging stick, and was used to extract edible underground roots and vegetables, to ferret out small lizards and rabbits for the evening meal and to lean on when walking long distances from camp to camp.

At first I couldn't imagine what use would be made of a crowbar when hunting for a kangaroo, but I knew enough just to observe and learn. Much of the conversation as we walked along would consist of sign language, pointing to various desert creatures as they scurried in front of us, or laughing at small talk about their children and teaching me more of their tribal language. Then suddenly the dog would appear, the women would point and nod their heads and confirm that he 'got one'. I never knew how they could tell, because I couldn't see any hair or blood around his mouth.

We would come around a thick clump of bushes, and there it would lie, a young kangaroo ready to be carried home for the evening meal. The older woman would take a stick from the brush, slit open the stomach and pull out the guts, tie the roo's feet with the entrails, put the crowbar through the legs, hoist it up on her shoulders and then we all walked home with the prize.

A few days after one such hunt, one of my best friends and language teacher, Rhoda Green, came to my tent and motioned for me to follow her.

A few metres away, she handed me a crowbar. 'It's mine,' she said, 'but I want you to have it.' She smiled and disappeared along the creek bed.

I carried that crowbar for a number of years until a 'family' obligation meant that it changed hands. The gift bonded us together and reminds us of the stories of hunting time and time again.

Our camp was nestled at the junction of bush roads on the outskirts of Laverton, which meant that we often had visitors who stopped for water on their way to Warburton, to borrow bullets to go hunting, to have a yarn about God or to pray for a sick child. Trucks full of men, women and children would often arrive in the middle of the night after driving the six hundred kilometres through the desert road, tired, thirsty, with children crying and dogs jumping around everywhere.

I would often be woken in the middle of the night by the loud noises and sounds of smashing bottles of a fight or domestic argument. The language would be hot and fast, and my meagre understanding of it did not help me to grasp the real story. However, a few minutes after the shouting, a shy, quiet voice would whisper from the tent flaps: 'Sister Diana, are you there? Can I camp here tonight? That fella gonna bash me.' The voice would then take shape and the woman would put her blanket on the floor of the tent and go to sleep.

❂ ❂ ❂

After my meeting with Ron on New Year's Eve in Kalgoorlie and our first exchange of letters, I continued to ask many questions about hope for the people of the creek. 'What is there for the people here? What will be their future?' I kept pressing him. Many ideas had been tried, studies had been done, and reports had been written. But those reports never changed their lives, and they never contained the dreams and visions of the Aboriginal people themselves. Everyone seemed to have an answer for the 'Aboriginal problem'. Teams from overseas, teams coming from the east to the west, or the other way around, continually wrote hundreds of sheets of paper called 'feasibility' studies. But where was their dreaming for today and for tomorrow? 'Without a vision' (without a dreaming), 'the people perish,' says the Good Book. Over the years, from these early days in Laverton and during the many trips Ron and I were to take around and across Australia, I would try to catch the whispers in the hearts of my Aboriginal friends, try to hear their vision, try to see the world with their eyes. The view from their heart was so different from mine.

The highlight of my week was going to the post office after hearing the mail plane circling over Laverton. My romance with Ron grew through the written word. I lived for his letters and he lived for mine. We poured out our dreams and our love and commitment to one another, sometimes in more than twenty pages. After he had asked me to marry him and I had said yes, we decided to get engaged over the phone. Laverton was thousands of kilometres away from the Cootamundra Bible College, where Ron would remain for the next six months, and we didn't know when we would next see each other. So, on the night of our planned engagement, I donned the one dress that I had brought from America, put on my 'Sunday best' sandals and walked through the bush to a friend's house, where I waited for Ron to ring.

We talked for what seemed like an eternity: plans for the future, dreams for our life together, whispering our love to each other, trying to remember that five-minute meeting four months earlier. I then took from my right hand a small diamond ring that had been my grandmother's, the only ring that I had left from the Before-Australia days, and slipped it onto the ring finger of my left hand.

Ron prayed for strength to face all the tomorrows. 'It won't be easy, Diana. There's a lot against us.'

As I walked back to my tent, I wondered at those words and reality nudged its way into my thoughts. How could I be committing myself to marry a man I barely knew after a meeting of only five minutes on a New Year's Eve? But Ron had told me he wasn't getting any younger, and neither was I, so there was no time to 'beat around the bush'. There seemed to be a hand guiding us, a hand bigger than ours, gently pushing us together. Every step into the future is a matter of faith, but this was an extra big step that needed a huge dose of faith.

Diana, my love,
I'm excited about the future ahead of us, for the best is yet to be. As the late Winston Churchill said during the war, 'I was born for this hour.'
That is the way it is with us. I believe we were born for this hour, for this time in history. My life feels incomplete without you, honey, and I am so glad that you love me. I feel so enriched and privileged to have a woman like you, who I can call my own.

The first cloud that gathered against us came from some of the missionaries and church workers. The topic that raised their ire was my previous divorce. That word seems to toll the death knell for those unfortunate enough to fall short of a happy and committed marriage. I had always believed in Christ's words of forgiveness and promise of pardon and a new beginning. When I read of his blessing to the woman who stood by the well at Samaria, knowing she had had five husbands, and to the woman who wandered in from the street, spilling her tears of loneliness and rejection at his feet and spreading the aroma of her own scented oil, I felt released from my own past. Free to pursue the blessing of marriage with Ron.

The word of our engagement spread like wildfire around the churches throughout Australia who knew Ron Williams. The word of his impending marriage to a young divorcee from America reached the many places around this country to which Ron had travelled. One missionary wrote Ron a scathing letter. 'I've never met Diana, but it's better that way. It would seem that she's quite a bit younger and that may be glamorous, but think about when you grow older and she is still a young chick.' I didn't consider that being five years younger than my future husband would classify me as a young chick. The hierarchy of the UAM also expressed their disappointment to Ron regarding his plans to marry me. One other missionary told him there were plenty more fish in the sea—why did he have to pick me?

For over twenty-five years Ron had been loyal to the mission, even in earlier years when others were leaving because of its patronising attitudes. Ron had been considered their 'star' property, proof that an Aboriginal could succeed. 'That's *our* Ron,' they would say. Now he was being threatened with dismissal. It was very hard for that realisation to sink into Ron's heart. One winter night he had to drive to Melbourne to meet with the mission board, and later he wrote to me of how he felt.

I felt as if I was being interrogated. I sat by myself with other men sitting behind a table, one of them looking over the rim of his glasses at me, telling me I was making a big mistake. He said the judgment of God would be upon me and my ministry around Australia would be finished. As I rose to leave, no one shook my hand, no one thanked me for the years I had served them, often with no money or help of any kind. There was silence as I left alone. When I made it to my car, I couldn't move. The tears were coming down as fast as the rain in Melbourne that night.

The only person Ron could share this pain with was another Aboriginal pastor, David Kirk. David was from Queensland and·had experienced his own heartaches from the mission where he had grown up. He had served for years as a church worker, had gone to Singleton Bible College, was well spoken, well dressed and had many visions and hopes for the future of his people. But over the years, as he pushed forward step by step to raise the dignity of his people, he was knocked back time and time again, not being trusted to bank the church offering, not being given a position of authority in the Bible college, because he was told that 'Aboriginal people would never make proper leaders'. Years later, these many experiences joined together to crush his spirit and finally his body. But he encouraged Ron to stick with me, to follow his heart and to 'stand up for what you believe is right'. Ron never forgot David for being his mate, and neither have I.

The rejection didn't only come from Ron's circle of influence. The couple who had led our team from America were also unsupportive. I had wanted Doug to help officiate at the wedding, but at the last minute they· booked their flights back to the United States, leaving their missionary work behind. Doug's last words to me were: 'I don't object to your marriage to Ron—he's a lovely man—it's that you are really marrying all the social problems, political problems and difficulties of the cultural situation that worries me. You are not just marrying a man.'

The negativity in the wake of our engagement fuelled my deep-seated insecurities about love but Ron did his best to tell me in his numerous, lengthy letters that his commitment to me was genuine. He revealed his own difficulties with rejection, the pain of not being able to have a child of his own, the long days and nights of seeing his first wife trying to cope with her terminal disease, and the patronising attitudes of white people. He thought of us as 'fellow soldiers trudging through the mud and muck of trench warfare' in the struggle for the survival of the forgotten and the marginalised, encouraging the troops as we moved from place to place.

Diana,
I have asked God to bring a special kind of woman into my life to be my
wife. So she would be a blessing to both men and women of many different
races. I want us to reach the highest goal that we can for others. We have

*great privileges and with that comes great responsibilities. In your background
and in mine is a rich heritage, all woven together by Providence. Interwoven
in you is England, Scotland and Europe. Just as Robert Bruce, the Scottish
king, was encouraged by the untiring effort of a spider weaving a web, when
he was a fugitive from the English soldiers, so am I encouraged by the
weaving of the web of our lives and what we can do together.*

Ron dreamed of travelling the world, visiting the places that our lives
represented, to see America and my people, to visit the Germans, the
English, to acknowledge the mix of his own background. His vision of
our partnership was to unlock the music in other people's lives, to tell
them that they were special. My vision was much more practical. I
wanted him to love me, and I wanted to love him in return.

It never ceased to amaze me that this man from the bush, born in an era
when his race was despised by the majority of Australians, should have such
love for people, from all sorts of backgrounds, countries and conditions.
On the surface, there was never a barrier, racial or otherwise between him
and the other cultures of the world. He has always reached out to the rest
of the world with no apologies or hesitancy. One of his letters to me
contained a beautiful story that captured the music of Ron's heart,

Dear Sweetheart,

*Many years ago the Prince of Wales landed in Darwin's airport (not Prince
Charles). Many Aboriginal people came to see him. A red carpet was rolled
out to the steps of the plane to welcome him. A naked little black Aboriginal
boy broke away from his mother, ran out onto the red carpet and sat down
near the steps. The Prince stooped down and picked up the little naked boy
and carried him for most of the day. Where the Prince went, the little boy
went and later he was given back to his mother. When the little boy grew
old enough to understand, they told him how, when he was a toddler, he
was picked up and carried by a Prince. From then on the boy, as he grew to
be a man, lived and acted like a prince. When he did the corroboree, he
danced with his chest out, proud of who he was. This what I want my
people to know, to be proud of who they are.*

In between receiving letters from Ron and writing lengthy replies, I
continued with my life in the bush. Every morning the families living in

the creek bed would walk barefoot across the rocky, barren ground to the Aboriginal community centre to have breakfast, take showers and wash their clothes. The centre was the daily gathering place for all the creek dwellers, a transportable structure complete with kitchen, dining area, wash house and toilets. The large verandah in the back was where one could hear the news of all the local families. The children would bolt down their meal and then be off to school, running and pulling tin cans with long bits of wire attached. I helped in the kitchen, talked to the women sitting on the grassed lawn when the weather was good, and visited the local gaol.

Around the gaol there was a wire fence bordering a concrete slab where the Aboriginal men and women could sit in the sun. Sometimes they were lined up, sitting on the footpath outside the fence. I could seldom discern who was in the lock-up and who wasn't. When I brought my guitar into town, we all sat together, playing and singing, while the guitar pickers performed for us. Later in the day, my friends would wander into the pub to find a cool spot out of the sun, meet with their mates and have a few drinks, usually leaving with a carton under their arm headed for the shadiest tree. There were two doors to the pub area, the one for white fellas and the other one with the sign that read 'Coloured Bar'.

❂   ❂   ❂

Almost two months after our engagement, I was finally going to see him. The Bible college was preparing for a week of celebrations at the end of May. Many visitors would be coming to and fro, and Coral would be travelling from Marribank to spend that time with 'Dad'. Ron had begged me to come, paid for half the fare, and promised that 'it would be a great time to spend together, the three of us'.

The bus trip lasted for two and half days, traversing the flat Nullabor Plain. I gazed transfixed at the monotony of the countryside, read magazines and tried to calm my nervous thoughts. It was all well and good that we seemed to have such compatible visions for the future and similar needs for the present, but I couldn't even remember what Ron looked like. I hadn't seen him since the last day of December. I felt crumpled and tired after sitting so long in the same seat.

I tried to freshen up at the final roadhouse stop before Cootamundra, where our expected arrival time was three in the morning. As the coach turned into the deserted street at Coota, I pressed nearer to the window, my eyes searching for this person I had promised to marry. Somehow I felt I had to have the edge, to see him first before I actually had to stand before him. I didn't recognise what I saw.

When we had met more than five months ago, he was clean-shaven. Now there was a small beard sprinkled generously with grey. I had met him in the summer and now the breeze told me of the approaching winter. I hugged my jacket around me, felt the tightness growing in my stomach and nervously descended the steps of the bus. As we stood there facing each other, neither of us seeming to know what to do, he seemed bigger and taller than I remembered. Maybe it was that I felt smaller and more scared.

We drove silently toward the dark outline of the college buildings, which had once been a hospital. Ron led me to the backyard of the principal's house to a little area at the base of a large tree, which was surrounded by a green army tarp set up as a windbreak. In this outdoor setting, Ron had kept a small fire going and arranged an early-morning breakfast. We sat down together on the ground sheet, he reached over to the fire and pulled out a camp oven, lifted off the lid, and served me a meal of damper, possum and billy tea. We talked until the sun began to peek over the distant hills. It was there that we had our first kiss as a couple, an engaged couple.

The week became a blur of activity. How could I ever get to know him in such a short time with so many people around? We took bush walks and met the students and the staff of the college. We toured Sydney, walking from the harbour to the tower for lunch. The slowly rotating tower high above Sydney was the most expensive restaurant Ron had ever been to in his life. The world below seemed so far removed from us. The contrasts of our two separate worlds seemed to be drawn together in that moment. Ron and I, representing the bush and the city, the opposite poles of life experience brought together by common goals, held hands across a linen-covered table. That night we took a walk through Kings Cross. We sipped cups of coffee at the Wayside Chapel in the Cross, laughing and swapping stories with the women of the night and the drug addicts seeking a bit of warmth from the street. It seemed

as if I was back in New York City, and the sights and sounds of inner
city life touched a chord in my heart. Neither of us really knew the
corrugations that lay ahead of us as the parallel lines of our life-journeys
seemed to be coming closer together, almost touching.

Our first disagreement occurred during the preparations for our
wedding. Before I left Cootamundra, Ron had presented me with a draft
of some fifty or sixty pages of scribbled handwriting containing vignettes
and verbal portraits of people from the goldfields that he had met through
the years. He placed them like treasures in my hands, wanting me to edit
them for printing in time for our wedding. 'We can launch the booklet
at our wedding, Diana, as a symbol of reconciliation. Especially with the
police. We can have the sergeant do the honours as a healing for what
has taken place at Skull Creek in the past.'

I was so shocked that I didn't know how to say no. I would eventually
learn that this was how Ron usually got his way, waiting until such a
moment that I could not possibly refuse his request. On my way back
to Western Australia, I scanned the pages. I began to see how his mind
worked—so many memories, and he seemed to leap all over the place.
The stories seemed to pour out of him, in no special order, thoughts
bursting onto the scene in the most unlikely places. I had to break up
the pages into smaller bits and then put them back together like a jigsaw
puzzle. He had written his first—and final—draft in only a few days. It
took me the next few months to make sense of it.

I only wanted a wedding, not a book launch, or anything else that
might overshadow the significance of our love for each other. I wasn't
even overly thrilled with the idea of having reporters there. I was already
becoming somewhat nervous and confused about the future, and some
of the plans that Ron shared with me were much too grandiose and full
of symbolic meaning. A whirlwind of unwanted demands threatened to
overtake me. Where were we as a couple, just husband and wife, man
and woman?

In the last weeks before our wedding, Ron and I negotiated over the
final plans in Kalgoorlie. His eyes danced as he showed me stories about
us in Christian newspapers, responses from around Australia from well-
wishers and those who couldn't come to the wedding, notes from the
reporter and photographer who would be there. I burst into tears and
walked away. He followed. Through my tears, I explained that I just

wanted a wedding, a special day for us with our friends in the desert, not a media circus. We compromised, we hugged, we walked and talked until we understood each other just a little more.

In the end, the covers on the booklets had not dried, so they couldn't be ready in time for the wedding day, and the police sergeant took sick and couldn't make it either. So who won? It didn't matter, because when Ron and I joined hands at the bush altar, the heavens were beginning to touch the earth. The promise of our future was filling the sky, even though the earth, the bush roads, the detours and the bogs we would still have to travel were just beginning to appear. The horizon was there, but far away.

CHAPTER 5

Homecoming

I awoke to the first day of my married life aching from head to toe. Sleeping on a mattress of bushes was not the most comfortable—or the most romantic way to begin a honeymoon. The first light of dawn had appeared at the edge of the cave on top of Mount Margaret Hill, and the flies began to buzz around my ears.

'Day's gonna be hot,' said Ron, matter-of-factly while he gathered up our belongings, looking like he had been awake for hours.

The walk down the mountain was much easier than the walk up and soon we were packed into our green panel van. We sped down the highway toward Esperance on the south coast for a few days camping by the ocean. Perched on the mattress behind the front seats were our two panting dogs, one black, and one tan and white. I had picked Ron for a dog lover at Cootamundra when I met Maru, his black kelpie heeler cross. Maru was Ron's minder and watched over him wherever they went. If anyone had dared make a sudden move to Ron they would have had to deal with Maru first. Everyone at the college was afraid of him. He must have sensed that Ron and I had a special 'thing' between us, because he nuzzled up to me right away. A few months before our wedding, Ron had picked up Toby, a labrador bull-terrier cross puppy sitting in a basket, at a street stall in Katanning, just for me. 'I don't want you to feel left out. Besides, I have a mate now, and Maru needs one too.' Never mind that they were both males.

We would often joke about how our two dogs were mirror images of their bosses, both being of different colours, having their little tiffs. Actually, Ron's dog, the black one, kept a close paw on Toby, the light coloured one. Despite their small arguments over which one got in the car first, when one went walkabout the other would search for him. They provided us with many hours of fun, laughter and storytelling.

'Did you hear the one about Maru repenting of his sins?' Ron used to be known as a fiery preacher, especially when he called people to come to the altar, repent of their sins and meet their God. One evening at a camp meeting, he gave his invitation. The crowd sat silent and then the dogs that were fighting outside suddenly stopped. Out from a darkened corner of the tent flaps crawled a black blue heeler, ears flattened, head down. It was Maru, crawling toward his boss, obviously repentant. The crowd burst into laughter and applause and so did Ron.

The interior of our car would become our honeymoon suite as we travelled thousands of kilometres around the south-west, over to Port Augusta and back, before finally going to a place called home. Every situation would reveal just how much I needed to learn about this man I married and his cultural ways. During the months I had spent living on the creek bed in Laverton among the fringe people I had barely touched the surface of Aboriginal life. Now I had opened a door, walked into a different world with a new set of rules, and the door had shut behind me. There was no turning back. It was left up to me to find my way because Ron just kept moving ahead. After all, we were in his territory, his land, his world of over forty-four years of experience.

In Esperance, we pitched a small tent near the sand dunes that bordered the Indian Ocean. In the evenings, we watched the sun setting over the shimmering waves, ran with the dogs along the beach, tossing bits of wood into the ocean for them to retrieve, then stared into the brilliantly coloured coals when the billy had boiled. During the night I snuggled up to Ron's wide chest, listening to the waves crashing on the dune, so loudly that I thought they might sweep us away. I had never camped so close to crashing waves before.

Ron chuckled at my fear. 'There's a lot you have to get used to, Diana. There's a lot of country to see, lots of mountains I want to climb. Before we settle down, honey, I want to show you Australia. We'll do it soon, or we might never go otherwise.' I was too sleepy to answer and I didn't know what to say anyway. I could only follow blindly, since I had no clue as to where he was headed.

I climbed out of the tent, washed my face with water, bending over the four-gallon plastic container, while Ron turned the toast on the open grill. Not far away from us were three kangaroos enjoying their morning feed. I grabbed a piece of bread, walking slowly towards them, thinking I would make friends. The two smaller greys perked up their ears and then hopped away, but the big boomer stood his ground. I hadn't appreciated the signs of danger as he stretched out and suddenly threw a boxing jab, missing me by a whisker. Startled, I jumped back, stumbled and watched as he loped heavily across the clearing to join his mates. I turned toward Ron with a pained expression that asked if he was going to help me and heard the click of his camera.

❂ ❂ ❂

'Along this way is where my great-grandfather come from. Peaceful he was. His people didn't want circumcision. That's why they went the coast way, not up in the desert.' As Ron told me his stories, he drew maps and pictures in the sand, then pointed in the directions where his family used to walk.

I was fascinated by this man I married, his profile dark against the setting sun. He was slightly balding, with a sloping nose and dark, shining eyes set deep beneath his forehead. His eyes were often piercing, as if he could look right through a person. His features were those of the desert Aboriginal, whose eyes were shaded by bushy eyebrows from the heat of the sun and were protected by a strong, sloping forehead. As we jogged along the beach, throwing the sticks to the dogs, his legs took long strides, like those of an emu. He had slim desert legs built for long-distance walking. Above his waist was the mark of the whitefella life, a rounded belly caused by a diet of bread, tea and sugar. Ron had just begun to battle the diabetic disease that plagued many Aboriginals at middle age.

During the next two days we must have visited everyone Ron knew in Esperance. Parked outside his brother Henry's house, I noticed that the curtains were tightly drawn, giving it a deserted look, but when Ron knocked at the door I glimpsed the tips of someone's fingers pulling them back slightly. The Noongar way, determining if it's safe to open the door. Before long, a tall, younger version of Ron emerged.

'Bro,' cried Henry, and gave Ron a big bear hug. Glancing surreptitiously over his shoulder, his eyes gave me the once-over. 'Well, is this your new missus?' He reached out his hand to me, but his eyes darted around as if he didn't know how to greet me, or what to make of me. I was conscious of trying not to make whitefella's blunders: talking too much, being too direct, or failing to listen. The safest approach in most community situations is to remain silent, observe in order to learn the protocols, and wait.

'I didn't make it to your wedding. No petrol. Sorry, bro, I wanted to be there.' The lounge room was sparse, a mattress on the floor and a large, old television stood in the corner. Taped onto the walls were family photos, a poster of Johnny Cash and a Perth Noongar footballer advertising Aboriginal week. Henry grabbed two kitchen chairs, plopped them in the lounge and called to his girlfriend to make cups of tea. Henry talked fast, yarning about the news of family from around the south-west. Things I never dreamed of, stories my family never would have included in their conversation. With tears in his eyes he talked of relatives who had died or had been killed. Friends in prison, wrongly accused. Sightings of tribal magic and power surrounding the Noongar houses late at night.

I had nothing to add, nothing to contribute to this visit, other than my presence. After a while, following Ron's lead, I got up, told Henry how much I enjoyed meeting him while he shook my hand, vigorously this time, and we walked out to the car. As I got in, I heard him whisper to Ron, 'Look after her, bro. Y'got some woman there.' Their talk continued in the car, with Ron leaning out the window, Henry slowly backing toward his front door, as if they didn't want to say goodbye. This was the way Ron ended every visit and conversation, especially with his own people. As if he didn't want to say goodbye.

We met more family, some elderly missionaries ('We've known Ron Williams for twenty-five years, dear') who had retired by the sea after decades in the dry desert, and even strangers when we went window shopping on the main street of Esperance. Since a pictorial description of our wedding had appeared on the front cover of the *Daily News*, we were stopped numerous times and asked, 'Did you really spend your first night in a cave?' When we nodded, the reaction was usually a smile or a grin, but also a puzzled look which said, 'How interesting!' before the inquisitor walked away loudly discussing the doubtful success of such a liaison.

Our next stop was Perth. Ron wanted to visit some of his friends and relatives in prison. As we waited behind the gate while the guard found the right key for the lock, I saw one dark arm after another appear through the bars along the far wall, followed by dark eyes peering out to see who was coming. Once they saw Ron, a chorus of voices echoed in the courtyard, 'Kurta Kurta' and then 'Uncle Ron'. Smiles were obvious and Ron was in his element. I stood quietly waiting, knowing that women, and particularly white women, should not make the initial greeting or gesture. Just wait.

There were handshakes all around, and some, with tears, told Ron of their auntie's death, or trouble in the family. Then there were more handshakes. Ron put his big arms around them and prayed for them and their families while each man in respectful silence bowed his head. Tragedy is an everyday occurrence in Aboriginal life and it is never handled easily or taken for granted. The pain is real and community protocol dictates that it must be acknowledged by all before any further business is transacted.

After a number of minutes, Ron finally turned to me, grinning at his audience of men gathered around him. 'This is my missus.'

The mood changed almost immediately and there were hands reaching out to shake mine, nods of approval to Ron, tears starting again as they told me the same stories of deaths, trouble and pain. I cried too, even though I didn't know the people they were talking about. It was the sense of family, the sense of shared destiny that I was feeling. Somehow they were drawing me into their pain, trusting me to share it with them, to understand. There in the cold prison cells, the shadows of bars stretching across the floor, arm in arm with Aboriginal men and women in prison greens, drawn into their suffering, a startling contrast flashed across my mind. It was the contrast of institutional life painted against a backdrop of a once proud people camped in the freedom of the bush, never suspecting what the future would hold for them.

Ron got a message from the news reporters, who asked for more details of our personal lives, future plans and wedding comments to send to newspapers in the UK, America and New Zealand. My head was spinning with all this, but Ron was delighted.

We continued to drive hundreds of kilometres through the south-west toward Mount Barker where I would spend my first Christmas as Mrs Ron Williams. We stopped at small towns all along the way, having cups of tea with Ron's old friends, family and acquaintances. Names were getting jumbled up in my head, and it was increasingly difficult to store in my memory all these life histories as Ron recited them day after day, mile after mile.

The description of our wedding and the night in the cave entertained everyone and then the conversation would turn to the past twenty or thirty years, outside of my realm of experience. I could feel the looks, sizing me up, silently making an assessment of just how long Ron and I would be able to travel this road together. Most of these people were whitefellas.

Already I knew that I was taking second place in his life, after the needs of his people. Not that he loved me less, or had changed his mind. I just hadn't proved myself yet. Ron would never explain what we were about to do next, but just announce it on the day. Then he would watch to see my reaction, how I coped, if I could be trusted. I didn't like this constant testing, but there was no alternative. After many lengthy letters promising his love and emotional support, I was suddenly left to find my own devices in order to navigate this new relationship.

❂ ❂ ❂

'Come meet Aunt Florie,' Ron called out as we pulled into the driveway of an unpretentious government house in Mount Barker. Our dogs jumped out from behind me, raced around the house, and Ron gave a whoop as he saw his cousin Reynold. It was Christmas Day. Tables in the backyard were piled high with bread, salads, chooks, ham and cool drinks. Aunt Florie was the matriarch of the Williams clan, and all the kids and grannies (Noongar slang for grandchildren) were crowding around, waiting for her to shout the directions over the noise. There were children of all sizes and shades of colour.

Florie had a large family and many of her daughters lived with her from time to time, when their men were off shearing, in prison, or had simply walked out one day. Her home was the place to come when someone was bereft of companionship.

I was enveloped at once by Florie's warm greetings, then she called out for someone to get me a chair, sent a daughter to get us cups of tea and continued making final preparations for the feast. The paper plates and plastic forks were handed out and the children surrounded the tables. One slyly reached out to grab a chicken leg, and Florie slapped his hand. When Ron finished saying grace, the assault on the food began.

Most of the talk was of family. Slowly I was beginning to piece together the puzzle pieces of Ron's history and who was related to whom. At first, not many questions came my way. No one seemed interested in stories about New York City, except for the kids. One by one, as they watched me eating and whispered among themselves, they gradually slipped over toward me.

'What's it like in America?'

'I want to go there some day.'

'Did you ever meet Elvis Presley?'

When I said no to the last question, there was obvious disappointment. Anyone who lived in America *must* have met at least one movie star.

Being around Ron's nieces, nephews and cousins helped me to loosen up and forget my nervousness about whether I would say or do the right thing. I started to play frisbee, joke and tickle, tell stories and blow up balloons. Soon, sitting on my knee, several of the little boys and girls were showing me their treasures, found in nearby paddocks or behind the neighbour's shed. 'Auntie Diana, tell us more stories.'

Ron motioned to me that it was time to go. We never seemed to stay long anywhere we went, I thought to myself, hugging Florie, shaking hands with Reynold, and giving loads of waves and hugs to the kids.

During the next few days we shopped and packed our car with food, washed our clothes. Then we picked up two friends, Liza and her daughter from Gnowangerup. They made themselves comfortable in the back of the panel van, along with our two dogs, as we headed across the Nullabor for Port Augusta, halfway across Australia. It was New Year's Eve day, one year and a day after we had first met, and our destination was the Port Augusta convention, where Ron had received his first letter from me, also one year ago. Liza had been desperate to go to the convention but had had no lift. 'We have room in the back', Ron had said, averting his eyes from mine.

We drove all night. Such was the beginning of our married life and what looked like the end of our honeymoon.

The weather was stinking hot. We had no air-conditioning in the car and the hot air blowing through the open windows was so dry that my throat stuck when I tried to talk. The only remedy was to soak our bath towels at the roadhouse wash basins and hang them in the windows to try to cool the air. That, combined with very little sleep, no privacy, and waiting to wash up at the crowded roadhouses several hundred kilometres apart, led to frayed tempers. I was being forced to get to know this man I had married while living in a fish bowl. Liza tried to give us space, taking her daughter for a walk or a ride on the swings, or sitting in the car while we went for walks.

It didn't seem to bother Ron, I began to find out. He had lived his life in full view of his family and other people for so long that he didn't seem to understand or acknowledge my need for attention or privacy with him. Even sexual life had not been all that private for those who grew up in the bush. When a family lived all together in a tent, intimate sex took place under the blankets while the kids were asleep on the next mattress. My whitefella ways of dating, private affection, sipping coffee in the afternoons, or long conversations about our hopes and dreams for the future were not part of his culture.

Port Augusta is the meeting place of east and west, the home of a Brethren mission and the scene of Aboriginal Christian conventions since the early 1970s. The mission was built on the flat, government houses providing the backdrop for the grassy oval where a wooden stage had been erected at one end and a cooking area at the other. Along the edges of the oval a tent city gradually came into view as Aboriginal families began to arrive from all over Australia for this annual January event. It was a modern-day corroboree, with singing, stories and preaching. Sophisticated Kooris from Sydney and darker tribal men and women from Central Australia sat together on the lawn while their children played chasey and leap-frogged over each other in the front of the stage.

The first night some folks from Ernabella, a community near the top end of South Australia, shared their life stories, sang in their language and preached up a storm in desert lingo. I didn't understand much of what they said, but I could sense the passion and authority of their orations. Their dignified stature, their heads held high and their lack of shame surprised me. This demeanour was so different from the Wongi people, who lived along the creek bed in Laverton or who walked with their heads down along the streets of Kalgoorlie or Perth. I had learned a Wongi word that constantly sprinkled their speech, old and young alike. That word was 'kurnda', meaning 'shame'.

Shame has pervaded the Aboriginal soul from the time when William Dampier set foot on the north-west coast of Australia, and, upon seeing the bush natives, declared, 'They are the most miserable people on the face of the earth.' Those words have filtered down through the generations, bringing a sense of shame that has blocked many Aboriginal fellas from sharing their talents with the rest of the world. It has kept many young teenagers from completing their high school education and applying for jobs. Many don't even try because they know they won't be chosen no matter how qualified they are.

Shame is a concept that is very near the surface, ready to explode. When Aboriginal teenagers see a white person looking at them, their heads turn away, eyes toward the ground and one of them whispers, 'Kurnda.'

Some Aboriginal men would rather be lost than ask a whitefella for directions, or walk into a full room on their own. But there in Port Augusta, that night when the Ernabella people sang, I observed a difference, something I wanted to know more about. The dignity of the Aboriginal man and woman of Australia.

❂ ❂ ❂

We drove along the dirt and gravel road, watching as the landscape turned into wheat crop, windmills dotting the horizon. Ron and I both felt excited as the last sheep grate was crossed. We were approaching Marribank Family Centre. Finally we were home. The narrow, wooden bridge welcomed us, even as the car seemed to steer itself toward this little community nestled in among the tall trees, off the beaten track. On the left the shearing shed loomed as one of the largest and newest buildings in the compound, flanked by fences and gates that guided the sheep toward the shears each season. Along the left of the dirt road was a number of houses, some demountables that sheltered families, group homes for children who were sent there without their parents, and a few stone houses that were the original buildings from early in the century.

The road continued to loop around, enclosing a large field where children would run, swing on the tyre that was tied to the tallest tree, or build dirt ramps for their push bikes. At the junction of the loop road and two other tracks, one leading to our house, the other heading out of the community over another river and beyond, there was the store, the office and an extra storage room that had once been the gaol. The bars were still there, perhaps to remind us of what had gone before.

Formerly a penal settlement called Carrolup, the reserve had been taken over in 1952 by the Baptist Mission Committee of Western Australia, in order to look after children who had been removed from their families by Native Welfare or who had been left there by young mothers who did not have the resources to raise them. A couple from Swaziland, descended from the Zulus, came to manage the place. It was at their suggestion that the name was changed to Marribank Family Centre, a Door of Hope, to reflect a new attitude for the future. The five thousand acres of bushland were nestled between two rivers, long since gone salty, with the marri trees planted along their banks.

Turning toward our house, which stood standing like a solitary sentinel at the very end of the lane, we drove past the stone church with its attached wooden hall, an old louvre-windowed kitchen, more demountables and small stone houses. Set apart from the rest of those buildings was our weatherboard house, with a two-room flat on the right-hand side and a couple of outbuildings.

We had arrived just before dark and slipped into the community unseen. Streaks of light bounced between the tall river gums and paperbark trees that stood at attention about a hundred metres behind my new home. Ours was actually the oldest house on the settlement, having once been the superintendent's residence, then relegated to serving as the hospital, the VD clinic and finally the morgue.

'This is it. Home sweet home,' Ron called out, opening the back door and with a sweep of the hand ushering me forward.

I stood in silence. Living out of a car had been serious business and had proved to be a source of irritation between us. Ron's method of organisation was to haphazardly toss in everything he needed—clothes, towels, food and tools—in a heap in the back of his panel van and drive into the countryside on his pastoral visits. A lot of time was spent searching for the right spanner, a tape to give a fellow traveller, the box of teabags or a spoon. The somewhat romantic idea of a nomadic life roaming the back roads of Australia had quickly faded and I had tried to make sense of how I could manage my wifely role. But the disarray in the back of the car seemed insignificant when I stood at the doorway of Ron's home, now *our* home.

I was in the kitchen. I gazed around the room, noticing the cobwebs huddled in each corner, the broken louvres and torn flyscreen on the only window and the pervasive smell of mouse urine. Besides the kitchen the house consisted of a small lounge of three and a half metres square, two small rooms facing the front and the master bedroom, with what one might call an 'ensuite', except that it lacked a toilet. The rooms were sparsely furnished with only the necessities, but there were boxes and bookshelves everywhere. Piles of newspapers and magazines were stacked in the corners, and boxes blocked the entrance to the third bedroom. The only room that looked the least bit inviting was the large bedroom.

'Well, what do you think? Our little home, huh? Some of the ladies here told me they would try to clean it up a bit before we got home.' Ron smiled and looked around. 'Maybe they didn't have time.'

'Oh, it's okay.' The words stuck in my throat. What a mess, I thought to myself. How could he ever live like this? I sat on the bed, the only space in the house that didn't have boxes piled around it, suddenly feeling exhausted.

All I could manage that night was to put clean sheets on our bed, have a cup of tea and wish for sleep, a desired interlude after a hectic two months of married life.

In the morning I found the toilet a few paces out the back of the house in a small brick enclosure built on the side of an old shed. The outside wash house consisted of two huge cement basins surrounded on three sides by corrugated iron. A discarded copper stood to one side, propped under an enormous gum tree.

I was grateful that no one came to see us the day after our home-coming. Perhaps it was sensitivity to our needs, or perhaps they knew the house was in such disarray. But it gave me time to think. Ron disappeared early in the morning with the dogs. I walked from room to room, wondering where to start. Ron had probably not done any house-work in two years. He had rarely been at home, the mail had piled up and he was usually in too big a hurry to read it, or even unpack from trip to trip. Letters were stuck in between pages of books, at the back of shelves or on top of the refrigerator.

It appeared that Ron had kept every piece of paper, book, photograph, magazine or lesson material that he had ever owned. Household furniture and personal items of clothing had no meaning for him compared to these records of his past. Many of the papers were of historical value, but others were outdated advertisements, church bulletins of long ago and unread requests for donations to American television preachers. As I began to sort through the books on the shelves, out from their pages would fall unopened letters containing cheques given to Ron for his travel and ministry expenses sent from a few kindly grey-haired ladies. The cheques were so old that they couldn't be cashed. 'I can't believe you could live like this!' It was going to take weeks to sort it all out.

During the first week of our homecoming, visitors had begun to stream to the door. Our house hummed with activity. Children came to watch me paint the walls and taste a slice of American apple pie. Gifts of freshly made damper wrapped in steaming tea towels found their way to our table. When Ron killed a kangaroo, our neighbours knew about it. Often we had a houseful for stew and damper. One afternoon as I stirred the stew pot, I glanced up at the ceiling in my little kitchen and counted about three hundred flies. It was impossible to keep them from coming in between the cracks in the louvres, even with new panes. I quietly thought to myself, 'If my mother could see me now, she would personally buy me a plane ticket back to the States.' Then I laughed out loud at the thought of her waging war on one fly. Having to face three hundred of them would give her a heart attack.

In the kitchen, while drinking endless cups of tea with the local men and women who came to have a yarn, there was a constant flow of family narratives. 'Ronnie, you remember when you sang that song by Buddy Williams at my wedding?'

'Now, George, when Ron married us you couldn't even kiss me 'cause you were too shamed in front of all them people.'

'Remember that time when we chased all them charnacks away. Well, they ain't been back since.'

'It was those good times, out on that Tambellup reserve. Never had much, but what we had, we shared.'

There were tales of when Ron was young, walking around the bush always followed by six dogs, when he used to shanghai the parrots and tie their frail bodies together on his belt like trophies, and when he used to pinch cabbages from an old man's vegie patch.

Laughter made our sides ache and brought tears rolling down our cheeks. There were memories of jokes they played on one another. 'Ronnie, boy, you were the biggest tease around. I remember when Uncle Barney used to grab you by the ear and drag you away from the little kids, tellin' you to leave 'em alone. You had 'em cryin' all the time.' The comedy of the past pushed the shame back into a corner for a short while. In the midst of these yarns was the whisper I've heard so many times around so many camp fires, the whisper of dignity, the whisper of survival during tough days. These were the whispers of a people proud of who they were. Always the story of survival.

Because the house had once been the morgue, not many Aboriginal people wanted to stay overnight with us. Every one who did would invariably have some sort of eerie experience of tribal visitations or past ghosts and spirits on walkabout. I had never been a person who got easily frightened, although as a child I had never wanted to sleep with my feet uncovered, even in the hottest Oklahoma weather, but after hearing from our guests the stories of all the bumps in the night, it took a bit of courage to walk out to the toilet after dark when I was alone.

After a few weeks I began to settle into life at Marribank. Surrounding the small Aboriginal community were over two thousand hectares of bush and paddocks. Our two dogs loved the fresh air, the thousands of birds waiting to be chased and the kangaroos that often hopped through our back yard. The kookaburras would wake us up early in the morning with their constant cackling laughter. The setting was breathtaking and alive, so opposite in many ways to the desert life.

The water we used for cooking and drinking was piped into the kitchen through a rain water tank, but the water for showers or a bath came from a dam on the Marribank property. Often the water was brown, bordering on the consistency of thick soup. When I took baths, my legs disappeared. I could get used to washing in muddy water, but I couldn't get used to the mess, so I decided to tidy up in earnest. I made a pathway between the boxes, moved bookshelves and designed a plan of attack. I bought paint for our bedroom, vacuumed and swept the entire house, walls, floor and ceilings, replaced the louvres in the kitchen and the two front bedrooms, and stitched new curtains. Ron just smiled, stood watching for a few days and then went hunting with the dogs.

I moved the heavy bookshelves myself since Ron always made himself scarce when I threatened to reorganise the house. He owned more books than any blackfella I knew about, on topics ranging from American history to religion, photography, men's health issues to Aboriginal folklore and legends. But they were covered in dust.

'If all these were my books, I'd take care of them. Dust them off once in a while.' I started to pull them out, one by one, trying to group them according to topic. I found more uncashed cheques and old unanswered letters. Then a photograph fell to the floor. I picked it up.

I was looking at a pretty young girl, her fair, fine-featured, heart-shaped face framed by dark, wavy, shoulder-length hair. She was wearing a black lacy negligee and smiling at whoever was behind the camera. On the back of the photograph was written the name 'Jasmine', in Ron's handwriting. I sat down immediately, a knot suddenly forming in my stomach.

After what seemed like hours, Ron came through the back door and produced a kangaroo leg, a trophy from his hunting expedition with the dogs. 'Toby got this one! You should have seen him. Went right for the neck.'

'What is this?' I demanded, tossing the photo on the kitchen table.

His eyes went from the table to me and back to the table, before he quietly put the leg in the sink, shooed the dogs out through the back door and sat down. 'Where'd you find this?'

'Where do you think? Hidden away. Who is it? Why do you have this?' My mind was racing and my mouth couldn't seem to form anything more intelligent to say.

'I was going to tell you about this. Sometime later, but I guess it better be now.'

Ron tentatively began telling me about when he was a kid, his mother, some of his aunties, other Noongar women who played the game of prostitution, only not as sophisticated as the game is now. How they gave favours to men in order to survive, to get some food to eat. How so many were beaten up and eventually died from the years of abuse.

'Yeah, I know those things. You've told me. Lots of times. But who is this?' I jabbed my finger at the photo. 'What does she have to do with you?' I was almost screaming. I had learned that when Ron was trying to convince me of something he started way back at some obscure moment and worked his way slowly around, nibbling at the edges of what I really wanted to know. I was imagining so many possibilities, most of them sickening.

I knew that Ron had always been one to seek out people who were on the fringes of 'proper' society. 'I know what it feels like to be on the outside, where nobody wants to know you, so I try to help those wherever I can,' he had told me a number of times. When I watched him talk to the drunk huddled in the shadow of a doorway of a shop long boarded up, or purposefully walk into heated arguments when two people were ready to strike at each other, or squat down to look into the eyes of a crying child, I marvelled at his untiring energy and an almost-driven commitment to those who had no one. He was bold in the face of the problems of living, bold in ways that I was not. A bold, Aboriginal man who had grown from a timid child, his brown face pressed against a window pane, looking in at white society, never being invited in, but having something to say. As an adult, he had invited himself in.

'Diana, after Marj died, I was confused, knowing that I needed a wife, but . . . where to look, I didn't know. No one seemed to want to go to the places I went, talk to the people I wanted to talk to, so, I sort of, well, gave up. I used to take little Bibles, poems and flowers to the girls in the red lights to cheer them up. Show them that a man doesn't always come looking for sex, like the whitefellas did with our women. But I came to tell them they are special people to God.'

The explanation was taking too long, and getting too spiritual. I was impatient. What did all this have to do with an erotic photograph of a young woman hidden between the pages of an obscure, dusty book in the back of his bookshelf? I fidgeted, indescribable anger and fear overtaking my thoughts. Anger at the possibility that I had been deceived by the apparent goodness of this man; fear that somehow I was the second choice to a more-desired sensuality. 'Ron, get to the point.' I couldn't follow him around this waterhole anymore.

'Well, Jasmine worked at a massage parlour and I met her one night when I was giving out flowers before Mother's Day. She was American, friendly, interested in what I was doing and we talked. I guess, I thought, well, Diana, the honest truth is that I thought I wanted to marry a prostitute. At least she wouldn't turn up her nose at others like her.'

I couldn't believe what I was hearing. On an impersonal level, the explanation tugged at my heart, remembering the nights I had spent around Times Square and my own commitment to those on the edges of mainstream life. But on the personal level, I couldn't give it permission to come any closer.

Ron sighed, sensing my tension, and went on. 'I asked her to think about marrying me, I wrote her some cards and talked on the phone. The last time we talked, I told her I'd see her in a week for her answer. I knew I was treading on thin ice, Diana. The mission was aware I was visiting the brothels and I had even hinted at a future relationship. All my friends said they wouldn't touch those places with a forty-foot pole. But, when I went back, she had disappeared. Her co-workers said she had gone to America and hadn't come back. I waited, but never heard anything more from her. So, that was it. Not long after, I met you.'

I got up. I walked through the rooms, not knowing what to say. The dysfunctional world of the street had suddenly made its way into my house through the back door. What I had welcomed before, I couldn't now.

Ron followed me. 'It has nothing to do with you and my love for you, Diana. I knew that it wasn't the right road and it worked out the way it should have. The corners I had been looking in, well … they were just too dark. I prayed God would send me the right woman, that she would write to me, seek me out. I couldn't trust myself any longer. That's when you came along. Don't you see? When I got that letter from you in Port Augusta I knew you were the right one.'

He went on. 'You remember Wilf? He told me that the mission breathed a sigh of relief when Jasmine disappeared. But when I met you and you didn't disappear, well, that was different. What they might have accepted in a prostitute, they wouldn't in a divorcee. But this time I wasn't going to give up, no matter what they said.'

The wall of tears that had built up during Ron's disclosure finally broke. My body stiffened slightly at the touch of his arm around me. It would take time for me to digest this. The disarray in Ron's house mirrored the disarray in his heart, not to mention in the people we wanted to help. There was nowhere to go to find some salve for this gaping wound. Ron slowly got up, took the photo and tore it into little shreds and tossed them in the bin.

With a rush of adrenalin, I pushed past him and walked swiftly out the back door and then ran along the path behind our house into the thousand-acre stand of trees. So there it was, a terrible exposure of my insecurities. Waiting so many years to find a man I could trust. Giving up a life of promised promotions and prestige to come to Australia and live in a tent. No regrets, mind you. The spartan life didn't bother me. No, it was trusting in love that I needed. How many years did it take Dad to leave? One minute you think a man will be there forever, the next minute he's gone. I let my guard down and Ron walked in. Marriage made in heaven, I thought. Then rejection, even by men and women who had had a string of de facto relationships, children by a myriad of partners. Now they passed judgment on that word 'divorce'. If you were unlucky enough to have committed yourself to marriage, hoping for a lifetime, but in the end, you crashed, divorce was not the option. They said it was God's judgment. But I knew God was not like that. He forgave. It wasn't the end. But I was all alone in this. And now where did Ron stand?

Could I go back to that house? Were there more photographs yet to find? Full of memories, that house. But not my memories. Ones I had to struggle with. A past that wasn't mine, but it lived there anyway, intruding into our new life together. How long, Lord, how long until it's just us.

I found a log and slumped down on it. The tall, leafy trees seemed to envelop me as I wept under the pressure of it all. Wrapped in the pain, I didn't hear Ron approaching, but I felt wet noses and the lick of a tongue as Maru and Toby nuzzled under my arms. Ron sat down on the log, and wrapped his arms around me. Not a word. It wasn't over, but it was a beginning. I let my body go limp, exhausted from the emotion and we wept together as our two dogs, one black and one white, stood guard, while we both made a step toward becoming 'one'.

✪ ✪ ✪

'Come on in, honey,' said the madam who opened the front door to Aphrodites after we had rung the bell. 'We're expecting you.' She was a woman in her fifties, attired in a lace top over bikini briefs, trying to conceal her age with heavy make up. Her copper hair was piled in curls.

Her long fingernails dug into my hands as she shook them. We were led into the waiting room of this fancy brothel in Perth where a number of women in various states of dress or undress were reading magazines, talking to customers or watching a small television. There were ornate mirrors covering one entire wall, and the lights were fairly dim, glittering from a fake chandelier hanging from the ceiling. Large artificial palm trees decorated the corners of the room, and a statue of the Greek goddess Aphrodite stood guard on the opposite side of two dark-green velvet lounges. Glass coffee tables were strategically placed in front of each lounge. The madam introduced us to the girls as 'Pastor Williams and his wife'. Behind us through the door came a reporter, our friend from the *Daily News*.

I later found out that this reporter had written other articles about Ron before, particularly about his pastorly visits to the brothels. Now he wanted to write about both of us talking to 'God's forgotten people', as Ron has called those behind prison walls and brothel doors. Even though I had spent a couple of years walking around the dangerous streets of Times Square listening to the problems of the working girls and trying to help them find a more positive side to their lives, I had never ventured into a brothel.

'You have to see it, Diana. To know what these girls face. You have so much to help them with, stories of your own life even. Many of them have run away from broken marriages, fathers that didn't love them or abused them. Living a life with drugs. You'll see. We can do this together.'

That night the girls asked me questions about New York City, talked about their children, and listened to Ron and I sing songs together. Ron told how his mother and his aunties had fallen into prostitution at the time when there were no jobs or relief of any kind, except begging. When some of the women had to leave with their customers, others stayed and told us about their personal lives. We drank coffee and drew the amused looks of male customers while the reporter was taking our photograph.

When it was time to leave, the madam embraced us both. 'Don't forget to come back for a visit,' she called out as the outside gate clicked shut behind us. The first part of our drive home was in silence, both Ron and I meditating on the night's events. Then, ever so gently, he touched my hand.

'I'm glad you are with me, Diana,' he said. 'The women really liked you, and I could see that you were loosening up a bit. We can do this together, you know.' The apprehension I had felt at the beginning of the night had gone and I even began to plan our next trip to the brothels, sharing my ideas with Ron as we drove into Marribank, well past midnight.

In some ways the visit broke the ice between us. Ron, carrying the need to lighten the load of his mother's beatings at the hands of men who took advantage of her and to throw off the guilt of never acknowledging her or her real pain, saw this ministry as a 'calling'. I, on the other hand, could identify with the women whose lives had been tangled in such a way as to push them into choices that had devastating consequences. Slowly we were beginning to acknowledge each other's needs.

CHAPTER 6

On the Road

I awoke with a start, sat straight up in bed for one moment and then flopped back on the pillow, wondering where we were. Slowly my eyes adjusted to the light and I peered around through my eyelashes, remembering that we were in our caravan, parked beside the road in one of those places along Australia's highways called a 'rest stop'. I felt beside me for Ron, but the bed was empty. Yep, I thought, he's gone walkabout again. Ron was a very early riser and went out for a walk in the bush at every opportunity. It had been dark, very late, the night before when we sleepily pulled off the bitumen, let the dogs out of the car and then crawled longingly into the inviting bed.

A mere five months into our married life, we were back on the road again. The plan entailed a nationwide walkabout until the end of the year, with an itinerary of speaking, singing, and preaching in numerous churches, missions, out-of-the-way cattle stations, capital cities, prisons and remote communities. Ron wanted his 'woman' to see Australia—or maybe for Australia to see his 'woman', I didn't know which. I hadn't allowed myself to get too settled in the house at Marribank with this trip in the back of my mind.

On previous trips around Australia, Ron had either slept in his car, had thrown the swag on the ground, or called into some unsuspecting friend's place for a cup of tea and a night's camp on the floor. Now he had a wife to consider. Not that I minded camping on floors. I had been doing that for almost two years. But now I viewed everyday life through the eyes of a wife, with all the attendant 'nesting' instincts.

We had begun to sort and pack for the trip when a message came from the office at Marribank. 'You have a phone call, Uncle Ron, from Kalgoorlie.' There was only one phone for the community, inside the superintendent's office and we knew that people were serious when they went to the trouble to track us down. The call was from Kevin Ewings, a friend of Ron's for some twenty years. Kevin had spent most of his working life on bush property and stations, carting sandalwood and fixing everything that creaked and moaned from being years out in the desert sun and wind. He wanted to give us a gift. 'Ron, we want to give you our old caravan. It's not flash, but it'll get you around. You know, you have to look after that wife of yours. These white women take a bit more lookin' after. You can't just go livin' in every-body's back pocket now. We thought you two might need a bit of privacy.'

Ron had thought this over for a while, not really wanting to give in to this change of lifestyle, but he realised how much I would like a nest of my own as we travelled, so he said yes. The Marribank house was not really my own. Already I felt like I was sharing it with some unresolved events from the past. The furniture, the appliances, the pictures on the wall hadn't changed with my arrival. The past was all around us, extending its tentacles into the present. Remnants of Ron's previous marriage, memories of his people taken from the bush through Katan-ning, then dumped in front of Marribank's gaol. I needed a 'room of my own' as the writer Virginia Woolf once put so well. Not just the physical space, but the emotional space.

Living in a tent in Laverton had not been conducive to interior decor-ating and I began to think that a home on wheels was just the way to go. I had observed many Aboriginal women as they moved about, gath-ering their belongings into a blanket or bag, tossing it into the roaring motor car and heading off to make a new place for themselves. When they reached their destination, the first order of business was to stake the family spot under a shady tree. I could now have the best of both worlds. A 'room' where I could retreat, decorate, call my own. And a 'room' that would move with us.

The caravan was over twenty years old, silver-grey in colour and about five metres long. At one end was a couch that turned into a double bed and at the other end was a table lined on two sides with green vinyl seats. Fitted neatly in between was a wardrobe, a sink, which was fitted with a water pump, and a hot plate.

After pulling it from Kalgoorlie to Katanning, we had surveyed our new treasure. 'This is great,' said Ron, approving of the prospect of travelling in a bit more comfort than he had previously. 'Now we can invite the mob in for a cup of tea wherever we go. Have some yarns, and even a Bible study.' I glanced at the table and counted the number of spaces where people could sit. Just how many 'mobs' did Ron think would eventually crowd into our small caravan? I shuddered at the thought.

The launch date was 1 June 1985. We had crawled north from Perth on the highway, caravan behind, the panel van's roof rack loaded with five extra second-hand tyres ('you never know when we'll have a blowout along these roads'), three jerry cans full of petrol ('so we can drive all night'), and a variety of poles and tarps ('for when we set up a stall at the Katherine rodeo').

Like most men who lived in the outback, Ron was a bush mechanic, which, in his case, meant that he could repair almost anything on the car from items that he found in the bush. During my years of travelling in the outback of Australia, covering almost every corrugated, dirt track that exists, I have come to appreciate the abandoned cars, utes, and four-wheel-drives that punctuate the roadsides. These serve as the outback mechanic's 'roadhouse', providing the needy traveller with bits of wire, hubcaps, engine parts, brake shoes, windshield wipers (if you're lucky enough to still have your windshield), pieces of steel and iron. Ron was well-versed in all these tricks of the trade. So as we set off for remote parts without a two-way radio, or even a CB, somehow, I knew that he would be able to fix whatever went wrong.

Toby and Maru had found their normal spots right behind the front bench seat, crowded in between well-organised plastic containers stuffed with copies of *Nuggets from the Goldfields* (our little book, finally delivered to us two months after the wedding, to be given out as we travelled), cassette tapes of Aboriginal singing, gospel tracts and the all-important photographs. In one corner was a large wooden box containing a cassette tape fast copier, one of Ron's treasures, which had been given to him by a Baptist church in Perth. In such an oral culture as that of the Aboriginal, sharing stories by tape was an important communication tool. Ron's years of speaking on mission radio for the United Aboriginal Mission had contributed to his huge collection of songs, stories and messages he loved to share.

There had not been an inch of space left available after we had added the microphone stands, two guitars, amplifiers and loud speakers and the boxes of my special puppets. Harkening back to my drama days at the high school where I taught, I knew that puppets could speak about problems of living in a light-hearted yet insightful way where sometimes a person couldn't. One of the gifts I had received from an American church when I was in Laverton was a Mickey Mouse puppet for me to use with the children. That was the beginning of my collection. I slowly gathered Australian animals, the familiar kangaroo, a koala, and a kookaburra, then expanded to include a Muppet-like Aboriginal family complete with tribal grandfather, a small boy and a teenage girl with striking black ringlets sweeping across her face. They were to prove a big hit in the remotest of communities.

When I emerged from the caravan on that day parked alongside the North West Coastal Highway, I could hear the dogs barking in the distance. A beautiful rocky outcrop, which was turning marvellous shades of red as it reflected the rays of the rising sun, was directly opposite the door of the caravan. Beyond the rocks was a great expanse of flat land, low shrub and then bluish, grey hills in the distance. On the top of one of the smooth, large rocks stood Ron, waving at me, with Toby and Maru beside him, wagging their tails in excitement.

I pulled the folding table and chairs from the back of the car and positioned them where we could see the sun's play of colours, and far away from the roadside rubbish bin, which was already starting to attract the flies. Out came the picnic basket, filled with knives, forks, spoons and plates. Next I carefully spread the blue and white checked table cloth over the small table and prepared for breakfast. I chuckled to myself as I thought of the times I had sat in the creek bed in Laverton and eaten breakfast with the mob that lived there, sharing hunks of damper with black coal marks, a slab of margarine and a dribble of golden syrup. Never mind about the knives and forks, plates—or tablecloths. But now I was a married woman, wanting to take care of my husband and provide those

On the Road

103

things that I associated with being married. My own cultural ways were bubbling to the surface.

By the time I had put out the cereal and boiled the billy, Ron had come down from the hill. He presented me with a small bouquet of wild flowers that he had collected that morning. 'For you, my dear.' Bowing slightly, he took my hand and kissed it. I laughed and wondered to myself if his Noongar friends knew what a romantic he was.

There we sat at a table in the wilderness, complete with flowers, dogs at our feet, as the sun continued to rise over our car and caravan. The black bitumen lay not far away, stretching out its arms in opposite directions, connecting the roadhouses from the south to the north. While we were enjoying that peaceful moment we could just barely hear the low hum of a motor car in the distance, signalling its approach long before its appearance. As the white ute came into view, a horn sounded, we waved and sailing over our caravan, landing almost at our feet, was the morning newspaper. What surprises the roads of Australia hold for its travellers!

❋ ❋ ❋

We had left Perth with one thousand dollars in our pocket. Ron had never worked a steady job for pay. His years with the mission had been financed by sporadic donations to cover costs of petrol, food for the road and literature. Ron had great faith that, if he was working for God, then God would provide for him. After all, he never wanted much, and whatever he had, he usually gave away to someone who was needier. Shortly after we got married, I had begun to notice the way in which he handled money. In his view, it really wasn't 'ours', it belonged to whoever came along. In the pocket and out. As simple as that. He had never opened a bank account and had only put in a tax return that one year when he was principal of the Bible college in Cootamundra and had drawn a regular salary for the first time in his life, rather than living on gifts of milk, cream, chooks and tea bags.

'I don't know how to handle money much, Diana. It never lasted long enough to worry about. Never any extra anyway.' He had assured me that we would make it around Australia. He had done it before. I didn't want to doubt that, but I didn't want to be stranded either. All I could do was dutifully follow my husband, on this, my next adventure. I'd have to worry about money matters later.

One of the difficult moments in our preparations for the trip had been receiving notification from Community Services that Coral could not go with us. She had continued to live with the Minniecon family at Marribank after our wedding because of our travels, but now we tried to plan for her to come on this extended journey around Australia. I had worked out a schedule for her schooling as we went, but the welfare department would not hear of it. According to them, she did not actually belong to Ron or to the family looking after her, or even to her own flesh-and-blood in Hall's Creek. She belonged to the department.

Ron became angry and I was disappointed. I knew that the three of us needed to work at being a family. Without any words being spoken, there was a hint that facing another family move seemed daunting to Coral. Besides her biological mother, she had already had two additional mothers. The prospect of a fourth mother, a white one on top of that, would certainly be a venture into the unknown. For my part, even though I had taught a number of high school students and listened to adolescents as they recounted their various hormone-inspired entanglements, I had never raised a child of my own. During the whispers and rumours that Ron should not be marrying me, Coral began to ask questions. It was difficult for a fourteen-year-old to understand the politics of religion. In the complex rush of planning a wedding, trying to get to know my future husband and coping with rejection and insecurities, I honestly had not known how to handle this new family of mine.

Ron was bewildered as well, since he had not been Coral's official guardian for over two and a half years and didn't understand much about the changes that take place inside teenage girls. We were all three groping in the dark. Ron and I had thought that a trip together would help put the pieces together, but it was not to be. Coral had to stay at Marribank.

We headed up the coast with plans to pull into Shark Bay to visit Tim and Maggie, the unofficial caretakers of a little church made out of shells. I was driving when we turned off the highway along the last stretch into the small coastal town.

'Look, Ron, up ahead. It must be a tumbleweed.'

Ron peered through the windscreen and laughed. 'Where do you think you are, back in the Wild West? That's no tumbleweed. That's an echidna. Better known as a porcupine to you. Pull over. We'll get it.'

I couldn't believe what I was hearing. What on earth were we going to do with an echidna? Ron explained what a delicacy they were to eat. As we came closer, I pulled off the road and Ron jumped out, rolled the animal over, hit him on the head with a large stick and put him in a plastic bag.

Tim and Maggie lived in a Spanish hacienda-style house near the sea, not far from the beautiful Anglican church made from white stones and shells called St Andrews by the Sea. In the dining room of their home was a long, smoothly finished mahogany table decorated with native flowers, and set with bone china, crystal glasses and exotic place mats.

Later that night Ron boiled a bucket of water, dunked the echidna he had caught, painstakingly pulled out the quills, made a delicious stuffing and baked it in the oven. When we were all seated for tea, the contrast of serving native-baked echidna while sipping a drink from a crystal goblet brought hearty laughter and an appreciation of each other. This was the first of many such scenes that would be replayed throughout our life together. A combination of bush and city, simple and sophisticated, spontaneous and planned, open and cramped, old and new. At times it made us cry, but most of the time we laughed.

✪ ✪ ✪

All along the western coast of Australia, Aboriginal tribes had once roamed. The land was lush with plants, alive with kangaroos and other wildlife, and the sea reluctantly gave up its bounty of fish and pearls to the divers among the tribes. The region from Shark Bay through to Exmouth and on up the coast had been first discovered by the Dutch, the name Dirk Hartog a familiar one in early Australian history. In 1942, the United States Navy had occupied the area around Exmouth and built a submarine base complete with early warning radar. In 1943, the Japanese bombed the area and two years later, the shores were lashed by waves from a cyclone.

There were no Aboriginal people there when we drove in to visit the navy base. Their history of the area was not recorded in print, but was often told in ceremonial legends or around the camp fire. They told of the numerous caves carved into the coastal rocks that line the beaches and extend inland, which contain many drawings of early Aboriginal life. The stories also tell that those who know the area never go there because of the sadness.

Some time in the past, during the time that huge tidal waves came from the islands of Java, a number of families were wiped out. Those who did manage to escape could not find their people to bury them properly. Their spirits still roamed the land. The sadness was too great for them to return and the fear too real. The Dreamtime stories of the Aboriginal clans told of the frightening spirits that lived in the breakaway caves, an intermingling of beauty and terror, hauntingly lonely.

Ron told me many stories of the spirits in the bush, and how his people know that spirits can bring mischief, can roam the bush unsettled, sometimes looking for revenge. I did not discount the reality of that belief or the fact that the fear was so real. I just had never had that experience. Until Shothole Canyon outside of Exmouth. Shothole Canyon is a tourist attraction. Visitors drive in, wonder at the stone formations, and listen to the echoes of their voices bouncing off the canyon walls.

Ron and I drove through the canyon one morning, along with other tourists, after leaving our dogs with a friend and arming ourselves with a video camera we had borrowed for our journey. We happily took a number of shots and soaked up the beautiful scenery, talking about what it must have been like in pre-colonial days.

'I can feel the spirits of the old people in this place,' he said, looking up at the hills. I couldn't feel or see anything, there were only rock formations there.

Later that evening, when we reviewed the footage on the videotape, we found, much to our dismay, that the picture was jumpy and distorted. Perhaps a loose cable was the cause.

Ron was disappointed. 'When we leave tomorrow, let's go early and drive through the canyon again. I really want to get this on tape.'

The next morning, we drove to the canyon entrance, a huge sign stared at us: 'NATIONAL PARK: NO DOGS ALLOWED'. We hadn't noticed this before. Should we risk going in and be accosted by a ranger?

'I'll wait here with the dogs. You just drive in, take some shots of the canyon and drive out again. Then we'll be on our way,' suggested Ron. No problem. I could do that. I got the camera ready and began to drive down the narrow, one-lane dirt track that made a loop into the heart of

the canyon and came back the same way. For a short while, I relished
the view, took a bit of footage, then came to a stop about halfway into
the canyon. The early morning rays of the sun were dancing across the
hills and I could see a kangaroo father and joey enjoying their breakfast.

As I reached for the camera, I suddenly felt as if there were a thousand
eyes watching me from the top of the hills. Some sort of pressure was
preventing me from looking up and when I did manage it, I had an eerie
sense that the rim of the canyon was lined with tribal warriors, waiting
to see what I was going to do. My ears were ringing with chanting and
I could feel my hair start to bristle. Involuntarily, I shivered. I couldn't
go any further. Something sacred was going on. I was being told to leave,
to get out of this place. I twisted and turned the steering wheel, reversing
my direction and headed toward the entrance. My hands gripped the
wheel while I took one more glance at the hills. There was nothing
there, but I could almost sense the warriors with their hands raised,
clutching spears, in victory. They had won. When I pulled up in front
of where Ron was sitting crouched with the dogs, I was out of breath.
As my story poured out, he nodded and stared at the hills behind the
'NO DOGS ALLOWED' sign.

'It's real all right, it's real,' he said softly. I didn't know what to make
of it all, but I couldn't deny what I had felt. I had so much to learn yet,
so much personal adjusting to do, so much dismantling of my own world
view in order to accommodate the Aboriginal paradigm.

❂ ❂ ❂

The word 'missions' brings a strange mix of reaction from Aboriginal
people. To many, it reminds them of separation from family, of rigid
schedules, and a loss of cultural connections along with sometimes very
cruel treatment. To others, it brings thoughts of thankfulness for education received, a place that was a safe haven from the encroaching
prejudice of white Australia. Western Australia had many such missions
dotted throughout its vast territory. When Aboriginal people greeted
each other for the first time, the proper etiquette not only included the
individual's name, but also who their family was, where they came from
and what mission they had been raised on.

Ron had been associated with or had visited almost every mission in

Australia. His travels had made him one of the most accessible Aboriginal
pastors in the country. His loyalty was impeccable, remembering the
kindnesses he had been shown and rehearsing the stories year after year.
The missionaries would often describe my husband as 'our Ron', as if to
imply ownership, not wanting to let him go, always with a restraining
hand upon his life.

'I know they think I belong to them,' he began to reveal as we drove
along the never-ending bitumen through the Pilbara. 'I've heard some
of the mission leaders, leaning across the table, peering over their spectacles at us, saying that we might as well face it. Aboriginals would never
be leaders in their own right. That we would always need whitefellas to
do things for us, to open the doors for us. As if we can't have any ideas
of our own.' Ron's voice was tinged with anger as he spoke these words.

'Well, what did you say? Didn't you take a stand? What about all these
things you tell me about Martin Luther King? How you respect him for
how he spoke out? Couldn't you have done that?' My American background had taught me to speak out, for justice, for rights. I could hear
my friends in Harlem shouting out their anger at police harassment,
patronising attitudes and black tokenism.

'What could I say, Diana. I've learned, and you'll learn too, that they
would never listen to us. So I said nothing. Most of us said nothing.
That's why I would just smile, nod my head and then do what I wanted.
When they think we agree with them, then there's peace. They leave us
alone and we can do what we would have done all along.'

Little by little Ron shared his heart with me. What was said in the
confines of our car, lying next to each other in bed at night, or watching
the play of the camp fire's flames was much different from what he said
behind the pulpit or to anyone in authority. I struggled to make sense
of not only the contrast, but also the internal conflict.

❁ ❁ ❁

Ron taught me that the camp fire is healing to the Aboriginal soul. No
matter where we camped, in the desert, on the coast road, or in the bush,
no matter what time of year, or what the season, the first activity of the
evening was to make a fire. The camp fire is the centre of Aboriginal
life. It is not only where the food is cooked, but where the family gathers

for news of one another, where history is told and retold, where warmth, both physical and spiritual, is found, and where one can find safety from the spirits that roam in the dark. Children were taught to stay around the fire if they didn't want the 'mamu', (the devil-devil) to get them. No one ventured very far from that circle of light.

I have grown to love the camp fire just as much as Ron does. To sit for hours, staring into the fire brings peace and calm to the heart. The colours mingle together and then separate into blues, oranges, and reds; the leaping flames form pictures and designs. The fire definitely assists in telling exciting stories. The feeling around a fire is the same as sitting by the ocean for coastal people, staring into the undulating waves, receiving timeless offerings from the sea.

To be Aboriginal was to love the fire. For Ron, it was sitting by the fire, poking a stick at the broken wood as it was slowly consumed and retrieving a few of the glowing coals momentarily abandoned by the others, that released his desire to be heard, his deepest feelings of struggle with prejudice and stories of people who had meant the most to him. 'It was old Bob Williams who helped me the most. He was a tribally initiated fella, and a Christian as well, whom I respected. Finally I saw someone, my own colour, not afraid of anything or anyone. I wanted to be like him. He was a lawman too, in tribal way, and he wanted to understand how the Christian religion fitted with Aboriginal understanding. He paved the way for me, in a sense.'

In tribal custom, boys become men when they go through initiation. If the boy never goes through the ceremony, then he isn't considered a man. He is still called 'boy' in the language and not allowed to participate in important tribal decisions. If the 'boy' inadvertently walks through ceremonial ground, he could be seriously punished, or even killed. Ron had never been initiated because his Noongar tribe didn't normally follow that custom. So, by law, Ron would have been considered a 'boy'.

'Normally the tribal fellas wouldn't take notice of men like me. But somehow for me it was different and I think it was because of my friendship with Bob. The men accepted me as their brother and shared their secrets with me. Bob was instrumental in helping me to see that being a Christian doesn't mean I can't be proud of being an Aboriginal,' said Ron.

Bob Williams had been initiated in Cue, Western Australia, one of the region's most powerful law areas. He was given the role of featherfoot, a henchman, who could bring justice in some very mysterious ways. The featherfoot was the most feared of the tribal warriors in traditional Aboriginal life and remains so to this day. Bob had a legal right to speak in firm tones to other initiated men. Some time during the late 1950s he called a meeting of the desert lawmen to discuss the issues of Aboriginal leadership on the missions and the communities and how they, as traditional people, understood the relevance of Christianity versus tribal law.

Ron continued throwing small sticks on the fire while he talked, 'Those men came from all around the desert and sat down in a huge circle, in the flat, right in the dust. It was like a meeting of parliament, a tribal fellas parliament. These men weren't the lawmakers. They don't make laws now, but they carry the law, they look after it. All of them respected their own tribal law and some of them were Christians. They respected Christian law, too. But all of them despised whitefella law. They thought it was too weak.'

Another important figure standing before the group was Dooley Bin Bin, who had initiated the strike of Aboriginal workers on Pilbara sheep and cattle stations after World War II. That strike had ended the 'slave' labour of the stockmen who had received only tea, flour and sugar for their hours of hard work. That strike had brought in 'proper' wages for stockmen on the properties. And it had crippled the stations of the Pilbara.

'They stayed there in that flat for days,' Ron explained. 'They talked about the white man's religion and how they could ever accept it. They wondered how it could fit with their own ways that had lasted them for thousands of years; traditions, rules that helped them survive. One fella said that the Christian religion took more away than it gave.'

At one point in this meeting in the flat, a Bible translator, our friend Noel Blyth, in his early days as a missionary, stood up to read from the book of Mark in the Bible. He had just helped to complete its translation and it was the first time these tribal men had heard something from the Scripture in their own language. As Noel finished reading it, old Dooley Bin Bin, tears glistening in his eyes, stood up. A heavy silence hung in the air as he spoke to Noel.

'Give it to us slow, Kurta, my brother. We want to digest it, not vomit it out. We don't understand all this white man's religion, but we want what this language book is saying to us.' They listened some more and then they picked Bob Williams to go and walk between the tribes, to tell them the Christian law in their own language. Ron reflected that Bob would be like a bridge between two worlds.

Bob took Ron on many of these trips, opening the doors for him to all the tribal leaders in that area and then extending the network through the Northern Territory and South Australia. 'After Bob got too old and too tired to travel any more, I remember the day that he came to me and put his hand on my arm. He told me it was time for me to go on my own to see the old people, the elders. But he said to me, 'Just tell 'em, Ron, tell 'em I've given the word. Me, old Bob Williams.' That was the tribal way, to tell them that the old fella had given the word.

The coals were glistening on the ground as the fire began to die down. Ron was quiet, the air was still. There were tears in Ron's eyes. I was only beginning to understand. Just beginning to see what the past meant to him. Years before Ron had walked this path of 'spiritual initiation' into this desert land. I had only begun my journey. We sat closer together, savouring the last moments of the fire. A shiver went through my body.

Ron slept easily that night, gently snoring. I tossed and turned, trying to settle my thoughts from all that I was learning. We were only three weeks into our trip. I had already heard so many stories and met so many people, and we still had a long way to go.

CHAPTER 7

So Much All at Once

We continued to travel the highways of the north-west coast, our dogs leaping over us as they scrambled to gain their respective positions in the back of the panel van. Our trip was often interrupted by a blowout or an impatient wait by the side of the road while an overheated engine cooled down. Periodically Ron would crawl beneath the car, sliding along the dirt underneath, to check the oil leaks, the wheel bearings and the springs. Sand and red dirt were permanently ground into his shirts and trousers. Ron could fix anything on the road, at least for long enough for us to get to a mechanic, a friend's place or a burnt-out car for spare parts. One kind person even took a brake out of his own car he had parked in the back yard so we wouldn't have to wait for a delivery from Perth.

Ron often made detours when travelling, stopping to collect bush berries, gather a clump of wildflowers, sit by the edge of a waterhole savouring a few peaceful moments, or to pick up wounded birds. Outside of Onslow, we drove past a little chicken hawk with a broken wing. For a few seconds we discussed whether or not to take on this little hitch-hiker, but Ron was already making the U-turn. Chicky was with us only a few days before succumbing to shock and pain.

The small village of Onslow was once used as a port for the sheep stations, then pearling and, later, for gas exploration. The coastline had often been battered by cyclones and the deep-water jetty had been repeatedly damaged. Some of the Aboriginal people there had inter-married with the Japanese who came to Onslow after the turn of the century to search for pearls.

As he did in most of the towns we visited, Ron sought out the local Aboriginal people, to refresh his acquaintance with the elders and make plans to conduct a good old-fashioned tent meeting, only without the tent. Usually, we would meet in the church building, the CWA hall or in one of the Aboriginal homes. It was always low-key with little or no preparation, just a time to talk, to sing, to pray. And, of course, for his American wife to tell how she came from New York City as an 'airmail package' for this Aboriginal bush preacher. It was also a time for me to hear their stories.

That night in Onslow a young man named Bert joined us. He was a delightful fellow who had once been considered the town drunk, burning out some of his brain, and later, his throat, on grog. No one had been able to control him, and because he was violent, he was sent to a mental hospital in Perth. One day, walking behind the hospital afraid, lonely, wanting to run, he noticed a black object lying out in the middle of the oval. He walked toward it, bent down and picked it up. It was a small Bible. He believed it was a sign for him.

Aboriginals are spiritual people who believe in a realm beyond that which is discernible with our Western logic. Events, circumstances and objects are viewed as signs of that unseen world. Bert recognised that this book was meant for him and day by day as he read it, his mind improved, much of his sanity returned and he was released from the hospital. Bert is now well known to everyone in the Pilbara, and visits all his extended family wearing T-shirts designed by his own hand with slogans and signs of God's special touch one day outside a mental hospital.

'This is a present for you,' he said, his eyes down, while he pressed a small, white box into my hands. I opened the box and there was a tiny, green ceramic frog looking up at me holding a sign, 'God loves you.' My eyes filled with tears. He had given me something precious.

Ron nudged me. 'They are reaching out to you, Diana. They know that you have the same desire to be loved and accepted as they do.'

Every little gift was important, the chance to share someone's special story.

We left Onslow the next day and headed toward Roeburne, Broome and Derby. At each stop we made, I could see that Ron was in his element, hugging old friends, crying for those who had passed away since he was last in the area, meeting the new spouses, and pinching the fat babies. He reminded me of a politician, but he gave them no empty promises, just his attention and love. We drank endless cups of tea while we waited for someone to arrange the night's meeting.

In Broome, we finally went fishing, and took walks along the beautiful Cable Beach in our shorts and bare feet. For two short days, we were alone with no one to visit, no meetings to go to, no one's problems to solve.

'If I could just forget about all my people's sorrows, this is what I would like to do every day. Enjoy nature, go fishing, do a bit of gardening, walk with the dogs. What a life!' Ron threw a line into the water from the far end of the jetty. We had been sitting in the same spot for two hours, soaking up the sun, neither one of us saying much. Even though the fish weren't biting, we were content to stay put.

'You wouldn't be able to do this every day,' I chided him. 'You love being in the centre of everything too much.' This new revelation from Ron had startled me. I couldn't imagine that he would ever want to be left alone. I couldn't imagine that he would even want a holiday. For months I had been hinting about enjoying a few days just to ourselves.

'No, you're wrong. I could handle it. That's something about me you don't know. If I had the choice . . .' his voice drifted off. 'But I don't.'

And I knew that I didn't have the choice either. Wherever he went, I wanted to be with him.

Broome was a sacred Aboriginal site. When Dreamtime history washed up on the shores of the north-west coastline, it brought with it the people who traversed the landbridge from Mesopotamia and then moved on into the desert following the footprints of the dinosaurs. Along the rocky ledges lining the shore out from Broome are slabs of rock on which a series of depressions can be seen when the tide goes out, some of which are outlines of huge dinosaur footprints. Alongside, as the legends tell, one can see the shape of Aboriginal footprints of a time long ago.

While Ron fished, I viewed the surrounding landscape through my camera lens. I still had the somewhat hidden desire to be a photographer, to produce visual stories, almost with a hint of surrealism. In the distance, I saw a derelict lighthouse that had seen better days. I glanced at my historian husband and asked if there was a story attached to it.

'Back in the seventies when I was here, some of the old fellas told me about that lighthouse keeper and how he looked after his crippled wife. They said this was a healing place.' It seemed that the only source of comfort for the wife's crippled legs was the salt water of the ocean. Every day the lighthouse keeper would carry his wife to one of the rock basins where a pool had been carved out, and there she would soak in the water as the tide came in.

'Quite a man, he was. Quite a man.' And Ron gave me a squeeze. Just then he hooked a small fish, held it up to announce his success, and then threw it back into the ocean.

I have quite a man too, I thought to myself. I was seeing so many facets of Ron, each glimpse a seeming contrast to the previous one. He loved people, but desired to be alone. He readily gave his dollar to a needy friend, but he jealously guarded his stash of photos, tapes and books, even outdated letters. He wept almost as a child when he thought of family members or close friends who had died, but his countenance could turn icy and hurtful when trying to ward off pain caused by prejudice or when he was defending his ideas. He had boundless energy when travelling on the road and preaching to crowds or telling stories over numerous cups of tea, but he often feel asleep in the chair, covered by the day's newspaper.

The two of us were like separate pieces of a jigsaw puzzle, bumping up against each other to see which parts might fit together. Though from opposite sides of the world, there were many passions that did match. Music, photography, dogs, reading, writing, moments of quiet, God. Being the woman, I sensed that my puzzle piece would have to do the changing, become fluid enough to fit into the vacant crevices. While Ron was moving within his own comfortable environment, old friends, family relationships, roads he had travelled before, I was the misfit super-imposed on the landscape of his world.

Ron packed the car the next day with extra water and fuel and informed me we were driving out on a dirt track to the One Arm Point commu-nity, to try some turtle fishing and call in at the Catholic mission at Beagle Bay. This stretch of land jutted out toward what is known on the maps as the Buccaneer Archipelago, trailing off into the Indian Ocean. The contours of the land looked amazingly like one arm pointing toward Sunday Island, the original home of many of the Aboriginal people brought to Catholic missions of the north.

I didn't have a clue what the road was like. Ron had called it 'bulldust'. The air was dry as we hit a section of the road, extending for two hundred kilometres, of the thickest, reddest dirt I had ever seen. As we ploughed through it, the fine particles poured over our car like flood-waters. We couldn't risk slowing down or stopping, or else we might not get started again. My chest began to wheeze, my breath grew short and I could sense the remnants of childhood asthma creeping through my lungs. I couldn't risk opening the window or we'd be covered in more dust than we already were. Every two minutes I had to take my glasses off and wipe them so I could see. I finally took a small towel, soaked it with water from our jug and held it up to my mouth so I could breathe. We had driven almost one hundred and twenty kilometres when, in the distance, I could see a small patch of green grass off the side of the road. It was neatly mowed, like a welcome mat rolled out in front of the Beagle Bay mission church.

The Trappist monks had established the mission in the late 1800s. Half-caste children from all over the north-west were brought there, some of them attached together with dog chains, coming from Derby to Broome. Then they were taken across the water by small boats, or over-land by horse and cart. The mission nuns and priests educated the children and taught them to work. During World War I the church was built using thousands of hand-made, limestone double bricks. Each brick carried the invisible fingerprints of an Aboriginal child of the north-west.

Our dust-covered vehicle came to a stop in front of the church, and I was grateful to open the door and breathe some fresh air. The church was inspiring. Paintings by local Aboriginal artists depicting Christian scenes decorated the walls and the altar was covered with mother-of-pearl shells in various hues and shapes. A dignified elder showed us around the church and the grounds, head held high, obviously proud of the mission surrounds, as he shared its history with confidence and authority. I made a mental note that it seemed that wherever the people had been able to express themselves, their spirituality, and their Christi-anity in their own way, their dignity soared.

The Bardi people in the north had always been a proud people, proud that their spirit wasn't broken by the whitefella. They knew the sea, the way it behaved and what it had to offer. But, after the war, the local trochus shelling and turtle farming had been taken over by the Indonesians and other fishermen, who drove the Bardi people out. They had no choice but to drift into Broome and Derby searching for work, food and welfare. Over the years, living in town, their spirit was crushed, no longer proud, but rather bereft of hope. They turned to drink, dying out at a fast rate.

'One of my friends, old Dave Drysdale, loved them and helped them to make a home out here at One Arm Point,' Ron explained as we drove to the jumping off place to Sunday Island. Dozens of children and teenagers greeted us, and some of the adults, coming close behind, recognised Ron from his days as a pastor in Derby. That night the whole village invited us to sit around a campfire, which burned outside the community boughshade against a backdrop of waves breaking on the shore. It was the land of the turtle and dugong.

Ron preached a sermon that night on hope and retold the circumstances surrounding the settlement of One Arm Point and the commitment of the man named Dave Drysdale. I could see the old people nodding their heads in agreement and wiping a tear from their eyes from time to time.

When Dave saw these beloved people fighting, going in and out of gaol, all their dignity stripped from them, becoming a laughing stock of the communities, he vowed to get them out of such a negative environment. He started to take small groups of people from Broome out to the point in a small boat, making hundreds of trips back and forth.

Eventually he cleared a road, with the help of the people, part of the bulldust road that we had just driven on. When the Bardi people saw his commitment to them, it gave them hope to establish their own community once again. This was years before the homeland movement started in other parts of Australia, a movement that was to see many hundreds, if not thousands of Aboriginal people who had been taken away or driven away from their hunting ground and ancestors' homes gradually come back to find their identity and hear their songs once again.

When Ron finished this ceremonial story, the silence hung in the air, like a moment from the Dreamtime, the old people quietly weeping for the memory of their old friend. The long intervening years had not dimmed their devotion to him for the sacrifices he had made. In these days of the fly-in and fly-out government worker, politician and short-term missionary, such personal memorials to those who had stayed through many faithful years and much hard work with only a few personal rewards stand out like diamonds against a dark sky.

Early the next morning, Ron went fishing with the locals and I spent time alone walking along the winding coastline. The foreshore was a beautiful blend of sand and smooth rocks bordered by small shrubs and clumps of pink and white wildflowers before sloping toward the village, where the sand gradually turned to dark soil. Large shade trees dotted the community, with government-built housing scattered throughout. The lifestyle was simple. No busy supermarkets or standing in a queue at the checkout. No cars spinning around the corners going nowhere in a hurry. No time-clocks regulating one's every move. In many ways, it was what many westerners dreamt about. Simplicity. Peace. An unfettered life.

I was fascinated by all the history and stories of people that Ron could remember, not only of his own family, but of those all around Australia. He had gained the reputation as a custodian of Aboriginal grassroots history. Not an author of anthropological treatises such as are published by universities, or of the political diatribes printed in the newspaper headlines, but a keeper of stories from the heart, treasures held secret within the Aboriginal consciousness, guarded carefully lest they fall into hands of exploitation.

'There are some things we don't tell the whitefellas,' said Ron. 'Too many times they have taken this history, *our* history, and made it their own. Making a name for themselves, getting their degrees, making their fortune by taking it away from us. The important things we don't tell anymore.'

He is truly an elder of his people, I thought to myself. It is not just because of age or maturity that an Aboriginal man becomes an elder but also in recognition of his role as the repository of the threads of Aboriginal life. Elders are the libraries, the memory banks of an oral culture, containing the riches of spiritual life, personal anecdotes, complexities of relationships, anchors that keep the community stable in the midst of the storm. Those who study the culture may be able to describe the garment it's wrapped in or analyse the vessel that holds the memory, but they cannot know the life force that fills it. Only those living it can truly know it.

❂ ❂ ❂

Me at four, looking incredibly pleased with myself. I'd just been for a ride in my grandfather's Pontiac during one of his many visits to my family in Oklahoma. His work on oil drilling rigs took my grandparents all over the country.

Ron, aged nine, in Albany, holding his favourite toy, a 'Ned Kelly' gun. He used to love hearing stories about the notorious outlaw. Because of his own treatment as an outsider Ron has always related to the stories of people on the fringes of society.

One of the few photos of Ron's grandmother, Grannie Grace, and a powerful reminder of the strong woman who guided Ron's life with such skill and love. I discovered this photo of her with two of Ron's cousins by chance in the deserted Bremer Bay cabin of Ron's Uncle Barney after his death.

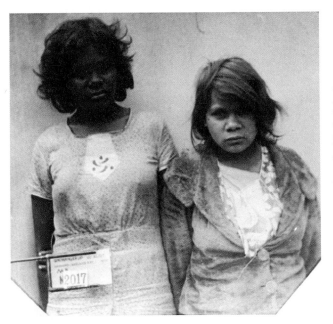

Ron's mother Cissie (left) and her sister Josie in Albany in 1939, photographed as part of a study of Aboriginal clans by anthropologist Norman B. Tindale. For many Aboriginal families, such impersonal, serial-numbered images are the only tangible reminders of their loved ones.

Grannie Grace in Albany, 1939, also photographed for the Tindale anthropological study. Like many Aborigines during the war years Gracie and her family were pushed out of towns to live on poverty-stricken reserves. Having been forced into so many mission homes and settlements, Gracie was determined for her family to live an independent life.

In contrast to Grannie Grace, my mother, Jean Greer, lived a comfortable life in Oklahoma City. This high school graduation photo was taken in 1942, not long before she met and married my father while he was training for the United States Air Force.

After three years of marriage, Ron and I saved up enough money to travel to America. One of only two occasions I've seen my brother John in the last seventeen years was at San Francisco Bay in 1988.

At Ron's first American Christmas in Oklahoma, he took one of the last photos of my mother and my sister with me before their deaths. From left, my mother's sister, Norma, who has been like a second mother to me; my sister, Pat; my uncle Jim (Norma's husband); me; my mother; and Bruce, my mother's second husband.

The track leading to Windjana Gorge was narrow and bumpy. Our car creaked and rocked from side to side as we came toward a stone building standing alone in the middle of tall grass and high rocky outcrop. It seemed to rise out of nowhere, like a submarine surfacing unexpectedly from a gently moving ocean. The stones had been removed bit by bit over the years.

'Follow me,' Ron beckoned. 'And watch out for the snakes.' He had climbed to the top of the rocks.

'Thanks for the warning. Couldn't you wait for me?' One thing I hated was snakes and I certainly didn't want to be caught alone on the ground trying to figure out how to deal with one. But Ron wasn't listening. He was starting to go into another time, another story.

'This whole place is sacred,' he began, sweeping his arm across the landscape. 'I can almost hear the cries of my people.'

'What do you mean, hear their cries?' I asked. I was still getting used to Ron's spiritual sensitivity and link with the land and its people.

'Whitefellas don't understand it. They think it's all superstition. But we can hear the spirits of our people. We can feel the past all around us. You wait, you'll see. This was Pigeon's place. Jandamarra was his tribal name, but his nickname was Pigeon.'

We were sitting on the remains of Lillimilura Police Station, where Pigeon killed a policeman in 1894, an action that began the most legendary manhunt in Australia's north-west. The provocation for that action and the events that followed turned Pigeon into a hero to his people, seeking justice from the destruction brought by the whiteman's stock-whip and shotgun.

'He lived in these caves. Up there, running along the edge of the cliffs. No one could get to him,' explained Ron, as we walked along the floor of the gorge, looking up at the cliff face that jutted straight toward the sky. I could see no way to climb up or down. The entrance to the gorge was flanked by jagged, vertically layered, multi-coloured limestone, ancient formations holding treasures of shells and fossils of marine life dating to a prehistoric flood.

'He eluded everyone,' Ron went on proudly, patting our dogs as they walked close to our side, sensing something in the air. Ron took me from one rock to another, obviously following the steps of this Aboriginal hero, the last stand of a man who didn't want his people to lose their culture. His choice of hiding places along the gorge was of Dreamtime significance, following the steps of the spirits who left their images as they touched the rocks. He ran along the limestone reef of the Oscar Ranges and came to his final resting place in Tunnel Creek.

'Let's walk through the tunnel,' beckoned Ron, as I peered into the dark abyss. 'This is where an Aboriginal police tracker from Roeburne shot him.' We walked a few metres into the cave, but a sudden chill came over me and I froze there on the spot.

'I can't go on, Ron.' Fear crept over me and I groped in the dark to find Ron. Maybe I was spooked by the story. Or maybe I was just tired and couldn't walk stooped over to the end of this tunnel. Or maybe I could hear the cries of the people. Water trickled over my feet and my small torchlight would not penetrate the darkness.

'I'm turning back, Ron.' No amount of coaxing could convince me to keep walking. Ron reluctantly came back with me. I took a deep breath as we walked out into the light, feeling safe again. He continued to talk.

'After Pigeon's death, there was unrest between his mob and those who killed him. There had never been any payback for it, never any ending to the story. Aboriginal people always have to have an end to the story, even if they have to wait for years.'

The custodian of Pigeon's story was old Banjo, a good friend of Ron's and his first wife's relation. In 1971, Banjo wanted Ron to take him to Roeburne, to make things right between the tribes. Sitting with the elders, they talked, they nodded, spoke the right words to bring the killing of Jandamarra 'Pigeon' full circle.

'They included me in the talk that night,' explained Ron. 'Old Banjo knew I wasn't an initiated lawman, but he told them I was "God's lawman", a peacemaker for them.'

'I'm glad to be leaving here. It's too spooky,' I said, as we drove away from Windjana Gorge, its cliff face receding in the distance. No sooner had the words left my mouth when the car came to a stop right in the middle of the dirt road. Ron crawled underneath and checked all the hoses.

'Looks like the water pump's broke. We'll have to camp here.'

'Here?' I said. 'It can't be.'

'Yeah, it'll have to be here. We sure can't go anywhere with the water pump broke.' I walked around the car praying that it would start. Ron started to laugh. 'You're getting just like a blackfella, scared of the dark.' He rolled out our swags.

My sleep was fitful that night as Dreamtime images crowded into my mind. Cattle bellowed in the distance and, occasionally, a dingo howled. I could feel my western, whitefella skin slowly slipping off, like a lizard moulting, while, at the same time, struggling to get used to a new kind of skin, the one my husband wore, the one that cries out from the ground.

✪ ✪ ✪

Just out of Derby, we came to Looma, the place of the Lizard Dreaming. 'You've gotta meet Limerick,' said Ron. 'He'll sing you some songs. You'll like him.' He took me by the hand, sensing my tiredness. I didn't know if I could meet anyone else or remember any more stories. There were a number of people sitting under one of the large trees in the middle of a clearing, which was surrounded by rectangular demountables, a similar arrangement to most remote Aboriginal communities. The familiar boughshade stood empty, a dozen dogs wandered aimlessly around the buildings while a dozen others sprawled lazily on the warm ground next to their owners.

Limerick had once been a much-feared tribal warrior who had lost his eyes as punishment for the people he had killed. When he stood before the elders, expressing sorrow for what he had done, they decided to blind him with fire sticks rather than 'do him in'. That act led him to acknowledge God, who was powerful enough to save him and compassionate enough to love him. Limerick was a linguist, fluent in six tribal languages, and after he became a Christian, he was the first man to use his language to write hymns for church and play the clapsticks. Without ever knowing the word 'contextualisation', he had forged the way to linking his tribal understandings with the Christian religion.

'My son,' he called out. 'Over here.' Limerick had heard us coming, recognised Ron's voice, and he greeted us warmly, touching my hand. Every time I thought I couldn't handle any more people, or that it was all too much too soon, a warm handshake, the small gift of a frog, or cup of tea made the difference.

'Come on, brother, sing us some songs,' Limerick commanded. 'We'll all join in.' Ron brought out both guitars, signalling our partnership, and we began to sing, with Limerick joining in with the rhythm.

I marvelled at this old man who had obviously been through so much agony, but who could sing with such joy and gusto. For the next few hours, I enjoyed the companionship of this remote village of gentle, caring people sitting on a carpet of red dirt. I could just stay here, I thought, while Ron drove on, on around Australia. I wanted to get to know them better, to catch their whispers. We were not even halfway around the country yet, but I wanted to stop. Stop, to give myself time to absorb some of the life that Ron had already lived for over forty years. Would I ever be able to catch up?

❂ ❂ ❂

The road to Halls Creek was dusty. Fine silt seeped under the car door and through the seams around the windows, even though they were tightly closed. The washouts were extremely rough since the road had been alternately softened by the rains and then baked by the sun. I wasn't really looking forward to going to Halls Creek. Not only was I aware that the church would not accept us, but I also knew that Ron's first wife was buried there. I sensed that Ron would expect a lot from me.

It was proving to be difficult enough for us to establish our life together at our 'mature' ages of thirty-nine and forty-five, along with adjusting to the cultural differences, the demands of our public ministry together, the absence of close family support from America, without coming face to face with rejection by many of Ron's church friends.

We parked the caravan near a toilet block about fifty metres behind the mission church. While Ron went to see who was around, I wiped the dust from the counter tops, restacked the shelves, which were in total disarray after the rough trip, and made myself a cup of tea. I sat in the doorway to the caravan gazing along the road that ran in front of the mission church. Toby and Maru were asleep at my feet, lifting one ear whenever a car backfired. Sputtering white Holdens and Ford panel vans of various colours sped down the road, packed full with blackfellas. Almost everyone wore cowboy hats, the trademark of the tough Kimberley region.

'Where you come from?' I was suddenly stirred out of my reverie and saw a little dark girl wearing only a pair of blue shorts and carrying a teddy bear that used to be white. She approached me with a timid look, warily poking out her finger to touch Toby on his head. Toby opened only one eye, saw the small hand and went back to his canine dream.

'Well, I come from a long way. Do you know where Perth is?' She shook her head from side to side, obviously never having gone out of her family's territory.

'Well, you ever heard of America?' She broke into a big grin, vigorously shaking her head up and down. Strange, not to know where Perth is, but America drew the nod.

I reached behind the door of the wardrobe and brought out one of my puppets. Mimicking a few voices, I made the puppet dance, cry, sing and tell stories. She pulled on its arms, put her own hand in its mouth and begged to take it home. Just then, Ron walked toward us, the little girl ran away, and the puppet rejoined its friends in the wardrobe. Behind Ron, an Aboriginal man hurried toward us.

'I'm sorry, Kurta,' said Jonathan, not looking at Ron's face, or into his eyes, but down towards the ground. 'You can't preach this Sunday. You know ... the mission boss.' Ron graciously put his hand on his friend's shoulders, letting him know it was all right. I could tell that Ron was deeply hurt through all this, but it hurt him even more that his own Aboriginal people had to carry this message.

Neither one of us could force the wounds to heal. We had to find ways to live with them. We still had many disappointments to weather, but when the moments of despair surged through us, Ron was often the stronger one. A small bouquet of flowers, the offer of his shoulders to cry on, an understanding silence while I exploded with anger at the pain I was feeling.

'But they don't even know me, Ron. How could people who call themselves Christians pass judgment on someone they have never even met, or tried to understand?' Not being given a chance to speak was the depth of the pain. Placed on the fringe as an untouchable without having a fair trial.

Ron cried too, but much more silently and with a much different kind of grief. In moments of honesty, he held his head in his hands and wept, 'If it came from people I didn't know, I could maybe understand. But it's from my own spiritual brothers. We've worshipped in the church together. We fought so many battles together, but we were always loyal to each other. That's what hurts the most.' Ron's answer to rejection was to love them all the more, to move toward those who hurt us.

'What?' I croaked. 'Have cups of tea? Visit them? Go out of our way? For people who have prayed for an accident to happen so we wouldn't get married?' I couldn't believe what I was hearing. It was too much for him to ask of me, but Ron would not be deterred and I dutifully, if not happily, followed. The strategy of 'loving our enemies' was followed faithfully for the next decade, wherever we travelled. I have thanked my Maker many times for the man He pointed out to me. A man who has the love to withstand the cyclonic struggles of this white American woman, the square peg, as she has tried to fit herself into the round hole of Aboriginal life, with all its complexity, struggles, and cultural pressures.

At the evening twilight, there was a knock on the caravan door, a few whispers to Ron, and within a few short minutes we were following a small group of men to a camp of blackfellas not far from the mission church. Underneath the trees there were twenty or thirty people, among them several children pulling on the dogs and throwing sticks.

There was a makeshift table fashioned out of tree trunks stuck into the dirt at four corners, logs spread across the top and then covered with branches. Perched on this were plastic bowls, blackened billies, bags of fruit, instant Sunshine milk tins and a variety of tin mugs and bowls. Blankets covered the ground nearby and a few upturned milk crates were scattered here and there.

As I contemplated where to sit, I knew that I was being watched to see how I would fit into their community. At that moment, a little girl in dark shorts tugged on my hand and pulled me down on the blanket next to her family.

'Puppet,' she said to me. I searched Ron's eyes and he quickly ran back to the caravan to bring out our little friend. That night the people let us know that they wanted us. The puppet was a hit. Requests for hymns and old country and western songs continued until our throats were hoarse from inhaling smoke from the camp fire. While Ron gave his last message of encouragement to his friends, my little friend brought me a cup of tea in a chipped tin mug, which had seen many tea-drinking days. She scampered back to her mother, whispered a few words and then returned and stood in front of me, a big smile on her face. In one hand she held out a piece of damper, dripping with golden syrup and dangling in her other hand was a piece of lizard recently taken out of the fire. From the corner of my eye, I saw the women watching my reaction, as I gladly took the kindly offered gifts and began to eat. More initiation into the Aboriginal world.

❂ ❂ ❂

'I know that this is going to be tough for you, but if you can do this with me, it'll speak to the people here.' Ron wanted me to meet his first wife's relatives and visit her grave with him. He didn't think that anyone had cleaned it up over these three years and he had brought some stones and wildflowers to place there. Even a rake to clean around the grave.

That afternoon we drove out to the cemetery. A knot began to form in my stomach. Ron's past was taking over our life together. If it wasn't staring me in the face, like today, it was never very far away. On the other hand, I had no grip on my own connections or familiar landmarks. Ron had never even met any of my people, had never seen where I came from. For all he knew, I was a woman without a clan, no past and no future, except his. The closer we got to the cemetery, the worse I felt.

It was a sad-looking place, dry, covered with gravel, no grass or trees. The area was fenced off with sagging lengths of wire and a locked gate. We climbed over the fence. Ron carried the shovel and a bucket of rocks. I gripped a bag of wildflowers and a jug of water. First, he had to find the grave. There were not many headstones or inscriptions, just small round markers with numbers on them. He had written down the number on a small scrap of paper, but couldn't find it. He seemed to walk around for ages. I just wanted to get it over with.

Finally, he stopped and started to clear the area around a mound of pebbles. I went to help him, placing a few rocks around the grave and emptying the bag of flowers. Suddenly a rush of grief came over me and I felt suffocated. I didn't know if I was grieving for Marj or for me or for all of us. But I knew I couldn't stay there.

Ron has too many unfair expectations of me, I thought. I walked away to a distant hill and cried, letting go of the tensions of the past weeks, the struggle of balancing our life among the burdens of the

Aboriginal people, and the desire to have a happy marriage just between a husband and a wife.

Ron leaned on the rake and watched me go, knowing the difficulties, and continued to pull on the rake and arrange the flowers.

I slowly walked back to join him, he held me in his arms, right there in the middle of the cemetery, next to Marj's grave, and we wept together.

Later in town, he nodded to the relatives and they nodded back. The story had come a complete circle. It was finished. I was accepted by his former in-laws. We could now go on.

Our plan was to meet Coral's parents, Bill and Maisie. Their little house on the edge of Halls Creek was deserted and someone nearby said they were away. Disappointed, we pulled into the roadhouse for a pie, knowing we had to be on our way. But while I paid for the pie, Ron spotted Bill and Maisie across the road in the park.

Maisie greeted me warmly and when she smiled I could see Coral's lovely face all over again. Bill was a tall, rather lean man and spoke only a few words before motioning to Maisie that he had to go. Ron shook his hand, but it was obvious he didn't want to stay. It was an awkward moment, but Maisie started to laugh, told me to say hello to Coral and then posed for a photograph beside our car. There was nothing more to say and she took off down the road to catch up to Bill.

'Maybe they didn't like me.' I said to Ron in the car. I had been nervous meeting them, and I didn't really know the whole background of the family situation, only that Coral had four other brothers and sisters, and that her parents had been together for a long time.

'No, no, that's not it. Sometimes I think they would like Coral to come back, but Bill knows there's not much for young girls up here. That's why he was willing for us to have Coral in the first place. They probably miss her, though. Tribal blood's pretty thick. But don't you worry about it.' We drove away from Halls Creek.

❂ ❂ ❂

Through the rest of the Kimberley, we followed the tour books, visiting Lake Argyle and Hidden Valley, before we stopped for a while in Darwin. There were more friends to have tea with, more visits to missions, this time where children were raised who had been removed from Croker Island, and more stories, this time of Cyclone Tracy.

'Let's go to Kakadu. You'll love it. Water buffalo come right up to the car on the way there. The scenery is beautiful, and we'll have a day to ourselves.'

I was thinking we needed a week, not just a day. An Aboriginal tour guide named Johnny took us up the Alligator River and cooked buffalo steaks and barramundi on the open fire. Along the river by the side of the boat, crocodiles jumped straight up out of the water, trying to catch the bait that Johnny held out on the end of a rod.

Later in the day, we drove to Obiri Rock (Ubirr); walked silently over the ancient formations and gazed at rock paintings. Ron went on for a short distance, climbing over the larger rocks, looking for caves. I stood on top of Obiri, alone, gazing deep into the horizon before me, where deep reds consumed orange streaks in the sky as the sun dipped low.

In art, the horizon exists where the sky appears to meet the ground and there is always a vanishing point near the centre. This is the point where parallel lines appear to converge in the distance like train tracks heading toward the furthest hill. Yes, I thought, Ron and I have walked along parallel, but similar paths throughout our lives, but now we're heading for that vanishing point on the horizon. That's where we'll come together, if we keep walking.

I turned in what I thought was a westerly direction, looking out along that road from Perth. I thought not only of how much distance I had covered, but also of how many people I had met and how much history I had learned. While the cloud formations kept drawing my attention to the sky, my mind was full of stories of the past, and emotions of the present.

I could see the downcast eyes of the Aboriginals sitting along the edges of the streets in small outback towns, the laughing and the tears of the old people in the bush as they spoke with pride of their beloved country and cried for the days now gone.

In the background I could hear the shouts and screams of children at play, innocent of the world they would one day have to face. I could see the past when men and women were chained up and led away to a destiny unknown, and the early missionaries, as they battled the physical elements to build schools and hospitals throughout the north-west. I could see in Ron's eyes and in his heart the love and appreciation for his people all through this region.

I had learned so much in so little time. How could I process it all? There had been no time for these encounters to be filed away and digested. It was as if the pages were scattered everywhere and I was trying to retrieve them before they were blown about by the wind. Could it be that one day, long ago, a tribal woman stood on this very rock, asking these same questions, with these same thoughts?

Did the white person's way ask too much, too quickly for the Aboriginal heart to process? I could answer a definite 'yes'.

We had only been married seven months and there was a lifetime before us. I turned toward the south, the direction we were headed for the next few weeks. What more would I learn, who else would I meet, what did all this mean for us?

Only the horizon ahead held the answer to these questions.

CHAPTER 8

From the Never-Never to the City

'Hey, bro, didn't I see you in Katherine at the rodeo?' drawled the slim, dark, cowboy looking in our direction. He was dressed in R M Williams' moleskin jeans, Akubra hat and bright blue polyester shirt. He held out his hand and grinned.

'You know who I am?' was the familiar question. Everyone seemed to recognise Ron and want to be known by him. This young fellow just 'happened' to be related to someone who had just 'happened' to attend Bible college in 1978 in Gnowangerup when Ron just 'happened' to be the principal. Surely Ron must remember him! Wouldn't we like to have a cup of tea with him at the tourist cafe? You know, to catch up on the yarns.

Ron and I had been meandering through the remains of Elsey Station, south-east of Katherine in the Northern Territory, a name synonymous with the Never-Never—when the outback dream grabs hold of someone, they never never want to leave—looking for the headstone of Aeneas Gunn, who was the focal point of his wife Jeannie's book, *We of the Never Never.* I had seen the movie in New York City over a year before I actually came to Australia. When I had emerged from the movie theatre on Seventh Avenue, facing the blur of yellow taxis and being bumped by throngs of people as they hurried past on a Saturday afternoon, my thoughts were still among the tall grasses, white gum trees and small humpies surrounding a weatherboard station house in the middle of nowhere.

'Yeah,' said Vinnie, our new-found friend sitting across from us, refilling his mug of tea. He had selected a table a good distance from the rest of the tourists. 'This is a big country out here. But changed now. Not much work for us blackfellas. Not like it used to be. I was a good horse breaker in my time. Still hang around the stations, though. No, not like it used to be.'

Ron nodded in agreement. 'Yep, those were good days. We had a lot of spirit, close to the land. You done any buck-jumpin' lately? Those fellas from Hooker Creek were really somethin' at the rodeo. Smart dress too.'

The Northern Territory in its early days was a dream that faded for the Aboriginal stockmen, as cattle stations were developed, and the land pushed and stretched into a shape that would fit the life of the newcomers. From around the edges, many dark eyes had watched as the dust rose from the paddocks and the native animals flew and ran from their hiding places. They watched as wagon wheels made deep ruts in the land they loved, and as trees were felled to build strange-looking fortresses surrounded by wide flanks, verandahs, the whitefellas called them, and then enclosed by wooden fences. Some approached this new scene with fear, others with curiosity and still others with anger.

'I think we blackfellas have lost out twice,' said Vinnie. 'Our bush land went and then the stations went. No more work, no more cattle to muster. Helicopter, motorbikes now. Too bad, they were good times, those.' He shook our hands. 'See ya back at the rodeo.'

The dust was thick near the Katherine rodeo stands and the smell of horse dung and bull sweat was heavy in the air. Blackfellas and whitefellas were everywhere, laughing together, holding their stubbies of beer and ogling each other's boots and spurs. Ron had backed our panel van in alongside the caravan that sold cool drinks, ice cream and corn dogs on sticks.

'This will be a great spot. Everyone is walking by here. We can give out some of our books, sing some songs and talk to people,' he explained while he shouldered two speakers up to the roof rack and adjusted the microphone. He had dressed in a beige western-style shirt, the last button near his belt undone as usual, and a red bandanna poked out from under his collar.

After the table was arranged with a number of copies of *Nuggets from the Goldfields* and Slim Dusty's lyrics were blaring from the tape deck, scores of blackfellas started gathering around. Ron grabbed my Ovation guitar, the preferred acoustic brand for rock stars, and started to sing.

Ron's voice was a mixture of the twang of Hank Williams, the American country sound of Wilf Carter and Ron's Aussie hero, Slim Dusty. I could never understand why everyone wanted him to sing. He was usually out of tune, always missed the beats, added his own words and never learned any new chords. No matter how hard I tried, I could never interest him in the more modern, up-to-date ballads, folk music or soft rock. As a teenager, I had spurned country and western songs, considering them not worthy of the refinements of a true musician.

'Come on, Diana, join me. Let's sing this one together,' Ron winked at me and signalled with a nod. 'Hey, everyone, my wife from New York City' (with emphasis on New York) 'is going to sing with me. She's got a beautiful voice. She's come all the way from America to be with you today.'

Ron never allowed me to say no. How could I refuse to join him when he had just announced it over the microphone? Curiosity-seekers were beginning to crowd around us.

Ron strummed on the guitar, finding a range that would suit us both. Once in a while he would forget that he had a partner and be well into the first verse before he realised that it was the wrong key. Most of the time I just had to follow along. Never any rehearsals for anything. 'Just be ready,' he'd say to me. Those who had ever travelled with him would hide behind the crowds of people lest he call them up in front to say something.

One of my few treasures from America was my Ovation guitar. It had survived for almost ten years, through the streets of New York and the heat of Central Australia. I had cradled it carefully in its tough plastic case all around the world, not so much for the sake of the guitar itself but that it was one of the few items from 'home' that remained with me.

'Hey, man, I sure like your guitar. I'd like one of them some day.'

That was an Aboriginal man's way of saying, 'I'd like you to give that to me.' Tribal obligations. That's why I cringed every time Ron opened the case and started to play. But he never offered the guitar to anyone, knowing what it meant to me.

Fifteen years, many desert concerts and at least twenty sets of new strings later a tribal singer from the centre borrowed my guitar, strummed too hard and the entire bridge broke away from the body. By then, that special guitar had lost its New York vibrations.

As we came to the end of the song, I saw a whitefella sauntering toward us. He swayed from side to side, obviously having had a few too many stubbies. 'Hey, sweetheart, what you doin' with this blackfella? You're too good-lookin'. How 'bout givin' me a kiss.'

I started to back away, glancing in Ron's direction as if to say 'Help'. He didn't seem phased by the incident at all, but moved nearer to this man, who had a slight sneer on his face and a chest puffed out like a fat goanna.

'Hey, mate,' said Ron. 'You must be pretty good at riding the horses. You come here every year?' Those words seemed to completely disarm the man, and soon Ron had cornered him into conversation about his family, his horse-riding expertise and station properties he had worked.

We often encountered these moments of racism. Sometimes they occurred when Ron was alone, at the local hamburger stand, the fast food outlet or a chicken shop, where he patiently waited to be served. The furtive looks and whispers were loud enough to hear: 'I think he's an Aboriginal, you know.'

Other times they occurred when we were together, mostly from men with icy stares and snarling lips, who mouthed the words 'You black bastard' toward Ron, making sure he understood. And I could always see the look of surprise on the face of the person behind the counter at a deli when Ron was short-changed and he would turn to me in conversation or touch my hand. Suddenly there would be profuse apologies and obvious blushing cheeks as the correct change was handed over.

✪ ✪ ✪

'BUDDY WILLIAMS PLAYING HERE TONIGHT': the sign greeted us as we drove along the Stuart Highway into Tennant Creek. Everyone, including Ron, loved this blackfellas' friend. They would travel in from miles around to hear him sing in the outback communities, the Aboriginal hostels or on the cattle stations. Some of the men had worked with him in the Wild West rodeo shows when he was on tour. When Ron wrote one of his first songs, 'You Can't Help Me Now, You've Come Too Late', he had borrowed the tune from Buddy's song 'The Wandering Gambler'. Many a night as a young fellow he listened to his Aunt Josie and Uncle Allan crooning that song at every Noongar gathering.

That night on the little reserve outside Tennant Creek, we found Buddy singing his favourites to the motley mob of Aboriginals from all around the area. Young fellas dressed in their cowboy best cradled bottles of beer. Teenage girls huddled together for safety, pointing at the thin and wiry young teenage boys who glanced periodically over their shoulder at the bevy of females.

Couples were seated on the ground, just below the microphones, singing loudly with the band. In the shadows, children would get up and dance to the music for a few seconds at a time, bobbing up and down like small pistons as they giggled to one another. As the night wore on, some of the young women who had been sipping on their cans would saunter towards the small stage to join the band, or they would dance with each other, since most of the men remained seated, maintaining their dignity.

There was plenty of noise and laughter, the familiar sounds of men and women calling out to one another. 'Hey, bro! Over here!' someone called to a relative, patting the ground beside him.

'Hey, Buddy, ya doin' good. Sing that gamblin' song.'

There was a feeling of security, of community, that was not found in the daylight walking down the streets of the outback towns. Once in a while along the dark edges of the group, an argument would start up, perhaps caused by jealousy over someone's mate, or a boast about one's skill in horse breaking, or a wrong word spoken to the wrong person. The argument was soon quelled by a word from one of the elders, or by a mother-in-law wielding a hitting stick. A few listeners would growl in the direction of the fray, 'Sit down!'. 'Come on, listen to Buddy!' and then all would be back to normal, laughing, drinking and singing.

Aboriginal camp life was tugging at me, pulling me in with the jostling, the fun, the humour, the fights and the tears.

The next day I stood by our car, which was parked on the main street running through Tennant Creek. I was just digging into my bag to find some money to buy a coffee for the road when a young woman came running toward me, calling my name. I couldn't imagine who would know my name out here in the middle of the country.

'My sister, my sister,' she whispered as she planted a wet kiss on my cheek and threw her arms around me. I recognised Delores, a friend from Laverton, my Australian 'birthplace'. She had been one of my kangaroo-hunting buddies and had spent many hours sitting on the ground next to me teaching the desert lingo and telling me stories of her family. I had never been loved so much, greeted so profusely or felt so much a part of Australia as at that moment. It was special, when an Aboriginal arm embraced this white woman from New York City.

I was vaguely aware of the stares from the white folks walking down the street, questioning the sight of this rather dishevelled Aboriginal lady hugging and kissing a white woman for all to see. Our common 'home-land' of Laverton had brought us together. We came from the same territory. With her I had just experienced the embrace of one who had suffered exclusion at the hands of others. I was not a stranger any more. She wasn't obligated to notice me. She didn't have to cross the racial divide in the middle of the main street. But she did.

Tension fell away from me. When our car pulled away from Tennant Creek, Ron and I started to sing. We were slightly out of tune and the key was too high, but we were doing it together.

❍ ❍ ❍

Three blowouts on the way to Mount Isa. The last one burst as I was driving along the continuous flat, ribbon-like strip stretching out through the desert-brown background, dotted with rocky mounds reflecting in the sun. Even though it was the middle of winter in Australia, it was hot on the road. While Ron walked around the car a few times, checking hoses and kicking the tyres, I sat beside the road, learning to be patient. 'Someone will come soon,' he said.

That someone was an Aboriginal family from Camooweal. The over-crowded ute slowed to a stop as it approached, the driver called to Ron to find out the trouble, then they parked right behind us. It was quite a while before there was any talk about our tyre problem.

'You come from Western Australia, do you? I got a cousin in Bassendean, Perth, I think. You ever hear of him? Name's Johnson.'

'Well, there's some Johnsons down south. Any relation?' explored Ron.

'Maybe. So whatcha doin' out this way. Y'seen any 'roos along this stretch?'

'Nope, not a one. We're headin' to Mount Isa for some meetings. I'm a pastor. This is my wife. She's from America.'

'Really? I always wanted to go to America. What's it like there? There was a teacher once in the Walpiri country that came from America. You ever hear of her? Can't remember her name, though.'

'Say, you wouldn't happen to have an extra spare with you. We just blew out our last tyre.' Ron finally got to the need of the moment.

The conversational pattern among Aboriginals is much different from the 'get to the point' style of the western-trained mind, which cuts out all the frills. The extras can come later after the 'real work' is done. In my newly adopted culture, greetings were very important. There were precedents to follow, relationships to sort out. It was a circular pattern, not a straight line. My own culture had taught me to think in straight lines, to get from one point to the next in the quickest, most cost-effective approach. Not so among the original people of Australia. The pattern involves waterholes, circling around them, until you get to where you want to go.

Relationship is much more significant than the actual reason for the conversation. The intricate kinship structure of traditional Aboriginal society dictates the need to establish who the other is, where they come from, what links they have to your country or your family. Then business can proceed. That was the transaction on the side of the road in Queensland on our way to Mount Isa.

The driver found a spare tube and gladly gave it to us, along with another gift as well. A kangaroo tail. That signalled a feast, a celebration. The passengers of the ute jumped out of the back, kids played along the dirt road, we dug a hole in the ground, lit a fire and covered the tail with its coals.

The unwritten law of the outback roads and the time-honoured tradition of Aboriginal life is to stop, share and help each other. Such a different attitude from the city, as I was to find out years later, when the engine of our four-wheel-drive blew up along the Geelong Freeway. No one stopped. How I longed for the bush roads at that moment!

❂ ❂ ❂

I had been waiting for news from America. The mail took several weeks to catch up with us, being sent from Marribank to various spots around the country, where I would eagerly stand in the queue at the post office hoping for a large parcel of letters. In Mount Isa I finally collected letters from both my parents. I surprised myself at how eagerly I ripped them open. I had never been a regular letter writer and neither had they, but now I found myself wanting to connect with my family. Was it because I had learned so much from my Aboriginal family, their closeness and love for one another? Was it because I had seen so much suffering as a result of removal, scattered communities and one-night stands?

I recalled when, in a little house outside of Cloncurry, gentle, soft-spoken Auntie Kate had ushered me into her bedroom to show me some photos of her family, and whispered a secret. 'My dear, I just want you to know that my son is American.' She held out a photo of a handsome, smiling young man dressed in a uniform. 'This is his father. He was an American soldier passing through this way during the war. He wanted to marry me, even gave me an engagement ring. But the mission wouldn't let me. They had the last say, you know, on our lives and that. Then he went away one day. My boy never knew his father.'

The ache was real, within her heart and within mine. Over and over I would remember the events of my own childhood, the separation of my own family. In some small way I could understand what Auntie Kate had experienced.

Our busy schedule and nights of travel precluded much letter writing to Coral or other family members, except for a post card once in a while. We tried to keep in touch by phone whenever we could get through to Marribank and link up with the Minniecon family when they were home.

'Coral mentioned she wants to go back to live in Halls Creek.' I had suddenly decided to tell Ron about the impending demise of our family before we had even had a chance to retrieve it.

'I didn't want to tell you,' I went on, 'but that's what she said when we rang up last night.' Ron continued to drive silently, so I made another attempt.

'Shouldn't we go home? We don't have to make these other stops. Maybe the family is more important.' I desperately wanted to establish ourselves as a family, beginning with the two of us and then providing for Coral. The tour of Australia, the work in the church, and my growing understanding of Aboriginal community life and social history was valuable, but the details of family life were getting swamped in the process.

I knew that Coral was unhappy, probably growing frustrated with Ron's travels and lack of family life. Perhaps the anticipation of any changes that would occur when he and I had married had long since disappeared, and the prospect of reconnecting with her birth family in Halls Creek was more inviting.

'We'll work things out with Coral when we get home,' Ron murmured. 'We've made our plans, so let's keep going. You can make it. We both can.' When Ron made up his mind about something, he didn't want anything else to interfere. Even advice from an Aboriginal pastor and his wife, knowing Ron's background, urging him to go back home and concentrate on his family, fell on deaf ears. Ron nodded politely, but then walked away and did what he wanted. Family would have to wait.

❂ ❂ ❂

The lights of Tamworth appeared over the hill. We had driven hard all day to get there in time for a small gathering at one of the local Aboriginal churches. My thoughts were still on Coral, and the desire to turn west and cancel the rest of our journey was gnawing away inside. These other people did not need us as much as she did. How many more times did I need to share my story of New York City, my migration to Australia or my spiritual journey? Besides, my experiences could never match theirs and I never knew if they really wanted to hear about mine. I didn't feel that I had anything left to give.

Ever since the days at Laverton, seeing so many Aboriginal people shuffling along the footpaths of life with bowed heads, their spirits crushed, I had been searching, as many others had done before me, for answers. These things were on my mind that night in Tamworth while

I told my story again, laughed with Ron about our wedding and the cave, sang our usual gospel songs and ate chunks of damper with jam.

When the people started to leave, a dark hand took mine and a gentle voice caused me to look up into the eyes of Auntie Pearl. 'My dear, thank you so much for coming tonight and sharing your story with us. You and Ron make a good match.' With that she squeezed my hand, turned and walked slowly out, steadied by her young grand-daughter. When I looked in my hand, there was a twenty-dollar note, probably a fifth of her pension for the week.

This 'widow's mite' showed me what was important in life. To be able to give. For over two hundred years her people have been on the receiving end of someone else's hand-me-downs. At first it was cast-off clothes and bags of flour with weevils in them, then it was spent bullets and chains marked with old blood, and finally the dole cheque and 'sit-down' money. The system of paternalism, welfare and handouts, no matter how well-meaning, has sapped the richness of the Aboriginal gift to Australia. Auntie Pearl had more dignity than I did when she took my hand. She wasn't ashamed of her gift and I reached out to receive.

It's not just receiving their gifts of dot paintings to hang on walls of wealthy homes, without ever knowing the artist. It's not just receiving the gift of an Olympic gold medallist, yet never knowing the potential Aboriginal runner who lives in the same community. It's not just receiving the gift of the didgeridoo, its music travelling over the oceans of the world, without appreciating the struggles of its maker. Nor is it taking these gifts and claiming copyright for ourselves, thereby committing one more act of dispossession.

It is also receiving the gift of their Dreamtime history, their gift of the knowledge that relationship is more important than *what* you do, their gift of hearing and seeing the signs in the bush that speak of a glorious Creation and Creator. It is also receiving, even embracing, their gift of pain. The pain of a people who have survived. They have so much to give us, if we will only receive.

❁ ❁ ❁

'Hey, man, you don't wanna park your car here, unless you want to get it ripped off by the Abos,' was the greeting from the old man watching us as we locked the doors and looked around the neighbourhood. We had arrived at the Block, the end of Eveleigh Street, Redfern, in the heart of inner-city Sydney.

The old man leaned on his walking stick, peered at us both, then looked at Ron. 'You a blackfella, eh? Well, I guess you'll be all right. They look after their own around here, but just watch your back.' With that, he spat on the footpath beside us and hobbled away, muttering something under his breath about, 'Damn tourists, puttin' their nose in everywhere.'

Redfern has been the centre of much controversy over the last few years. The small community of Aboriginal people sprinkled with a few whites and other nationalities have lived for the past sixty years in a number of two and three-storey tenements on one rectangular city block. Some of the buildings are burnt out, abandoned long ago. Others are marked with graffiti, Aboriginal flags and neo-rock paintings on the outside walls. Children run in the streets playing with tins, marbles and, once in a while, a basketball. Men and women of various ages lean over the dividing walls just in front of their flat, as if to stand guard over the community, watching the comings and goings of strangers.

I followed Ron's lead as we approached, watched as he shook hands, saying where he was from, who he knew in Redfern, where we had been travelling and where we were going. Out of his pocket he drew some photographs of Noongars in Western Australia, some of our wedding, and two or three of his family in Kalgoorlie. That broke the ice. Photographs make connections with the Aboriginal sense of relationship. They provide context and reality and mere words do not carry the same weight. Soon their previously suspicious eyes relaxed and their hands shook mine.

The whole area reminded me of New York City: the streets of Harlem, the stoops of West Side apartment buildings, where ancient residents would survey their neighbourhood. I thought, I could live here. One of those second storey flats would do me just fine. Right here in the middle of the action.

'Go around the block, man. Lots of fellas over there to talk to,' was the advice. A few minutes later, we were warming ourselves around a small fire burning in a cut-down 44-gallon drum sitting in the middle of a patch of dirt where once a condemned building had stood. Men and women were seated on the ground or sitting on milk crates, playing cards, drinking beer. One moment there'd be a laugh, the next a push and a raised voice and then a man and a woman were pulling each other down the street.

When someone in the group realised we were from Western Australia and they could possibly be related to Ron, there were more handshakes all around and shouts of joy at finding a relation from so far away. There was the hushed discussion between tears for family who had died, then laughter and slaps on the back when recounting the problems of life in Sydney.

I had been standing dutifully to one side, taking in the scene, when Ron introduced me as his wife. Suddenly I became 'Sister Diana' or, more often, 'Auntie Diana', since Ron's white beard had earned him the title 'Uncle' from every Aboriginal he met. I was then reckoned into their kinship system, immediately admitted into the larger family, with arms around me, a sloppy kiss on the cheek and a comment in Ron's direction. 'She's boss, Uncle.' That didn't mean I was in charge, but that I was 'all right'.

All around the Block, the word went out that fellas from the west were there. Blackfellas came from everywhere, wanting to see the photographs, hear the stories of our travels, interested in New York City. Was it like Sydney? Did I know any blackfellas over there?

Against the background of the surrounding gutted grey buildings, the elevated train tracks behind the dirt patch, the piles of tins and bottles scattered along the streets, hidden to the rest of the world, there was a family. A family just like any other one, who loved, who fought, who protected each other, who shared a life in meagre circumstances. A family proud to tell you who they were, where they came from and to invite you into the history of their lives if you were interested, to let the tears stream down their cheeks at the reminder of their pain. My shoulder was wet with their tears.

'You know, Uncle, they wanna move us from here, those bloody government mob. They say we're eyesores. But this is our home, this is where my family was long time. We belong here. This is Aboriginal land. We can't let go of it.' It was the spirit of the Never-Never here in the city streets, their homeland.

At that moment, a police siren pierced the air, the black eyes darted from one to another, muscles began to tense and the talk ceased. The fear of the chains, of removal, of the gallop of the police trackers' horses was now a fear of the screeching of tyres, which brought the same message down through the generations, from desert land to the city streets. 'No you don't, you don't belong.'

○ ○ ○

It was early November when we arrived in the nation's capital. Our focal point was the Aboriginal tent embassy, the controversial tin shack that had been planted beneath the steps of the imposing Old Parliament House in 1972. Then, it had only been five years since Australian Aboriginals were first counted in the census and recognised as citizens in their own country. During those few years, the rumblings of discontent were being felt all across the land. Communities in Arnhem Land had begun to issue petitions to the government regarding the mining of their land. In answer to a petition and legal action from Yirrkala, Justice Blackburn had declared the land 'terra nullius', literally, 'the land of no one'. According to the ruling, Australia had been without an owner in all the previous generations before 1788.

Aboriginal poets and writers were beginning to emerge, speaking of injustices and pain that the rest of Australia didn't want to hear about. In 1970, in the heart of Redfern, the first Aboriginal Legal Service, followed by the Medical Service, was established. In 1971, on National Aboriginal Day, the red, black and yellow Aboriginal flag was hoisted for the first time in Adelaide.

'We were starting to realise we had to do things ourselves,' Ron explained. 'No longer act like "Jacky-Jacky", just taking handouts, always saying, "Yes, boss." It was time to take action.'

It was in 1972 that the Queen planned to come to Australia to participate in the Australia Day events and open the next sitting of parliament. It was also in that year that the Department of Aboriginal Affairs issued an invitation to ten Aboriginal men, some of them products of the government reserves and missions, who had trained in Bible colleges and were dedicated to serving their people.

'They flew us here to talk to the government. They said they wanted to know what we Christians wanted to do to help our people. It wasn't easy for us. When we left our homes, the missionaries and other Christian organisations called us Black Power. Huh, Black Power, what a laugh! We were just wantin' to have our say, for someone to listen to us. It's *our* people who's dyin'.'

The representative from Senator Cavanagh's office brought them into a large office, where he heard the plans of these men. Men who had lived on next to nothing while they searched out the corners of Australia to bring comfort to the disheartened and dispossessed.

'We didn't want our people to be in gaol all the time, or drunk on the streets. I can't tell you how many of my people I've buried over the years. All of us had. We had no regular support from the church organisations. Most of their money went to white missionaries. We wrote out all our plans before we came to Canberra.'

The men had outlined a strategy for employing chaplains in the prisons, improving basic education skills, training in social services and developing spiritual understanding and leadership. This was more than a decade before the Royal Commission on Deaths in Custody, a study that outlined much of what these men already knew were the needs of their people and how to provide for them.

'That politician leaned back in his swivel chair, sucked on his cigar a couple of times, and thanked us for coming. Then he closed the folder that contained our plans, and said that he really couldn't help us. We were too religious,' explained Ron.

'What did you say?' I pumped him, not believing what I heard.

'What could we say? No one could say anything. We were too stunned, so we left knowing that most people didn't listen to us anyway. Very few of us blackfellas spoke up in those days, me included. When we were on our own we complained plenty, but around the whitefellas we had been trained to be quiet.'

Ron and the others didn't feel like celebrating during that Australia Day. Most Aboriginals stayed away from the marches, the speeches and awards to the citizenry. Others had long since refused to participate in re-enactments of the First Fleet landing.

'The people organising Australia Day went out to the camps and the tin humpies in the bush and along the river to bring the blackfellas in to welcome the ship when the Sydney mob said they wouldn't be in it. Those poor fellas from the bush didn't even know why they had been brought there. They were locked up overnight and they got a feed, and when the day was over they took them back to the huts along the river.' Ron's voice grew louder as he told me the story.

'I was right here in this spot when it was erected,' he pointed to the embassy. 'The Aboriginal flag was raised, we all gave a cheer. We knew it was sacred land. All our roads led to Canberra that year. 1972. I'll never forget it.'

Ron didn't forget. None of the Aboriginal people forgot. The tent is still there, symbol of the longest protest in history. A tent similar to the one Ron had grown up in as his family moved from farm to farm looking for work.

In 1972, underneath the soil of Australia came volcanic rumblings, gathering energy from all parts of the country. Energy from the attempts on the part of Aboriginal leaders to make things right, to piece together the remnants of a nation, to bring healing to their own soul. They wanted a home in their own land. The volcano erupted in the political heart of Australia, surrounded by the ancient hills of Canberra. The ancient hills formed by the heat and pressure beneath the earth's surface. What a significant time and place for the heat and pressure of a whole society of people, having endured generations of pain, to explode on the surface!

'We can't allow it to keep happening. Somebody has to listen to us!' Ron's voice spoke firmly, remembering the moment. He had been there when it happened, he was part of it and the rumblings could still be heard in his heart.

What my friend from New York had said before I got married was true. I hadn't just married a man, I had married a culture. As Ron's wife, I knew that I could never escape the political aspects of his life, the injustices against his people or the frustrations of not being heard. Even though I had seen these problems first hand along the creek bed at Laverton and knew something of what I was facing, and I had freely chosen to link myself to Ron, wherever our pathway would take us, it would not be smooth sailing. Indeed, I was being stretched to the utmost, and challenged in my thinking. I was experiencing the bitter taste of prejudice and rejection, hatred and misunderstanding.

❂ ❂ ❂

There was one more stop before we set our sights toward Western Australia. Across the Tasman. The reason? To see Frank Cole, the man who had led Ron to Christ, the man who had walked across racial boundaries to be his friend in a meeting that had radically changed the direction of Ron's life. It had been almost thirty years.

Frank had returned to Tasmania by the end of 1958, married, became a fisherman, and had lost track of Ron Williams, the mission and the church. Then one day in 1984, receiving a Christian magazine from a friend, he read an article about an Aboriginal evangelist, Ron Williams. He wrote to the publisher. Was this the same Ron Williams he had known in Western Australia?

After we had married, Ron contacted Frank and a reunion was planned. I had seen a photo of Frank, short, stocky and rugged, dressed in the traditional Aussie shorts, standing next to Ron, tall and thin, with black wavy hair, against an old weatherboard hut on the Gnowangerup mission. When Frank greeted us at Launceston airport, so many years after the photo had been taken, I saw the same jovial smile and friendly eyes.

Ron and Frank talked non-stop, bringing each other up-to-date after all those years. As much as Ron had struggled with bitterness toward white people who snarled and jeered him, bitterness at being born into a disadvantaged life, bitterness toward the police who had chased him as a child, he still reached out to those who had shown him kindness, to those who had treated him as an equal, looking at him eye to eye. Frank was one of those men.

✿ ✿ ✿

The Nullabor Plain stretched out before us and I could smell the water-hole called home. I couldn't get my foot off the accelerator. I wanted to run to home base and allow all that I had seen and heard to work its way into my life. We camped alongside the roads, walked to the edge of the cliffs lining the Great Australian Bight along the southern coast, climbed the sand dunes at Eucla and anticipated a more settled life at Marribank Aboriginal Community near Katanning.

The roadside scenery had gradually changed from flat plains country to jarrah trees and farming properties. It was our last night on the road and we camped around the usual fire. While Ron stirred the stew simmering in the camp oven, he said gently, 'You know, I never let up on you this year. I never really told you how to act, or what to expect. And I never rescued you when you made mistakes.'

I didn't know how to answer. I could only agree. The whole year had been a tough one and I had said to him many times that I would never want to repeat it. Sometimes I had woken at night crying for no apparent reason. Other times I had dreams, sometimes nightmares, of tribal warriors, destruction and sadness. 'I felt like I was sinking many times,' I murmured. 'All I could think of was to run. Why didn't you help me?'

Ron moved nearer. 'To see if you could pass the test. It's like initiation, Diana. When I first saw you, you were sitting on the ground with the Wongis in Kalgoorlie. That's why I knew you were the woman I wanted to marry, because you weren't afraid of dirt, you weren't afraid to get close to my people. But now, if we're going to make it together, you have to go through initiation. Like climbing the mountains, sleeping in caves, travelling the roads, listening to their stories. And there are a lot more miles to go yet.'

Ron, along with other Aboriginal people, had learned to sit back and wait. Wait patiently to see how the whitefella would handle being in their territory. They gave no clues, no signposts to mark the way, only the way of initiation. To put the would-be warrior out in the bush and wait to see if he made it home. That is the way to learn survival, the only way to make a man out of a boy. To make a woman out of a girl.

Initiation is part of the journey of faith as well. Many a servant of God was initiated in the wilderness of life, enabling them to understand the struggle of others. Moses, brought up in a palace, cut his feet on the desert floor for forty years. A Chinese leader once said that the only way to cross a river is by feeling the stones.

Initiation was painful, but it was the only way to embrace the journey and each other.

CHAPTER 9

Life and Death Among the Jarrah Trees

Driving through Katanning toward the final thirty kilometres to Marribank, I felt I had just been through a time warp. I was coming home. I looked forward to 'settling down', to having time to get our life in order. There was so much to do.

The first stop was in Katanning and the nearest store. Katanning is in the heart of Noongar country. Before white settlers had begun to clear the land for farms, it was the meeting place for the ceremonial activities of three tribal clans. These clans formed part of the Bibbulmun tribe, one of the largest in Australia, its territory stretching from Perth down the coast to Albany, across toward Esperance and up through the wheatbelt, forming a triangle as it reconnected to the Perth Swan River location.

Bibbulmun meant 'many breasts', the name reflecting a land that was plentiful, generous and fertile. Today, the adventurous bush walker can follow the Bibbulmun Track and see dense forests, lush foliage and hundreds of birds and creatures of the dirt as they scurry away at the vibration of footsteps. For the spiritually sensitive traveller, there may be a sense of a people gone before, whose echoed laughter, songs and rhythmic dance steps can still be heard as the wind gently blows through the tops of the tall jarrah trees. It was the place of Ron's childhood memories.

As in other parts of Australia, the Noongars, as they were eventually called, held to the intricate kinship patterns and survival customs that enabled them to live with the land. There was a communication with the elements of nature and the contours of the land that the non-Aboriginal did not know and usually didn't take the time to learn. This language was taught from the moment of birth, as the child was cradled in the earth, dust gently blowing across the newborn's body, the parents and the extended family welcoming their offspring into this eternal Dreaming.

The people of the south were a strong race, in stature, in wisdom and in spirit. They had long ago decided against the circumcision rites and tooth removal that the desert tribes engaged in during initiation. Even so, the Noongar men still held man-making ceremonies, and still sang their songs of creation and the history of their forefathers. This was their school, their system of education, which enabled the younger generations to understand their significance and purpose. It was also a means of cohesion in the midst of new and strange philosophies that appeared with the coming of the tall ships and the galloping of horses into the bush lands.

The Aboriginal people of the south-west did not understand the coming of these strange men of white skin, who at first seemed to be spirits of the dead returned, but then watched as the situation quickly turned to mishap and mayhem. The Noongar people did not understand the process of hoarding, as they watched the newcomers saving up grain and stores until the morrow, nor did they understand the marking of fences that went up across the fields, keeping possessions in and keeping them out. They had lived for generations in cooperation with the land, using only what was needed. Their natural boundaries had sufficed to keep respectful distance between clans and still provide for movement from season to season.

They had learned to have patience with the bush game, to sit when sitting was needed, to hunt when the signs were right, to straighten their spears in the fire and to chip away at a precious spearhead while resting during the heat of the afternoon. They watched in hesitation as the farmhouses sprang up and the tall trees, where the birds sang the coming of dawn or approaching danger, were felled with loud crashes resounding from within the dark forests.

Yellagonga, the tribal leader of the Swan River area, had once embraced James Stirling as he descended from a small craft lowered from the tall ship that he navigated to the upper reaches of the river. This leader thought that Stirling was the vision of his dead son returned to bring hope and life to his clan, a message from God.

At first Stirling was impressed by these people of extraordinary dignity, vowing to live side by side. The tribal people, thinking these white spirits were sent from their Creator, watched. But the hope soon turned to sadness, and then to despair, as their lands were stripped, their rivers gradually emptied of the teeming marine life. As their food supplies dwindled, they helped themselves to the produce of the farmers and, from time to time, a sheep from the paddocks. Just as they had not understood the ways of the white man, neither did the white man understand the ways of the Aboriginal man.

These misunderstandings eventually led to open warfare, culminating in the Pinjarra Massacre of 1834, with James Stirling leading his men to break the strength and spirit of resistance among the Noongar leaders so that white settlement could begin to extend from Perth toward Albany. Many a good fortune, many a prosperous farm or station property was built on the misfortunes of Aboriginal people who once belonged to those places.

His spirit destroyed and hopes lost, Yellagonga carried his sick wife on his shoulders through the streets of Perth in view of all, both black and white, past the English-style parliament buildings, down from Kings Park hill, toward what is now St George's Terrace, in the centre of Perth, to lay her to rest. The tall warrior, carrying himself with the dignity and pride that was slowly ebbing away from his race, did not take notice of the jeers, the disdain, nor even the gasps or the tears of those who watched.

It was a sad moment, a story still passed down in the ceremonies of the Noongars, or when sitting around the camp fires telling and retelling their history. The outward resistance of the original custodians had been quenched, but it was the stories that would keep their inner spirit alive, a flicker of the old ways, the spirit of the Aborigine. Stories always make a place for people in one's memory.

It did not take many years before the dignified warrior-like Aboriginal man and the graceful Aboriginal woman had become a people of the camps, almost gypsy-like, moving from reserve to reserve, herded out of town like animals. Carrolup, later to become Marribank, thirty kilometres outside of Katanning, was such a reserve, and it was there that the descendants of Yellagonga and others were sent. It was another meeting place of Aboriginal tribes, but this time they were mixed up, confused, lost and without pride.

❂ ❂ ❂

The residents of Marribank were overjoyed to see us. Their love of stories dictated that we would be telling and retelling the adventures of our travels for many nights to come. A photo night was arranged in the church hall. There were children racing in all directions, kangaroo stew cooking on the fire just outside the door and cakes galore. It was so good to realise that I didn't have to pack up the next morning and move on to the next town.

The mice had taken over our house again, kids had broken into the shed and a variety of bush gear, as well as a tent, a portable engine and some old blankets had gone missing, as well as the electric washing machine. Even then I was happy. Home at last.

I continued the redecorating that I had started almost a year ago, trying to launch a new life together for us both.

'Auntie Diana.' A little black face was pressed against the screen door. 'Can I have one of those gingerbread bickies you makin'?' The smells from the oven must have travelled down the path, I thought to myself as I opened the back door. Little Hazel, a ten-year-old from a big family, came shyly into the kitchen, perched herself on the chair and watched eagerly as I opened the oven door to reveal six large gingerbread men. She helped me to place sultanas and Smarties in various strategic spots on the shapes, making her own designs as she went.

The children were always around, hungry for attention and eager to see whatever new concoction I was brewing, or dabble in the water-colour paints that I kept by the door in a box. One by one young girls and boys would ride their makeshift bikes up the path to the last house on the turn, lay their bikes at our front doorstep and call in for a 'treat'. I had several boxes of treasures, including my ever-growing supply of puppets, storybooks, and ample paper and crayons to keep children busy for long periods of time.

By default, I was put in charge of the children's Sunday school and the after-school activity time. One of our favourite pastimes was walking in the bush to spy out a nest of eggs, to follow the tracks of the kangaroo or to listen to the special sound of a small bird perched somewhere up in the tall trees.

'Do you *really* come from New York City?' would be a usual question.

'Are there birds in New York?' was another question.

'Oh, yes. But most of them walk on the ground, like the pigeons. The swallows fly around the tops of the buildings.'

'They must have headaches all the time from running into the buildings. They are so high up!' was the conclusive remark.

As we sat on the bank of the Marri River, I would hear the dreams of what the outside world would be like for them. The dreams were always wonderful, a place where there was fun, the chance to see movie stars, and no more troubles. For these children, who had never been out of the Great Southern except maybe to Perth a few times, like the children who grew up in the high-rise tenement buildings of New York but had never seen red soil, the rest of the world seemed only a dream.

One of the pressing issues for us, now that we were home, was money. Ron's view of 'waiting for the Lord' to provide might have been sufficient when he was on his own, but now our needs were more extensive.

'The community wants you to be the teacher for them,' announced Ron returning from the community social worker's office. A two-year grant had been given to Marribank for an education officer to liaise between the school and the community, to tutor the adults in tertiary skills and to develop community-based learning programs. It was to be full-time. Ron advised me to take the position—after all, his main talent was 'talking, and there's not many jobs in that'. Besides, maybe we could save toward a trip to the United States to see my family.

A small community cottage was set aside for an adult tutoring centre. After rummaging through second-hand shops and putting out a call to the local church families, I installed bookshelves, arranged a few desks, hung curtains on the windows and nailed up a blackboard. On cold winter days, Ron stoked up the fireplace so we could read and study in comfort, and in the warmer weather we sat under the trees.

Every day the children were bussed into town to attend the local primary and high schools. Part of my job was to liaise with the teachers as a support to the Aboriginal students from Marribank. I found that many of them did not have any expectations for the Aboriginal students, having already stereotyped them as academic failures. It was enough just to have their physical presence in the classroom, without presuming any academic success. My years of teaching in high school, especially with those 'difficult to handle' students, had instilled in me the 'strange' idea that everyone deserves a chance, and if the right button is pushed then everyone, even those who've had a difficult run, can succeed.

This was the challenge when I approached the small groups of teen-agers standing huddled together near Chicken Treat, negotiating over who would buy the chips. Or when a young Aboriginal boy or girl would look into my face and ask, 'Why should we bother about school? My dad never finished high school and he gets the dole.' What incentive could I give to these young people when they knew that someone—the government, the community, or a relative—would look after them?

❂ ❂ ❂

Coral joined the family. Soon after we had unpacked and I had begun to make sense of our house, she left the Minniecon's, where she had lived for over three years, and moved in with us. With great anticipation, one of the small front rooms facing the path to our house was transformed into her bedroom. I had a sense of expectation of being the 'mother' to a teenage girl, of helping her to achieve where others her age might not have, for us to have some sort of cohesion as a family. How little I knew!

Coral would be at home for a few days and then she would disappear. Not disappear like 'running away' but just not show up at the house. A message would come later that she was at Aunt Minnie's house or off in the bush with the other teenagers. Most of the time I never knew if she got off the school bus or not until much later toward the evening.

Most of us learn to parent from the way we were parented. My ideas of family structure and responsibilities, academic achievement, and adolescent social relationships were formed within my own family of origin. On the other hand, even though Ron's dreams for Coral were generous, the pathway to achieving them seemed to elude him. He had no experience negotiating with high school teachers, finding his way through the homework dilemma, or providing much-needed discipline.

As soon as we had returned from our trek around the country, Ron started to plan all sorts of trips to Perth, Albany, or small country towns in between. In addition to starting a full-time job, every weekend I was packing and unpacking the car, on our way to spread the 'good news', visit some old people before they passed on, or cheer up the inmates of the regional prisons. Since we no longer were attached to the UAM, and because Marribank was supported by the Baptist mission committee, Ron was licensed as a Baptist pastor, with the expectation that we would be available to speak in their respective churches. In the midst of all this activity, there was hardly any family time together. What I had longed for so desperately after our first year of travel, was to be a 'normal' couple with a 'normal' family.

'I want you to come with me, Diana,' said Ron, when I offered to stay at home with Coral on the weekends. 'We're together in this. I don't want to do it without you. I've had a lot of years travelling on my own already.' He didn't seem to have an answer for what Coral should do while we were away. He just expected the extended community would always be there to take up the slack.

I found myself caught in the middle, with expectations of somehow filling a mother's role as well as being at my husband's side in the work of pastoral ministry, caring for his needs and finding my own place of significance. I seemed to be getting no help from him. 'Don't leave me to figure this one out alone!' I exclaimed to Ron in the heat of one of our discussions about the situation. 'You're the common denominator here. I need to know what I should do or even think. The school says Coral needs help with her homework and some of her friends have been luring her away from school during lunchtime. You'll have to talk to her.'

Ron would nod his head in agreement, and he would start his speech to Coral with good intentions, but would usually end up preaching her a sermon. I could almost pinpoint the moment she switched off, smiled at him sweetly and then went on her own way. Sort of the way Ron himself did.

On numerous occasions Ron had told me that Coral always wanted to be a police officer. A role model, that's what I want her to be, Ron would say. A role model for her people. Then he would look at me as if I could wave a magic wand or at least teach her a few things that would make it happen. I felt that he was placing a weight of responsibility on my shoulders, that the future of this young girl was somehow in my hands. Every time there was tension between Coral and me I felt a tremendous guilt.

I tried the motherly approach, sitting on the edge of the bed, asking how she was getting along. But I would receive only a monosyllabic answer. One weekend I had convinced Ron to go on a trip by himself so I could stay with Coral. 'You want to learn how to bake lasagne, Coral?' I got all the ingredients, sorted the bowls and the baking pan, and we set to the task. We slapped the noodles around a bit and mixed up a luscious sauce.

'What's this stuff?' Coral pointed to the ricotta. I gave her a quick lesson in Italian food and we waited while the oven put in the final bid. Later we dined together on a perfectly turned-out lasagne and tossed salad.

I decided to ask her a question that had been sitting on my tongue for a long time. 'Coral, how did you and Mum—Marj—feel about Ron going away so much and leaving you two here? I don't want to pry, but I need some help with how I should feel.' It was the wrong question to ask. The mood changed immediately.

'I don't wanna talk about it. I didn't ask to be brought up in a pastor's house anyway,' was the sullen reply.

I cleaned the kitchen by myself that night, while Coral stayed in her room.

While I was trying hard to understand Aboriginal family values, the complexities of mixed clans, the unique dilemmas of children raised in two opposite life styles or away from their blood relatives and tribes, I didn't always respond correctly. So far, I had been able to superficially put on some of the Aboriginal ways of life, but they hadn't soaked into my skin yet, into the core of my being. It's like learning a language. At first we have to translate it in our heads before it can come out of our mouths. We know it has become a part of us when the word bypasses the brain and comes from the heart and straight out of the mouth. I hadn't reached that point yet.

For Christmas, after our first full year back at Marribank, Coral wanted to fly home to Halls Creek. I stood there waving as she walked toward the plane. I wondered if I would ever be able to enter her life. It was a strange triangular relationship in our home with Ron as the pivotal point. The harder I pushed for him to step into the middle and guide us as a family, the more he retreated, leaving me to stumble in the dark. When I didn't understand, I asked her forgiveness. When I pushed too hard, I tried to step back. When I did step back, others tried to coax me forward. From time to time there were a few momentary flickers of hope between us. When we went shopping or I was able to show her a new way to solve a maths problem, I was the best 'mum' ever. But then I realised that she called everyone 'mum'.

'I want to go back home, Dad,' Coral announced a few months after she had returned from the north. Her father was getting sick and she wanted to get to know him more before anything happened to him.

'There's nothing there for you,' said Ron, repeating her own father's fear of her ending up in some old tribal man's tent. But her mind was set.

We watched her go. The sting of failure stabbed at my conscience periodically over the following years. I had prided myself that I knew teenagers and what they needed. I had gone through a childhood battling a sense of rejection and confusion of identity. Shouldn't I have been able to provide a safe place for her? The thought haunted me, and Ron hinted a number of times that he had expected me to have the answers, the ability to transform a life that he had left a few years before.

Coral never permanently lived with us again, except that every two or three years, she would walk back into our lives with a distress call. For a few short weeks the three of us would connect and then she was off again, weaving her own story. But she still called us 'mum' and 'dad'.

The month that Coral left, I received a letter from my mother.

I wanted to tell you this, Diana. Pat is losing custody of her children. I can't help her anymore. God knows that I have tried, but it's for the sake of the children. She may do something terrible. But she won't talk to me now, because she thinks I'm behind it.

My sister, Pat, had been diagnosed as being manic-depressive. The psychiatrist had put her through two bouts of electric shock treatments with no visible improvement. She had become unpredictable in her behaviour, one time gathering her young children still in their pyjamas into the car and driving with them late into the night to another city, wanting to leave them in a hospital. Finally, their father filed for custody. My mother did not want to stand in the way, no matter how much she was grieving for her daughter.

The letter seemed to burn in my hands. It was so close to the bone, touching the pain of what I had seen and felt in families all around me in the Aboriginal communities. Now my own family was again in pain. My mother, who had helped to look after the children since they were babies, from the day Pat walked out on her husband, was saddened by the turn of events. The children were bewildered and confused. Pat was hurting and blaming everyone else for it, her psychiatrist, our mother, her children's father, social welfare, our dad, and even me. But the truth was, she couldn't handle the children. Separation didn't affect just Aboriginal families, but it was just as devastating, no matter what culture it touched.

I rang Pat from Marribank. She yelled at me, listing the crimes of the family, which she believed had led to her situation. I just listened, kept saying that I loved her and I knew that somehow things would work out. Eventually she stopped. There was weeping on the other end of the line. Both of us were crying together when we said goodbye.

The word 'separation' rings throughout Australia's history. From the very beginning, this was the land to which those who were separated came. Convicted felons separated from their families and children separated from their relatives and sent as orphans. Women who came were separated from their children, never to see them again. The sentences of justice were handed down as 'Transportation: seven years', but in reality they were forbidden ever to go back to their homeland. When a people has been separated from its roots, I wonder if it is then easier for them to separate others from their roots.

In the wake of my family grief, a message came from Laverton. On the day of our anniversary, 15 December, there had been a head-on collision on the road between Mount Margaret Mission and Laverton, which are seventeen kilometres apart. One car had tried to pass another, and as it swerved to overtake on the right-hand side, out of the clouds of white dust billowing up from the gravel track suddenly appeared a car coming from the opposite direction. It had been too late to stop and the crash was horrific. Eleven of thirteen Aboriginal occupants were killed instantly. A man and a baby survived. Most were friends who had been to our wedding.

The grieving in Laverton was to continue for years. Another devastating sadness for the people who lived on the edges of Skull Creek.

❂ ❂ ❂

The knocking seemed far away as I stirred in our bed. The night was bitterly cold. Ron and I both wore fleecy track suits and snuggled under a pile of blankets to keep warm during the winter nights at Marribank. I nudged Ron to wake him. 'Did you hear that, Ron?' I asked, in his direction. He just mumbled and turned over.

When I opened the door, Jenny was there with her little girl in her arms. At first I thought the child was sick and they needed a ride to the hospital in town. 'Ya gotta come pray,' her voice quivered. 'Them charnacks are walkin' around and there's cryin' under my window.'

I brought her into the house, wrapped a blanket around her shoulders and made her a cup of tea. We sat in the kitchen waiting while Ron went to her house to pray through it. Most of the Noongar people respected prayer, especially when it came to frightful spirits. They also respected Ron, who possessed the wisdom of the elders, complete with a white beard, was a 'real' Christian and was more willing than others to face the spirit world. By virtue of his standing in the community, his strong faith, his inheritance as a Noongar warrior and his familiarity with Australia, he had the right to confront the spirits of the land, the fights between spear-throwing wati (initiated men) and the whispers from the departed spirits occupying the sacred sites that dotted the country.

'I always hear that cryin',' explained Jenny, pulling the blanket around her. 'That's where someone died, long time ago. Never got a proper burial, that one. Must be her spirit, cryin' for her children.'

Even though I had not seen any charnacks, those little black, hairy spirit men, I had felt their presence. I also knew that Ron, who had no fear of such things, nevertheless recognised their reality among his people. Old Grandfather Joe had taught Ron to stand up to those meddlesome spirits. 'I tell you, son,' he'd explained. 'Go after them, chase them. Your Auntie Josie, when she was small, one little charnack bin followin' us. Down that old track to the Stirling Ranges. Me and your Gran, we was takin' the kids, followin' the sheep down to Albany. We heard little Josie yell. I knew right away they got her. I grabbed the fire stick and chased after it, wavin' that stick around. That little charnack, he left her stuck in the vines.'

Noongars knew that spirits lived in the bush and the coming darkness of the night brought fear. If children were prone to wander away from the camp fire or the makeshift camps in the bush, and later from the proper community houses, the oldies would whisper the words 'Charnack might get you', and back they would come, huddled together, exchanging knowing looks.

When young fellas went hunting for kangaroo in the bush, sometimes the shots, no matter how many there were, wouldn't bring it down. Then they would know. 'It must be a spirit, time to get home, quick as we can.' The Aboriginal spirit world had the power to harm as well as the power to heal.

The calls of the birds would warn of danger, of someone coming, of a death in the family. The trees, the animals, the changes of the sky all spoke a special language to the Aboriginal soul. Spirituality was all encompassing, not a separate religious act as so many missionaries had presented it. It was an all-pervasive way of life, which gave support and guidance, warnings of danger and sickness.

When Ron came back from Jenny's place, she seemed to breathe easier. We walked home with her and prayed again before we left. The night was clear and the sky, loaded with stars, was like a shimmering evening dress, its silver threads twinkling. The horizon was not visible, but was guarded by the tall shadows of gum trees, which swayed from side to side in time with the night winds. The hoot of the night owl would break into the wind's rhythm, accented with the calls of the smaller night birds. This was the Noongar bush, mixed with beauty and fear.

Death seemed to hover around the Aboriginal community, waiting to snatch someone away. Grandmothers knew that deaths came in 'threes' in a community and they would stoically wait for news of the next one. Children grew up knowing death intimately. It was never far from them.

Many nights we were awakened by a car driving around the loop in front of our house, a toot of its horn and a shout from the driver's window. 'You there, brother Ron?' That signal usually meant some sort of trouble, either with the spirits or the drink, or a death.

Funerals were the rule, rather than the exception. There was no other situation in the life of the Aboriginal community that could bring so many together in one place at one time. The whole clan was acknowledged, not just the one who had died. In a sense it was a corroboree of grief, a gathering to reaffirm one's identity, to reconnect with those who had been taken away, or who had drifted to another tribal country.

At funerals, young men would come from gaol, handcuffed to the police officer. Police vans would be sandwiched between the long line of cars moving slowly through the cemetery entrance.

Funerals had always been a major part of Ron's pastoral ministry throughout the south-west. If anyone could be described as an 'expert' in conducting funeral services, he would be it. He had even buried at least three men who had claimed to be his father. By virtue of being Ron's wife, I was now attending funerals, arranging flowers, writing eulogies, providing the quiet organ music, joining Ron in singing the favourite hymns, 'In the Sweet Bye and Bye', and 'God Be with You'. But I faced each funeral with a sense of fear and dread, remembering my first rather shocking experience of being in the presence of death.

I was eleven when it happened. At that age, I had never thought about death. Like most children, I thought life just went on forever. That is, until my best friend from primary school, a doctor's daughter, died of acute pneumonia two days before school was to start. When I entered the funeral parlour, the smell shocked me first, then the darkness and then the quiet. I thought I had entered another world. She was so still, and so pretty, dressed in a yellow chiffon dress edged in lace, and with a ribbon in her pale yellow hair. She must be asleep, I said to my mother. Then I saw her parents, sitting in the corner. Her mother wore sunglasses, I guess to hide her eyes, puffed from so much crying. For years afterward, as long as I lived in my home town, my friend's mother wore sunglasses.

The night after the funeral, in my attic bedroom, I had a dream, or it might have been a ghost. I awoke with a start, half sat up in bed and saw a figure of light standing across the room. It wasn't that it looked sinister or monstrous. It was just that it shocked me so much that I bolted from the bed, raced down the narrow staircase and collapsed in a heap on the bathroom floor. I never went to any more funerals after that. Until Australia when I went to many, many funerals, Aboriginal funerals.

'Diana,' called Ron from the back door. 'We have to go to Perth and pick up a body. The family want him buried in his home country, Gnowangerup. They can't even afford a funeral and certainly not cartin' the body there. They rang to ask me to take it down there. It's no worries, I've done it plenty of times.' I could only stare at him in disbelief. My mouth wouldn't open.

Ron wanted me to come, said it would be fine. 'Only one thing. There's no coffin this time. But they'll put the body in a heavy bag and lay it on a stainless steel tray in the back of our panel van. I'll take a blanket to cover it up, so there won't be any smell.'

When the body was in the back, I couldn't bring myself to turn around. We drove through the streets of Perth, out onto the highway going south. Ron announced calmly that he was thirsty and promptly pulled into the deli.

'Why didn't you think of this before?' I asked nervously. 'I'm not staying in here with this . . . this . . . body.' In the end I sat glued to my seat, eyes staring straight ahead, not daring to turn around, while Ron went into the shop. Had I become fearful of spirits, like the Noongars were at these moments? No blackfella I knew would do this, and certainly no Aboriginal woman would ride or sit in the same car with a dead body. Ron teased me. Said I was turning into a blackfella. But everyone knew that Ron was different. He would do these things that no one else would. They must have thought that his wife would be the same. After all, she was white.

On our way to Gnowangerup, the blue light of a police car came up behind us. Since we had no air-conditioning Ron had been trying to get to the undertakers as quickly as he could. The police officer sauntered toward the driver's side, requested Ron's licence, which he always forgot to carry, and asked Ron how fast he thought he was going, with a slightly cheeky grin on his face. He leaned over just enough to catch a glimpse of a white woman sitting in the passenger seat.

Ron just smiled at him. 'Well, officer, you see, I'm a pastor, and this is my wife, and, uh, well, you see, we have a body in the back of the van. One of my relatives. We're taking him to the undertakers, Coventry's, to be buried in Gnowangerup. I often help our people out this way. They want to go back to their home to be . . .' Before Ron could finish, the officer was peering in the back window, recognised a body bag and, obviously flustered, told us we better get on our way. He would radio ahead to tell his mates what we were carrying. We took off down the road, chuckling to ourselves.

❂ ❂ ❂

William Farmer was a big man, muscular, well-built, a Noongar respected by all the tribal clans throughout the south-west and in the goldfields territory. In his early days he had been a street fighter, making room for himself in his own world through his fists. Later, he was given links to tribal power through his relationship to desert warriors. Whoever he would hit, would die. Not so much by the power of his fists this time, but through the supernatural knowledge of the bush and its secrets.

As he grew older and his health began to fail, he often grappled with this power he had, no longer wanting to bring pain to others, wanting to help them instead. Often he would seek out Ron, asking for help, for prayer, for understanding of how to cope with the power his own tribe offered him and the power of compassion and mercy that was at the heart of the gospel, the words of Jesus.

Late one night there was a frantic sound at our front door. As I tried to make out who the shadows were I heard, 'Ya gotta come, it's him, it's Uncle Willie, he might not make it. They gonna fly him out.'

I took hold of a woman's hand and drew her inside. The hushed voice and anxious looks told the story. It was after midnight when we arrived at the entrance to the Katanning Hospital, which was always locked up after 9 pm. When Ron touched the door it swung open and we rushed through toward the ward, following our night caller. Outside the room where Willie lay the corridor was lined with extended family, some standing, some leaning against the wall or seated on the floor. Children were lying asleep on their mother's laps.

The damage to Willie's heart had been extensive. There were not the facilities at the little country town's hospital to treat him so the flying doctor had been alerted and was on his way.

When Willie saw Ron, the tears ran down his face and he held his hands out. His slurred speech could barely escape from his throat, but his frightened eyes caused Ron to bend his ear to Willie's lips. Head to head, Willie whispered halting words: 'I don't want this power any more, this one here, in my hands. This anger ... gotta go ... only help my people now ... pray for me ... brother ... pray for me.' He held out his hands to Ron, motioning with his eyes and his bottom lip for Ron to hold them, to pray for them.

Willie's immediate family was in the room, standing around his bed, sitting on the floor. There were maybe twenty people in a room meant for five or six. The room was full, but there was a respectful silence like one might observe in the presence of the divine.

When Ron and I had arrived, the relatives had made a pathway for both of us to come near the bed, to mourn, to pray, to speak words of comfort and courage. As I glanced around at the grieving faces, the wrinkled brows, the eyes that bore the pain of generations, I could scarcely think how I could comfort them. One by one they offered their hand for me to hold, the women drawing physically near as if to make it easier to bear the intrusive pain of impending death.

'Look at him ... his face,' someone whispered. Willie's face had begun to relax. His voice had momentarily gained strength and he spoke to his wife. 'It's okay now ... I'm gonna be okay.' He took her hand and then turned to Ron. 'Thanks, bro. I'm at peace ... I'm free.'

Outside the door, shuffling noises and the sound of squeaky wheels announced the arrival of the orderlies to take Willie to the airstrip for the flight to Perth.

As he was wheeled away, we talked together in hushed tones with those left behind. No one wanted to leave. They were still standing in small groups in the car park, comforting each other. 'We can't lose him ... we don't have many men like him anymore.'

'He still has kids that need a father.'

'God will answer our prayers.'

'Anyone goin' to Perth tomorrow? Can I get a lift?'

'He's a good man.'

We had just started our car to drive the thirty kilometres toward home when the message came. William had died on the stretcher as he was being put into the plane. He never took that flight to Perth.

Ten days later, the police in Tambellup, a thirty-minute drive from Katanning, lined the short main street in front of the town hall. Over a thousand Aboriginal men, dressed in black trousers, white shirts and ties, and women in black dresses, or black skirts and white blouses were standing along the footpaths. Even small children were dressed in the proper mourning clothes. All the pension money for the fortnight had been used to outfit each family and, in some cases, to drive over a thousand kilometres to pay their respects. It was a tribal obligation that has maintained the solidarity of the Aboriginal community. At least they would be together in times of death, if they couldn't always be together in life.

The small town was bursting with carloads from all over the state, driving slowly around the streets, sharing cups of tea in Noongar houses, congregated in the town's only park, buying cool drinks at the deli or filling petrol tanks at the roadhouse. There weren't many whitefellas in sight.

Wailing came spontaneously, in cycles of hushed moments followed by tears and waves of emotion. With each new visitor or family member just arriving, the entire process would begin again.

Most of the time, I had no tears, but instead felt subdued by the enormity of the burden of pain that the community carried. Death was not just experienced by the immediate family, but it affected an entire population of people. The immediate death was always linked to someone related who had died some time ago. It was ancestral, down through the generations. That was why, no matter how close or far away a person was related, an Aboriginal was obligated by his kinship system to be present, not just to honour the dead or comfort the family, but to reconnect as a people. In death, there was the paradox of survival.

Early in the day, Ron and I had checked last minute details with the family. I had distributed the booklet of Willie's life to the family, the pallbearers were named and the last wishes of his wife were heard. We walked into the town hall along with the undertaker and his helper, who wheeled the chrome trolley holding the coffin. Everyone else waited outside. Not a sound could be heard.

When everything was in place, Ron signalled for me to begin playing the small portable organ which had been brought in for the occasion. My hands shook as I began the familiar tunes. As soon as the first people came through the double doors, the low wail began to roll through the room like a tidal wave in slow motion. As the people continued to pour in, the louder and more undulating came the waves of grief. I was caught up in the waves and began to cry, not just tears for this man whom I really didn't know all that well, but for the entire Aboriginal community.

Ron stood in front like an anchor, completely familiar with the entire scene before me. Once in a while someone would stagger up to the front, touch the coffin, cry loudly for his brother, his cousin, his uncle, whatever relation to Willie he happened to be. Some had been drinking grog that morning to ease the ache of what they had to face that afternoon. The hall was jam-packed, men standing along the back walls and children crowded onto the floor. A young man, head down, walked through the crowd, his right wrist manacled to that of a prison warden. They both stood quietly while the entire hall waited.

The front row was still vacant. Then slowly, one by one, the procession of immediate family came down the aisle. Willie's wife was supported by friends, the children walked together. The cries got louder, the wailing reached the ceiling, permeating the walls, pushing itself out into the street, where those who couldn't get into the building joined in. No one rushed this process of grieving, no one hissed for quiet, no one tapped the microphone. The undertaker and his mate stood patiently, accustomed to the Aboriginal way, their diary already marked out for the rest of the day. The room groaned with grief.

Then just as gradually, it stopped. Ron stood at the microphone and began to speak. He knew all the family, he told of their history, William's mother and father, cousins and brothers. Ron knew the journey to take, the Dreaming journey of this man, telling and retelling the important parts of his life, the times he gave his last dollar to a friend, or told Noongar yarns around the fire. All these events, these stories, made a place for him in their memory. 'The peace of God passes all understanding, more than we could ever muster ourselves,' Ron spoke. 'It is a supernatural power that we know. It's our heritage and it comes from God. He can comfort us, even when no one else will.'

The cars lined the cemetery road, weaving toward the grave site. Another few hundred people waited by the grave. The sun's rays warmed our backs while several specially chosen people gave eulogies, sang a song, said a prayer and then quietly dropped flowers into the grave. More hugs, more tears, more handshakes, until the last remaining members of the family filed out of the cemetery to their waiting vehicles. Some of them helped fill in the grave, crying their final tears together.

The closing act of the funeral ritual was the gathering immediately afterward, with cups of tea, cakes and bickies. Usually held at the Aboriginal function hall, tables were pushed together and laden with plates full of food. The children who arrived first were making off with handfuls of goodies while the adults queued for a cup of tea. Conversation spilled out the door, into the car park and beyond. The achievements of the deceased were recounted with pride and children who had grown taller in the past year were admired and gloated over. Family and community life regained its spark.

Would I ever get used to this, I wondered as we drove home. A whole day for the funeral, two weeks in preparation. Everything else in our life had come to a standstill in the midst of the grief. Attending funerals and its accompanying sorrow was not what I would choose to do. I had never even attended any of the funerals for my own family in America.

Ron and I walked hand in hand through the trees, disappearing into the bush behind our house. Our dogs were leaping in the air, catching the sticks we threw some metres ahead. We sought the healing of the silence guarded by the gum trees. Silence is necessary at times like these. Ron needed the medicine that time in the bush could bring to his soul. This man, who felt comfortable in any environment, who had buried scores of his own people, who had travelled throughout Australia and would talk to anyone, no matter what colour, social status or background, whether a former ambassador to England or a drunk camped under the Sydney Harbour Bridge, needed the bush to replenish his spirit with his Creator. I understood. I was beginning to need the bush too.

Today I had learned that I was part of a whole. Aboriginal communal life was sanding off the square corners of my world view. I could no longer live for myself, not even just for Ron, but for a community. This funeral, and many others to come, had taught me that the group comes first. That was a hard lesson for this whitefella to learn.

'You're doin' okay, sweetie.' Ron put his arm around me while we walked. 'There are not many who would stick with me the way you do. In fact, I don't know of anyone. Life with me is pretty tough at times, I know, but I want you to know how much I love you.'

I buried my head into his burly chest and wept. Yes, it was certainly true that life with this man involved many heartaches. He didn't think that white people had any problems, certainly not as many as his people faced every day. Consequently, my struggles were usually faced alone.

But sprinkled in the middle of the struggles, he was also the one to whom I could turn, be enveloped by his love and find momentary peace.

At this moment in the bush, there were no white people or Aboriginal people. There were no 'racial' tensions or anyone holding out their hand to us in need, no political issues screaming into our ears, no rejection from those who were still 'protecting' the blackfella. There were only two people, a man and a woman, a husband and a wife, comforting one another.

It's hard to lose your cultural underpinning, even when you voluntarily give them up. Ron lived for everyone else, and he required me to as well. Even his own family—sister, cousins, uncle, and aunties—took second place to the world 'out there'. There was no planning for the next day; instead, we responded to the crises of the moment, of which there were many. Ron had expectations that we would be able to meet everyone's needs, which, in turn, meant that we should not have any for ourselves.

When Ron climbed the 'hills' of his life, he dreamt of how much ground he could cover, touching as many people and relishing as many experiences as possible. In some ways I looked at life the same way, except that I dreamt of how deep I could excavate each of those experiences. The clash of the horizontal with the vertical, in some ways, was cultural as well as personal.

'Look at that,' laughed Ron, pointing to our dogs, who were sitting together further down the path, one black, one white, heads slightly tilted, looking at us eagerly and waiting for our next move. We collapsed with laughter.

'Well, isn't that a picture of us?' We hugged each other in the middle of the pathway, overshadowed by the towering trees, branches creaking, frogs croaking in the distance, kookaburras adding their chuckle.

'It's so good to laugh,' said Ron with a slightly serious tone. He faced me squarely and took my hands. 'It's so good to laugh, Diana. That's why I like being with you, because we can laugh at our mistakes as well as love each other. If we couldn't laugh at something, we would drown in our own tears.' With a concert background of sounds from the bush, our steps were converging closer together. While we often walked along the cracks in the earth, at times they gave way to the joy of heaven. At that moment, deep in the forest of the old Carrolup settlement, we saw a glimpse of the horizon.

CHAPTER 10

Door of Hope

The weatherboard kitchen at Marribank had come alive with artists. There were at least six women bending over the six-metre long work table, with fabric stretched from one end to the other and pots of paint lining the edges. In one corner an electric skillet was slowly heating the wax with several metal styluses perched on the side, each waiting to become the implement of design in one of the young women's hands. The length of silk was to be designed with an intricate pattern of swirls and shapes that would bring to life a Noongar legend or a reminder of the landscape of the south-west.

Gabrielle and her daughter Tina, along with Audrey and Cora, were the artists. The cooperation among them seemed to take place without any planning or direction. Gabrielle would nod her head and take her place along the side of the table, then the others joined her to begin the design. Tina was the creative one. The metal stylus loaded with wax would glide easily across the silk, steered by her expert hand. The hot wax, melted to a milky consistency, would soak into the white silk fabric and almost lose its way, only to be retrieved again by the designer.

'Hit's just there, in 'er 'eart,' explained Gabrielle, using h's at the beginning of words that had no h's and dropping them from other words which did have h's, part of the Noongar's modern dialect.

Gabrielle Farmer Hansen was the matriarch of Marribank. She and her husband, Ernie, had the most children, six in all, five daughters and a son, and they occupied the house on the corner lane where they could see all the comings and goings in the community. As a young girl, Gabrielle had been determined to make something of herself, living in a hostel in Perth, almost finishing high school. 'Then Ernie came and stole me away . . . and we had lots of kids.'

One day she grabbed me by the arm. 'Now that you're the education person around here, how about you help me. I want to graduate from high school so I can get one of those papers, then maybe go to college.'

We became good mates 'in school' together. She told me the Noongar yarns and I tutored her in high school subjects for the leaving certificate. We'd sit down together, head to head, mainly working out the grammar and ideas for her writing projects. Then we'd have a warm by the fire and she'd tell me about the relatives, how she knew Ron, the old Noongar ways and some of her dreams.

'I don't wanna just sit down and do nothing. We gotta show those fellas that we can run things around here.' When her girls were reluctant to get on the school bus Gabrielle was known to take the kitchen broom after them, until they had no choice but to jump on at the last minute.

Gabrielle, along with the Baptist-appointed superintendent, Courtney Nunn and his wife, Pat, the social worker, plus the residents of the small community in the bush had formed Marribank Aboriginal Corporation in 1984. During that decade the term 'self-determination' was the favourite word among Aboriginal communities. Government-funded bodies were sponsoring work projects, small business packages and the development of arts and crafts.

The people of Marribank had a dream, a dream to change the reputation of that piece of property from being the dumping ground for unwanted Noongars living on the outskirts of town to a door of hope for the future. Even the incorporation documents embodied the dreams for a community-based education centre, a place for revival of the Noongar language, a governing body of Aboriginal representatives, a museum of Aboriginal history of the south-west, and an artists' colony. Tall dreams for a small group living in the bush.

Pat Nunn had come to Australia from South Africa. She also had gone to a mission school and knew what it was to battle discrimination. She and her husband had run a boys' home in Perth for some time before being asked to manage the Marribank property on behalf of the Baptist churches. They were quite a team: Courtney's happy whistling, which invariably revealed his whereabouts as he made repairs on the property and guided the sheep-shearing activities and Pat's uncanny penchant for finding funds for much-needed projects and skill development so the people could fulfill their dream of becoming the decision makers and shapers of their own destinies.

Once Gabrielle had started her lessons, many others wanted to study. One by one the mothers, grandmothers and even a few men came into the makeshift 'school'. 'We want to learn. Show our kids how to do it. We don't want them to be at the bottom of the class.' Always their children. The most important reason for doing anything was for the children.

Ron and I opened a learning centre in Katanning to give support to the Noongars in town who wanted to get their leaving certificate. Ron dubbed it the Nuni Centre, from the Greek word 'nuni', meaning 'now, right now'. He even created an acronym: Noongars United, Noongars Initiative. At the centre, we both presented cultural seminars, while I taught the academic lessons and Ron gave workshops in radio communication.

Ron's love for the radio and his lifelong quest to communicate through this media began in the early 1960s thanks to Keith Morgan. During World War II, Keith had operated a radio on a destroyer. Several years later he completed Bible college and married Margaret Schenk, the daughter of the pioneer missionary who had started Mount Margaret Mission, outside of Laverton. From that setting, Keith initiated a radio program called Mission Church Hour, which was broadcast throughout the outback areas, featuring Aboriginal voices, gospel songs and Bible stories.

It was during the late nights in 1955, just after Ron's grandfather had been murdered, that Ron would lie in his swag gazing up at the vast array of constellations, and listen to this man's voice, coming across the air waves scratchy and scrambled through an old valve radio. He never wanted to miss it: the Aboriginal singing, the stories told with such a warm but authoritative voice. He didn't know then that one day he would work alongside this man, or that Keith would be so instrumental in his life.

'Ron, if you want to do a good job at this, you have to put some effort in. Don't just think you can come in here and talk off the top of your head. I won't accept it. You can do better next time.' Keith had had no qualms about 'growling' at his protégé or challenging his limits. Keith always had a special place in Ron's heart over the years. Now Ron wanted to pass on this knowledge and love of communication to other Noongars.

At Marribank, hobby classes in pottery, painting, and textile design were started, and soon the mediocre pottery greenware gave way to experimental designs from the gentle hands of the budding Noongar artists, designs that emanated from somewhere in the past, echoing the patterns of Aboriginal life.

The streams of language, education and art were working simultaneously to unlock the creativity of the community. The numbers of artists grew. Young Noongar men and women even drove thirty kilometres each day, sometimes staying overnight, in order to learn the art of throwing clay on the wheel, designing jewellery, batik and silk screens. Swirls of colour greeted the visitor to the old kitchen, and ochre and earth colours were splashed across large pots and bowls sitting on the shelves in the pottery shed.

Hundreds of metres of brightly painted cloth emerged from the work tables. Stylised pots, created by Jenny, with distinctive patterns and earthy colours sat on everyone's shelf. Tastefully boxed silk scarves were sent to craft outlets in Perth. Orders were coming in. Thoughts of overseas marketing were voiced at community meetings. Soon government funding bodies were driving into Marribank almost every week.

The Aboriginal Development Corporation, funding from the Lotteries Commission and other private sources wanted a piece of the action. Along with the money came many forms to complete, ledgers to quit, receipts to tally. The creativity of the artists did not extend to such tasks and most community members had never handled a ledger before.

The work buildings were in desperate need of repair. They had been adequate when the projects were only hobbies, but now the thought of exporting hundreds of pots and metres of fabric from buildings built in the 1940s or earlier with wide cracks in their wooden floors, windows with no screens and doors that didn't hang on their hinges properly didn't seem to make the best business sense.

After every expedition to a gallery in Perth or to attend art workshops, the questions were raised. 'How can we manage our own business?'

'Why do we have to work in these conditions? These building haven't changed in forty years.'

As land ownership for Aboriginal communities began to surface during the decade of the 1980s, many funding bodies resisted making any capital expenditure, such as upgrading workshop areas, unless the leasehold on the land was found to belong to the community.

The lease became the topic of conversation in the classes at our learning centre, over the dinner table and around the camp fire. Night after night the community leaders would sit in our lounge room to discuss the future. How could they present their case to gain this property and begin to run this business for themselves? Most had never even seen a five-year plan, which was required by the government.

'What's this five-years mean? Sometimes I don't even know if I'll have money for food for my kids tomorrow, much less five years. Who knows where we'll be in five years!' A very logical statement from a people for whom the past and the present are the most important aspects of the evolution of time. There was no inclination to read mounds of paper about land issues, future plans or legal implications. Besides, the language tended to be convoluted and abstract, while the community people were grappling with just the day-to-day problems of living.

I sat listening to all this, trying to hear the needs from their perspective and the difficulties that threatened to strangle their creativity. Once in a while a suggestion or word of advice or caution would form itself on the tip of my tongue, ready to spill out. But I didn't want to be the one with the answers. They didn't need another white person giving their educated theories about issues they hadn't even thought of yet.

Most whitefellas are used to taking the lead, walking into the room ahead of the others, taking charge, speaking their mind first, getting their say in as quickly as possible. Indigenous people sit back, waiting patiently for the leaders to emerge from the group as the interactions take place. Relationships are established, the lines of generations are acknowledged, trust is recognised and everyone has their say. No tall poppies are wanted.

A few months earlier I had learned the hard lesson about how to step back and wait to be invited for my opinion. It was a lesson that was difficult to swallow. During our many trips to Perth, we often stayed with our good friends Denzil and Shirley. Denzil attended Bible college with Ron in 1960, became a well-respected Noongar leader, travelled the country and married Shirley, a nursing sister from Victoria. Shirley had become somewhat of a mentor to me, having walked this rocky road of cross-cultural marriage a number of years ahead. She often filled in

Ron's background for me, the history of her struggles as a white woman in an Aboriginal world, the issues facing her children as they grew up. Often, she was a lifesaver in a moment of despair.

I felt comfortable with them, able to express my opinions, give what I thought were good 'answers' to the dilemmas of Aboriginal church life, sharing what I had experienced in New York City and its cultural variety. One evening I had launched into my 'speech'. 'We've just been to this great seminar on church growth among indigenous people. Now, what I have experienced in New York ...' I kept talking. I failed to see that Denzil was growing increasingly agitated, until finally he glared at me and exploded with anger.

'Look, I'm tired of all these answers you seem to have. Who do you think you are? First you're a woman, and a foreigner on top of that, and you haven't been around long enough to know even what the questions are, much less the answers.' He continued on and on.

I was shocked into total silence, as if I had been slapped across the face. My mouth wouldn't even move. Hot, bitter tears began to ooze between my eyelashes and slide down my cheek, no matter how hard I concentrated on holding them back. I had thought Denzil was a friend. I had felt comfortable sharing my opinions. Shirley was silent, but slipped her arm gently around my shoulder.

After that momentary explosion, Denzil continued more calmly but in clipped tones. 'Look, Diana, I know this hurts, but it has to be said. You have to learn. There are a lot of people, Christians and all, who tell us what to do, have all the good ideas, but I'm sick of it. I don't want you being like that. So I have to say it. I'm sorry.'

I barely heard those last words. All I could think of was to get out of their house and into the safety of our car.

Ron spoke quietly to them both and then slipped into the driver's seat and put his hand gently on mine. I drew it away, huddling myself into a ball like an echidna rolls itself up, protecting its soft underbelly, leaving only the spikes to fight the invader.

'They are waving goodbye to us, Diana. Over there, Denzil and Shirley.'

I couldn't look up.

It was some months before I consented to go with Ron to see them, and it was even longer before I realised that Denzil had taught me one

of the best lessons I was ever to learn from an Aboriginal person. When
we walked in the door, the four of us hugged each other, no word was
spoken about the incident and life went on as normal. But I had changed.

For years afterward, I realised that this had been a turning point and it
was because of Denzil's truthful outburst. It was a cultural shift, to be able
to follow their lead, not try to make the pathway myself. It was a lesson
that I have heard the blackfellas say over and over again: 'We wish the
wadjala [whitefella] would learn to listen more, walk with us, not in front
of us. We know what our own people need, more than anyone else.'

And I realised that us whitefellas don't really learn that lesson until we
are made to see it with their eyes and made to hear it from their voice.

❂ ❂ ❂

'What we need is the land. We got nothing if we can't have this place.
Anyway, my family come from here,' was the common thread through
the conversation in the community.

Ron felt the same. His own relatives were buried somewhere on
Marribank in unmarked graves, old Auntie Mary, and Willie Kikar. Even
though he had been brought to Marribank as a child imprisoned, there
was a connection to this land and to all the people who had once been
through its gates.

A delegation appeared on our doorstep. 'We want you to be our
chairman, brother Ron, you can talk and you can help us. And we want
Diana, too, to be the secretary. Help us with these forms and dealin' with
these whitefellas.' That was how I got involved, through their invitation.

Ron didn't really want to chair the corporation. We already had
enough to do, teaching classes and caring for the spiritual needs of three
church congregations. Trying to balance these roles was difficult and did
not leave much time for anything else.

When the big government bosses from Perth met with the people in
the church hall to explain business plans and marketing techniques, I sat
at the back, drawing diagrams and circles, attempting to transform the
many words into visual images. My days in the desert listening to the
women while they told their stories and drew dirt maps of significant
moments in the journey had taught me to think and speak visually. It
was through this method that more effective communication could take

place. I started to carry a small whiteboard to every meeting, tucked underneath my arm.

'We can't win against the whitefella's words,' Ron explained to me. 'That's the reason for circles, dots and lines. We can say lots of things with those few marks. Looking for a pattern.' I started to look for patterns, to make connections. All the nights in our lounge room, drawing the plans, explaining the issues, listening to the people, the journey was like walking around the waterhole. A circular pattern, enclosing an issue within ever smaller circles, all-inclusive of relationship before actually getting to the destination.

The decision was in their hands. Did they want the community badly enough? Did they want to take on the responsibility? Would the government give them a chance? Only time would tell.

❂ ❂ ❂

Three or four times a week Ron and I travelled into Katanning and then on to Tambellup another thirty kilometres away to conduct the classes in adult literacy and then to hold church services, pray for the sick, grieve with those who had lost family members or to mediate family arguments. The faces of the Noongars of the south-west took on more and more life for me, especially George and Alma Farmer, and George's sister Emil and husband, James, better known as Bimble.

George was one of those special people, with a kind, shy, almost boyish face, although he had a tribe of kids himself. He kept us supplied with legs of kangaroo whenever he went hunting. At any Noongar gathering he always stood quietly to one side, seeing that the children did not get out of line. All he had to do was 'growl' in their direction and they would scamper back to their places. His sister Emil became my best friend, taking me under her wing to teach me the ways of the Noongar women.

She pointed out all the relationships to me: who was married to whom, whose child was screaming in the backyard, whose funeral had been held last week with a whispered 'real reason for his death'. Emil was my teacher, and she wanted me to teach her. 'Help us with our faith. We don't want to be shame anymore, sittin' back like we got nothing to say. We gotta believe we are somebody.'

We began to talk, study the Bible, discuss our faith, hear each other's stories, and pray together. Their strong faith in God helped shape their leadership in the Noongar community and bring meaning to their lives. None of the Noongars there really believed in the theory of evolution and when the children came home from school with such talk, Emil would proudly announce, 'We don't believe in such rubbish. None of us came from monkeys. If those wadjalas want to believe that, then let them. We know that God created us.'

'You ought to be a speaker in the church, Emil. You're not afraid, are you? It's time for you fellas to come forth, tell the world about yourself. Encourage others with what you've experienced.' I had come to believe that the way toward any sort of reconciliation or sharing the future of this country together would be when Aboriginal people could give and the whitefellas could receive, and each could respect the other for it. Starting with small victories, even here in Tambellup.

'Let's have an afternoon tea in our Noongar centre and invite the white ladies in town. We can sing for them, share our food and give a little talk.' Emil's idea was applauded by them all. 'And Diana can deliver the invitations. After all, she's a whitefella.'

'No, no,' I retorted, holding up my hands. I knew they had to face this fear in order to conquer it, but after bantering back and forth, I agreed to deliver half the invitations.

The Noongar centre was decked out with long tables covered in white paper plates loaded with triangular-shaped sandwiches—egg salad, tuna, sardines, cheese and salad—jellyroll cakes, cream biscuits, and at the end of the table, in a place of honour, sat a warm damper wrapped in a tea towel, surrounded by a plate of butter and two jars of jam. In the centre of the table were a few sprigs of purple wildflowers arranged in an empty vegemite jar. A number of chairs facing a small podium were arranged in a semi-circle at the other end of the hall.

The women waited nervously for the first guest to appear. I observed, making myself scarce in the kitchen so I wouldn't automatically be expected to act as greeter. The first white woman walked in, rather timidly, looking as nervous as Emil and the others were feeling. One by one, others came and the atmosphere slowly changed as each one showed their appreciation of the other. The conversation turned to school children, the Tambellup store, shopping trips to Katanning, or Perth, and how 'my grandfather always had Noongars on his farm helping with the sheep a long time ago. Maybe they were some of your people.'

Emil led the singing while I played the guitar. I followed the program that she had written out, dutifully performing the tasks they had assigned to me.

Then we enjoyed her message to the women. 'I grew up around here,' she began. 'But it wasn't always easy ... being kept out of town ... sometimes not much to eat ... but I thank my God for my family and for the wonderful life ... He has given me.' Emil described her childhood, close family who had been in gaol, and experiences of discrimination without bitterness, revenge, or anger. Some of the women from the town were struggling to hold back their tears. They applauded when she finished, and when the cups of tea were served, it was as if they had all been friends for a long time.

Some weeks later, Emil was invited to speak at the local Anglican church on Australia Day. When she finished, there was a standing ovation. No shame anymore.

George and Alma had raised their own kids plus a number of nieces and nephews who had wandered in from time to time. When they decided to get married, whitefella way, legal and all, they asked Ron to do the honours. As they stood together trying to repeat their vows, nervous and conscious of those looking on, all they could do was giggle.

Ron loved to build up these romantic moments when it was time for the nuptial kiss. 'You may now kiss the bride,' he proudly announced, waiting for them to comply. Instead, George and Alma burst into embarrassed laughter, unable to look at each other.

It was yarns like these that kept the songline of the Aboriginal family going from generation to generation. George and his sister Emil kept the Farmer family story alive. I gladly helped to serve the cups of tea, or cradle the little 'grannies', nieces and nephews on my lap, as the yarns began to spin. When George played his country and western tapes, especially of old Hank Williams, the memories would begin to flow. Stories of his father and uncles who had served in the war at Gallipoli. His father, Kenny, had been shot in the mouth during that campaign. An uncle was killed. But when the troops came marching home again, among the banners and the reception of the white soldiers, again and again the black warriors were met with silence—no music, no marching bands to greet them, no standing ovations of honour.

The telling of the yarns around the Noongar kitchen tables, as the storytellers were plied with large tin mugs of tea and chunks of warm damper, was the honour, the celebration. In quiet and remote corners of Australia, men and women wept at the memory of their brave men, who had not only lost their battle to retain their own land, but had also lost any recognition in fighting the battles alongside their conquerors. 'If only Katanning could have welcomed them back, recognised them for what they did.' George always ended the story with tears brimming in his eyes.

Every Noongar family seemed to have someone in gaol, someone on the grog or someone who had been taken from their mother at birth or soon after. George's Auntie Eva had only one son, Graham, who was taken away from her when he was only a toddler. He was too fair in colour, they said. He needed to grow up like a whitefella. 'There's a lot of stories about them days,' said George, 'but I know that Eva tried to see him.'

Apparently Eva took many trips to Perth, knocking at the door at Sister Kate's home, desperately wanting to see her son, to hold him in her arms. Each time the answer was the same.

'He's not here.'

'He's on a picnic.'

'He's on an excursion.'

One day she gave up and didn't go back anymore.

Some mothers have never recovered from those experiences and some children have never known what their mothers really felt. Intimidation, fear and apparent rejection drove a wedge between separated families that was often never overcome.

George took a sip on his cup of tea. 'Yep, it's too bad, what happened. She never really got over it. But my cousin, he made it.' He was talking about Polly Farmer, one of Australia's finest and most decorated Aussie Rules footballers, who played in Perth and then for Geelong. A ruckman, king of the handballers.

❂ ❂ ❂

In June 1986, Ron and I led the Marribank artists on a tour through the desert communities, especially to visit the Ernabella community in South Australia, where traditional desert batik had been in production for a number of years, and then on to Alice Springs and our eventual destination of Hermannsburg community, once a Lutheran mission and the home of Albert Namatjira, the most famous Aboriginal artist of all time.

The small caravan of cars bumped up and down on the corrugated road heading to Palm Valley, one hundred and twenty-five kilometres west of Alice Springs. Palm Valley was a spiritual place where Namatjira used to roam and reflect on the blues, oranges and reds of the hills of his homeland. It was this inspiration that the artists from the south-west wanted to capture.

Namatjira was born in the country of the Aranda people and became a man courted by the wealthy of Australia and presented to the Queen of England, a man whose paintings continue to symbolise the landscapes of Australia. At the Hermannsburg Mission Namatjira learned to use watercolours and when his tutor exhibited his paintings in Melbourne, his success grew. With increasing fame and money coming in, he tried to help his family and his people, first by leasing a cattle station and then by trying to build a house in Alice Springs. The laws governing Aboriginal ownership caused confusion and, in the end, Namatjira was refused the right to build. Perhaps to clear their conscience, the government granted him full citizenship rights in 1957, a full ten years before Aboriginal people across Australia were given citizenship in their own country.

Albert Namatjira was then caught between two worlds, a disturbing but common place for Aboriginal people to find themselves in. In those days, it was against the law to have certain associations between 'citizens'—whitefellas—and the 'native' population. By becoming a citizen, Namatjira had to abide by these rules of conduct and separation. In his case, it meant black against black, against his own race. But as a tribally initiated man, he had obligations to family and clan members. In 1958 he was charged with supplying alcohol to his people. On the one hand, the government expected him to act like a whitefella, but on the other, his own culture had rules to follow as well. Even though the case was appealed to the High Court, and support came from all over the country—from women's groups, churches, advancement leagues—the appeal was rejected and he was sentenced to prison.

Something happened in his spirit. Namatjira lost the will to paint; his spirit was broken. When I sat on the rocks of Palm Valley in thought and then walked through the stucco buildings of Old Hermannsburg, I could feel the echoes of this man, whose artistic spirit had been freed for only a short time. I could never see these places through the eyes of a tourist again, but with 'blackfella' eyes, in touch with the spirit of the place, the thoughts of those who had gone before.

Namatjira never painted again and within six months of his release from prison he died a broken man.

'Will this happen again to other people who try to make it? It seems that there will always be competing loyalties and responsibilities, won't there?' I asked Ron while we walked through the valley. So many times I had seen Aboriginal men and women who had just made it to the doorway of success in sports, art, teaching, or health and then, because of a setback in their family, lack of support from their community, or having to choose between two worlds, had failed to walk through the door.

'Only somebody who knows who they are and where they come from can survive and make a go of it. Only somebody who knows his people and his community,' answered Ron.

❂ ❂ ❂

Marribank Aboriginal Corporation began to push toward recognition. The Lands Trust Department in Perth was in discussions with the Baptist Union on the future of this two thousand-hectare portion of land. The arts and crafts business was growing. The University of Western Australia hosted a spectacular fashion parade of Marribank fabrics draped across slim, stunning models—evening wear, long shirts, trousers. Their designs were bursting with colour, reminders of the south-western skies, and geometric shapes of lizards, crabs, and desert animals seemed to move with the flow of the garments. Perched along the borders of the sunken garden at the university were both small delicately formed and large chunky-shaped ceramic pots with traditional patterns and modern Aboriginal responses to the earth.

Business managers and Aboriginal artists were brought in from various parts of the country and from overseas to help boost the vision of what could be done. School groups from all around the south-west were coming for an 'excursion' to this Aboriginal community, watching artists at work, having a taste of damper and hearing Aboriginal legends.

'What we need is a museum of Aboriginal culture,' mentioned Pat. The idea caught on like wildfire, especially with Ron. His interest in history, his love for the south-west and his desire to honour the achievements of the Noongars fuelled his enthusiasm, which he shared in abundance with his people.

A small grant was given to the corporation to open a museum of early Aboriginal art, photographs from Carrolup days as well as the contemporary art of the community. One of the small original stone cottages on the property would be transformed into a museum-cum-art gallery. Once the remodelling work had been done, the historical research completed and the early art documented, a grand opening was planned for the Back to Carrolup Day.

The Back To Carrolup Days were an unusual phenomenon. In a sense they were reunions, planned by the Aboriginal people who had been raised in the various mission homes around the south-west, along with the missionaries who had looked after them. When the fear of being taken away by the government was no longer a factor, there was a desire to 'come back home' again, especially to see their mates again and to reconnect with their history. During the days of removal, children were sometimes sent far away from their home country or their family's territory, and then when they left the mission where they had been raised, they scattered once again, sometimes never reconnecting back to their original homeland and losing touch with their own blood line. The Back to Carrolup Day served as a slender thread of identity for those who had not been nurtured by their own mother and father.

Besides the dismal moments of its history, Carrolup had had a brief rise to fame in the 1940s. After the war years, during which the settlement had been closed, the education department reopened it with the particular view to involving young native children in some sort of worthwhile activity. In an effort to bring some order to his class and give the boys something to do, the teacher, Mr White, had handed out some butcher's paper and crayons. That act ignited a release of talent that was to make headlines around the world. This almost accidental introduction to drawing to keep the boys occupied sparked an expression that none could have predicted.

As they bent over their small desks in the weatherboard schoolroom at Carrolup, they made broad strokes across the page, which became the haunting shadows of the Stirling Ranges, the squat outlines of the spiny blackboy trees and the trios of kangaroos huddled on the distant horizon. The bush life, reflections of the setting sun, with deep reds, and deep purple streaks across the sky, took shape inside the confines of the cold, stark schoolroom.

Their work was noticed, sent to galleries, picked up by educators and taken to England. The boys were boarded onto buses and taken to Perth to special showings, dressed up and marched into the hall to demonstrate their talent to the proper authorities, as if to prove that it was indeed these boys who did this remarkable art, not some well-taught whitefella. At the word of the teacher, the boys stood up and filed out of the hall, having delivered what was asked of them.

For a few short years, Carrolup was in the public eye. The future of these boys and the institution was on everyone's lips. And at the same time, across the great deserts in the centre of Australia, Namatjira's name was on everyone's lips as well.

As quickly as the fire had been ignited so too did it die. The government authorities in charge of Carrolup began to introduce new activities, more structure, and vocational training for the boys. Some were conscripted to Perth to work in offices, but escaped at the first opportunity, homesick, back to the bush and their families. The Department of Education decided that art should certainly not be the foundation of the future for these native bush children. No further improvements were provided for the arts program, and in 1951, Carrolup was closed and the artists scattered.

Simpson Kelly, who was related to Ron through their grandmothers, was one of those boy artists. He came to talk to us and inspect the stone building that would be the museum for some of his work and others who had been his mates. He cut a striking figure standing in our kitchen, warming himself by the fire. His white hair flowed down the back of his neck in pronounced contrast to his dark skin.

'Hey, Ngun,' he began. ('Ngun' was the Noongar word for 'brother'.) 'I've got a gift for your missus. There by the door.' Simpson grabbed a fuzzy, yellow blanket, folded neatly, and put it in my arms. 'This is to keep you warm when that Albany Doctor comes through the hills.' It was his way of welcoming me into the family.

Simpson alternately yarned and cried while he walked with us through the museum. 'There's old Parnie, and Reynald Hart. Yeah, and Revell, too. Whatever happened to him? You know, we had lots of dreams in them days. We wanted to be somethin', somebody. They promised us lots of things, art classes, jobs. But nothin' ever happened. Maybe there weren't enough of us to worry about.'

I followed behind as the two men talked and reminisced about those days long ago, made more real by the presence of the boys' own drawings. Most of them had died, some in tragic circumstances.

'You know, Sim, we saw ol' Revell when we went around Australia. It was in Melbourne . . . there he was at the drinkin' park, in the middle of all his buddies. We had a yarn . . . he asked me for two dollars, to "fix" his head.'

I remembered Revell well. A very articulate man, gaunt from the drink, all but the light of his eyes growing dim. He was once interviewed for an ABC program that focused on why Aboriginals drink so much.

'Y'know what I told those fellas, bro?' Revell had said as he recalled the program. 'I told 'em we drink to escape reality. That's why. We been branded with shame since the beginning . . . only white lady metho our comfort now.' And he had cried on Ron's shoulders.

Ron had called him the 'Namatjira of the Noongars', but one day he had gone missing. Eighteen months later a whitefella 'doing time' in Long Bay Prison confessed to killing him and hiding his body. Such was the end of a man who had been one of the most promising teenagers at Carrolup.

It was always a mystery to the authorities how the boys were able to draw so well when no one had taught them. As with Namatjira, the tools were only placed in their hands and the talent was released.

Simpson reckoned he knew where it came from. 'From our old people,' he explained. 'We watched them when we were little. My own mum. They told us stories and drew in the sand. They talked to us about the bush. Their stories were in us, their spirit talkin' to us. It was in their blood, my own mum's blood. It was in all our blood.'

It was a legacy that lay dormant for thirty-three years, to be resurrected as Marribank Aboriginal Corporation. In the intervening years Marribank had operated as a farm school, a children's home and a family centre. When the Marribank Noongars joined together in 1984 to form MAC it was founded on the dreams, the talents and the spirit of those who had gone before. In the 1950s the door of hope had closed on both Namatjira and the young Carrolup artists. Would it stay open for the artists of Marribank as the bicentennial year was approaching?

Back to Carrolup Day was a huge success. Hundreds of older Noongars who had grown up there came, along with their extended families. Missionaries who had retired in Perth or Albany made the trip to celebrate with their friends. The anthropological department and museum at the University of Western Australia was represented by Dr John Stanton, who had provided ideas, materials and guidance along the way.

Aboriginal dignitaries planted trees alongside the concrete path to the stone cottage, children competed in a sports day, complete with prizes, while tours of the contemporary art works were conducted and there was, of course, a huge feed of lamb, kangaroo, damper and cake. Visitors bought posters and greeting cards printed with selected drawings from the early child artists. It was a day of activity, of memories, and of dreams for the future.

❂ ❂ ❂

It was now the third year of our marriage, the third year of the initiation process. When I wrote to family or friends in America, I didn't know what to say. More than the usual tourist description? How would they understand the social problems, the discrimination that we faced day by day, our house, which was open to all and sundry at whatever time of day or night it happened to be? How could I tell them that I often cried and wondered what I was doing here? Or, on other days, how I felt so privileged to be in another culture, where my own opinions were challenged at their very core?

Three years of travelling all around the country from creek bed, to mission, to community, to city had given me a glimpse of Aboriginal Australia that not many other white people had had, but each new day still brought new surprises. I could never second-guess what the thoughts of my husband or his friends would be; I could only observe and wait. It has always amused me that people who are 'tourists' into Aboriginal life—they might spend a few months here or there, might be acquainted with one or two Aboriginal people, or might have heard an Aboriginal speaker somewhere giving her life testimony—often think that the experience somehow provides them with 'expert' credentials. But the tourist hasn't walked barefoot in the red dirt. He hasn't felt the prickles and thorns pierce his feet or seen his blood mingling with the earth. He hasn't embraced the pain of the people to himself. Those experiences can't happen in a few short months, and many times not even in years.

I knew that I would always have more to learn, even when one of the little girls in my Sunday school class at Marribank sat on my lap one day and told me I belonged. 'Auntie Diana, you one of us now, unna? You not going to America anymore, 'cause you belong to Uncle Ronnie.'

CHAPTER 11

A Child of Our Own

News on the Aboriginal grapevine travels fast, covers a vast distance and is mostly very accurate. Whether it's in Wongi country (the goldfields) or Noongar country (the south-west and Perth), it's the same. Just after Ron and I had been engaged, one of Ron's friends had given me a little whisper that Ron had always wanted a child of his own. 'That's all, one of his own,' said the friend as he walked away.

That little sentence had put a moment of fear in my heart, because I didn't know whether I could have a child or not. Back in the 1970s in New York City I had made a decision never to have children. I was too wild and reckless then, and, besides, to me the word 'family' meant pain, and I didn't want any more of that. I was much too involved with my career at that time and didn't want to inflict my lifestyle on an unsuspecting child, a child worthy of more than I could give.

'Are you sure you want to do this?' the resident doctor had enquired as he leaned back in his chair. He had explained all the medical procedures for tubal ligation and was now pushing a form toward me to be filled out. I had made the decision that morning and walked the few blocks to the New York University Medical Hospital to book the operation. I nodded with determination.

'Well, we can't book it for at least one month. We're required to give you one month's grace period in case you change your mind.'

184

'Oh I won't,' I had said as I signed the form and left his office with the booking for six weeks away. I was sure that this was the best way to go: no hassles with sex, no worries for the future, neat and easy for me. I wasn't yet thirty years old, and had never been pregnant. These days, most doctors wouldn't do that operation on someone like me, but in New York in the 1970s it was different.

I had checked into the hospital on the assigned day, and as I was being prepped for the operation, the doctor looked down at me and rattled off the three methods of sterilisation. Which one did I want?

'Which one is one hundred per cent?' I asked.

Cut and tie, was the answer.

'That's the one,' was my reply.

I spent four days in the hospital then, recuperating, feeling very free and liberated, I rang my mum. Our relationship hadn't always been very understanding during that time. Every time we talked I heard the slight disapproval in her voice toward whatever I happened to be doing in my life at that time. I never thought she really knew her own daughter. Partly for that reason I had grown to love the cosmopolitan nature of New York City, a city that held so many marvellous sights and sounds, a city that was able to absorb so many lifestyles, cultures, and eccentricities. It was a city where I could be myself, a city that would not judge me as often as my mother had done. In my own way, that phone call to her was to again announce my independence and declare my release from the narrow-mindedness of the American Midwest that her life symbolised to me.

I'll never forget that phone call. Instead of gloating over my female independence, I heard the details of how she had gone to her doctor because of a lump in her breast. He had booked her in for a routine biopsy to test for cancer. She submitted to that small cut, trusting that all would be fine. When she woke up some hours later, her breast was gone. The cancer had spread so much that the doctor had done a mastectomy on the spot.

I began to learn more about my mother then. My view of her frailty and weakness was transforming before my eyes. She wasn't going to let this beat her. Her attitude was superb. The nursing sisters in the hospital working with her through her recovery glowed with praise for my mother. She was faithful in her exercises to regain muscle strength. She abounded in hope and faith for the future. She joined a support group and was an encouragement to other women who had gone through the same operation. This was twenty-five years ago, when very few books were being written about the subject, and no talk show hosts mentioned breast cancer. I began to see my mother in a different light.

Her strength began to stir a need within myself. A need to find an anchor to my life, to find a truth that was unshakeable. Like the gradual opening of a scented rosebud, the power of faith began to awaken within me. At the same time, I began to appreciate my womanhood. The more I could feel the strength in my mother, the more I accepted myself as a female. Careers could come and go. The corporate world was a fickle one, holding its adherents at arm's length. My desire to be some kind of corporate 'superwoman', who could do all things, both masculine and feminine, began to fade away. Life and relationships began to seem so much more important.

It was then that I realised the impact of what I had done that day in the hospital. My mind despaired. What had I done! Had I lost my womanhood forever, before I even had a chance to taste it?

Once in a while over the next few years, like a few raindrops in a bucket, I would hear a story of a woman who had had the same operation, or who couldn't for some reason have a child, and then a miracle had happened. One by one these stories boosted my faith, made me believe in my own femaleness, gave me hope that one day I might hold a part of me, a part of my own family, in my arms.

It was this story that I finally told to Ron before we got married. I told him with tears, with apologies, with fear that he might change his mind. When I finished, my head down, my heart racing, thumping so loud I thought he was sure to hear it, he put his arms around me and thoughtfully, quietly, said, 'It's okay, Diana, somehow I already knew it. If, in God's design, He wants us to have a child, then we will.'

Almost to the very day eleven years after that first abdominal operation, I checked into King Edward Memorial Hospital in Perth to undergo a three-hour operation by microscope to 'untie' what had been done back then in 1975.

I was still coming out of the anaesthetic and a bit groggy when the face of a young female doctor appeared and looked down at me, smiling. She had been the assistant to Dr John Yovich, one of Australia's leading fertility doctors, as he had performed the operation. I was only a Medicare patient with no private insurance and no choice of doctor, but God had been good to me, giving me one of the best in the country.

'We believe it's been successful, Diana. One side was very scarred and damaged, and with the other tube, we had to open it up more to make a pathway for the egg. If all is well, you should conceive within six months. But I must tell you the overall chances are less than thirty per cent.' I couldn't believe what I was hearing. Only six months! But there was another complication too, in that, with Ron being in his later forties and diabetic, his sperm count was lower and fewer. That meant that the percentage went down to about twenty per cent. We were told we could come back for more tests or drugs if we wanted.

Our decision was made. We felt we had done all we needed to do; now it was up to the Almighty. We were both in our forties and we were leading a hectic lifestyle, always on the go. Cross-cultural problems abounded all around us and we often met children who were of two worlds and having difficulty fitting into either one.

Children of couples who are in church ministry, or of doctors, lawyers or politicians at times feel neglected and short-changed of time and emotional energy. All those issues swirled around in our minds, but we both wanted a child of our own.

Our days continued as normal, with our calendar filled with travels from town to town and once in a while an excursion to Perth to speak at a church, to do some real city shopping or to teach a seminar.

Our only getaway seemed to be the walks in the bush. The dogs enjoyed our company, chasing the birds and the sticks that we threw high in the air, dodging the black boy trees that were dotted throughout the stand of gums and karris.

'Let's go grub hunting,' Ron would suggest. Since the first day I had been given a toasted bardi grub on the outskirts of Laverton I had developed a taste for this gourmet delicacy of the Aboriginal palate. Ron would spy out the black boy trees that were going brown and dying out. He would grab a heavy branch, heave it into the tree and force the top layer off. There we usually could find a fat, white, segmented grub trying to shield itself from the sudden intrusion. As we peeled off layer after layer of the trunk of the tree, dry and brittle in our hands, more and more of the grubs would be exposed.

Ron would dig them out of their hiding places, hand them to me and I would collect them into a 'baggie'. One day we collected over forty of the little creatures during an afternoon's walk. Once at home, we stoked up the fire in the old Metters stove and one by one I rolled them around on the hot plate until they turned a lovely light brown. What a feast! Pure protein and much sought after by the desert mob. The white-fellas who have eaten them describe them somewhat differently, but to me the taste was similar to a piece of crisp-fried bacon dipped into a soft-cooked egg yolk.

We attended a Noongar writer's conference along the North Beach area of Perth, meeting for the first time such people as Archie Weller, who described contemporary Aboriginal life in books with the titles of *Going Home* and *Day of the Dog*, and Colin Johnson (before he changed his name to Mudrooroo), author of *Wildcat Falling*, which was the first novel to be published by a writer of Aboriginal descent. That was in the 1960s.

Ron introduced me to Jack Davis. Ron had first met him in 1959 in Brookton during the days when many outstanding Aboriginals were in the church, giving 'Billy Graham' style orations and singing hymns with gusto. Jack was to become a statesman, a voice for his people through poetry and stage plays. The first collection of poems that brought his talents to notice was one called *First Born*, published in 1970.

Jack had the remarkable ability to gather the images from his people's oral history and craft them into a written odyssey, so that the world might understand, without anger or bitterness, the Aboriginal heart and soul. Two of the plays depicting life in the Moore River Native Settlement, *The Dreamers* and *No Sugar* received international acclaim as the bicentennial year approached.

Ron reminisced: 'I remember something Jack said a long time ago. It never left me. I think it went down into my spirit and has been there ever since. He told us that disappointments come and then they go. Disappointments will always be with us blackfellas. But the key is we can jump higher than these disappointments.' Jack certainly jumped higher, and so have many others.

The 1980s would be known as the time when Aboriginal writers were emerging, the traditional message sticks of the tribal people, sticks carved with signs and symbols, giving way to a river of words and print. Jack

Davis's words of his poem 'First-Born' were to be echoed over the next sixteen years with words such as 'first peoples' and 'first nations', a reminder of the custodianship of this land. These words revealed another cultural world beyond what the whitefella could see and understand of the Noongars of the south-west. What made a person an Aborigine? It wasn't the colour of the skin, but the spirit within. This is what the written 'message sticks' were tapping out.

Ron's words were changing as well. There was a rumbling somewhere in his heart. We started to collect books of Aboriginal history from all over the country. Stories of massacres, of children stolen from their families. The history that I had learned from Ron's storytelling as we had travelled the country was being written down now and brought to life by writers of all variety of tribal backgrounds. As we sat around the camp fires at night, or the kitchen tables in a number of Aboriginal households, the heart of the blackfella was being released, with bursts of pain and anger.

Even Ron seemed angrier. His preaching gradually changed from comfortable topics to more strident treatises on injustice and incidents from the past. Especially in white churches. He would stalk the platform, arms swinging, voice modulating in volume from loud to louder. I don't know if anyone else noticed that his nose would flatten, his eyes would flash, and his chest would seem to swell with the pressure of images trying to force their way out.

At times I would think, where has my husband gone? He was changing before my very eyes. The more I read about the 'black history' of Australia, the pages written by the Aboriginals themselves, and listened to the rumblings of anger around the country, I, too, felt it rise within me. But I didn't know what to do with it.

❁ ❁ ❁

Ron came running back to our house after being called to the phone. 'David's dead. Might be suicide. They found him back in the trees.'

He was devastated. He wept for a long time. David had been the one to encourage us when we had met so much opposition to our marriage. Now the opposition that he had faced all his life as an Aboriginal pastor, a pioneer in leadership, struggling to extricate his life from the control of the missionaries, had exploded over him. His spirit had been crushed and now his body.

Ron flew east for the funeral. All the Aboriginal church dignitaries were there and the memorials lasted for hours. Tributes from all over Australia honoured this man, who most believed was a fallen warrior.

When Ron returned, I sensed a distance, even a wall between us. He was angry, even angry toward me. His voice was curt, his sentences clipped, and the atmosphere was morose. I felt as if death was all around me.

I went to hug him, but no longer was he gentle. Our intimacy that night was harsh and painful, as if I was being punished for what he had experienced at the hands of whitefellas all his life.

For a long time I didn't understand. He started to blame the whitefellas more. He would talk about David's life and the discrimination he had been dealt. His anger spilled over into our personal life together. When we made plans to travel, or prepare for ministry, seminars or classes, and I made a suggestion or gave an idea, he would bark out the words, 'That's what the white missionaries always said.' I knew what that meant to him and those words were like a slap in the face. There were times that I thought I was being made to 'pay' for others' attitudes in the past, and sometimes in the present.

I could sense that Ron was struggling with his identity, and, perhaps even more than that, struggling to feel comfortable with his identity. For almost forty-seven years he had battled, like most other Aboriginal people, with prejudice, with feeling unwanted as his own person, feeling unwelcome in his own land. Maybe he had tried to be what others wanted him to be. Now the volcano was beginning to erupt and the hot lava was starting to flow.

My reaction was to try harder to be accepted, to be like a blackfella. I too felt some bitterness at the past and the actions of the government, the wrongs of the reserves and mission settlements, mainly because I could see where it was still affecting our own family, our friends and even my relationship with Ron. I too would shake my head in agreement every time our friends would criticise 'those government mob'. I too would 'feel' the barrier between white and black when I went into town.

The path between two worlds is a hard one to manoeuvre. The bumps, the corrugations often throw the traveller to one side or the other. The grip of the hands on the wheel needs to be tightened in order to stay in the middle.

While Ron was continuing to grieve over David, a phone call from the United States told me of my friend Doug's death.

I hung up the community phone. I was shocked by the news and was silent as I got back into our car. Ron's reaction was totally out of character. Driving off down the road, he suddenly shouted, 'Hey, look, there's a rabbit in the road. Let me knock him down,' and he swerved the car, bumping my head against the window while I cried for my friend. When we got home I jumped out of the car, slammed the door and ran to our bedroom and locked myself in. I didn't want to see him any more, I thought to myself then. All I could hold in my head was to get out and go back to America.

I had come to Australia with Doug and Joyce, a missionary couple whom I had been close to for a number of years. Doug had not wanted to stay in Australia to be part of our wedding, but left to go back to the States, sounding a warning to me of difficulties ahead in a mixed-race marriage. He had been in the Special Forces serving in Vietnam, and had seen many of his mates killed during a rocket hit to the hospital. He had heard a voice telling him to get out and, just before the rocket hit, he had jumped out of his bed, run to the end of the hospital ward and dived under another bed. That action had spared his life. Only he and one other soldier were saved.

During those war years Doug had tried heroin a number of times before giving up later when he came back to the United States, was converted to a Christian life, married and had children. But the terrible effects of contaminated needles produced the insidious disease that had attacked his immune system, eventually causing his death.

The house was silent well into the evening. I had intermittently slept and cried. Why was I expected to grieve over all his people, many of whom I didn't know? Why was I going with him, helping him in all these funerals, when he couldn't grieve with me? Did he only have room for his own people, as well as his own anger?

There was a light tap on the bedroom door. I turned the key. He took me in his arms and, as we so often do, we cried together, wiped our tears together, relaxing the tension of two worlds trying to fit as one.

The links to my past were being cut and Ron's links to his were being renewed and released, causing us both to grieve in different ways. I was experiencing change and loss of my own cultural ties, and Ron was experiencing change and renewal of his. Sometimes our paths collided while other times we walked together. This would be the cultural heritage of our child if God so granted one.

❂ ❂ ❂

'When you gonna give us a baby?' was the whisper from some of the Noongar grandmothers. 'We all waitin'.'

Children are the most important aspect of Aboriginal life. A man or a woman is not fulfilled unless there are children from their loins. Some who can't have children are given nieces and nephews to raise so they won't be bereft of family. We were offered children from a number of families, but Ron was waiting. Each month went by with no glimmer of hope.

One year after the operation, I gave up. The whole year had been tense, as if my identity as Ron's wife was all wrapped up in being able to produce a child. I could sense the looks from the Noongar women, looks of expectancy that any day now we would make a big announcement.

Even beyond the looks were the questions, even from children. 'You gonna have any babies?' Every question and every look reminded me of possible failure. I heard how the other women talked about those who didn't have a child, and who should have. 'Oh, nyaru [*too bad*], she got no child. Lonely one, she is. No grannies either.' Then a shake of the head or click of the tongue would follow.

In my world in New York, achievements rather than children were the mark of success. A child was just an extra bonus. Now I had actually made a decision, not a haphazard one, either, to put the birth of a child in first place in my life.

When Ron and I had discussed the issue before the reversal operation, I made it clear that we wouldn't bring a child into the world unless he was absolutely sure he wanted to. 'This isn't just for me,' I had said. 'It's for you too. Maybe even more important for you to make the decision. With our lifestyle the way it is, I can't possibly bring up a child by myself, travel and work, even part-time, without you really wanting to be a father.' He had reassured me a number of times.

It seemed that babies were appearing everywhere, at church, in the community. Every time I turned a corner at the supermarket, I would almost bump into a stroller. As I searched the aisles for powdered milk or a different brand of cereal, my eye would fall on baby formula or miniature T-shirts with Pooh Bear neatly embroidered on the sleeve.

Every day that my age crept over forty-one, it seemed that all chance of experiencing motherhood was fading away. I even shook my fist at God and said to Him, 'Well, if that's it, then fine. Just forget it! Because I'm going to forget it.' And forget it I did.

A few children at Marribank knocked on our door late one night. 'We just been huntin', Auntie Diana,' they all said in unison, giggling to each other. I couldn't see much in the dark, but they kept passing back and forth some sort of bundle. It looked like a jumper. 'My dad killed a mother kangaroo. We want you to have this joey. You'll look after it for us, unna?' And with that, they scampered away, leaving me standing with a squirming bundle in my arms.

'It's a sign, y'know,' commented Ron when I asked him what we were going to do with this joey. I didn't want to look after any more animals, just to have them die on me. Many of the joeys that the Laverton mob had tried to raise died with the runs from drinking Sunshine milk. I had enough to look after without adding this furry bundle to the list.

'What do you mean, a sign?' I asked.

'Well, tribal way, when a joey, or other animal, appears across a woman's path, it means you'll have a baby. And the child will have a kangaroo totem, a sacred dreaming.'

'Oh, sure,' I murmured to myself.

I named him Joshua, the only boy's name that I liked. He attached himself to me, hopping wherever I went. Everyone at Marribank howled with laughter, seeing me walk down the dirt lane to the school or the church, little Joshua hopping in my footsteps.

'You sure have a mother's instinct there,' said Emil when she saw us. Joshua slept in a beanbag with a hot-water bottle during the winter months and I made hanging bags that I looped over the door handle of our bedroom. When we travelled he would swing in a bag that hung from the hook Ron drilled into the back of our old Landrover we had purchased. I surprised myself at how maternal I became, planning my every day around Joshua and his needs.

At the same time I was trying to keep my distance in case the little thing died: the success rate of raising joeys was not very high around the community. But more and more he captured my heart. One weekend we visited Fremantle when the USS *Carl Vinson* carriership was in port. The US Navy boys combing the streets stopped to talk to us after noticing Joshua's face peering out of the green canvas bag slung over my shoulder. He became the star of many photo shoots.

Our life was freer than most of the mob living at Marribank. We were often away, travelling across the dry, bumpy desert roads or along the sparsely travelled bitumen of the Nullabor Plain. Families came and went from Marribank, seeking help with problems caused by alcohol or for seasons of work in the shearing shed or crafts, or having a bit of respite from the pressures of the world at large. The core community was continuing to produce submissions to the government for leasehold of the land.

Ron had always travelled and most of his adult years had been spent away from his homeland and extended family. This was unlike most Aboriginal people, who were obligated to their families and didn't like to be separated from them. Even if they took on good jobs in another part of the same state, a family trouble or funeral brought them back, more than likely never to leave again. Ron came and went, known to all as the 'walkabout man'.

'I knew you wouldn't have your own family around when I married you. So in a way, you'd be stuck, have to come along with me ... Anyway, it wouldn't be so easy to run home,' Ron had hinted.

I didn't know if that was good or not. There were plenty of times I wanted to run home, but, Ron was right, it wasn't so easy since we never had enough money. I was coming to understand that Ron wasn't really the typical Aboriginal either. So when Ron announced another desert trip in September of 1987 it was no surprise.

We planned for some weeks, buying many boxes of supplies, since at that time the stores in the desert communities were not very well stocked. Our esky was packed with ice placed around the bottles of cool drink, margarine and meat packs. I neatly arranged Ron's favourite cereal, two loaves of bread, and tins of fruit and sardines into a cardboard box, items that would suffice if we got stuck on the side of the road.

There were no phones in most of the communities at that time, except for radio phones, and it was a very long way between petrol stops. Ron tied several jerry cans for fuel, extra tyres, tools and swags on the roof rack. On this trip we were driving an old Landrover that he had brought back to life with the help of a friendly mechanic in Bunbury.

A few days before we were to leave, I had finished a big wash and hung all the clothes along the fence line next to our house. I had given up trying to make 'capital' improvements on our living quarters. We had no spare money to buy a crank-up clothesline or a new washing machine, and we were always travelling anyway. Even the tomato bushes we so carefully fertilised burned up in the sun while we were away. I had started to feel that there was no use.

When I took the last basket of washing to the fence, I felt quite queasy and uncomfortable, like the beginning of some sort of sickness. In fact I was sore all over. I immediately thought about the trip and had visions of being airlifted out of the central desert writhing in pain. I rang our doctor in Katanning and made an appointment for Thursday. Saturday morning was departure time.

I was halfway to town, along the dirt road, when it suddenly dawned on me. When was my last period? I thought. Could it possibly be, could I possibly be . . . pregnant? It was hard for my mind to form that word, *pregnant*. I couldn't even say it aloud.

'I don't know what's wrong, Dr Ong, but I just sort of thought, well maybe, that I might be . . . pregnant,' I said to the doctor after he had sat me down and enquired about the reason for my visit.

He gave me a physical examination, ordered a blood test, then told me he suspected that I could be pregnant, but that the blood test would confirm it. However, Katanning had no pathology facilities and the blood samples would have to be sent to Perth. It would be several days before the results were known.

Dr Ong looked at me seriously. 'Do you think Ron would postpone this trip through those desert roads?'

'Oh, no,' I answered, shaking my head vigorously. 'You know him, he wouldn't postpone *any* trip once his mind is made up.'

Dr Ong was worried. He explained that the first three months of a pregnancy was a very important time. That's when most miscarriages occurred and, with my age, all precautions should be taken. 'You'll have to surround yourself with pillows,' he announced.

On Saturday, packed to the brim, we headed out of Marribank toward

Kalgoorlie, bouncing over the dirt roads through Western Australia and then on to the remote village of Amata at the top of South Australia. I had placed pillows all around me, just in case.

When we finally arrived, five days later, I rushed to the radio phone.

'Yes, Mrs Williams, the test was positive.'

I don't know whether it was the desert sun, or that I was a bit thick when it came to doctors' lingo, or that I thought that it was probably all a mistake, but all I could reply was, 'Does that mean I'm pregnant?'

'Yes, it does.'

I was struck dumb. I didn't know what to say. All I could do was hang up the phone after murmuring, 'Over and out.' I turned to Ron and nodded my head. He smiled, nodded to his tribal mates and, suddenly, his stature grew. He was going to have a child of his own.

CHAPTER 12

The Bicentennial Gift

W e had actually started to save money. To Ron, that idea had been foreign, as he had lived all his life from hand to mouth, sometimes not even having anything in his hand. Money to him was something to be used that day or the next, for fuelling up his car, buying a tin of meat, or putting a few dollars into the hands of one of his relatives. He never had much, certainly not enough to think about opening a bank account or saving.

With my steady job, the plan was to save enough to visit my family in America. None of them had met Ron; they only had seen photos of outback roads, the bush and some kangaroos. They couldn't possibly understand the intricacies of our lifestyle from those few images. No one from my own cultural connections had come to Australia; none of my family had walked the desert trails with me.

Our trip was in the wake of one of the greatest movie hits to ever come out of Australia, none other than *Crocodile Dundee*. After our friends saw the movie they kept asking us, 'Did they model that film on you two? You guys are the original. After all, the girl, Diana, from New York City meets, a "real" bush tracker, Ron.' We laughed all the way through the movie, probably understanding the uniqueness of such a relationship more than the rest of the audience.

As we planned our trip to the States, which would include that all-important stop in New York City, I kept pleading with Ron *not* to talk to anyone on the streets or on the subway. 'They'll pick us for tourists right away and then you never know what can happen,' I explained. After being away from the Big Apple for five years, I was more apprehensive about the potential dangers of the city than I had been when I actually lived there. 'And don't wear your Akubra hat!'

Well, that was like waving a red rag to a bull. Not only did he wear his Akubra, but he carried a knife in his boot too.

❂ ❂ ❂

We walked along Fifth Avenue, talked to the black American cops lining the street, then posed in front of the Plaza Hotel, on the south side of Central Park, where I took a photo of Ron standing next to the horse and carriage and the entrance to the hotel. Ron, with his Akubra hat and oilskin jacket.

'Well, you're the real Crocodile Dundee in my book. Too bad you can't afford to stay in the same hotel.' One of the cops had a good chuckle with Ron as they yarned about Australia. Everyone wanted to know about 'down-under' during that year.

One church that had farewelled our group of Americans going to Australia five years before opened their doors to us, and rolled out the red carpet for Ron. They were delighted to meet a 'real' Aboriginal and, as he ascended the steps to the pulpit, the pastor told him, 'Now take as long as you want, brother. We want to hear what you have to say to us.'

Ron looked at him in disbelief. No one, in church or out, had ever said that to him before. By the end of our trip, our expenses had been practically all reimbursed in gifts and hospitality by the American people to this lone blackfella and his Yankee wife.

I was four months pregnant when we had landed in Los Angeles, so I had experienced a bit of discomfort while we trekked around the country, to New York then to Seattle, San Francisco and, of course, Oklahoma.

When we boarded the plane for Tulsa, Ron asked about the snow. It was almost Christmas. 'It sure would be good to have a white Christmas.'

'Don't get your hopes up, Ron. In Oklahoma it only snows for Christmas Day once every few years.' As we descended out of the clouds in a landing pattern, I couldn't believe my eyes. There on the ground, all I could see was white everywhere, blending into the whiteness of the sky. When my mother met us, she explained that if we had come one day earlier they wouldn't have been able to drive the two hours from Ponca City to pick us up, because the roads had been closed.

Ron was loved by my family. Any previous prejudices seemed to have melted away and my mother outdid herself to make him feel welcome. The house was decked out with Christmas decorations and lights everywhere. Ron couldn't believe how Americans spent up so big during the holiday season, with houses decorated with everything from Santas that literally climbed down chimneys to Nativity scenes that moved. On the morning of a new snowfall, he jumped out into the front yard, rolled around in the snow and built a 'snowy joey', complete with Akubra hat, guitar, and long tail. Holiday sightseers driving past to look at the decorations, nearly crashed their cars as they tried to get a better view.

Ron peered into my family's lifestyle from the edge, observing the American middle class who lived in very neat brick and tile houses with matching lounge suites, mahogany dining-room tables, and curtains that enhanced the décor. Both my mother and my father had always picked up every crumb that dropped and slapped at every fly that buzzed. Coasters with drawings of European cities were placed on the dark wood coffee tables, every eye making sure that the cold or hot drinks sat in the right spot. Not a vase or a picture frame was out of place.

'And this is the way you were brought up?' whispered Ron as we lay on the white ruffled sheets one night. 'Boy, have you come a long way!'

We combed the area for Native Americans. Ron was so anxious to meet the indigenous people that we spent time one day in a little pawn shop that sold local artefacts, off the main street, where a man could get his shoes shined, buy a string neck tie and see a wooden Indian. The proprietor assured us that some of the locals dropped in frequently.

When we left the shop, Ron saw a pick-up truck slide into the space in front of us, with a rifle slung across the back window and two men with long, black hair climb out. 'Excuse me, are you two guys Indians?' Ron gave them a big smile and held out his hand. They looked at one another, then to Ron and said, 'Nah, we're from the Philippines.'

Ponca City was a few minutes' drive away from a native reservation and we visited a number of times. I had once told Ron that if you fell asleep in an Aboriginal community in Australia and woke up the next morning in a Native American village, you would not experience culture shock. When we showed photos of Australia and the Noongars to the local people, we were welcomed, feasted and given gifts of jewellery, beads and blankets.

I have often thought how interesting it is that indigenous people love to give blankets, shawls, or coverings of some kind. It's more than just a gift, it's a welcoming into the clan, the family. Simpson had given me a blanket, a Mexican had given Ron a serape, and a Native American family gave us each a blanket. It's like a sign of protection—a blanket to keep out the cold, and sometimes to keep out the rest of the world too. Even in the days of the Hebrews, a tribal people, the blanket was a special symbol. Ruth, in her cross-cultural marriage to Boaz, one a Moabite, the other a Hebrew, was protected by him through the spreading of the corner of his blanket over her as a sign that he was connecting her life with his. Our friends in Oklahoma told us, 'You are now one of us.'

One person who was not 'one' with me was my sister, Pat. When we had arrived in Ponca City, she refused to come and see me or to meet Ron. The effects of manic depression would often take hold of her and she would lash out at every family member. In some way, she wanted to punish me. My mother tried to talk her into seeing me, but in vain.

On the iciest Sunday of the winter, we had decided to attend a small Native American church about sixty kilometres away. Ron had declined to drive the car, saying he would have to 'think' too much, so it was up to me to regain the skill of driving on the right side of the road. I gingerly propelled the car through the icy streets and back roads after the church service, heading toward my mother's house. The snow was deep on both sides of the street, bare tree branches covered in a coating of ice. When the sun shone through, it was like the glitter of crystal-clear glass reflecting the rays.

As I turned into the driveway, the side door to the house slowly opened, and there stood Pat, dark hair pulled back with a scarf, smiling at me, her features hauntingly similar to mine. That day we had a photo taken of the three of us: my mother, Pat and me. It was the last one we ever had taken together.

Manic depression is a strange illness, unpredictable at best. Pat's mood swings went wide and everyone had to watch what they said. But that day she greeted me as if there had been no problem and we had quite a good time.

For extra money to supplement her social services money and sickness benefit she would deliver newspapers. Ron joined her one day, trudging through the two feet of snow from house to house, making sure the plastic-wrapped newspaper landed on the front step.

But then just as suddenly she disappeared and didn't surface again until after we had left Oklahoma.

Since the day that I had received the congratulatory letter from my dad about my marriage to Ron, I had looked forward to the day when they would meet. My dad had seemed interested in Australia, and would report to me through his letters any documentaries about Australia that he had seen on television: 'Trains of the World,' which included the Indian-Pacific, something on the Gibson Desert and another on the life cycle of kangaroos.

Even after my parents' divorce, they both continued to live in the same town, but far enough away that they only met by accident, perhaps in a supermarket or walking down the main street. My mother and I normally kept silent regarding the past, so after our two-week visit with her, Ron and I made our plans to spend some time with my dad. It was to be another important step in our reconciliation. Dad served us his magic spaghetti bolognaise, made from an 'old family recipe', showed Ron his gun collection and spun him some childhood yarns about teaching me to shoot a rifle many years ago. Being with Dad and his wife Ellie was like getting to know him all over again, this time on new territory with my own bridges of resentment and revenge burned behind me. Forgiveness had cleaned the slate and we now could start over.

It was also the first time I heard him speak of Pat and my brother, John, with such sadness and the hope that they could desire to forgive as well.

'I've done all I can, Diana. I've written. I've asked their forgiveness. But do I have to be crucified again and again? Pat won't even bring her children to see me.' Dad's voice cracked as he hugged me and prayed for a safe birth for his next grandchild, one from his eldest daughter.

Before we left, Dad presented Ron with a Charles Daley shotgun, which had belonged to my grandfather. It was a family heirloom with double meaning.

On our way back to Australia, we touched down at Seattle before going on to the Bay of San Francisco to spend two days with my brother. I hadn't seen John in over seven years. While Ron took the ferry to Alcatraz to visit the ghosts of prison past, John and I walked the length and breadth of the harbour wharfs. John was still a loner, protecting himself from the painful mention of family. I walked beside him, or should I say 'waddled', with my six-month child in my womb, stroking my stomach from time to time as if to include this little life into the conversation. I ached to see a glimmer of forgiveness in my brother's heart.

It was time for me to leave America once more, this time with my husband and excitement about my impending motherhood. Our bags were full of books, baby clothes, toys and gifts from family, loaded to the limit for overseas passengers. Somewhere over the Pacific, Ron turned to me and said, 'I must say that I know more about you now. I've seen your background, and I can make more sense of you now. And I must say that you have had a lot of changes to make marrying me. You haven't done too bad either.'

After four years, innumerable trips around the country, a lot of laughter and certainly a lot of crying, he was just now beginning to understand me more. He had experienced my cultural connections, as I had been experiencing his. He had often quizzically commented that he didn't think whitefellas had any problems. Big problems only belonged to the Aboriginal population, created by the whitefellas. Now he had seen some of my problematic background, tasted the American middle-class lifestyle, witnessed the strains between siblings and the eccentricities of both my father and my mother. And now he appreciated me more. I settled my cramped body more comfortably in the airline seat and sighed, 'At last.'

❂ ❂ ❂

Ron kept patting my expanding abdomen and talking to his little 'son'. I had warned him that we could never be sure about the sex of an unborn child, and since we didn't seek any revelation from the ultrasound, he might be in for a surprise. But in the tradition of males desiring sons, Ron continued his little talks about sports, hunting and preaching. It worried me, but no matter what I said he seemed self-assured of the outcome. I even read to him studies that told of unborn children picking up tones, voices and emotions from the 'outside' and, of course, from within the mother's body.

The days ticked away as the supposed birth date drew closer and closer. The doctor had given us a projected date in May, which happened to be Mother's Day. What mother wouldn't want her child born on Mother's Day! There were many false alarms and various twinges and dashes of sharp pain, but nothing of significance to indicate this child's approaching entrance into our world. During the Mother's Day week, I continued to gather wood for the chip heater, to drive the Landrover over bumps along the dirt track, which did nothing to bring on the birth of the baby, led the Sunday school class and attended meetings of the Marribank Aboriginal Corporation as they fine-tuned the land request submission.

During that week, we were invited to a special luncheon by the church ministers and their wives in Katanning. Running late as usual, I tried to hurry Ron along. We were halfway into town, still on the dirt track section, when I felt the Landrover come to a screeching halt.

'Ron, the baby! What are you doing?' I cried out as I grabbed my stomach. At that moment I was frightened that I might have gone through the window or my stomach might have been rammed up against the dashboard. 'What are you doing?' I cried again as I looked around, thinking that he might have swerved to miss another car or something.

'Might be a goanna,' was the calm reply as he opened the car door and began to walk around to the back. I couldn't believe it. I looked out through the window and caught a slight glimpse of a shadow darting under our vehicle. I turned my head in the opposite direction, waiting for the shadow to emerge on the other side, but there was nothing.

'I don't see him, Ron. Come on, we're gonna be late. We don't need a goanna. Besides you could've killed us, stopping so fast.'

While I was saying this and mumbling to myself about goannas, he had opened the bonnet, spied the little creature sitting on top of the battery and, quick as you can wink, he had grabbed his tail.

'Get me a bit of rope in the back,' he called out. I walked around the car to him with a bit of rope that had been coiled under the back spare tyre for quite some time. I couldn't believe what he did. He tied that tail with the rope, wrapped it several times around the front of the engine and tied it to the front roo bar. Then away we went.

After a few kilometres, the steam between my ears cooled a bit, and all I could do was let out a little chuckle now and again. By the time we got to Katanning we were both laughing out loud about the goanna under the bonnet. We had our lunch, stopped at the supermarket, each time checking that our lizard friend was still there, and then we made our way back home. Ron couldn't wait to stop and tell the fellas standing around what was under the bonnet, and they all took turns peering through the front grill at two goanna eyes staring back at them.

By the time we drove around the lane to park out the back of our house, a dozen little kids came swooping upon us. 'Where's the goanna, Uncle Ron? We wanna see 'im.'

A few hours later, Ron came in through the back door holding a dead goanna by the tail. The poor thing had tired, loosened its grip and then Ron had bashed its head on a tree. That night we had baked goanna for tea.

Two days later I was in the hospital, waiting to have our baby. I had visited Dr Ong and, while moving his stethoscope across my belly, he had announced that he would induce labour the next morning. The baby was overdue and he didn't want to wait any longer he said, while he rang the hospital to reserve a bed for me that night. I hated the thought of inducement as I was hoping that all would happen naturally, at the right time. As I lay in the hospital bed, alone and waiting, trying to sleep, I felt a throb, then another, and again another. I lay there for an hour, timing each spasm of pain. Six minutes apart, to the second.

Ron had left me there a few hours before and had driven back the thirty kilometres to eat and sleep, planning to join me the next morning. I got up out of my bed and padded down the hall, looking around hesitantly for the nurse. I was so new to all this and there was no one there—no husband, no mother, to help me to know what to do. The nurse checked me and, sure enough, the birth was beginning.

I rang the superintendent's house and gave him the message for Ron to get to the hospital. Tell him to come quick, I told Courtney. I paced the floor. Then I sat. Then I paced again, growing anxious. What was taking him so long?

I was suddenly frightened. I had had to completely discard the idea of having my own mother there. She couldn't come on so long a trip and I had thought that this would be a piece of cake. But now it was all happening. I was going to be a mother. At forty-two years old!

What if there were complications? What if there were deformities? You know, a woman my age. One never knows. What was taking Ron so long? And what if our baby was a girl? What would he think then? I had told him not to be so cocky. So many fearful thoughts crowded my head while I sat waiting for what seemed like hours until Ron finally appeared.

'Oh, I decided to take a shower and have a bite to eat before I came,' he defended himself when I tearfully confronted him.

I had no one to hold onto but Ron. My familiar world seemed so far away. At a time when a woman wants her family around her, and particularly her mother, there was no one. Ron wanted to be there with me, by my side through the whole process.

All during the night, the pains continued. I gripped Ron's hand, then turned to the gas, then breathed in and out as I was taught. Our doctor arrived in the morning, listened to the heart beat, spoke to the sister and then walked down the hall, only to return within two minutes.

'Something's wrong,' he said. 'We've missed a heart beat and there seems to be some distress. I really think we need to do a Caesarean. I know how much you've been through for this child. I wouldn't want to lose this baby now.' Within one minute I was put on a trolley, prepped for the operation and was being whisked down the hallways.

As the needle took effect, I only remember seeing Ron standing next to me, dressed in hospital greens, armed with camera and tape recorder. After the cut was made and the baby was pulled from my womb, Dr Ong turned to Ron and said, 'Pastor Ron, you have a beautiful baby daughter.'

'Daughter, daughter . . . how can that . . .' was Ron's first thought. He turned to look at this child of his very own as the nurse held her out to him, and she, in turn, screamed at him. The nurse took her away to clean her up and wrap her in a pink blanket. Ron turned again and she wailed. Then, in the next two seconds, something of a miracle happened.

A voice spoke into Ron's spirit that this little girl was God's choice for him, to teach him many things. As he glanced sideways at her, peering through his eyelashes, lest she cry again, he could see in her face the shape of his grandmother Grace's face, his grandmother who had reared him, who had been his anchor in life. A tear came to his eye. He whispered a quiet 'Sorry' into the room and, as he went to pick her up, the clouds outside parted for a moment and a ray of sun shone through the window. Lydia Grace smiled at him.

In the nursery Ron leaned over my bed, his face barely coming into focus as I tried to blink away the effects of the anaesthetic. 'I truly love her, Diana. Here is our beautiful baby girl.' He nestled Lydia in my arms. He knew I had been worried about his attitude, but the joy and over-whelming gratitude of being given a healthy little girl filled our hearts. In the operating room, Ron had taken four photos of her birth and had captured her first cries on tape. Over the years, he has played them at very special moments, even on radio.

Lydia's little face peered through the soft folds of the blanket. Like every new mother I was overcome with awe as I examined every tiny finger, each soft nail, stroked her velvet-smooth skin, and silently begged her to open her eyes so I could peer into her soul.

A voice by the bed murmured with approval. 'She got your nose, Ron. Proper Noongar she is.' Auntie Emil had come to welcome our newborn and pronounce the Aboriginal blessing. 'But she got your skin, Diana.'

I wanted to squeeze her into my bosom, protecting her from the hurts that the world would eventually bring to her, but at the same time I was apprehensive of a baby's fragility. Every one of the past moments of my forty-two years, achievements that I had worked so hard for and had meant so much to me at the time, paled into insignificance as I counted Lydia's fingers and toes and put my lips to her chubby cheek. 'I'll be with you all the way, my sweetheart,' I whispered into her tiny ear.

In the hospital ward, I was placed between two women who were half my age having their second and third child. With all my educational degrees I knew next to nothing about having a baby. In fact, I could have read all the books on the shelf, but nothing would have truly prepared me for the next twenty years of my life.

'Oh, there's nothing to it,' one young woman said while her baby suckled at her breast.

I was struggling with breastfeeding, fully convinced of its worth and wanting Lydia's start in life to be as natural as possible. No sooner had I fed her, wiped the dribbles from the corner of her mouth and gently placed her in the small cot than she started to cry. What had I done wrong? Was she in some sort of pain?

The woman in the bed spoke up again. 'Have you checked her nappy? Maybe she's wet.'

Trying to hide my embarrassment, I dutifully changed her wet nappy. I have so much to learn, I thought, watching Lydia blow bubbles into her tiny rolled-up fist.

The day of Lydia's birth was 13 May in the bicentennial year. Australia was dancing its way through the year with celebrations of all kinds. Aboriginals had organised a protest march through Sydney, and over forty thousand people had walked together to celebrate a different historical marker—that of survival and 'Freedom, Justice and Hope' for the future. Most Aboriginal organisations were calling for 1988 to be named a Year of Mourning. As we flicked through some of the special booklets commemorating the year, we realised that Lydia had been born 201 years to the very day after the First Fleet had pulled up anchor at Portsmouth, bound for Australia.

In 1988, some wealthy Australians had paid thirty-three thousand dollars each to sail as passengers on the tall ships in a re-enactment of the First Fleet's arrival into Botany Bay. At that same moment, an Aboriginal child was born to us, not from the wealth of Australia but from the love between a man and a woman offering their own kind of grass-roots reconciliation. The fact that Lydia Grace, named after a biblical woman of independence and strength, and Ron's Noongar grandmother, made her appearance on that very day was special to Ron, who believed that nothing, absolutely nothing, happens by accident.

What was so special? What was the symbol? Was it that, as the arrival of the First Fleet had changed the life of Australia, the arrival of this child would change our lives? Was it that this fruit of our love and union, born of cross-cultural parents, would somehow symbolise a change for the better in Australia, through its children? Only time would tell.

Our bicentennial child was given gifts by the government as were all babies born in 1988. A special birth certificate was issued and a fifty-dollar savings account was opened. Gifts for a child whose father had never had a birth certificate, who had to prove his birth over and over again, and who had not been automatically a citizen of Australia when he was born on the edge of a lake in Albany.

❂ ❂ ❂

In the days leading up to Lydia's birth, we had been busy preparing to welcome our newcomer. Like any other mother of the first world, I was steeped in the lore of Dr Spock and, more recently, Dr Christopher Green, both of whom had spent years and hundreds of pages telling us women how to raise our children. I had dutifully gone shopping for a bassinette, a maroon and white woven basket lined with soft, padded cotton dotted in pastels. The chrome stand supported the basket at waist height, making it easy for a mother to place her precious baby safely within.

I had selected the small room in the front of the house that looked onto the pathway and down the lane to the centre of the community to be the baby's room. The wall above the bassinette I covered with an A-B-C quilt, and I hung curtains displaying dancing clowns. When I had finished cleaning out the room from its store of dusty boxes of old photographs, and books that were crammed into shelves vertically, horizontally and diagonally, I had stood back proudly, surveying its freshness.

Ron had sensed that there was some 'women's business' going on, so he kept well away during these preparations. When I had finally emerged from the room feeling very satisfied with these nest-making activities, he had quietly asked, 'Is that where the baby's going to sleep?'

When I answered in the affirmative, I heard him murmur, 'That's a bit far away from our room isn't it? Us Noongar families always slept in the same room.' With that, he continued reading his newspaper and didn't say another word.

A few days later, I moved the bassinette into our room and hammered a nail into our bedroom wall for the ABC quilt. The bassinette was within arm's length of our bed. I sat on the edge of the bed thinking about the problems of child rearing when Ron sat down next to me and said, 'It gets a bit cold here in the winter, y'know. Most of the time the Noongar babies sleep in the same bed with their parents.' I didn't dare tell him that all the 'experts' said never to let your child sleep in your bed.

When Lydia and I arrived home from the hospital and settled in for the night, I cuddled and kissed her before gently putting her into her little bassinette cocoon. After the first wake-up call for a feed, I realised how cold it was and from that first night, she was snuggled between us in bed.

Indigenous people look upon western child-rearing customs with suspicion. The practice of looking through the pages of a book, or going by the tick of a clock, or distancing yourself from your child as it cries is unheard of and shrugged off as so much nonsense. I struggled with the concepts of four-hourly feeds and leaving your child to cry in its cot as I tried to follow the dictates of my own inherent cultural patterns as well as the direction of seasoned missionaries who constantly gave me advice. At the same time, I was conscious of the glances of disapproval in my direction from Ron's family and community grandmothers.

Throughout the four years of living in an Aboriginal community, I had observed the beds all lined up together in the small bedrooms, lounge room, on the verandahs or out in the flat. When we had camped all together, I knew that the children snuggled into bed with their parents. Sometimes the mother even slept separate to the father, with children crowded in with each of them.

Babies were always held, passed from one auntie or grandmother to another. Skin touching skin at all times. No one left a child to cry alone and there was always a baby at the breast. The Noongar women showed no embarrassment about breastfeeding in public. No cloth covered this part of a woman's anatomy, there was no hiding away in the next room. Instead, it was a natural part of life accepted by the whole community. Some children were still at the breast at four years of age.

Children accompanied their parents and extended family to every function. Whenever and wherever a meeting was held, whether in the church or at a hall, children came. Even at community business meetings out in the flat, the children dashed from blanket to blanket while issues of land ownership, government funding or health problems were being discussed. Whenever their energy was depleted, they slept huddled next to each other on the blankets. When the session was over, the parents would dutifully place the children on their shoulders and cover them with blankets, before disappearing from the campfire light in all directions.

Once I picked up a brochure and invitation to a convention sponsored by whitefellas and read the inevitable announcement in fine print: 'Children Not Catered For'. I had to chuckle. No Noongars would go to this, I thought.

My Aboriginal friends and family never confronted me directly like my white friends did. But I could sense their bewilderment at my struggle. After all, we were living Noongar way. Their looks told me that something was wrong. There were a few hints. 'Here, let me take Lydia. She's cryin'.'

'She must be hungry. Come on, you can feed her.'

'She sleep with you now?'

After a few months of this balancing act, I fell in a heap one afternoon. I was so tense that my milk was starting to dry up, Lydia was crying more and I felt a failure. I turned to Ron, seeking for help, for answers.

'Well, I reckon you're makin' too much of this thing. Bringin' up a child should just be natural. Follow your heart, is what I say.' Blackfellas didn't worry about things like spoiling a child, or giving him too much attention, or how often he was fed. They just loved them, that's all.

That's what I decided to do. Follow my heart. Do what was right for my own child. In those beginning years, it was mostly the Noongar way.

❂ ❂ ❂

All tribes, white tribes included, celebrate in some way the dedication of their young into the family or community circle. Ron chose Albany, his own birthplace, to be the scene for Lydia's dedication in the church and into the Noongar community. We celebrated our faith and thankfulness to God for our Lydia in the midst of Ron's long-time friends and Noongar family relations. She was the first baby to be dedicated in the newly built Baptist church in Albany, with the prayers of Pastor Gary Keymer, who had been the administrator at the Gnowangerup Bible College in the late 1970s when Ron was the principal. Some of the congregation had been around to see Ron's family first work on the farms outside of Albany, Ron's first day at school, and his first fight with a white kid.

After the ceremony we walked through the park surrounding the town hall. We sat together, the three of us, Lydia cradled in Ron's arms, on one of the green painted park benches. Ron wanted to talk about another dedication.

'I chose Albany because of the spirit of reconciliation that is here. Not many people know it, but this place right here, at this town hall, is a sacred site.' Ron went on to tell me about Mokare, and one of the most peaceful encounters between blackfellas and whitefellas in this country of Australia. 'Lots of people talk about massacres and killing, but here, here is also a place to talk about. This is the story that gives us hope and pride in who we are.'

Mokare had been one of the leaders of the clan living around Albany at the time of the first settlement at King George Sound when Dr Alexander Collie was left in charge. Mokare had calmed his people, preventing them from attacking the white men with spears, and was responsible for those beginning years of virtually no racial conflict. He and Dr Collie became great friends, one translating for the other. Mokare lived with the doctor for a number of months, and they camped in the bush together as they explored the region. The doctor was suffering from tuberculosis and Mokare had contracted a sickness as well, and he sometimes crept away into the bush, endeavouring to bring tribal healing to his own failing body.

'We all knew about Mokare and how he warned the Noongars to accept the change that was coming. But he got sick then, and the doctor nursed him in his own hut,' Ron continued, touched that a white man would let an Aboriginal into his own bed.

'When Mokare breathed his last, the old doctor arranged his burial. Mokare's family and the white soldiers all together watching his body lowered into the grave. And then, the way I heard it, the doctor made the soldiers promise that when he died—'cause he was coughing and sputterin' with that pneumonia—when he died they were to bury him next to his friend.' Ron walked around me, pointing to the town hall site.

'But this is the spot,' continued Ron. 'The spot to celebrate what true reconciliation is all about. Friendship, relationship, brother and mate. This is where I want to dedicate my daughter, Noongar way.' Ron prayed at that spot and, with his own ceremony, his own remembrances of his childhood and his family, he celebrated the birth of our daughter and the path that would be hers for the future.

We felt a sense of completeness at that moment. The celebration of creation had brought the two of us together more than ever before. We were inextricably linked through the bloodline. The Aboriginal sense of 'ceremony' pervaded our every waking hour. Many had lost that sense from the days of dislocation, but here, Ron was recapturing it in the daily moments of our life. He was making his own ceremony, a ceremony to place Lydia's birth, and her story, into eternal history—past, present and future—of the Aboriginal story, the Dreaming, the eternal cycle of creation.

❂ ❂ ❂

The bicentennial year had begun with a sense of excitement and hope for the future, but as the year began to draw to a close, the atmosphere was gradually becoming yet another one of despair. While Australia celebrated the coming of the tall ships, Aboriginal people called it a year of mourning. The real truth has not been told, the activists repeated. Their real history was being trivialised by such ceremony. In Perth, in preparation for Aboriginal week, the slogan 'White Australia has a Black History,' was banned by the city council. There were demands all over the country for the truth to be revealed.

Representatives of Marribank Aboriginal Corporation submitted a number of plans to the government, staged more exhibitions of Aboriginal art, and sent more delegations to Perth bearing numerous folders with business strategies, architectural drawings and feasibility studies. A positive outcome did not seem to be forthcoming.

'Your membership is not large enough,' one report stated.

'Do you represent all of the south-west?' questioned the lands trust.

A power play was in the wind. Another Aboriginal body, vying to represent all the Noongars, wanted the land. Most of their members had never lived at Marribank and were not involved in the present-day struggle to gain credibility. It was a case of wanting to ride on the coat tails of someone else's success. Our small community was growing despondent, fearing a takeover.

Criticism had started to mount as well. The avid Christian Aboriginal groups who had learned their faith from some of the early missionaries told their people to stay away from Marribank. 'They're getting too much into culture,' they said. 'All you need to do is go to church, pray and wait for the Lord to come back. No use wastin' time learnin', paintin' and makin' pots. Those people there, they're not Christian enough.'

On the other side of the coin was the criticism from the government, who stated that the community was *too* Christian. The Marribank constitution recognised the basic tenets of the Christian faith and adherence to Christian principles of fair play in community development and self-determination. The lands trust was reluctant to grant the leasehold to a Christian community, no matter that they were providing a positive thrust to Aboriginal development.

The water that was so desperately needed at the community could not be piped in unless the lease belonged to them. In Ron's ears he heard an echo from 1972 in Canberra. 'Sorry, we can't help you. You're too Christian.'

The people of Marribank were caught in the middle. Their faith was strong. They recognised that it had helped to heal their families and bring them back together. There seemed to be a schism in the Aboriginal population between those who honoured the work of Christian missionaries and others who blamed them for all the wrongs that had been committed against Aboriginal people.

Years later, when some of these angry outbursts had run their course, even government officials and Aboriginal leaders admitted that the most positive and lasting work in the communities have been done by those who have a strong Christian faith, no matter what people believe about religious organisations themselves.

It was at that point that Ron began to speak out more. For decades he had lived under the thumb of missionary and government alike. He had honoured and revered the missionaries while at the same time often feeling dismissed or discounted as inferior. Ron was a man who had received virtually all his education from history books and the Bible. He could quote long passages from the Bible and link Biblical history with world history, and he preached a vivid sermon. But at this moment, the dignity of his culture and the contribution of his people were rising in his heart.

Ron called everyone together to the church. 'When all else fails, we must pray,' he said, then outlined the tracks that the community had followed to get to this place. 'We mustn't give up. Our people are buried here. It belongs to us.' Then he read an account of the exiled people of Jerusalem, who had finally been brought back to their land only to find destruction and desolation. When the exiles had approached the governor in charge, he made the decree to help this outcast people. Ron closed the pages of his Bible, took off his reading glasses, paused and spoke resolutely to his people. 'It was the governor himself who told the king to pay the expenses so God's people would not be hindered in what they were trying to do. Let's pray.'

The people of Marribank wanted to rebuild, to do something for themselves. They actually wanted to do what the government had been telling the Noongars to do for decades, but now the powers that be were slow, lax and seemed unwilling to help. The development of Marribank was being hindered. There we all stood, sojourners in our own land, in a land that cried tears for its people, standing alone in the middle of a paddock of red tape, flow charts, community networks, leaseholds, aims and objectives. Where was the door of hope?

At the final meeting of lands trust officials, the Baptist Union, representatives of the Marribank Aboriginal Corporation and those from other organisations in Perth, away from the energy and dreams of the Marribank residents, the decision was dealt. The final word was given. The leasehold of Marribank would be granted to the larger, more powerful Aboriginal corporation. Yes, composed of Noongars, but many who had never showed any interest in this little community ever before.

'Hope deferred makes the heart sick.' The heart of this community, indeed, fell sick. The brightly painted fabric slid out from under their feet and each ceramic pot with scenes of Noongar legends cracked ever so slightly. None of them wanted to work for someone else, not even another Noongar clan. The government's decision effectively brought division, as it had done all their lives.

Aboriginal people could knock on the door all they wanted to but the answer on the other side always seemed to have conditions. Churches were happy to dig into their pockets to finance the whitefella to go and deliver their message to the poor blackfella. But when those blackfellas wanted to go and do the same, there was no money to help them live or travel.

The government had a never-ending round of grants and contracts available for whitefellas to bring their 'skills' to the Aboriginal, but when the Aboriginal wanted to put those skills into practice, there was no money left. When the 'training programs' were over, the expectations of jobs seemed to vanish into thin air. The hopes of becoming self-determined, of completing what they had begun and worked hard for over the last few years, were crushed. The hopes of getting off the dole, choosing their own pathway in life, regaining their own dignity, vanished with that last decision from Perth. One by one they began to move away from Marribank.

We needed to say goodbye too. It was time to move on. We had lived in Marribank for four years, and the next journey would be to the goldfields. As the fire in Marribank seemed to be dying down, just before the last flame burned, a few live coals leaped out. Gabrielle would go on to finish a university degree and become a social worker. A few of the artists would take their skills and put them to use in other forms. And Lydia Grace, barely eight months old, born from Marribank soil, would carry some of this hope with her.

Ron and I stood by a deserted graveyard next to the Marri River to say our final goodbyes. The only indications of burials were a few metal numberplates.

'Somewhere here my great-grandmother is buried. Old Mary. She was the first of my family to greet me as she pulled me out of my mother's womb. Now I'm the last of her family to say goodbye to her. I wish this place could have made it.'

We turned to walk away, both crying for what should have been, Ron cuddling Lydia in his arms.

CHAPTER 13

Creating Our Own Space

O ur desert-gold Landrover grunted its way along the Great Eastern Highway, dragging behind it a grey covered-in box trailer loaded with most of our household gear so we could set up a semblance of a home in Kalgoorlie. The road was flanked by dry fields that waved with grain during the harvest season. Gradually, oh, so gradually, the scene before us changed to red dirt, scrubby mulga trees and spinifex bushes as far as one could see. Lydia was packed into her car cradle, eyes darting and hands jumping to the sounds of country and western songs playing on the cassette.

Music plays an interesting role in the background of life. One can drive faster and with more gusto to the beat of a good rock song, or a more leisurely drive can be accompanied by the strains of classical or ballad music. Ron loved country music. Slim Dusty and Charlie Pride, along with American cowboys, had been his heroes in his younger days. He knew every song by heart, all the verses, and could sing along at the drop of an Akubra hat.

I, on the other hand, fiercely resisted country music. After leaving the dusty plains of Oklahoma in the 1960s for cosmopolitan life, music of a more 'intellectually stimulating' variety began to appeal to me. I had immersed myself in classical music throughout high school, and had continued piano lessons until I left for university. This interest was punctuated by hits such as 'Jailhouse Rock', 'Love Me Tender', and music from the Beatles. Eventually jazz, protest songs, and the Eric Clapton guitar riffs of the 1970s was my music of choice.

Our lifestyles competed for prominence through music. The melodic strains of ballads, the African beat of Harlem, the twang of the country guitar and the choral arrangements of hymns were threading their way into our relationship. Ron and I often sang together in church settings and in singalongs around the fire and reminisced over our pasts in the lounge room. Ron had never heard most of the music I had listened to. His repertoire dated from the 1940s and 1950s and then made an abrupt stop. His memory for every verse of songs from Sankey's Hymn Book was uncanny. I quickly learned that I had to follow his lead if we were going to sing together. The D and E minor chords and variety of changes involved in the 'newer' songs were not part of his musical spontaneity.

'Do you really understand those words?' Ron would ask as I slipped my own music into the cassette player. I would give a slight grin as I continued to feed my musical soul.

The favourite music for Aboriginal people in general, was and still is, country music. The chords are simple, the beat is steady and the words tell stories that speak to the heart of the blackfella. Stories of lost loves, of wide open spaces, of broken friendships, of land taken and fenced. It didn't take me long to cry the tears that others were crying as we heard the relevance of these words to my Aboriginal family. On every table in every hut, on every bit of red dirt at the bush camps, surrounded by used 'C' batteries, and in every prison cell, there was a cassette player, volume turned to number ten, pouring out the strains of songs like 'Detroit City'.

Ron was singing along in his slightly off-key voice as we drove under the banner that called out to us: Welcome to Kalgoorlie-Boulder. The only break in the otherwise flat horizon was a man-made 'mountain' of mining dirt, the old Mount Charlotte hill which overlooked the widely built main thoroughfare, Hannan Street, named after Paddy Hannan, the Irish prospector who made the goldfields famous.

I was glad to be 'home', as I called it, since Kalgoorlie had been my first stop in Australia and where Ron and I had met. Kalgoorlie, with its kaleidoscope of history: the visit by the American president, Herbert

Hoover, and his memory of the bougainvilleas that grew in a park in Old Kalgoorlie; the concrete pipeline of water flowing from Perth; the brothels of Hay Street, which drew miners and women from all over the world; the fringe dwellers, who never seemed to find a home no matter what government department scheme was put into place; and pubs on every corner advertising the most vivacious 'skimpy' barmaids. This was the place where we were to stake our own land rights flag. But we had to pay for it.

When we had heard that the education programs at Marribank were to be phased out, the government funding was dribbling away and the lease was not likely to be handed over to the Marribank Aboriginal Corporation, Ron had decided we needed to spread our wings and go somewhere completely different. Another issue had always been support for our church work and on what church doorpost should we hang our hat. Among Aboriginal Christians, denomination isn't of major importance. It's the people that matter, but Ron wanted to work with others who would respect his ideas and talents.

The Christian and Missionary Alliance, a mission organisation that had started on the streets of lower Manhattan in the 1880s and had developed a presence here in Australia in 1970 wanted to support us. They didn't have a long history of church work among Aboriginals, only a lone missionary who had known Ron in the 1960s at Warburton and who had helped to translate that oral language into written hymns and verses of Scripture. He had also been the officiating reverend at our wedding.

The question that posed itself was what role Ron would play. Where would he fit in the organisation? What would be the relationship between Noel Blyth, this long-time missionary and Ron, whom Noel considered his protégé, as well as friend? The answer had presented itself during a retreat of church workers held in a bush lodge at Cooma, at the edge of the Snowy Mountains, one hundred kilometres from Canberra, in November 1988.

The days were still crisp, the village welcomed sightseers from all over Australia, the food was deliciously served cafeteria-style, the volleyball tournament was fast and furiously competitive between church leaders, and our spiritual thirst was quenched with gentle messages from Michael Maeliau from the Solomon Islands. Michael was dressed in white, a striking contrast to his chocolate black skin, and his eyes pierced right to the heart as he spoke of the revivals and commitment to prayer over decades in the Solomons.

It was during these moments that Noel, our friend and soon to be co-worker, stood up. With a broken voice, and tears brimming, he told of his own struggles with prejudice, his own feelings of superiority among Aboriginal people. The times that he never questioned the government policies, even though he did not really agree with them. The times he had been less than congenial with Ron in the past when they had worked together in the desert. Times he had had control over Ron.

Then, with a broken voice, he told of the time when Ron had come into his house when Olive, Noel's wife, had experienced a breakdown after years of looking after fifty boys in the home at Warburton as well as having five of her own babies to raise. 'I took her to Perth where she could regain her strength. It was too far to come back to Warburton so I stayed with her until she was better. But my Kurta here, my brother, Ron came into our family. He cooked, cleaned and looked after our children. He became an "uncle" to my own children,' Noel explained. In turn, his children had followed Ron like chicks follow their mother, never thinking that he wasn't their 'real' uncle.

Throughout the room, pastors, their wives and missionaries began to quietly weep. Ron and I sat stunned, never expecting such raw honesty. I glanced at him and saw the tears running down his dark face. Noel then turned to Ron and apologised. Both Olive and I were crying. I knew how much pride her husband had to swallow. I knew how much Ron had borne over the years, silently. Both of us knew the pain of reconciliation our husbands were experiencing, that we were all experiencing in that room.

A moment of honest, transparent reconciliation only happens in the midst of acknowledging the pain in each other. It was the first apology from a white man that Ron had ever received, long before the request for 'sorry' from the government, from church missions, from police or native welfare and any other official organisation was ever made. The two men hugged, prayed together, wept together, and others huddled around them, the room full of tenderness, tears and hope.

Ron was named Coordinator of Indigenous Ministries, then ordained as reverend. Noel would work with him in areas of developing new churches and language translation. In the words of Lester Coyne, a

Noongar friend of ours and long-time champion of his people, 'We can't walk ahead of one another, but side by side, sharing each other's resources and gifts.'

That was the reason we moved to Kalgoorlie, the gateway to the western desert, a jumping-off base of operations to connect with Aboriginal people throughout the country. To 'mine' the gold that we can find in Australia's people, as Ron once said.

❂ ❂ ❂

Ron had never dreamed he would own a home. All his life he had run from the authorities, had been given mission buildings to live in, or had camped in his car. Now we had to make a decision. The only money we had was five thousand dollars I had saved from working at Marribank. We had a steady income of a few thousand dollars a year from the church's national office, with the promise of an increase each year, and whatever I could earn teaching part-time. Lydia was less than one year old then, and I certainly didn't want to farm her out to day-care centres, so we juggled our time in order to be there for her. The rentals in Kalgoorlie were far out of our reach and Ron, particularly, couldn't bring himself to pay two hundred dollars a week for four walls that weren't his own, after living most of his life never paying rent at all.

Someone whispered to us that perhaps we could buy a house. The Aboriginal Development Commission was now giving low-interest home loans to Aboriginal families. We read over the forms, Ron oblivious to what most of the fine print meant. Even though I understood the legal jargon, I was somewhat resistant to join the mortgage queue, having to consult lawyers and conduct title searches. The years I had spent in voluntary simplicity, sleeping in a tent, driving off around the country with all my worldly possessions in one bag, living from day to day, all seemed to be slipping from my grasp. But we had a child to think of now.

We passed the tests. We could now own a home. We looked for a cheap one. One that didn't strap us with a high monthly payment, one that wouldn't take a lot of work to fix up, one that was just a small step beyond what we had lived in before, one that would not remove us too far from the world of the Wongi people of the goldfields.

House hunting was frustrating because most of the ones we could afford were listed in the 'handyman's dream' column. Then our agent contacted us. 'Look,' she said. 'I think I know just the house for you. I woke up in the middle of the night thinking about it. I just know it's the right one.' Ron's ears pricked up on that comment, for he still believed in the sacredness of every part of life, even in finding a house. If an image of 'our' house had interrupted someone's sleep, then it must be worth looking at.

We walked through the iron gate at number 7 Millen Street and stood under the two huge elm trees in the front yard. The front bullnose-covered verandah was half collapsed, louvres missing, unpainted. What a first impression! The backyard revealed a different story as we surveyed the landscape from under the sixty-year-old orange tree, which was heavy with still-green fruit.

A large bricked pergola with a massive barbecue at one end of it was the main feature. To the side of that was a brick two-car garage, flanked by a huge wire aviary that was almost covered from sight by a leafy grapevine. Right in the middle was a small concrete pond and a thin bare tree where birds could perch. Another wire birdcage was placed alongside the fence bordering the neighbour's property. Ron's eyes sparkled as he walked around touching the large lemon tree, dark grapevines, two almond trees and a number of other bushy plants.

'Our own bushland!' he exclaimed. 'What I couldn't do with this!' I had to almost drag him away from the yard to have a look at the house. It was very ordinary, except for the spacious kitchen with a dark slate floor and the bathroom large enough for everyone in the family, all at once, and sporting an antique four-legged porcelain and iron bathtub. Off the master bedroom was a small louvred alcove set apart by stained-glass French doors.

Ron and I looked at each other. All I could see in his eyes was the reflection of the garage—the Aussie shed—and the trees and bushes of the back yard. I knew that this was it—our home. We said yes on the spot, never mind the lean-to verandah in the front. One day we would have it fixed up.

The clincher that told us we had made the right choice came after we moved in and met our neighbours. Doreen Fraser had been born and bred in the house we had just bought. When she married Wally, they built themselves a home next door so they could be near her mother during her advancing years. When we met Doreen she was close to seventy-five years old. Some called her the 'mayoress' of Millen Street, a 'real' Kalgoorlie-Boulder woman. Better known as a 'local'. Her father had been a loyal and fervent member of the Church of Christ, driving his children to Sunday school in a horse and cart and sponsoring prayer meetings in their kitchen for the Aboriginal people and missionaries of Cundeelee, three hours drive along the Transline out from Kalgoorlie. Ron had worked with those same missionaries during the 1960s, when he had travelled through that area, connecting with the tribal mob.

This house was definitely meant to be ours: it had a history, a 'Ron' sort of history, it was a sacred site. Ron planted every sort of native plant and rosebush that he could find. Gardening became his passion, his escape from the pressure and demands of those around him. Eventually all of our artefacts, historical papers, books, photographs, ball and chain from early convict days, tools and guitars made their move from Marribank and we settled in.

Wally and Doreen looked after us as their own, adopting us as family, looking after the chickens that we raised, the kangaroos that hopped in our backyard and our two dogs, Toby and Maru, who now had to endure being chained up after years of freedom at Marribank. Over the next decade, we still would travel, crossing Australia again and again, flying to Japan, New Zealand and America, all the while knowing that our home and animals were safe in their care.

Another reason that Kalgoorlie was 'home' was because we had real relations, real family, there. Ron's sister Rosie had lived in Kalgoorlie for many years after meeting and marrying Hector Brennan in Leonora. Rosie had been born in Carrolup, only a month after Old Mary had died, during the settlement days, eventually coming under the care of Grannie Grace, just as Ron had in his early years. Rosie's father was old Paddy Coyne, from Albany way, a bush lawyer they had called him.

Rosie had inherited her dad's quick wittedness and had become a kindergarten teacher. In the mid-1960s she had made a trip to India with a singing group sponsored by Moral Re-Armament, under the watchful eye of the Beazley family. Rosie was the only Aboriginal in the group, which had been put together to support unity and reconciliation among all cultures and countries. Training sessions were held in Canberra where

Rosie heard leaders from around the world speak of peace. Her friend and another member of the group was Kim Beazley.

'Grannie used to stay at the Beazley's house in Perth waitin' for Rosie to come back. The old fella, Mr Beazley, he was a good man, friendly to us blackfellas,' explained Ron.

Even as a teenager, Rosie had a desire to 'have a say in how things turn out in this world'. She was attracted to the vision of Moral Re-Armament in regard to global transformation, seeing cultures unite and healing the wounds of history. Moral Re-Armament had an agenda for reconciliation long before the word became so popular. Its beginnings were marked by its important role in reconciling France and Germany after World War II.

Then, in the mid-1960s, during a threat of armed conflict in north-east India, the first Moral Re-Armament camp was formed to train young people to bring peace to their nation. This came on the heels of Mahatma Gandhi's grandson leading a march of several thousand Indians from southern India to New Delhi, a march that was to be the foundation of this peace movement.

Rosie was asked to fly to India to be a part of this camp, to sing of reconciliation and to stand committed to the building of community relationships, alongside a young Kim Beazley and others from Australia.

At this same time, Ron was living in the desert with tribal people, searching his own heart for the direction and healing of his people, and I was in Massachusetts, grieving over the shooting death of Robert Kennedy, questioning the American dream and struggling with the drama of the war in Vietnam.

Rosie and I had met a couple of months after Ron and I became engaged. 'I want you to go and meet my sister,' he said to me on the phone from the eastern part of Australia. 'She'll welcome you, no worries. Just tell her you're engaged to her brother.' As I stood at the coin phone booth in Laverton with the desert wind blowing across the receiver, I didn't catch the little chuckle that had escaped from his mouth.

I had written the address on a bit of paper: 16E Campbell Street. I had driven the borrowed car around and around the streets looking for the number. All the houses in Kalgoorlie seemed to be surrounded by high corrugated-iron fences, giving the impression that no trespassers were allowed. I didn't know if people were just unfriendly or they were trying to keep out the dust from the mining dumps. I finally decided to cross the railroad tracks. There I found it.

A tin house, blue paint fading from years in the sun, and scrawled in white paint on the front fence was 16E. The house looked dark and the curtains were drawn, giving an unwelcoming appearance. As I gingerly opened the front gate, the high-pitched squeaks brought a chorus of barking dogs from around the back corner of the house. All of a sudden I had second thoughts. What if she doesn't like me? What if she isn't home? What am I going to say? 'Hello, I'm going to marry your brother?' My mind was spinning in a thousand directions as I approached the front door. Little did I know that only strangers went to the front door. Once you know Rosie, you go to the back door. It's much more open and friendly. I knocked.

I stood for what seemed a long time. I knocked again and listened to what I thought seemed like scurrying and, through the corner of my eye, I thought I saw a curtain move at the window facing the verandah. I was almost ready to give up when the door opened a crack. 'Yeh,' said a voice.

'Uh, I was just looking for Rosie Brennan. Is this the right place? Her brother Ron sent me.' At that the door swung open, with whoever opened it standing behind. The room was dark since all the curtains were pulled. As my eyes became used to the darkness, I saw two men sitting on stuffed chairs staring at a television, not looking up at me at all.

Out from the next room, came a tall, imposing woman. 'I'm Rosie.'

There I was, in the middle of the room, with only the background of television murmuring behind me and I didn't know what to say next. I introduced myself again and haltingly told her that I was engaged to her brother Ron. She stared right at me, then turned toward the kitchen.

'Come through,' she said. As soon as we settled around the kitchen table, she relaxed. 'I think I saw you, on that New Year's night at Little Sisters. The last time I saw Ron. So you're the one, huh. I've been hearing something.' From that moment on, Rosie was my friend.

Rosie's kitchen became one of the focal points of our life in Kalgoorlie. An old Metters wood stove was embedded in the wall, a small electric stove next to it; there was paint peeling off the walls underneath posters of football players, old calendars and jigsaw puzzles that had been completed and glued together many years before. The floor was made of wooden planks that had slightly separated over time, the gaps providing a place to sweep the crumbs. Chooks and roosters strutted past and aimlessly pecked their way through the room, sporadically chased by the dogs that freely roamed the house. The fridge often contained the results of a night of hunting kangaroo, with legs, tails and backs covering its shelves.

The kitchen table, red top with chrome legs, took centre stage. A blend of mismatched chairs surrounded it, two of them snuggled next to the fire. Family yarns were spun around that table, police brought wayfaring youngsters there and an assortment of homeless strays eventually found their way to Rosie's motherly care. She was a social worker in her own right. Tears were spilled in her presence, teenage girls who had just found out they were pregnant received encouragement and comfort, young men just released on bail received their kindly lecture from her lips. Rosie knew everyone and everything that was going on.

When Rosie had turned the marrying age, Grannie had pleaded with Ron to take her to the goldfields, where she could get some more education, start to work and 'find a nice man to marry'. The elderly people of the tribes, particularly the grandmothers, held the kinship patterns in their memories and would usually direct the younger ones toward what 'skin group' they could marry. With the Noongar tribes being so mixed up with the removal of children and break-up of family and tradition, the grandmothers struggled to make sure that the young ones married 'right'. Often this meant being sent away so they didn't marry a relative.

Rosie had found work at a hostel that housed Wongi children who were attending school in Leonora, and that's where she met Hector. Hector was a hard worker, keeping the same job at the gold smelter in Kalgoorlie for over twenty years. Many a night he was called in to pour the gold, millions of dollars worth, which was dug up from the soil of tribal land throughout the goldfields. He came from a long-established family, keepers of the tribal legends, holders of much of the goldfields' lands' secrets. Their oldest daughter, Gloria, was the first Aboriginal to attend the University of Western Australia and, when she died of cancer, her life taken before her prime, a scholarship was established in her honour. Hector's father, old Jim Brennan, was decorated during World War II, a veteran of Tobruk and other 8th Army battles.

It was good to be around family after four years in the south-west, to celebrate Christmas together, to learn about gold-detecting in the bush, to have some place to relax and be yourself, where Lydia could connect with her roots. It was Ron's Uncle Barney who grabbed my heart, the uncle who had once pulled on Ron's ears when he was a kid and called him 'you little pig with big ears, always listenin' in', and who growled at Ron when he drank himself silly after his grandfather died. It was Uncle Barney who showered Lydia with affection, wrapping his big brown arms around her fair skin and ordering Ron to look after his family.

'Ya got yer own kid now. Ya gotta look after 'em properly. Don't get so busy wanderin' around that you leave 'em behind,' he'd say when I wasn't around.

It was a rather new experience for Ron to live so close to family since, unlike many other Noongars, he had travelled so far from his roots during his lifetime. But it was here in Kalgoorlie that we felt so much at home.

Uncle Barney was the quintessential bushman with a gentle smile, dark skin and eyes that twinkled with uncanny perception of the natural world. He often went barefoot, followed by a pack of dogs. Some would describe him as a hermit, for he shied away from towns. His knowledge of world news came from the radio, his constant companion, since he never learned to read or write. Like most other Noongar men his age, Barney had roamed the farms of the south coast, helping clear timber and stack bales, shearing and horsebreaking.

'Give me a horse with a bit of spirit,' he'd say. He came as close as any Noongar to being a genuine 'horse whisperer'. He had a way of talking to them, handling the meanest devil of them all with a gentle touch. The animals of the bush knew his voice when he tramped through the hills feeding the dingos and caring for their puppies. 'Dogs are quick to forgive,' was his wisdom.

Barney never married, but he was a true 'pop' for all the kids in the clan. Discipline in Aboriginal camps can be somewhat erratic, with tempers flaring and the odd whack now and then. Often a blind eye is turned, but Barney would just speak a word, never looking up from his wood carving as he sat around the fire. The kids listened, never gave him cheek, answered back or resented his presence. Just having him around brought peace and calm to the situation. When family anger burst open and fights started, a call would come up: 'Get Barney, quick!'

Barney faced danger many times: wild cattle in the scrub, wild bulls in a paddock, tidal rips in the ocean currents along the south coast of Australia. His advice when facing danger was 'don't fight against the current or you'll get weak and drown; swim out of it and catch an incoming one.' During a family outing at the coast, he had saved Coral and another girl from drowning when they had gone too far out. Drunk at the time, he jumped into the ocean and grabbed hold of them, yelling out a prayer to God: 'Lord, I'm just an old drunken man, but help me save these two little girls.' The distraught family watched while he battled the currents, carried along by a supernatural strength, then emerged on the shore with a little girl under each arm.

Barney's journeys had taken him from his old tumbledown cabin on North Garnett's farm at Bremer Bay where he had worked for a number of years, to the reserve camp on the edge of Kalgoorlie under the mine dumps. He and a few other drop-ins camped in tin sheds at the reserve. He would walk back and forth to Rosie's 'camp', followed by his mob of dogs, never going too far from his own turf. But that bit of turf was surrounded by gold, around and underneath, hiding deep from the mine blaster's dynamite. He told us that the mining company had promised some money to buy him a house, but in the end there had been nothing.

It was hard for any of us and especially Uncle Barney to understand the corporate manipulations of multinational business deals. The word 'buy' might have meant 'rent' and the word 'rent' might have meant 'sell'. Everything was vague; it was several years before the Mabo decision would make the headlines, opening the floodgates for land claims, and a long time before the Aboriginal people had any power to stop mining or change its direction.

The light in Barney's eyes had begun to fade when the bulldozers came and knocked down his tin hut, crushing it like a matchstick as he lowered his head. Against the background of the Kalgoorlie mining dumps and a western sky streaked with desert hues of golds and reds, reflecting the heat of the earth, we watched a lone, gentle, bearded Aboriginal bushman linger for a moment against the background of a large, rumbling metal machine of modern 'progressive' Australia, sweeping away whatever was in its path. All his dreams vanished as the huge bulldozer's blades dug into what he thought was his bit of red earth.

A 'room' of our own, a home, a hut, an area of space on this planet is what gives us reality. We exist if we have a place to be. Barney's meagre belongings were moved, the walls of his hut were crushed, and with them, came the crushing of his spirit. He never got over it; instead, he sought to dull the pain of 'no place left for me' through the anaesthetic of amber fluid swirling in brown bottles. It was eventually to take his life, lying on his cot in the back of a rented house surrounded by his dogs.

Uncle Barney's spirit still lives on, in his nieces and nephews, and in Lydia. He used to hold her in his lap, tell her stories of the bush and watch over her with the alertness of a father eagle. His love of animals lives on in our little girl, as she cares for the strays, mends the broken wings, and collects dogs wherever she walks.

For those who had lived on the reserve their 'home' had been shaken, torn open and fractured. The roar of the machinery of mining had blown their dust away, as smoke is blown away by the wind.

⭐ ⭐ ⭐

Number 7 Millen Street was our home, a space for us to be. Even though Ron had spent his life on walkabout, often quoting that 'Jesus had no home', he grasped this quarter acre home to his heart. It was his. Every bit of space in the yard was planted with a cutting from all over Australia and even from other places in the world. Ron not only had a green thumb, but a green hand. Every seemingly dead stick that he put into the ground eventually sprouted. He tended his garden with the care a loving parent shows his child. The plants grew and when visitors stepped inside our gate the bare world of the street in front of the house turned into a replica of the Australian bush of the south-west in front of their very eyes.

There was the rambling pink rose bush that had been in Grannie's garden at the Mount Barker reserve; a red bottlebrush that had been growing in the Stirlings; white dainty flowers, shaped like little kimonos, brought from Tokyo. Each plant spoke a story, a history of another time and another place.

Ron placed his stamp on the outside of the house, in the earth. I placed my stamp within the rooms and walls to make it my home. The last time I had owned anything was back in Massachusetts, and the colonial home on a hill surrounded by oak trees had disappeared from my view after the divorce. I had let it and all the unhappiness surrounding it fade from my memory. Now, fifteen years later, with two continents and an ocean in between, I was creating a place of my own. I painted, I sewed, I created, I bought. Our life was lived so much in the open, in another's territory, in another world and culture to mine, that I was desperately thirsty for a personal place of retreat.

Books began to line the walls, a computer buzzed in the corner, an antique oak table covered by a one hundred per cent cotton cloth from India sat in the middle of the kitchen. Aboriginal paintings hung alongside a framed cross-stitch of the Lord's Prayer, reminding us daily of our life's calling. Most of the furniture from Marribank had been left behind, donated to the community that was gradually disbanding. That furniture had reminded us of another life relationship and had no connection to me. The only piece we brought with us was a heavy wooden scroll desk with small cubbyholes for precious relics and drawers to hold future memories.

It was on this desk that I set my most significant momento, a studio photograph of my mother, taken at her high school graduation when she was eighteen years old. I lovingly placed it in a heavy ceramic frame, hand-painted with pale blue and yellow flowers on a cream background outlined in gold leaf. Her dark hair, reaching the nape of her neck and with curls and waves, parted in the middle, as was the fashion of the 1940s, was pushed back from her face, highlighting the soft squareness of her jawline. She was gazing into the distance, a slight smile at the curve of her lips and one eyebrow raised higher than the other, as if critically appraising what the future might hold.

Often a visitor to our home, on passing by the desk in the lounge room, would pause, then look at me. 'Is that you?' they would ask.

It must have been that question that caused me to think of my mother more often. Others followed. Who was I, really? How do I walk between two cultures? Do I have to give up my own in order to embrace another? What should Ron be gleaning from my culture? What stand would our daughter take? What I had previously considered as weaknesses in my mother's character were now becoming strengths. I could see myself in her, only brought to my attention by our visitors' comments. Our move to Kalgoorlie had intensified my need for family identity—my own.

Living in an Aboriginal community was slowly loosening my grip on western patterns of life—emphasis on the individual, orientation toward material success, tight organisation and linear thinking. Even so, there were a few connections that I still had to hold onto, a part of me that I could not let go. It was only much later that I would realise that I didn't have to let them go. They were a part of my own 'dreaming', and I could still be myself and be a part of Ron's mob too. I could respect the gifts of my own culture as well as those of the Aboriginal culture and hold them in balance, even though that proved to be the most complex challenge of all. How well I handled this balance would, no doubt, become a model for Lydia to follow. These conversations within myself were prompted by the photograph of my mother. When I saw her eyes penetrating my thoughts while I walked through the lounge day after day, I gratefully celebrated the gift of my birth and the gift of my own daughter.

There was another photograph that took its place in our lives. After Uncle Barney's death we drove to Bremer Bay along the coastal waters somewhere between Esperance and Albany, mainly to visit the spirit of the old man in his cabin. Ron wanted to meditate on the past, recapture his uncle's memory and honour his story. We had walked through the remains of the cabin years before, during our first year of marriage, and the place hadn't changed. Remains of camp fires were scattered under the trees, old clothes were piled in the corners between the walls, which were cracking with age and lack of care.

'That's where Barney's pet snake used to sleep. And this must be the old fella's bed,' Ron reminisced as he pointed to the rafters in the ceiling and then to the corner where a blackened metal bed frame lay crumpled.

I gingerly walked through the rubble, careful not to disturb any spiders' nests and half in fear that a snake would start to uncoil at the intrusion. From a corner, on top of a pile of cloth, rotting away with mildew, my eye caught a glimpse of something shiny. I looked again, stooped to grasp this small metal object and realised it was a photo frame. I picked it up and there staring up at me was an aging, slightly water-marked black-and-white image of Ron's grandmother, Grannie Grace, and two small children.

Her eyes too, just like my mother's, were focused beyond the camera to a distant scene. Her face was strong, a firm set to her jaw, fair skin, the round Noongar nose and gently flowing dark hair parted slightly left of centre. It was a family 'find', a reminder of one who suffered, but survived, through government removals, to become the woman who had guided Ron's life with such deftness of hand, and the one whose great-grand-daughter would carry her name, as well as some of her character, into the next generation.

Two women who had featured prominently in our lives, either directly or indirectly, had come into our home, following the gaze of their eyes toward their future generations, a constant reminder of our inheritance.

❂ ❂ ❂

I began teaching at Kalgoorlie College in communications and general office skills. Even though I needed a job, I could only manage part-time as my responsibilities toward Lydia had become immensely important in my life, both practically and emotionally. In my earlier years, being part of the 1970s liberation of women, I had thought that a true modern woman would never allow the entrance of a child into her life to curtail what she considered as an equally or even more-important career life. Not that a child wasn't important, but somehow I thought that all these facets of life would mingle together happily. For the modern woman, that is.

I had never considered that spending my days teaching, counselling and speaking was mere 'work'; rather, it was 'my *life's* work.' There was a sense of destiny in my mind even as a young girl, as a university student, during my teaching career, in my move to New York, and in my landing in Australia. They were all pathways of destiny. I hadn't anticipated the even greater influence my daughter would have on that destiny. Each day that I left her behind, albeit in her father's care, I felt a pang of guilt. But I had to work to live.

'All I can do is talk,' said Ron. 'I can do that pretty good, but no one pays you much money for it.' Even though Ron had traversed Australia and was well-known in Aboriginal communities and church circles, he had never had a steady income to live on. Sometimes driving along the back roads he would find a drum of petrol that had fallen off the back of a truck, just in time to fill his car. Other times, not having any money left for food after travelling all night, he would pray for someone who would pour out his story of a lost love or a lonely life, and that grateful soul would buy him a meal.

Most of his life, Ron just trusted that somehow he would be taken care of, that as he went about answering the needs of others, his turn would eventually come. His days had no time clock, no punched-in hours, but instead they were fluid, organic, a schedule that made itself as the day wore on.

My days were the opposite. The bell rang, the time clock ticked, the deadlines loomed, the paycheck came on time. I came home exhausted after teaching class, visiting students, paying bills, buying food, planning the evening meal, checking that I had enough nappies for Lydia. I welcomed the moment I could walk through our door, to my safe place, a retreat from other demands, but even there, the world followed me in.

'Auntie Diana,' a voice would whisper on the phone. 'Can you or Uncle just pick us up, down by the pub. We gotta get home. I'm sick.' Most phone calls and knocks on the door were signals for help.

'It must be midnight,' I would think as I rolled over to the sound of the phone ringing and began groping for the phone.

'This is one of the prison wardens. Could Ron come and talk to some of the girls here? Something's spooked them . . . saw a spirit or something . . . they won't sleep.' Ron would be up and dressed and out the door, returning to our bed a couple of hours before daybreak. Another call answered. Until the next time.

I would have just served our meal, a special one. Fish, one of Ron's favourites. A slab of barramundi. There would be a knock. It would be Gillian. 'Anybody with you?' She never came alone. Out from the shadows would step Maitland. 'We don't have anywhere to camp tonight. Can you put us up?' Maitland was Ron's cousin. They usually camped under the railway bridge, but it was cold that night, raining.

Juggling an organised, time-clock existence with spontaneous, moment-by-moment turns of events was difficult. We set up an extra room for those who turned up in the middle of the night. We kept extra chops and bread for those who had no food. There was always fuel to make a 'taxi' run in the early hours of the morning after a distress call.

The only time I had to say 'no' was when I was home alone and Lydia was asleep and too young for me to leave her alone. Other times I would bundle her up in a blanket, gently deposit her in the car and drive to perform whatever service was required at the moment. It might be a carload of fringe dwellers who suddenly decided they needed to go to a relative's house or were fearful of the local miners doing 'burns' around their camp.

Our four-wheel-drive would hold sometimes twelve or more adults and children and a baby or two. Sometimes a dog would jump in as well. The ladies who usually sat in the front with me would cuddle Lydia, giving her a sloppy, somewhat inebriated kiss on the cheek, while Lydia looked on with suspicious eyes. When the destination at the town camps, the railway bridge, or the hostel at the end of the main street was reached, one by one the vehicle was relieved of its load, with many thank-yous and a request for a few dollars for some 'mayi'—a bit of tucker to fill the stomach for the night.

The times that I was away or at work and Ron was called out to prison, to the hospital to visit a dying patient or a hit-and-run accident victim, or to the lock-up to comfort a distraught teenager who had been apprehended in a stolen car, Lydia went with him. She was too young to remember the event, but I could imagine what her dark eyes were taking in.

These were the times when the tensions would mount and our tempers would fray. These were the moments when the clash of cultures came with a fury. The opposing forces of timelessness and spontaneity against schedules and planning created its own electric energy. I found it harder than Ron to adjust. I had to live in the two worlds more than he did. There was not an expectation for him to be organised, to be on time, to answer a deadline.

It was just the opposite for me. There was not only the expectation that a white person would handle pressure and deadlines but the expectation I had for myself coming from my own culture. Even when I understood it intellectually, the physical and emotional toll was draining. It was only in the depths of my home, back in my bedroom or in the little nook behind the French doors, that I could find a refuge, 'a room of my own'. Sometimes that room shook with anger, many times it swirled with tears, at others it was calm, quiet, healing. It was much easier to find one's space in one culture or another. It was the precarious tightrope walk in the middle that presented the greatest challenges.

I could understand fully the dilemma that the fringe dwellers faced, as 'people in between', walking their own kind of tightrope. They were a hot topic in the goldfields press and at city council meetings, if the letters to the editor berating the 'Aboriginal eyesores of Kalgoorlie' were anything to go by. No sooner had one solution been mooted than a barrage of headlines would appear, blaring comments like: 'Drunks in the Shop Doorways Again' or 'Hit-and-Run: Dark Shadows Hard to See Crossing the Road'. I approached the college for permission to develop a series of seminars on Aboriginal culture and society, which would be offered to the community in an exercise of 'raising awareness'. It was a great idea, they thought. The college had been instrumental in developing programs in recent years for Aboriginal people to learn skills in running small businesses, mining operations and human resources.

The Aboriginal elders were enthusiastic and eager to be the lecturers. Perhaps people will listen to us now and understand, they said. The topics they chose ranged from stories and songs, health and law, land and traditional life, to reserves and the future. Laurel Cooper, Reg Johnson, Myrtle Brennan and others who had lived through the government settlement days, who had been taken from their mothers and communities, who had walked the hard miles to achieve what they had, would share their experiences.

The build-up was exciting. For the Wongi people to have their say, to be the teachers, when most of the time they were ignored, might make a difference in Kalgoorlie. Or so we thought!

The course was never offered. The college had to cancel it because only two whitefellas registered. It was not 'economically viable', said the registrar. Economics continued to be the balance beam of social interaction and understanding. Ten years later a prominent Aboriginal matron commented: 'Kalgoorlie is still not ready for reconciliation.'

◉ ◉ ◉

Kalgoorlie was almost one thousand kilometres from the south-west, but distance didn't stop us from being called on to take funerals for Noongar families. At each visit we heard of more families moving away from Marribank, some finding work in Katanning, others drifting to parts unknown. The new leaseholders had no vision for its future, providing only for a caretaker to make sure the houses weren't vandalised. The caretakers came and went every few months. The pottery wheels had stopped turning and the brightly coloured fabric expressing the Noongar way had disappeared.

I asked myself over and over why it had happened, why Marribank hadn't worked. My thoughts wandered back to Lester Coyne from Albany—who was, as I found out, Rosie's cousin—'No one should walk ahead, even if you have good ideas'. That was it—even well-intentioned help can drain the energy of the heart, where ideas originate and where dreams are formed.

The Noongars, and maybe most Aboriginal people around the country, didn't feel they were trusted to do what needed to be done. Over the years many of their ideas have been hijacked and become someone else's, and then it was easier for Aboriginal people to back off with the attitude, 'Let's see what the whitefella's gonna do with this'. Not many government programs let them walk the pathway themselves, make mistakes if they had to, but still with encouragement to keep going. They didn't own the dream, lock, stock and barrel. If anyone truly wants something, if they really have a dream of their own, they'll usually go for it, even if it means sacrifice.

I've seen Aboriginal people sacrifice plenty for each other, for what was really important to them. They've had to do it through all their generations. But these government programs, 'package deals', were too big, too complex, designed for the whitefella. Once these big rocks started to roll, it was too hard to keep up and definitely too hard to stop. To stop the government machine requires a big voice and at that time the Aboriginal voice had to fight hard to be heard. And sometimes people get tired of having to fight so hard.

CHAPTER 14

Let My People Go

L ydia had just turned two years old. She was a bright button, a
keen observer, and talked a lot, both in English and desert lingo.
Even at this age, she sometimes would play happily alone while
at other times she craved the company of other children.

The morning had passed uneventfully, but by lunchtime I felt strangely
exhausted and ill. I crawled into bed, something I often wanted to do but
never had a chance to. Lydia dragged her stuffed dog next to me and then
went to play with her extra-large pieces of Lego. What was wrong with
me? Why was I so tired? The days and weeks had been going so fast
and had been so crammed that I could barely remember where we had
been, what we had done, or problems that had been solved. I knew I was
physically present, but I felt that my spirit hadn't caught up with my body
and the next day I was scheduled to fly to Warburton.

There's no room in our lives for anything except social problems, I
thought to myself. The emotions are getting more than I can handle.
Death, prison, violence. Always on our doorstep. I need family time, too,
for the three of us. And so does Lydia. And so does Ron, I thought
emphatically. He's just letting it slip by. He has told me so many times
that God has given him a second chance to be a husband and a father to
his own child. He never took much notice the first time around.

What had he said to me? 'I never saw how a family was supposed to
be, Diana. The missionaries never taught us. We never saw them with

their families much. They sent their kids away to school. And some of us never knew our fathers or our mothers. I just don't know how. I guess I run away from it sometimes.'

Maybe that is what's bothering me, I pondered. I feel like I'm being smothered under all these demands.

I was desperate to find a balance between the demands of our work and the desire to find a pathway of normality for Lydia. I was keenly aware of the need for her to accept her Aboriginality, to embrace it as wonderful, special and unique, but I also wanted to shield her from the harshness of its reality. Even at two years of age she sensed the traumas of life that were played out around her.

At times she would hide in fear under the seat of our four-wheel-drive when we picked up people along the street who were drunk, angry or cut in a fight. 'Why he drink that yucky water, Mum?' I had no answer.

At other times, she grinned when a tribal grandmother waving a stick to keep the dogs away planted a very wet kiss on her cheek.

❂ ❂ ❂

I climbed out of the six-seater Ngaanytjarra plane, clutching on to Lydia, reassuring her that this would be fun. I had flown to the desert community of Warburton to teach basic business skills for a week. Ron was to follow in our vehicle so we could spend an additional two weeks travelling through the red dust country.

'You gotta call, Diana. Come quick.' One of the ladies who worked in the community advisor's office puffed out the words.

I couldn't imagine what had happened or why I was getting a call. Ron was supposed to be already on the road to Warburton, so it couldn't be him.

I cradled the receiver of the radiophone in my hands listening to Ron break the news, his voice crackling over the phone.

'Your mother's very sick, Diana. Family rang up. She went in for a heart operation, but the pathologist found cancer in the bone marrow. So they stopped the operation just in time. Your mother has cancer.'

I was stunned. My family links seemed to be stretching thinner, almost to breaking point. I had been so consumed by everybody else's problems,

I hadn't even had time to think of my own family. And they were so far away. It had been years since I had seen them.

'Over and out,' I whispered into the phone.

There was no one to help me grieve. Ever since Lydia was born, my mother and I had spoken together on the phone once a month. One month she called me, and then the next month I called her.

Our conversations were usually about the past. She kept me informed about Pat and how her illness was being treated, rather unsuccessfully as it turned out, and I usually asked her questions about my own childhood. Information about my own antics, mishaps, childish ways and dreams took on new importance as I worked my way through motherhood.

I knew I had to see her and that I wanted her to see Lydia, her only grandchild from her first-born daughter. When we got back home to Kalgoorlie, I made plans to go to America.

We landed in Tulsa, greeted by Bruce, my mother's husband, dressed in his usual cowboy hat and boots. He was a quiet man, with a gentle way about him, but he hardly smiled, and I didn't know him well enough to tell what he was thinking. 'She's sicker than you think, Diana. You'll see when we get home. She was too weak to come to the airport.'

We travelled the two hours toward home. My mother's home. It was never mine. I had moved away before my parents split, before she bought this house.

I walked in the back door from the garage, and made my way toward the lounge room, where I heard the voices of my mother and auntie and uncle. She had her back to me, sitting on the edge of the sofa. When she turned to look at me my face smiled, but inside I was crying out, 'No! No!' She was like a skeleton, her eyes sunk into her head, her skin pale, drained of any colour. Her thin frame was covered by a cream-coloured cotton gown and matching robe and the fingers of her hand as she reached out to me were bony, veins protruding. I gently held her to me, trying to smile. I greeted my aunt and uncle and then excused myself as I raced out to the back and convulsed in tears with a helpless feeling churning in the pit of my stomach. My mother! How could this be!

Day by day, she improved. We talked continuously of old times, of childhood memories. She wrote out a family tree for the Greer genera- tions, we took photos together, she beamed over Lydia. The night before we left, she dressed up for the first time to join us for dinner at her favourite restaurant.

Later we sat together on the bed, sifting through her jewellery, turning the pages of photo albums, laughing and intermittently crying. 'I want you to have this when I go,' she said, as she placed her hand in mine. She showed me her diamond ring. It was huge, almost a carat, a beautiful solitaire held by six gold prongs. Her aunt had passed it down to my mother and now it was her most prized possession. I shook my head and cried. I couldn't acknowledge the gift because I didn't want to lose my mother. She cradled me with her arms like she used to when I was a child.

⦿ ⦿ ⦿

A year later, I was awakened at four in the morning by a phone call. It was the voice of my uncle. 'Diana, I have bad news to tell you, honey. Your mother died just after lunch today. It was sudden, nothing we could do.' The day was 28 May, Memorial Day in the United States, remembrance for those who had fought in the wars. She had spent the morning writing letters, arranging the top of her dresser in the bedroom. She and Bruce had sat down for lunch and as she finished eating and pushed her chair back from the table, she just leaned over and stopped living.

I screamed into the phone. Part of me was gone. I was being left by one whom I had struggled with, one whom I had misunderstood and had misunderstood me, one whom I had grown to love and who I knew loved me. I felt suddenly so alone.

That day, a leader in our church from the Koara tribe in Leonora put his arms around me and wailed in the Aboriginal way for my mother. He had never met her, but he knew *me*, and he grieved for my loss. I didn't have the money to go to the funeral, and the whitefella tradition is to get it over and done with in three days. But two months later, due to my mother's will, there was enough money for Lydia and me to go together to stand by her crypt, touch her name, place the flowers and cry together.

Lydia was only three and she didn't understand, although she had attended many funerals. As we sat on the ground in front of the crypt, she gently placed her hands on my face, touching the stream of salty tears, and then stroked my cheeks before laying her head on my breast.

'Don't cry, Mummy,' she whispered. My mother's ring glistened in the sunlight.

❁ ❁ ❁

I came home again. Along with me came four large boxes packed with relics from Vermont: the cherry-wood chair, the brass lamp and the gold-framed oil painting of a New England cottage by the lake. Connections to my own past that were as important to me as Ron's photographs were to him. Stuffed in between each of these objects were a few items from my mother's closet: a lap rug I had knitted for her a decade ago, two pairs of her shoes, and a mink jacket with her name embroidered in the lining.

'It's rather silly to have a mink, isn't it, Ron?' I slipped the jacket on and paraded in front of him. 'Especially here in Kalgoorlie. When would I ever wear it? Can't imagine wearing a mink to Nanny Goat Hill to visit the fringies.'

I couldn't bear to part with it. My mother's name was stitched inside. I couldn't bear to wear it, either, but somehow just having it made her seem closer. One by one, the objets d'art were placed around our home, and each room came to contain a mixture of Aboriginal art, American colonial treasures, and photographs of family members.

I went back to work the next morning. I was running a playgroup at Ninga Mia village, three kilometres outside Kalgoorlie, past the mines. Twice a week I met with the mothers to plan the program and introduce new ideas that might capture the creativity of the young minds of the community with the hope of giving them an extra boost before starting in the primary school.

In traditional Aboriginal life, the parents and relatives of a child, partic-ularly the mothers and grandmothers, were the primary educators. The children were not sent away to a professional in the way that Western society does. When the mothers searched the country for food, they sang and narrated the stories of their ancestors' travels. When they prepared and shared the food during the day, they drew their boundaries in the dirt and demonstrated the significance of the land and its produce to their children. These were important years.

Female solidarity came with sharing activities like childcare, food collection and preparation. Women's business was an important part of life. In their ceremonial, as well as in their daily ritual, women unflinchingly bore their role as nurturers of community, land and relationships.

'Hey, Linda, who we got comin' today?' The tapping sticks tumbled out of the bag onto the tarp that covered part of the verandah in front of the building where we met. We usually met outside, in full view of all the houses. No bells rang, no signal was given, just the slow movement of women walking across the flat when they saw my four-wheel-drive. I often brought Lydia with me. The joy of working with Aboriginal families is that children are always welcome.

I spread out the ingredients for play dough, various pots of paint and large sheets of paper. Mobs of children swarmed around us like bees, momentarily resting on one flower of activity before buzzing off to the next. They appeared and disappeared at the whim of their friends, grabbing a handful of play dough right out from under the noses of the dogs that sniffed around our feet.

When I packed up to leave, after sweeping the concrete verandah of crushed biscuits, pools of cordial and strips of coloured paper, I was usually faced with a few men and women quietly whispering about wanting rides to town.

I turned to see that Spurs had planted himself in the middle of the road, a few metres behind my vehicle. He slowly raised his arm toward me, clutching a rock in his hand. His medium-sized body was slightly bent with the effects of years of drinking. The matted hair that protruded from his head in all directions had begun to turn grey and his eyes penetrated mine with a kind of defiance that he seemed to be mustering up from somewhere in his mind. 'You give me a ride to town,' he growled.

I had first come face to face with Spurs in the Laverton lock-up, before I married Ron. He usually sat along the fence outside the police station with the others, dressed in a T-shirt and khaki trousers. He always asked to play my guitar while he told stories about 'Kurta Ron' when he used to be at Warburton, looked after by Spurs's family. Spurs's father was old Possum, who had worked alongside Ron during the 1960s, clearing wells and planting trees. They had treated Ron like a son, gave him a good feed and admired his singing and guitar-picking.

Spurs had also played Ron's guitar on numerous occasions and had considered himself the best country and western guitarist of the desert, decked out in a silk shirt and cowboy boots. In his prime, he won a buck-jumping contest in Noongar country, shared his prize money with his mates and was awarded a gleaming pair of silver spurs. His Noongar mates had given him his new name. 'Call me Spurs, bro,' he had told Ron.

Twenty years later, an older and angrier Spurs had picked away at my guitar, the one I had brought from New York City.

When he had been released from the Laverton gaol, his celebration at the pub had left his walk a little wobbly and his temper somewhat frayed. When he had demanded that I produce my guitar for him to play and I explained that it was back in my tent three kilometres away, he had given a swipe of his hand near my face, knocking my wire-rimmed spectacles to the ground.

For a moment I had been stunned, not knowing if I should slowly back away, turn and run, or stay and pick up the fallen spectacles. Mustering my courage, I had looked back at him eye-to-eye and said, 'Spurs, you know I'm your friend, and you know I'm marrying Ron. He is like your brother, so I am like your sister. We're family.'

His eyes met mine, and I observed just a glimmer of gentleness begin to shine through. He stooped down to retrieve my glasses and, as he handed them to me, he took my hand, bent his head and mumbled, 'Sorry.' He had been a strong man in those days. His shoulder muscles bulged through tan work-shirts with the sleeves torn out. But the more he ventured into the towns, joining the fringe dweller camps and sleeping under the old railway bridge in all sorts of weather conditions, his body slowly became the victim of disease and sores.

The citizens of towns and cities like Kalgoorlie thought of men like Spurs as 'eyesores'. At best, they were tolerated, as long as they didn't come too close. During the local shows and racing rounds, the city tried to clean up the 'rubbish' that hung about, with complaints appearing in the newspapers and diatribes being aired on the local radio talk-back shows.

Most of the time there were references to the older 'good' Aborigines, the tame ones, the ones who didn't talk back, and who accepted any handout humbly and gratefully. There was always a sigh, a click of the tongue, and a reference to the past as the voice on the radio denounced the appearance of the 'dark shadows' at the edge of town, who dared to find shelter at night in the doorways of the local shops.

Now I faced Spurs again, ten years on, and this time he held a rock in his hand, his only defence against what he saw as a hostile world where he expected rejection at every turn. Since we had moved to Kalgoorlie, he had been a regular passenger in our vehicle. Sometimes he flagged us down in the middle of Federal Road going from Kalgoorlie through to Boulder, barely dodging other cars, which sped up as they passed him by.

Most Sunday nights, he trudged through the front door of our church, bringing his dog and his blanket, making himself a cup of tea while the hymns were sung. Then he would loudly call out for us to sing his favourite, 'The Old Rugged Cross', and would stand up at the microphone and tell us for the fifth time how he had been raised from the dead in the hospital and how he had given the orderly a shock when he sat up on the morgue stretcher when the white sheet was pulled back. 'So you fellas still have me around. I'm not dead yet. I think Jesus saved me, for something, but I'm not sure what.' Everyone clapped for Spurs while he sat down and cried for the lost glory of past days. The past days in the bush, mustering cattle, travelling the roads with one's mates, and the security of traditional life. Someone would sit next to him, put an arm around him and say a prayer. The gift of the Aboriginal church is the patience and acceptance of one another in all their weaknesses and sorrow. Seeing Spurs struggle in the midst of the prison of alcohol and disease, we all loved him.

At the end of the service, he would drink his cup of tea and then wait for us on the front footpath after everyone had gone, the lights were turned off and we had carried our sleeping daughter to the car. Then his bushy head would appear at the driver's window.

'Kurta, can you give me a ride to Ninga Mia?'

'Kurta, can you take me to Brown Avenue to get my blanket before someone takes it?' Most Sunday nights it was past ten o'clock before we slipped our daughter under the covers into her own bed and said goodnight.

This morning I knew he was angry and had had his fill of grog as he stood there clutching the rock. I walked toward him and stopped about two metres away. 'Spurs, you want a ride, huh? What? To town? Now, how about you put that rock down. Ron wouldn't want to see you with that in your hand, and I don't either.' I talked softly, thinking how many times I had been through this before. Then I saw Lydia's head peek over the front seat, her wide eyes staring straight at Spurs.

'Mum, come on,' she shouted.

Spurs dropped the rock, mumbled to himself, hitched up his trousers, which had inched down over his hips, and allowed me to help him into the vehicle. A few other women and a couple of men had joined the scene, respectfully, perhaps fearfully standing back to see what would happen. Then one by one they piled into the vehicle and we were on our way.

'You remember us, sis? We was at your wedding. That was really good, huh? Out in the bush. Laverton, huh?'

'You take me to the hospital! My uncle, gotta see him.'

'You teach me in prison, remember? When you comin' there again? We all wait for you to come.'

The talk going into town ranged from memories to family relationships to recent funerals or a son who was in prison. The voices uttered a mixture of desert lingo, Aboriginal English and sign language. One by one my passengers unwound themselves from the darkness of the back of my personnel carrier, like soldiers emerging from the Trojan Horse, trying to hide from me the fact that they were heading for the pub for their daily 'fix', to dull the pain of living in a world that didn't want them or even care.

The last person to leave was Spurs. He hobbled around to the passenger window and put his hand on Lydia's arm. 'I'm sorry, Yilkari. Your daddy's my good friend.'

Not long after, he spotted Ron across the main street, called out to him in a loud voice, gesturing with his hand for Ron to come. As he approached, Spurs clung to his side, weeping into Ron's chest, stammering out the words. 'It's Colin, my nephew, our nephew. He been finished. He's gone, last night.' Ron guided Spurs to the brown painted park bench that was welded to the footpath outside the shops of the main street. They sat together to mourn Colin.

Ron wept for Colin, remembering him as a white-blond-haired desert boy with bandy legs, who was always running after him at Cosmo Newbery, two hours out of Laverton, where Ron had mustered cattle and dug wells. He would jump up into Ron's big arms, nestle against his chest, and wait to be tickled. Then he would wriggle with laughter, jump down to the ground and skip around to continue the play.

When Ron left the desert and the goldfields, he only saw Colin sporadically, until we moved to Kalgoorlie. There, at Yamatji Ngurra rehabilitation centre, in the early days of our church, we met him again. This time he was struggling with the grog, had a wife, scars from too many fights, and harshness in his eyes.

When Colin and his wife had dropped into a singalong, they listened to the hymns sung in the desert language, the tapping of the sticks, the Aboriginal flavour that permeated the air, and they politely smiled. They also listened to other voices who said that real Christians didn't do that in church, that Aboriginal expression of worship, with sticks and didgeridoos, was wrong. Gradually they had both drifted away.

Colin held no power in white society. After growing up in Cosmo Newbery and drifting into Kalgoorlie and the other mining towns of the goldfields, he had become caught up in the fringe dweller camps, living a life on the edge, standing in the queue at Social Security every other Wednesday morning. But a man needs power over something. A man has to be able to make decisions for his life, to have a reason for being.

The men of the desert once were the warriors, the hunters of their society. In the white world, they had nothing, they had no place of power. So Colin asked for magic power, the power of the darkness, the unspoken power of another world, a world that the naturalistic mind does not comprehend. With that power, he could be boss in his own world, over those immediately around him, and over his wife. That power, combined with the effects of alcohol, exploded one night at Ninga Mia.

The fight had started in the middle of the night. Screaming and yelling, back and forth, between husband and wife, jealousies remembered, accusations hurled, punching and hitting. Colin took a knife, like a spear in his hand, and the power flowed through his arm, through his hand and into the knife as he plunged it into his wife's neck. The blood flowed into a great circle on the ground around where she lay. The relatives screamed, grabbed Colin and beat him senseless, unleashing the fury that lashes out from within a people who have suffered, have lost direction and power and have nowhere to express it, except among themselves.

Ron and I had been called immediately to the scene. The body of the wife had been removed, Colin had been locked up, the blood on the ground had been covered with the red dirt of the community and there was a deathly silence covering Ninga Mia.

Colin was given a twelve-year sentence. When he awoke from the beating, lying in the cell cot, and was told what he had done, his eyes turned glassy, as if, at that moment, his mind had retreated to another world. He never remembered what happened that night. He had loved his wife so much, beyond any words that his mouth could utter. The pain was almost too much to bear.

It was a story we heard many times in places like Laverton, Kalgoorlie and Alice Springs. In each town, I had cradled a woman's head in my arms, blood oozing from the back of her head, her fella raging on while Ron held him and walked him away from the scene. There was always a 'sorry', there was always a decision to never do this again, yet so many Aboriginal women carry the scars of violence on their bodies. The 'sorrys' continue until one day the woman is no longer there, no longer in anyone's camp.

It would be so easy to blame the men for this, to turn the violence back onto them, but the reasons are so complex, entangled with the dark threads of many injustices from the past. The pressures of living in a society that does not really want them continues to sap the hope from the heart of the Aboriginal male. Within a few short generations, the heads of the clans and Aboriginal families have been moved away from the authority of the warrior-hunter. Then moved again from the illustrious life of the drover and the horse-breaker, to finally end up as a circle of men, gathered under the trees on the fringes of town, dreaming of their past and what could have been, staring into the brown liquid of the bottle.

Colin was sent to prison in Perth, not to return again to the goldfields for more than six years. In prison, not a day went by that his wife's face did not appear to him, that he did not think of her and his guilt. It was all he could do to put one foot in front of another throughout the sameness of his days locked up.

His dark eyes deepened within his skull, the top of his head showing signs of balding, while he grew a long black beard. If he ever looked like a warrior from the desert, it was at that moment. But while he was tall and straight on the outside, on the inside he was suffering. Gradually the grief and fear of tribal punishment began to take its toll on his body. His diabetes was crippling him, and illnesses didn't seem to go away. After six years, he was finally transferred to the regional prison in the goldfields so his family could visit him.

They came in droves. His mother, Nancy, who had sat for years amid her circle of friends on the fringes of Kalgoorlie and cried for her son, was finally able to touch his hand. His mother-in-law stepped quietly into the visitor's room, cried with him, and forgave him. 'You have suffered too much already. I know you loved my daughter.'

He called for Ron to come and see him. 'Kurta, I'm getting sick. I don't think I have too much longer to go. But I want to talk to you.' Ron stayed with him for hours as he spilled out his life, the memories wrapping themselves around them both, as if to free Colin from the past.

'I've given away the magic powers that made me kill the wife I loved,' he said. One night he had had a dream, a very clear vision, the sort that speaks reality to the Aboriginal heart and mind. He was in a clearing somewhere in the desert, facing a line of tribal warriors, all with spears, dust rising from the ground shimmering with the heat. It was the time for punishment.

A voice, a strong, but gentle voice, spoke in his ear. It wasn't a voice to be afraid of. It wasn't a voice to harm him, but a voice to guide him. 'Walk on,' the voice said.

In the tribal way, he would have to dodge the spears if he wanted to live, but he knew that was impossible. As he walked toward the line of warriors, the first spear came flying toward him. He didn't dodge. The spear flew past with a whistle and then it was gone.

'It took something away from me, that marbarn, magic,' said Colin. 'I knew because that smell went, smell of death went past.'

Another spear and another. They all passed him by as he closed his eyes to each one. Then the last warrior stood before him. It was his own cousin, a man who never missed. They stood eye to eye, warrior to warrior, death to death. The spear left his hand, whistling right toward him. This time Colin did not take his eyes off his cousin. He could feel the breeze of the spear as it flew next to his ear and hit the ground behind him.

He continued to walk toward the men, reaching down to pick up one of the spears that had dropped onto the dirt. When he stood up, the spear turned into a cross in his hand, and he smiled at his cousin. At that moment he awoke and he knew he had been forgiven. He was now free, free from the custody of guilt. A few days later, his cousin rang him up in prison and spoke the words 'I forgive you' into the phone.

Spurs gripped Ron's hand as they continued to talk of cousin and friend's passing. 'In hospital, Kurta. He died in hospital. Sick, weak, couldn't walk much. Royal Perth. That's where he died.'

After Colin was transferred back to Perth, his life had begun to ebb away, diabetes wasting his body. He was transferred to the hospital, along with a prison guard. He could hardly walk, his legs weakened by the disease. In spite of that, the prison guard stood by his door both day and night. Colin died during the night, his leg shackled to the hospital bed. He died with his body in custody, but his spirit had been set free.

❂ ❂ ❂

Ron's collection of photographs helped him keep alive his memories of people like Colin. Ron treasured his photographs. From his early days, the box camera, later replaced by a reflex lens, captured and framed significant moments, family groupings and dusty roads, visual contacts with the past. His collection dated as far back as the early mission days and captured glimpses of the first white people to meet the tribal elders. When we married, Ron had shared his plan with me of producing his own people's history first hand.

'Everyone comes and studies us, writes about us, takes our photo, then goes away with their own mark on our life. I don't think it's any accident that I have collected all this material or that some of the missionaries entrusted me with these glass slides, stories and artefacts. When most Aboriginal people were burning the photos of their dead, I was saving them. I just figured that one day they would want to know about their old people. When I heard about you I thought you'd make a good wife for me. To help me put this together, because you would eventually know me like nobody else knows me and it would still belong to me and my family.'

The traditional Aboriginal still held to the custom of burning photos and possessions of their relatives after they died. It was their way of handling grief, and going on with life. But Ron had not only taken thousands of photographs and slides, he had also kept them.

In the brick garage in Kalgoorlie, we began to sort through this incredible historical archive. It was slow going, because every photo had a story and every slide invoked a memory, either from Ron's younger days, my first arrival in Laverton or our trips around Australia. It was not only a chronicle of grassroots contemporary Aboriginal history, but also our own history as a family.

One by one, the images cut a clear pathway through the years, lined with funerals, marriages, more funerals, dirt roads, bitumen roads, flooded roads. Each photograph dragged the past into the present. My hand touched a photograph that I had taken of a corrugated iron fence, scribbled with white paint graffiti telling the Aboriginal fringe dwellers to 'go home'. They weren't wanted. The stark reality of the photograph mirrored the harshness of fringe dweller life.

From the first moment we arrived in Kalgoorlie and now that we had made our home here, we had followed the attempts of government, Aboriginal Affairs, and social workers to change the plight of the 'fringies'. But mostly the strategy was to get them 'out of sight, out of mind'.

When Warren Yates walked through the streets of Kalgoorlie, his feet shuffled slowly and he kept looking at the ground. His dark, bushy hair was usually tousled, looking like he had just crawled out of a swag. His shoulders slumped as if the weight of the world was balanced there, and he moved along with a silent resignation about life. Those who might notice him as they passed on the main street of Kalgoorlie, if anyone ever did notice him, probably would not be able to describe his facial features very well. He was undoubtedly wearing the only change of clothes that he owned, baggy trousers and a T-shirt that said 'Drink Jack Daniels'.

Each day Warren joined a few of his friends who formed a circle underneath the pepper trees on a flat piece of ground near Brown Avenue, silhouetted against the backdrop of the steel frames of Mount Charlotte Mine, which dominated the top end of Hannan Street. During the day, one could hear the clack-clack of the underground railway cars as they carried ore from one place to another.

Each evening, just at the time when most households were serving their family meal, like clockwork a blast was heard throughout the city. An underground blast of dynamite would shake the structures of homes nearby, loosening another bit of mortar and forming cracks in the walls. At night, the steel frame was lit up like a carnival, lights twinkling, search lights and beacons illuminating the entire hill. Along this strip of land, not far from the top-end pubs and two Aboriginal hostels, shuffled the homeless, the fringe dwellers of Kalgoorlie.

Warren was a fringe dweller. But he hadn't always been. Ron remembered Warren as a little boy at Warburton during the 1960s. Warren took hold of his little brother's hand and guided him around the mission, shyly asking for a piece of fruit, to hear someone play the guitar, or to play a game of spears. Everyone knew him as a timid little boy who didn't get into real fights; always holding his head down, as if that act itself would keep him out of trouble. His parents were tribal people, couldn't speak much English, and relied on the help of the mission and government direction to guide their lives. Warren and his brother led fairly carefree days in the bush, learning a little English from the mission teachers, attending Sunday school, at peace with the environment. Then Warren became a young man.

He stood at the edge of the Warburton community watching the dusty, muffler-rumbling Holdens drive in and out along the Laverton road, the one that eventually ended up in Kalgoorlie. Older men came back to the community with flagons and stories of exciting nights in Kalgoorlie, meeting up with mates from prison, having a stand-off with the group from Coonana, a community on the other side of Kalgoorlie. Sometimes they told of women that they had met, kisses they had stolen, nights under the Railway Bridge. Some of the teenage boys sported shiny cowboy shirts, Levi jeans or a new pair of leather boots. Warren's mind began to drift into Kalgoorlie and soon his body followed.

The old folks in the tribal communities sadly shook their heads when they talked of their young ones drawn away by the lights and promises of town life. They reckoned that even Laverton, a mining village of a couple of thousand, and especially Kalgoorlie, soon to reach a population of thirty thousand, were evil places for their people. But the bright lights, the grog, the nights under the trees, meeting up with friends, following the lead of the older men, they were all a sort of 'initiation' into manhood for them. Warren drifted into Kalgoorlie, squeezed into the back of one of the Holdens, with not even a blanket to his name, never knowing what to expect or how it would end up.

Not far from Mount Charlotte Mine was an 'infamous' mound named Nanny Goat Hill. This place was probably mentioned more times in the local newspaper, *The Kalgoorlie Miner*, than almost any other landmark. A generation ago, before the mines began to encroach on the residential areas of Kalgoorlie, this mound of earth was inhabited by a number of families, especially by one man who boasted several daughters. When the daughters became of marriageable age, the fellas in town came to court the 'nannies' on the hill, as the local 'yarn' was spun. The fellas were called the 'billies'. Even after the old houses were torn down and the landscape was taken over by mining equipment, that mound of earth was still called 'Nanny Goat Hill'. As the tribal men and women began to drift into Kalgoorlie, many of them were seen camped at night in the crevices and cave-like impressions of Nanny Goat Hill.

Once in a while someone would drop off a bit of wood for the 'residents' of the hill to have a warm around the fire or cook a few chops. Small piles of dust-covered, flea-ridden blankets littered the landscape, forming a pattern around the blackened remains of camp fires. Scattered throughout the scene were brown flagons, stubbies, and empty cans of beer. Late into the night a passerby could hear a cacophany of laughter, raised voices, shouts of anger, laughter again, a fight starting, accompanied by dogs barking and children crying. At the first peep of the sun over Mount Charlotte the next morning, the blankets stirred, arms and legs stretched, and crumpled bodies slouched their way to the safest place they could find for a wash or a feed. Trilby Cooper hostel and eventually the Brown Avenue houses were those 'safe places'.

Every winter a number of deaths scattered the little community at Nanny Goat Hill. The frail bodies of the fringe dwellers, soaked with wine to stave off the cold and the rest of society as well, were no match for the bitter desert nights. The news of the deaths would spread quickly throughout the Aboriginal community. Wailing pierced the air throughout the small clans huddled under trees around the city and drink was consumed in even greater quantities, easing the pain of relentless suffering in the midst of the richest 'golden' mile, the mining corridor of Australia.

The Minister of Aboriginal Affairs for Western Australia made regular trips to Kalgoorlie, specifically to address the issue of the fringe dwellers, the 'eyesore' of the city, according to the 'ruling fathers'. Consultations were held, sometimes behind the closed doors of the mayor's office, sometimes on the flat near Brown Avenue, with the local Aboriginal leaders. Usually these trips were up and back in one day. Only one day to try to repair a problem that had its roots two hundred years before.

The fringe dweller problem was not a simple one. There were several groups of displaced Aboriginal clans camped on the edge of Kalgoorlie. Most consultants proposed the erection of one camp, complete with ablution blocks, huts and even a park. That action would duplicate the mistakes of the past, when desert people from all regions were herded together into the one mission at Warburton and were expected to live together under a foreign rule and custom.

Many of us in the church brought corrugated iron to make huts, new blankets to replace the old, small trailerloads of wood, two or three heavy barbecue plates, a table or two, a cooler box of meat. Our friends often stopped us on the street.

'Come, hurry, old Molly, she dyin'. Please, take her to the hospital. Come, pray for her.'

We lifted Molly into the back of our four-wheel-drive, along with various children and grandchildren, a few old men and a dog, before we made the short trip to the hospital. We waited to make sure that the emergency room attendant knew what the problem was and that Molly would be seen before we left. Molly couldn't speak much English and neither did the rest of her family.

Eventually the Department of Aboriginal Affairs made their grand decision. A group of concrete dwellings, along with an ablution block was erected on the Nanny Goat Hill site. The bull dozer came and levelled the area, built the white concrete rectangular boxes, and erected a fence around the entire complex, supposedly to keep out sightseers, but mostly to block out this part of the world from the ever-watchful eyes of Kalgoorlie. A ceremony was held, a ribbon was cut, and the newspaper headlines shouted the news that the government had finally solved the fringe dweller problem.

'And this was the result,' I said to Ron as I held up the photograph of the white paint scrawled across the iron fence, facing the bypass road: 'KKK . . . Nigger go home'. It reminded me of another sign I had seen splashed across a metal plate outside of Merredin, halfway from Kalgoorlie to Perth: 'Keep Australia Beautiful—Shoot a Nigger'.

Warren spent his days shuffling from Nanny Goat Hill to the Aboriginal Medical Service, along the streets and back lanes of Kalgoorlie, once in a while jumping into the back of a Holden to visit his family in Warburton. One night his shuffling ended. He sought the refuge of a tree and the shelter of a fence along the back lane behind the Aboriginal Medical Service clinic building, two blocks from the main street of Kalgoorlie.

It was a Sunday night. Not far away in one of the local pubs, three white boys were having a night of drinking and carousing. As they laughed together and slapped each other around in the pub, seeking some thrills for the night, one of them had a suggestion. 'Let's go kill a boong.'

Their thrill-seeking led them to the tree and the fence along the back lane behind the clinic. Their heavily booted feet kicked Warren's stomach, their fists bruised his face and upper body, and finally one of the boys grabbed a nearby jagged boulder and fractured Warren's head, opening his skull. He breathed his last.

Ron and I sat with his family, talked with the police, calmed the other fringe dwellers and cried with the 'people of the shadows' of Kalgoorlie for many days afterward. Deep down Ron was not only grieving, he was angry. Another deep wound to his heart, and the heart of his people. It wasn't just the bodily wound, but the wound of the spirit.

A proverb asks this question: 'A crushed spirit who can bear?' The fringe dwellers of Kalgoorlie and in every town and city of Australia shuffle through the streets with a crushed spirit. 'Let's go kill a boong' echoes through the streets as they walk. Not long after, an Aboriginal man sleeping in the doorway of the Uniting Church, only one block from where Warren was killed, was spray painted with white paint as he slept. Eventually the toxicity of the paint caused his death.

Two or three camp people often appeared on our doorstep with stories of big cars driven by white people coming through their camps at roaring speeds, tearing down tents, wheels spinning near a sleeping woman with her child and then taking off into the distance. Racial hatred would flare for a few weeks at a time, letters to the editor appeared in the *Kalgoorlie Miner* and then there was a space of relative calmness and the subject went underground.

One letter appeared in 1991 with the headlines 'Respect must be earned'. The author's comments ranged from suggesting that hooded raiders take over the law and order of Australia to the declaration that Aboriginal people should have nurtured this land by domesticating animals and planting crops and they should get no respect until they contribute something concrete to this country. I wondered what this particular author had contributed to the Aboriginal people in order to earn *their* respect.

❁ ❁ ❁

The prison door clanked shut behind me and the guard motioned for me to follow him into the women's cell block at Boulder Regional Prison. My eyes gradually adjusted to the darkness of the room. A television sat in one corner on a table pushed against the wall, surrounded by five plastic chairs, and several ashtrays grouped together in the middle. Two Aboriginal women slowly appeared from their rooms, obviously as lookouts to see who was now invading their space.

Jenny's face lit up. 'Hey, it's Diana, Kurta's missus,' she called to the others in the room. She pulled me by the arm into a double room where there were four beds. Six or seven women were either lying on the beds, sitting at each other's feet passing the time of day, or painstakingly pulling nits out of their bunk mate's hair.

Once or twice a week I entered the prison through the electronic sliding gate that separated over a hundred men and women, eighty per cent of them Aboriginal, from the rest of society. When my car slipped into an available parking spot, the eyes of the 'men in green' who were serving their time tilling the soil, making concrete slabs or cleaning the grounds, would peer in my direction to see who was coming to visit.

Most of them waved, called out my name, asked where Ron was, how big Lydia was getting to be, and reminded me of the last time I was out in the desert. I would try to focus on who they were, what family they belonged to. In my mind's eye, the background setting dissolved from the grey prison walls and garments of green to the deep red hues of the desert and chatter of community life, helping me to remember their names.

The reason I went to the prison in the first place was because of Ron. He had a 'calling' for the prison, similar to the brothels, and the men and women who ended up there. 'The women want you to come and counsel them,' he said to me one day after he had spent the afternoon talking and singing his way around the cell blocks. 'They reckon you know all about them, you've seen them in the bush and you know their stories. How about it? I think you should do it.'

That meant that I had no choice. There weren't many times I could say no to Ron, particularly when it came to people in need. I spent hours listening to the women and their stories of surviving domestic violence, jealousies, children taken by welfare, and fights within the prison itself. Fights usually started over jealousies, when they caught their man evaluating the physical virtues of another woman. I had witnessed several times a woman's pension money and child endowment being taken from her by her man, who bullied her as she tried to hide her last bit of money inside her bra or under her blouse.

I discovered that some of them even sought refuge in prison from the difficulties of everyday life when the weather began to turn colder. On my journeys around town, I once gave Susan a lift to one of the fringe communities and she told me of her plans for the winter. 'Getting cold now. I guess I better do something so I can get into the Regional. At least I have a place to sleep and food to eat. A bit warmer than sleeping on the ground.'

The prison became another fringe dweller camp, a revolving door in a love–hate relationship. Within its four walls were incredible stories of pain, of hate, of anger, of violence, of rejection. Every day, they suffered the pain of facing the fact that a wife had been killed, a child had died, a woman had suffered cuts, bruises or broken limbs, a man had taken another woman, an uncle's funeral had just finished.

The reality of payback and tribal punishment played on the mind, and the spirit of death stalked the cells. But we didn't know whether to laugh or cry when we got word that one of our friends had actually broken *into* the prison to growl at her boyfriend because she had heard he had taken another woman within the confines of the prison walls.

Most of the time the reasons for the prison sentences resulted from owing fines, driving without a licence, drunkenness or assault on one another. Echoes from the past haunted the prison cells, echoes of incarceration for sheep stealing, jumping a fence to grab a few tomatoes or carrots, or running away from a farm with a chicken under one's coat. Imprisonment extended in some states to include young teenagers caught taking a few pencils, a packet of biscuits or a can of spray paint. Young teenagers, defiant but frightened, ended their life with a belt, a rope, a torn sheet, never stopping to think that there could be hope for the future.

The footsteps of the past two hundred years had led from one kind of custody to another. From early settlement days, when the boundaries of Aboriginal life began to shrink ever so much smaller year by year, through the moments in Ron's younger days, when his Uncle Fred would say that 'prison was the high school, where you could learn lots of things', to the present-day anguish from within the confines of the Aboriginal soul, came the cry 'Let my people go'.

Why do so many Aboriginal people end up in prison? Why was there a Royal Commission into the abnormally high number of black deaths in custody? Why would a woman try to commit a relatively minor crime in order to spend the winter in a prison cell? Why would a single mother, trying to raise her teenage son, lash out in frustration and impatience when he appeared in court yet again, screaming to all who could hear, 'Just let the welfare take you. I can't do anything with you anymore'? We lived with these questions every day.

The nights we spent together sitting on the floor of the garage sorting photographs, looking through slides, brought many tears to Ron's eyes. I would chatter away, make comments about picture quality, the number of spiders in the boxes, the extraordinarily large number of photos of four-wheel-drives and dirt roads, when I would see his head go down, his hand go over his eyes, and I knew that he was remembering. Sometimes I didn't know how to respond. Mostly I just reached out, touched his arm, sat quietly until he began to talk, or blow his nose, or launch into the memory, bringing it back to life.

'I don't know of another Aboriginal person who has so much history, Ron. So many images, footprints that have gone before. Your people can't afford to burn photographs anymore. They can't allow their dust to be blown away in the wind. The survival of the future depends on the heroes of the past.' Sometimes we would dream of a historical centre, a waterhole of memories where one could draw fresh water, a heroes' hut of Aboriginal lives, where young people could embrace their story and receive encouragement from the 'cloud of witnesses' who have gone before.

Aboriginal people have fought many battles. They have survived with incredible ingenuity alongside the harshness of the sunburnt land. They have survived the onslaught of a foreign invasion, the tearing apart of the fabric of their society, and even the proclamation that they are 'a dying race'. But when their story is told and proclaimed across the pages, interwoven among the words put to song, and proclaimed through the artist's brush, the battles will become the pearls that decorate the fabric of Aboriginal life and give hope to the next generation.

A pearl is made from suffering. Irritation from a grain of sand grinds its way within the prison of the pearl shell and there is weeping. That weeping, over a long period of time, deep within the bed of the ocean, forms a treasure, highly desired and worn with pride.

The treasure of Ron's life, along with the rest of the Aboriginal community, has been formed through the irritation of grains of bitterness, anger, rejection, causing suffering and weeping. Our own marriage has endured many grains of sand that have almost destroyed the pearl, so much weeping that the pearl shell should have burst open before its work was completed. Only by determination and commitment 'till death do us part' have we been able to allow the weeping to form the pearl, and, by God's grace, to glimpse that pearl once in a while.

CHAPTER 15

Tribal Ground

T he spiritual thread of Aboriginal Australia moves silently but steadily beneath the surface of the visible, daily pattern of western life. It is hidden to all but those who are 'in the know'. Even when the encroaching tide of western civilisation threatened to drown out all remnants of ceremonial life and disregard the transcendent dimension of Aboriginal spiritual cosmology, it was carefully preserved within the collective consciousness of the tribal elders. And it went underground. That is, until it was safe to emerge once again.

'I found my identity in the desert with the tribal people,' Ron had told me many times. 'That's one way to understand ourselves, and know where we come from, what's made us who we are. Spiritually as well.'

It was a world I was still only beginning to learn about. I wanted to thrust my hands into the spiritual soil of this land, sift it gently and allow it to flow through my fingers that I might understand and know as well. Ron was starting to come full circle in his own identity from being the grandson of a tribal warrior, to being a Christian leader, and now he wanted to marry the two.

'I think we Aboriginal fellas know more about what the Bible is really talking about in the spiritual dimension. We are more like the ancient Hebrew people than the whitefellas are. Another thing is, God was already here before the whitefella came. We heard the Creator speaking to us.' In his role within the church to coordinate the indigenous world view in ministry, Ron had embarked on an exciting, but complex venture.

Some of the tribal ways were essential and helpful for sustaining life, but others brought harm. My first experience of this had occurred just after we had moved to Kalgoorlie, when we made an important trip to the central desert. 'My people want to see Lydia,' Ron had explained. 'She needs to be dedicated there too, to know who she is.'

The tribal people whom Ron had carried around when they were children, who had welcomed me when I travelled through the bush before marrying Ron, had all been eager to celebrate and welcome our child. Just after her birth one of the desert leaders had sent Ron a message saying they had given Lydia her Aboriginal name, 'Yilkari', a beautiful word meaning 'sky' or 'heaven', their acknowledgment of God's miracle of her birth.

Warakurna, the desert community that nestled under the rock of the warnambi, the water snake, not far from Giles Weather Station was our destination. The first night, as we sat on the ground, gathered together for a special time of singing, stories and retelling the story of God's miracle of birth, Bernard, our friend and leader of the community, took Yilkari in his arms and dedicated her as a child of the bush, and all of us as their family.

'We are all family. You are our family too. You will always be welcome here with us,' he said as the tribal grandmothers sang, wept and hugged us.

It was a special time, but a fearful time as well. The next day we were beckoned to join them as the community opened their first cemetery. In traditional burials, the dead had been taken out into the bush to selected spots to be buried. There was no cemetery as such. Now, in keeping with western ways and Christian burials, the community had decided to set apart a special area and have concrete slabs and flowers that would decorate the graves. It was an important gesture for us to be invited to go to the area, to cry with them as they dedicated this sacred place.

We parked a friend's van under a tree. Lydia was asleep on a mattress.

'Ron, I can't go with you. I don't want to leave Lydia.'

'She'll be all right. Just leave her on the mattress. I really want to get this on video and I can't work it by myself. I need you to come with me.' Ron was insistent, even though I had very mixed maternal feelings about leaving my child on a bed which was less than a metre off the floor of the campervan. He had permission from the community for us to include this in some of our media work and presentation of community events, and Ron wanted me to film his presence there too.

'Come on. Don't be silly. What could happen to her here? She'll be all right. We won't be long,' Ron said firmly.

I didn't want to leave her. The air was hot, and even though he assured me it would only be for a few minutes, I knew that those minutes could stretch. I was torn between the insistence of my husband and my maternal duties, but I reluctantly trusted his judgment.

I rapidly videoed the scenery—people walking amongst the concrete slabs, the quiet wailing as they remembered their loved ones. Someone was speaking, then someone was singing, then someone wanted Ron to pray—I was getting more worried by the second, sensing an urgency to return.

Finally, I couldn't wait any longer, so I turned to Ron and motioned for us to go along. As he pulled himself away, I hurried along the track, carrying the camera, the tripod, and the extra bag. Ron realised my concern so he ran up ahead, disappearing at the last turn of the bend toward the clearing where the car was parked.

Arriving only a minute behind, I saw him pick up Lydia from the ground about two metres from the sliding door of the van, heard her muffled cry and gasps for air, saw the dirt, mixed with saliva, caked around her mouth. I screamed. If Ron's face could turn pale, then this was the time, as he placed her in my arms. My eyes darted around, the questions hanging on my lips: 'How? Where? Who? How?' again. Ron shook his head. No one was around. No one except four children, a few cars away, standing up in the back of a ute, looking on. If they knew anything, they didn't say, but they didn't run away in guilty fear either.

I held Lydia close, while hot, desperate tears ran into my mouth. She was breathing better now, but my thoughts were of what could have been. The community nurse gave me a cool cloth to put around her head, checked her all over and pronounced her okay. No flying doctor service needed. 'But watch her. There could be dehydration or delayed reaction,' she advised.

Later that day one of the tribal women came to see Ron. 'Spirits,' she whispered. 'Spirits, tribal business. After your little girl.'

In everyday life, Aboriginal people acknowledge the sacred. There is no separation between the daily wonders of creation or the opposing struggles of living and the powerful spiritual forces that move in nature, between individuals, within communities or in the heavens. For every circumstance, whether in life or in death, there is a cause in the 'other' world. It was no different when Lydia and her parents were confronted with a power from outside the natural world.

The trips that we often took into the somewhat sequestered territory of the desert people presented us with many glimpses of transcendental life. However, most of the ceremonies are secret from the rest of society, not to be mentioned even in the midst of their own ranks. Academics and observers who have collected information over the decades would only have a slice of what these ceremonies are all about, because even the tribal warriors themselves are forbidden to talk about, describe, mention or depict them.

Another meeting with the 'other' world took place during one January, a hot, dry month of summer when we started our trek from Kalgoorlie toward Alice Springs. We often drove at night because we had no air-conditioning in our old grey Landcruiser, the air was stifling during the day, and there was certainly no shade by lunchtime.

It was almost midnight when Ron sleepily turned the driving over to me and crawled into the back of the cruiser to have a sleep. Lydia was snuggled beside him.

This old cruiser had seen better days: it ran hot, rattled a fair bit, but it kept us going. It had originally been a tray-back ute, but a goldfields prospector had covered in the back, put in a separate long-range fuel tank, added a single bed along one side and lined the other side with storage crates. As Ron settled himself into the back, I closed the back-door hatch and turned the handle. There was no way to talk to Ron now, as the cab was separated from the back section by two glass panels.

I was alone in the cab, both windows rolled down for the night breezes to flow through, the cassette player at full bore. I happily hummed along with the music, eyes peeled for kangaroos, potholes and washouts. About an hour later, I suddenly felt a cold shiver of fear begin to crawl over me, and somehow I knew that if I were to suddenly throw my glance in the direction of the passenger seat, I would certainly see an old tribal man with a flowing beard sitting beside me.

This is ridiculous, I thought to myself, but I couldn't shake it. I didn't even want to stop the four-wheel-drive to get out. By the time I would get around to the back and open the door hatch to call to Ron, I could be surrounded by fearsome spirits of the night.

'Come on, Diana, get a hold of yourself,' I thought. All I could do was to sing songs, light-hearted songs, ones we learned at church, songs I had taught Lydia to sing. I didn't want to meet anyone on the road. But what could I do? I knew it wouldn't have been following the code of the bush road to keep on going and not stop, especially if someone was parked there. They could be in trouble.

Lights appeared up ahead, campfires flickered in the distance to the side of the road. Must be someone camped, I thought. Maybe a flat tyre! Why was I so afraid?

My mind laboured to try to think of where I was along the road. We had travelled it so many times, that I could probably follow it in my sleep. We must be getting near a place called Peegal, I calculated. Peegal was a rock cave carved out of the side of a granite outcrop along otherwise flat, scrubby terrain. The path leading into the area was extremely rocky. It was known to be a sacred site of the watersnake, with drawings on the walls of the open cave.

We had stopped there a number of times, boiled the billy of tea, checked to see if the waterhole on top was full or not, and walked around to stretch our legs on the long trek to Warburton. One year we had found tadpoles in the waterhole. That same year Ron and a number of elders and church members from the goldfields region had planted a cross on top of the cave entrance, praying at that time that the bondages of alcohol and violence and deaths in custody would be loosened from around the Aboriginal communities. They proclaimed on top of that rock that God was already here in the Dreamtime, before the missionaries came. They also proclaimed that the Aboriginal spiritual story and the Christian spiritual story could walk together.

The road that passed by the side of this cave had seen numerous accidents and vehicle rollovers, sometimes causing the deaths of desert warriors. That road linked the pubs and bottle shops of Laverton and Leonora with the otherwise 'grog-free' lives of the western desert families. Ron had buried a number of his friends, men and women who had now grown up but whom he had once carried around as little toddlers during the 1960s. A few times we had arrived on the scene of an accident and had nursed a man or a woman, suffering and crying.

The road from Laverton to Warburton was littered with brown bottles of beer and coolers of wine. The ghostly remains of burnt-out vehicles told the story of deaths, maiming and headaches that took days to subside. That's why we prayed, that's why we planted a cross, that's why the church leaders drove the hundreds of kilometres into the desert. Because they were willing to try everything to put a stop to the 'genocide by alcohol' of their people.

So why should I fear this place? Why would I hesitate to stop along this road? I just kept singing. Then the flames of what I thought was a campfire seemed to disappear from sight, and I saw no one around. The car lights I had seen were no longer shining up ahead. I slowly turned to look at the passenger seat. No one sat there.

As suddenly as the fear had come, it seemed to fly out of the window, as surely as a bird that is let loose from someone's grip would take flight. I continued to drive until early morning, until I saw the sun, like a familiar friend, lift its shimmering golden head over the horizon. I let the car roll to a stop and got out. I was very tired.

Ron took the wheel and drove us into Warburton and we came to a stop a little way from the roadhouse and police station. It was too early for anyone to be awake or for the shop to be open. We stretched our legs, made Lydia comfortable in the front seat, and sipped a cup of water, when we saw a young man come out of the bushes toward us. His hair was matted and there was a tribal band around his forehead, ochre painted across his body. He held some leafy bushes and he was smiling at us.

'Kurta,' he called. 'Diananya.' A teenager, well-known to us, who had been to Kalgoorlie on detention for petrol sniffing. Son of a tribal leader. Gentle, soft-spoken. He greeted us. Hugged Ron. Shook my hand. Talked about his mum, dad, family. Then he leaned over to Ron, but still within the circle of my hearing. 'Tribal business,' he whispered. 'Just finished this morning. Men's business. Initiation.'

Now I knew. I had witnessed the spirits of the land in motion. The land of the desert was electric during the ceremonies, responding to the ceremonial line of tribal ancestors. As I had neared those rocks, a special place in their story, the winds had been dancing, the rocks had been vibrating in the spirit world, the unseen reality of the desert, as I drove past. And they had parted to let me through. I held Lydia close, realising that she was more a part of this reality than I could ever be.

A few days later we found that we weren't so welcome in the heart of the desert. After our usual drive into the middle of the night, exhausted, we pulled into a clearing off the track and set up our little tent. The day had threatened rain and we didn't want to take any chances.

Lydia fell asleep early and I tucked her in for the night in the middle of our swag. Our dogs roamed at the edge of the firelight, not venturing too far into the darkness. The night was still and quiet, except for the popping sounds of the sparks chasing each other from the heart of the flames.

'This place seems spooked. I can feel the spirits around,' said Ron.

'Come on, Ron,' I laughed. 'You must be paranoid. I don't feel anything. And beside, don't keep talking that way. I just might get scared!' I didn't like thinking about these sorts of things. I still figured that if I didn't think about them, then they would go away and not bother us.

I had been sound asleep when I was abruptly woken by Ron's movements. He was shaking my shoulder and telling me to get up. My eyes were slowly focusing and I was trying to remember where we were, when I suddenly realised that our tent had blown down around us.

'We're not welcome here. He showed me that. Let's pack up,' blurted Ron.

'Who? Who showed you what? What do you mean?' I was puzzled.

Who was Ron talking about? But he wasn't listening to me. I helped fold the tent up as the wind started to pick up speed and the trees around us creaked. Just as we got everything into the back of the ute, climbed in and picked up the track again at almost four in the morning, the sky opened and the rain pelted down, quickly turning the track into mud.

All this time, Ron hadn't said a word, but as we drove out of the storm, he explained what had happened. A noise had awakened him, almost like someone calling his name. When he looked out of the tent door he had seen a warrior, standing with a spear and a 'yakiri', tribal headband, just above his scowling eyes. A message, meant just for Ron, to say, 'Move on.'

'There are times when we are welcome, Diana, and times when we are not. I always respect that. I've always respected the tribal custodians of the land. Maybe I forgot to ask them if we could camp there.' Another glimpse, another time when the curtain to a hidden world was pulled back and a lesson revealed.

As a young man Ron had been destined to be a tribal warrior, in direct line from his grandfather Joe's side, to use the supernatural power of nature and the tribal spirits, even the power to kill. When he chose, long ago at the age of eighteen, not to accept that inheritance, but instead to embrace a Christian life and the supernatural power of God, he did not discount the Aboriginal spiritual realm. But he wasn't prepared to be the target of the tribal 'marbarn' spirit, the power to bring harm.

The following year, we packed for another one of our treks through to Alice Springs, where we hosted the Christian convention every January. This time we were also going to take a much needed holiday to Adelaide and then to Melbourne along the coast road. One night Ron had three dreams. He never had 'normal' dreams; in fact, Ron didn't usually dream at all. So when he did, his dreams appeared as realistic images from another world that stayed in his mind for a long time. The next morning during breakfast he shared these dreams with me.

At the time, I dismissed them as products of an overactive imagination, especially since my attention was diverted by the many tasks of preparing for this longer-than-usual time away from home. Three images had marched across Ron's mind: the first one led by a tribal warrior decorated for fighting, thumping his feet on the ground, which soon disappeared in the clouds of dirt rising up to encircle him. His eyes were piercing through Ron's eyes while Ron watched him fade into the image of a coiling snake, ready to strike, and then into a bull that seemed to race right toward Ron as he watched the scene from the sidelines. In each image, the eyes seemed to penetrate Ron's very being.

The next day he appeared to forget about it and so did I, but one week before we were to leave, Ron bent down to tie his shoelace, nothing strenuous, and the tendon in his left thumb snapped, leaving it lifeless. No effort or concentration on his part would move that thumb at all. Only one day before the surgeon in Kalgoorlie was to leave for the Christmas holidays he operated on Ron's thumb, stitching the tendon back together again then wrapping Ron's hand, wrist and forearm in a rock hard cast, not to be removed for three or four weeks.

The end result was not that we cancelled the trip, but that it was now up to me to drive the two thousand kilometres over the bush roads to Alice Springs in the heat of January, a journey of two nights and two days. Later we realised that that was the first in a trilogy of mishaps, reflecting the three images in the dream.

After we had arrived in Alice for the annual Christian convention of tribal people from all over the red centre and other parts of Australia, Lydia went for a swim with her friends from Kalgoorlie, who were staying at a caravan park. After she dried off and the families were preparing to pack up for the night meeting and bring her back to us, they gathered together to pray. They were praying specifically for pastors and Christian leaders and their families and for their protection. Lydia quietly sat with the kids along a metal railing secured into the ground with a concrete footing. All of a sudden, without warning, she fell straight back, knocking herself in the back of the head, just above where the nape of the neck meets the skull. Blood spurted.

'Quick,' said one of the mothers, grabbing Lydia's head and pushing it underneath the tap. Someone else wet a towel and wrapped it around her head. Lydia was still conscious, but dazed. They jumped in their van and drove out to the Alice Springs Showground where we were, some fifteen kilometres away.

I was happy to see the van drive up, still always a little nervous when Lydia was away from me. But when the door slid open and I saw her sitting there, head wrapped, looking a bit dazed, in a flash of a second I grabbed her, put her into our vehicle, barely hearing the details of the story echoing behind me, and rushed to the hospital.

The waiting room was full, children coughing, men hung-over with alcohol who had fallen and cut themselves, women who had arms and legs wrapped with layers of gauze covering sores and wounds.

'Our hospital looks like a war zone, sometimes,' said the nurse at the emergency desk. 'Take a seat. I'll see if I can get a doctor right away. Just see that you keep your daughter alert. You know, we treat more head injuries than anything else.'

I cradled Lydia's head in my arms, encouraging myself that this head injury was not like the others. It hadn't come about through anger or violence within the family or clan like most of the others in the room. Actually I didn't know how it came about.

I kept talking to Lydia to keep her awake, and praying silent prayers underneath my breath. Her eyes seemed slightly glazed and she asked me vague questions. She didn't seem to panic, but her hands wouldn't let go of mine.

Oh, God. Let nothing happen to her. You gave her to us, don't you remember? Please help her to stay awake. My brain was screaming to the Creator of all life to put His hand on my precious little girl.

The doctor appeared and led us to the last bed in the far corner of the emergency ward. He cleaned the wound and discussed with his assistants the next procedure. As each person walked by and looked at the cut, its depth and its location, their facial expressions were not encouraging. I held Lydia's hand and kept talking to her.

As the doctor applied local anaesthetic, she remained quiet. Then he proceeded to put five stitches in her head. I expected some yells of pain. I couldn't even look while he performed this task. Not a sound from Lydia. I thought she must have fallen asleep. When he finished, he spoke to her and she answered, not even realising what he had done.

'Is the doctor finished, Mum?' Lydia looked at me, still grasping onto my hand. I could feel my breathing, steadier now.

'I've never seen such composure with this kind of injury. You're some brave kid,' commented the doctor as he looked into Lydia's face.

When we turned to go, his last remark followed us out the door, 'Just keep an eye on her. You know we treat more head injuries here than any other kind.'

Even after this second mishap in less than a month, Ron still did not recognise the message of the dreams. The conventions were over for another year and we headed south for a break in the cooler weather.

After stopping to see friends in Adelaide we took the coastal road along the shores and around the hills toward Geelong and then Melbourne. Somewhere along the track, a strange knock developed in our four-wheel-drive engine. Previously we had sold the old grey Landcruiser and had purchased a 1988 Toyota personnel carrier, complete with dual fuel tanks, two batteries with wiring for an Engel fridge, a winch and, of course, air conditioning. We sailed along, not thinking too much about it, but the knocking would not go away and it seemed to be getting louder. We stopped at three different garages, but the mechanics were away because it was the January holidays.

'Let's just keep going. We'll be right if we can get to our friend's place in Melbourne.' Ron was confident we could make it.

I was driving when we passed Geelong and got onto the freeway, cars rushing madly in each direction. The steady knocking had faded into the background, like a constant dripping tap, when suddenly, there was an explosion. The four-wheel-drive rolled to a stop. Oil was gushing out from under the car and onto the bitumen. The eventual diagnosis was that a rod had gone through the block, causing massive damage.

No one stopped. Heads in cars passing by looked straight ahead as if we didn't exist. I was panicking and wishing we were in Western Australia, where the rules of the road meant that people stopped to help.

Ron headed down the highway for the blue phone, while I waited in the car with Lydia and our dog. Cars continued to whizz past, the moments ticked by, twilight approached. I could see dollar signs rolling through my head. I knew that we had no money to get this repaired. I feared it would take thousands of dollars, plus the inconvenience of where to stay, how long it would take and who would fix it.

Where was Ron, I thought to myself. Surely it wouldn't take this long to find the phone. The sun was setting. The years of living in the outback away from the occupational hazards of the city and its seemingly uncaring and impersonal attitude had left me unsure of its safety. I began to think the worst. What if someone had picked him up and kidnapped him, or even beat him up, or run him down? That wasn't such a far-fetched idea in my mind; we had seen it happen many times in other cities, especially to blackfellas. Over and over Lydia asked, 'Where's Dad? I'm hungry.' The usual comment from a seven-year-old.

A few minutes later, she called out to me, 'Mum, isn't that Dad? Over there. What's he doing?' I could just make out in the shadows of the setting sun a man walking along a fence line, some twenty metres back from the road, bordering a farmer's property. Tall grass edged the fence as far as we could see. He was beating the grass with a big stick, ambling along, with not a care in the world. Never mind that we had been confined to the car, anxious about the outcome to our plight.

'What on earth were you doing?' I bellowed as he came over to us smiling.

I began to wonder about his sanity when he answered, 'Oh, I just saw some rabbits. I thought I might get one for our dinner.'

I couldn't believe my ears. I didn't know whether to explode with anger or burst out laughing. Instead I just cried, and the tension began to melt away from my shoulders.

'It's all right.' He cuddled us both together. 'Help is on its way.'

We did get help. We were towed through Melbourne to Yarra Junction, where we stayed with friends for over three weeks. The repair was paid for by churches, friends and other people we didn't even know but who had heard of our plight and wanted to help.

On our way back home to the goldfields, we tried to make sense of all that had happened. Camped on the Nullabor one night, Ron made the connection when he settled into our swag after a walk in the bush. 'Those dreams,' he said. 'Now I know. They were a warning. A warning of danger and I didn't even recognise it.' As a potential tribal warrior, Ron was having marbarn thrown at him. Years of training in Western thought, and a fading recognition of the reality of the supernatural world, had dulled his readiness to 'take up arms' as a warrior. Now it seemed to come upon him all at once. It was a turning point.

His connection with his past, his identity and status in his own world swirled around him like the colours in a kaleidoscope. He took a hold of his rightful inheritance: his grandfather Joe, a man who had no fear of the bush; his great-grandfather Willie, a king among his people; uncles and great-uncles who were known for their strength in the face of danger. Faces, places, times and seasons all flew past, reminding Ron of his place in line.

Another piece of the puzzle of Ron's life turned up in the form of a family tree received from the files of the Native Welfare Department. It was crudely drawn on an oversize piece of paper extracted from the records of Norman Tindale's anthropological work throughout the southwest in the 1930s. Tindale had interviewed, photographed and sketched the family lines of hundreds of Aboriginal clans.

'Look at this!' I jumped up in excitement with an incredible find. Our detective work had unearthed a link in Ron's family history to American 'negro' heritage through Uncle Ned, listed on Tindale's genogram as 'three-quarter mix of Aboriginal and negro'. There was some confusion in the descriptions: Tim Harris, Ron's great-great-grandfather, 'may have been of negro extraction—according to a story'. Then his wife (unnamed) was described as possibly being American.

In any case, the 'negro' label had stuck throughout the family history, with a note written next to Grannie Grace's name, 'white and three-quarter Aboriginal and negro'—and another next to Ron's mother Cissie's name, 'full blood, white and three-quarter Aboriginal and negro'.

'And look, Ron, there's more!' At the bottom of the family tree was a glimpse into old Ned's character. 'During a dispute in Perth, Ned Harris was caught going into a bar. After his arrest, he took it to court and he won. He claimed he was of American descent. The court transcript said that he had all the appearance of an American negro.'

Ron was quiet. Thoughtful. I let him alone to consider this new piece of information about his roots. I didn't know what his reaction might be. He took the paper in his hand again and ran his fingers over the page, touching each name.

'If I had known this, things might have been different,' Ron said.

'What do you mean, Ron? Different how?'

'I was always too quiet, letting people walk over me, but underneath I was boiling. I didn't know what to do about that, so I just let people keep walking over me, like a pathway that gets worn down, trampled on, and isn't fruitful any more. Like my people have been.'

Ron paused and his voice sputtered out. 'This,' he shook the paper. 'If I had known this, I would have gone to university, become a professor and challenged the nation of Australia to look at our people differently. If I had known that one of my people, this man Ned here, had stood up and challenged the authorities when they wanted to throw him into gaol, I would have had the historical background to fight from. Freedom, that's what I think about. Freedom here in my bones, like the black Americans. No wonder my Uncle Ken never let anybody walk over him. Now I understand him better, after all these years.'

Ken Colbung, Noongar activist, outspoken fighter for Aboriginal freedom and recognition, related to Yagan and Yellagonga, tribal chiefs around Perth, Ken, whose history was the same as Ron's, a mixture of white, American negro, Aboriginal—his mother was Grannie Grace's sister. As a young teenager the police had put her in gaol at Moore River Settlement, nicknamed the Black Hole of Calcutta, for being pregnant to a white man, a man who had forced her into the bush for sex and then had run off and left her.

Tiny Colbung had nursed her little son in a bathtub in the cold cell

Ron's Family Tree

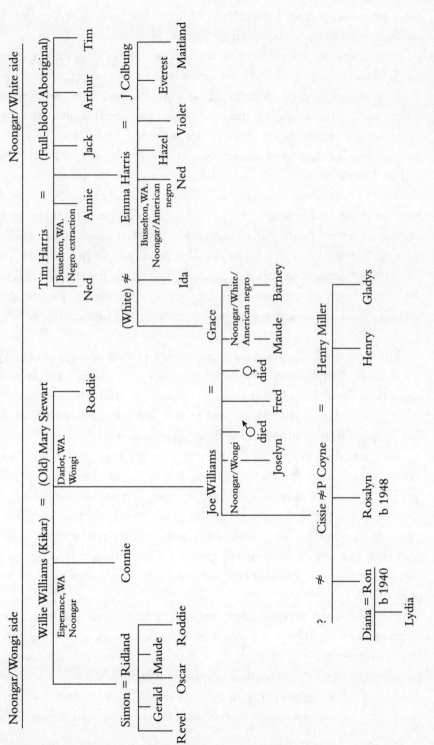

until pneumonia spread through her lungs, taking her life. Ken was left on his own in Moore River, then sent to Sister Kate's in Perth.

As a young man, Ken went to work on a ship, loading supplies down in the hold, when another fellow whispered to him, pointing to a white man working opposite to them. 'That's your father, Ken,' his Noongar friend said. Ken boiled up inside and thought about killing him, rage clouding his mind. A woman's image appeared before him and a soft voice called his Aboriginal name. 'Nungtjin, my son,' she said. 'He's your father. Don't kill him. It's all in the past now. Go up on top and calm down. Let it go now.' Ken had never seen his mother, but he knew she was speaking to his heart. He turned away. His dead mother's words stayed with him from that moment. He never wanted to pay back in revenge for the hurts that he or his Aboriginal people had experienced.

All this from a note on a genogram. To untangle the threads of Ron's life from so much diversity was like trying to separate the strands of knitting yarn that a kitten had pulled through the house from room to room.

And over it all, Ron saw the image of the Divine Warrior, a call from God to stand firm on the mountain of victory, to embrace the hope for the future for a 'Brand Nue Dae', as Jimmy Chi from Broome wrote in his popular play of that name, and to ride over the valley of tears and his people's history of exclusion from their own world.

To Ron, this now made total sense. The teaching of western Christianity had mostly presented rules to follow, separation from his own people and conformity to a thought process that was not what he was created with. But he was now looking past that, to what the spirit of God was saying to him, within his own 'tribe', not with a western garment, but with an Aboriginal garment. That brought freedom to his soul. I felt that my husband had just unlocked a cage door and was now free to soar.

Someone once mentioned to me that, when I married Ron, I had hitched my wagon to a star. Well, it was some years before the corrugations smoothed out enough for the wagon to take off. By reason of commitment and the definition of biblical marriage, we two were 'one'. Ron's world along with his Aboriginal world, had become my world. And he was connected to my world in ways he had never before imagined.

From the beginning, he was not like most other Noongars, Kooris or any other clan. Underneath the cultural shyness was a bold streak that enabled him to talk to anyone, of any race, any colour, any background. White kids at the shopping malls, elderly white-haired ladies waiting for the bus, returned soldiers on Anzac Day, Chinese waiters, politicians on the hill. He loves people whoever and wherever they are.

One afternoon on top of Anzac Hill in the centre of Alice Springs, looking over the scene that Albert Namatjira must have loved, Ron put his arm around my shoulder, and looked down at me. 'If you had it to do all over again, would you still marry me?' Whenever we had been through a rough patch, whenever the pressures seemed to be giving us an extra squeeze, or he wanted to see how I was processing all this information I was learning, he would ask me this question.

And I? I looked up at him and just smiled. 'I'm still here, aren't I?'

❂ ❂ ❂

As Ron learned more about his family, I grew to miss my own family more and more. Whenever I served sandwiches to grieving relatives after a funeral, listened thoughtfully to the women in prison tell me their fears and dreams, prayed in a house tormented by evil spirits, or tried to convince a young teenager that learning the maths table would somehow help him get along in life, I yearned for my own family to know some happiness.

Pat's struggle with manic–depression consumed her conversations with family members. I never knew what her mood would be when I rang her up. In ten years, I had received only two cards from her with descriptions of her visits to psychiatrists, bouts of electric shock treatments, three marriages, and purchases of stuffed animals and trinkets from outdoor markets.

After my mother died, I had wondered how long my sister could survive without her support, without someone to absorb her anger and frustrations. My mother's sister, Norma, had tried to take on the role, but it wasn't the same. Pat's third marriage was shaky, she didn't see her children that often and, without the help of our mother, the links were not very strong. Pat had never been able to forgive our dad for past family problems and, by choice, had closed herself off from all of us. In

many ways, she had become another sort of fringe dweller. Her coun-
sellor was often worried and concerned as to why the treatment and
medications never seemed to bring results.

One early morning, I received a phone call, again from my uncle, that
brought more pain across the world. My sister had walked into a large
department store in our home town, bought a handgun and had shot
herself that morning. I immediately rang my father, who then drove the
eight hours to the police station and then the funeral. A few days later,
he wrote me these words:

*Patricia went to Walmart on Sunday to buy a handgun. The clerk, noting that
she was nervous and didn't know much about guns, questioned her as to her
purpose. She made up a story that she was recently divorced and wished to scare
off someone who was harassing her. The clerk's boss was called in and she told
the same story, and finally the store manager also questioned her motives, but
she stuck with the story and finally got the gun. On Monday [Labour Day in
the US] in the early hours she was supposed to be at Kaw Dam with Brian
[her husband] fishing. On the way out, she apparently had a depressive attack
and started hitting Brian on the arm. He took her back home to calm down and
said he would come back for her later. I guess she felt rejected, because he didn't
come back. The police let me read the suicide note. It was lucid, neatly written
and short. I paraphrase:*

> I am tired of my life with no hope for the future. I really tried.
> I love Brian and my children and Auntie and Uncle Jimmy. I
> hurt too much. My dress I have chosen is set out and I want my
> hair done.

*She did not sign the note or date it. At the top, as an afterthought, she
wrote:*

> I thought I heard you honk for me, but you were not there
> when I went out.

*The police said she shot herself in the temple and that death was
instantaneous. She apparently lay there on the bed for about eighteen hours
before her body was discovered by her therapist. She had an appointment at
nine in the morning on that Tuesday. The police treated the scene as a
possible homicide, but then released her body for burial. I arrived too late to
see Pat, but it's just as well. I want to remember her as a little girl, playing
tennis in the Missouri Valley Tennis Tournament.*

Two years later, Walmart stopped selling handguns.

I sat alone outside our tent. We were camped with over a hundred Wongis and Noongars outside of Leonora for an Easter weekend service. Over a year had passed since my sister's death, three years since my mother's, but the grief was still so real. I thought of all the affinities that had brought Ron and I together. Our love for people, our inordinate sentimentality for dogs, the desire to capture moments through the camera lens, a voracious appetite for the written word, our faith in God, and our outrageous ability to laugh with one another. Added to that, and perhaps even more important, as I was beginning to understand, was our pathway of suffering—death, suicide, violence, rejection, and identification with the fringe of society, whether it was black or white, or somewhere in between.

These were my thoughts while my friends milled around, while guitars were tuned for the evening singalong and camp ovens bubbled on the coals. The moments of reliving my own memories contrasted sharply against the deep Aboriginal family ties played out in the drama of life from red dirt communities in the centre to the clans gathered in small city flats or rural farm houses. I had more contact with my dad now, taking the opportunity provided by telephone company price wars and a longing to reconnect to understand him more and to capture what was good in our relationship.

In the middle of my reverie, I felt a light touch on my arm. Miriam stood in the shadows, a grey-haired, gentle woman who often came to our house to pray for young people in prison. She spoke quietly. 'I've been watchin' you and I know you're sad and lonely. But you one of us mob, you know, you're black like us. Inside here, where it counts,' as she pointed to her chest. 'Don't ever forget, you one of us mob now.' With that she silently walked away, her touch still warm on my arm.

CHAPTER 16

Celebrations Dark and Light

When I had first set foot in Australia, I anticipated the joy of seeing and hearing the Aboriginal expression of the Christian faith. In New York City, I wandered in and out of a smorgasbord of singing, rhythms, instruments and unique expressions of experiences with God. My soul and body stirred with the black American gospel singing in the streets around Times Square, and the heavenly harmonies that flooded the neighbourhood tenements that surrounded the Brooklyn Tabernacle Choir. The rhythm of the steel drums from Africa and Haiti that echoed throughout Central Park and the gentle island beat and swaying hips of the Hawaiians had thrilled my heart. Now I wanted to hear the sounds of Aboriginal Australia.

I had been disappointed. There were no didgeridoos, clap sticks or boomerangs. It took years to discern what the true rhythm of the land felt like. In some mission churches these instruments had been banned. The message was that God only spoke in English and eighteenth-century hymnody.

'Those sticks are from the devil,' the natives were told. When the language and the rhythm of a people is banned, killed or destroyed, it is as if it never existed, as if the people themselves never existed. In many places the Aboriginal church of Australia had not been allowed to exist as God had meant it to be.

Most of the church services were conducted very much in the traditional British style. Hymns written two centuries before were sometimes translated into the local Aboriginal dialect, or otherwise sung in English. For years one man thought the words to 'The Old Rugged Cross' were 'The Old Rocket Cross'. No wonder the meaning of the song eluded him. Tribal people who could barely speak English, let alone read it, came to church carrying heavy, black King James Bibles under one arm, sat down on hard wooden pews set out in rows facing the front, and stood to sing to the melodies pumped out by a portable organ.

Changes began to take place in the late 1970s and early 1980s. An indigenous spiritual awakening, beginning in Elcho Island off the coast of Arnhem Land, spread down through the centre, catching fire in the west through Warburton, continuing down toward the south-west to Pinjarra. Aboriginal people began to get involved in their own church affairs, leading meetings, taking charge, making it their own, springing from their own indigenous soil. Basically, the missionaries still controlled many of the churches on the communities. Even if preaching and prayers were conducted by Aboriginal people, the missionaries were the organisers, the purse keepers and the ones who made the final decisions. Suddenly, a gust of wind broke through, the spirit of God, which blasted forth from within the midst of the people themselves. Like a bush fire, nothing could stop it. In the midst of such a determination and excitement, social structures in the community toppled. Hospitals were no longer full of men and women who had bashed one another; pubs were no longer full of blackfellas wanting to fix their head and dull their pain. The revival created such a stir that the TV current affairs program '60 Minutes', did a special report.

When I had first pitched my tent in Laverton in 1983, the tail-end of the movement was still rippling through the desert. It was exciting to see the bushy-haired, guitar-playing tribal leaders speaking with such authority, planning their strategies and carrying them forth. But underneath, there was a rumbling that all was not well. It was like an engine with the fuel running out, in fits and starts, sputtering, taking a few leaps forward, stalling, trying again and then eventually coming to a stop.

Later, when I asked a few of those revival leaders what they thought had happened, I knew there wasn't just one single answer. But I wanted to hear from their voice and see from their eyes and understand from their heart.

'The whitefellas were afraid of us. Some didn't want us to pray for them. Not many wanted to come and help us, to support us. Them fellas in charge got money to help them travel, preach, tell us mob about Jesus, but nobody helped us much.' I knew a few of the committed missionaries who had been in the desert for scores of years, had had their babies, had seen some of them die, who had seen the desert babies born, and some of them die. I knew that they had supported the efforts of this new movement, but there were not enough of them.

I contemplated the scene from their vantage point. Bureaucracy, aeroplanes coming and going, money for missionaries to travel in and out, papers being written, land being mined, resources being kept under lock and key. It wasn't an easy question, nor were there easy answers.

Later, Ron and I had tramped through the bush, debating these issues. We juggled a variety of cultural grids until our thoughts began to embrace ideas from each other's point of view.

'They couldn't speak up. They couldn't challenge the authorities, whether in the church or in the government. I know. I've been there. We were conditioned to keep our place, to keep still and not rock the boat. We didn't know how to negotiate. We couldn't win the verbal war.' Ron expanded my understanding.

'But why allow that?' I would retort. 'You're strong. I've seen you get angry. I've seen the strength in your eyes, and in the eyes of these men. They don't have any trouble confronting the supernatural in the bush. Why can't they confront what they see is wrong?' My view came from years of fighting inequality in women's issues, in speaking up for what I saw was wrong, in battling my way through education, career, moving out on my own. I came from a culture of freedom and with the 'you-can-do-anything-you-set-your-mind-to' attitude of the United States. But here, among the gentle but strong, the uneducated but wise people of the Dreaming, there were no Mandelas, no Martin Luther Kings, who had faced persecution, imprisonment, even death to see their people become equal in the eyes of the world. Unless you counted those who resisted genocide, resisted the takeover of the lands, resisted to the point of frustration, or to the point of taking their own life.

Ron's Uncle Barney (left) is joined by great-uncle 'Pa' Salty, for a last cup of tea at the reserve camp outside Kalgoorlie, just before a gold mining company bulldozed his home in 1988. Four years later the historic Mabo decision overturned the notion of *terra nullius*, that no-one owned the land before white settlement. Many Aboriginal families are still trying to keep their land and homes safe from encroaching mining conglomerates.

Our daughter Lydia was just a few months old when Ron showed her the resting place of her Aboriginal ancestors, especially Old Mary, her great-great-grandmother, at the overgrown Carrolup cemetery at Marribank.

Lydia and Soxy at the Duke of Orleans Bay in Western Australia. This was a welcome holiday from the problems of everyday community life.

Ron often visited the remains of Uncle Barney's cabin at Bremer Bay on North Garnett's farm. Before we moved to Canberra in 1999, the entire Williams clan gathered near this family 'sacred site' to celebrate Christmas together and farewell Ron, Lydia and me.

Lydia and me at the Pioneer Woman Statue in Ponca City, Oklahoma. For me the statue symbolises the pioneering spirit in my own heart and it has always inspired me to keep looking to the next 'horizon'. This is a vision that I've shared with Lydia—to boldly face what lies ahead.

Our great friends Wilf and Beth Douglas, who have worked among Aboriginal people for most of their sixty years together as missionaries. Wilf was the first person I wrote to from America for advice about the desert language of the Aboriginal people I was about to live with. He told his friend Ron all about me and encouraged me to write to him after we met on that fateful New Year's Eve in Kalgoorlie.

Our friend Livingston West, once a feared tribal spear thrower but now a tribal leader, pastor and community chairman in the Ngaanyatjarra lands of Western Australia. Livingston transformed his life so that he could bring hope to his people, rather than fear. His family looked after Ron in the 1960s and Livingston continues the tradition whenever our family visits his community.

Throughout our marriage and our travels, Ron and I have had many conversations around waterholes in the desert, such as this one along the Warburton track. Ron always has 'just one more story' to tell.

Ron continued to reflect on his thoughts. 'Someone will have to speak strong. But sometimes whitefella call us radical and angry and write us off. They only want to listen when they know we will say yes to them.'

I often heard the complaints the Aboriginal Christians had about their white counterparts, usually spoken only amongst themselves. One or two of them dared to speak out boldly for radical change, sometimes with anger that mirrored the deep cuts in the heart they had suffered from seeing their people die around them. Young men on the streets of Redfern, children and adults at Papunya, dying before their time, of disease, drugs and violence. No one wanted to listen to these 'so-called' radicals.

'What has changed in two hundred years?' one of our friends despaired. 'Handshakes aren't the answer. Who's going to be there for us, in the hard times?' The hurt within the Aboriginal people has been rehearsed for decades, around the campfires, in the bottles of wine, in broken family relationships, and has now reached the spillway, over-flowing across the land of Australia. Is anybody listening?

I alternated between anger at white Australia for what they had done and continue to do to my husband and our other friends, and somehow feeling responsible, whipped and rejected by the Aboriginal pain. 'I'm white,' I would think to myself out loud. 'How can I ever make up for this much pain? How can my angry Aboriginal friend, and others like him, ever accept me, or any of us?' I took the whole matter very person-ally. Ron could see that and he would rescue me. 'Look sweetie. These friends of ours wouldn't talk that way to most white people. They do that around you because you're their friend, they feel comfortable with you. You should feel privileged to hear the pain.'

I would nod weakly as my tears licked at my wounds. Privileged to hear the pain. I would ponder that thought for many more years.

One of our desires when we moved to Kalgoorlie had been to encourage the Aboriginal Christians in the goldfields and throughout the centre of Australia to take charge of their worship of God, and to let loose in free expression to their Creator. Ron had always been a bit of a rebel, secretly fanning the flame of indigenous Australia, experimenting with his own enunciations of his faith in God. His method of preaching wore a new garment of visual interpretation that linked the land, the people and their God. Creation began to sing with the language of his heart. Rocks and gnarls of wood were transformed into stories and his own starving people came back for more. Ron's two spiritual cultures, the land and its dreaming and the Creator and Christ, were blending together in celebration of Ron's growing freedom of identity. To pass this on to his people was Ron's desire.

'We want our own church, Kurta,' said Richard, Greg and Delson, and others nodded in agreement. 'We gotta be different from the missionaries. We have to be ourselves, do what God want us to do.' Our little church, Yiwarra Palya, the Good Road, began right there in the alcohol Rehabilitation Centre.

We were criticised, misunderstood, banned, rejected. We were break-aways, they said. We were evil, others said. It is hard for an Aboriginal person to walk alone, particularly when extended family members are the ones who turn away. But the church began to grow with rhythm, joy, tapping sticks, clapping hands and stomping feet. The Aboriginal preachers got to the heart of their people because they had walked the same road.

Making the transition from the 'mother church tradition' wasn't easy, and the accompanying imposed guilt took a number of years to pass. But eventually the church had its own unashamed identity. Born from within its womb was an Aboriginal dance team comprised of young boys and girls, re-enacting the Creation story in traditional mimes and rhythm, adding to it the movements of animals, birds and camp life. Some of these children, destined to walk with shame through the streets of Kalgoorlie, were now dancing with pride in their identity.

We planned a spiritual journey into the western desert communities to share the goodness of our Creator in song, dance and talk. Cattle trucks packed with people and dogs joined the caravan of four-wheel-drives, Holden cars and Ford stationwagons stretched along the dusty road toward Warburton, our first stop. Dark hands joined together against a backdrop of fear, isolation and generations of suspicion between tribal elders and children of the stolen generation.

The tuning of guitars signalled the beginning of the festivities out in the flat in front of the stone church building as evening settled at Warburton. One by one, group by group, the people of the community took their spots on the ground, wrapped in blankets, sticks resting at their side, picked up from time to time to keep the dogs at bay, break up a fight or point at the children. There was no such thing as a starting time. The ever increasing throng waited patiently for the leaders to appear.

'You mob, we're ready now,' Livingston called into the microphone. 'We all from everywhere tonight, Kalgoorlie way, Warakurna way. We need to pray together, to pray for me, for everyone who come tonight.' The dust between the microphones and the audience rose in bursts as children raced back and forth, sitting for a few minutes, playing chasey and listening to the growls of their aunties. Every family group had its turn to sing, to tell stories, to pray, to thank God for the land, the food, their families, to tell of their loved ones who had passed away.

'You have something for the children?' Livingston whispered through the microphone in my direction. The throngs of children immediately swarmed around me and started to pull at the bags beside me on the ground. Out came tapping sticks, tambourines, bells, shakers, triangles, all the percussion instruments I could find, the universal language of rhythm.

Western religious practice has so often stripped humanity of its rhythm, rendering it speechless, devoid of emotion and sensitivity. The craft of expression in its many forms is measured by beats, some long, some short. Life itself moves with rhythm, with appropriate rests, stops, crescendos and staccatos. That night the whole flat came to life, the women cupped their hands and beat the time on their thighs like they would do in their ceremonies and the dust rose higher under the feet of the children, as they danced their way into the hearts of their people under the stars of heaven.

During the preaching, children continued their play around the edges of the circle, not venturing too far into the dark, lest the 'mamu' get them. The dogs were closely guarded by Daisy, a tall, barrel-shaped woman who always wore a red cloth around her forehead, carried a stick, smiled while she talked and pointed to heaven to tell us that she still loved Jesus. No one batted an eyelid and the speaker never missed a beat while she broke up the dog fights with her stick and her sharp words, 'Payi, Payi, you stupid dogs,' as she pushed them apart.

Every small community joined in these celebrations, arriving in trucks with broken windscreens, tyres wrapped with bailing wire, exhausts hanging by a thread, trucks that were packed with men, women and children, each one carrying a blanket. Families camped around the edges of the community, tied tarps to the shrubs, bought an esky at the store to keep their kangaroo meat cool, and spent their pension money for the fortnight to celebrate their oneness as a desert people.

Conventions, funerals, football carnivals, land-rights meetings all take on the atmosphere of a corroboree or a celebration of community life, whether at a time of sadness or a time of joy. For ten years we made the trip every January through the desert to Alice Springs, and sometimes on into Arnhem Land, stopping at communities along the way, catching up with old friends, taking funerals, sitting under trees with tribal elders and their wives. One January, as we drove into Warburton, our first stop, the immediate impression was the stillness of the village. There were no four-wheel-drives in sight, only one or two dogs, and a heavy atmosphere. One elderly lady hobbling along the road supported by a knotted stick turned to look at us, but she didn't give us the usual wave. Ron stopped to talk to her in lingo.

'They all at sorry camp, nyaru, they sad,' she pointed toward the Warakurna road. One of our friends had been killed on the road coming out of the turn-off from the Olgas and heading toward the west.

We drove quietly and steadily over the bumps toward the motley crew of people sitting, lying, camping-of-sorts along a dry creek bed in the flat. When we turned off the engine, we could hear the background of wailing intermittently pierced by a scream or a shout. We stood silently by our vehicle for a few minutes until motioned by an elder to approach. Limping toward us was the deceased's brother, the guitar player at our wedding. His thighs were bandaged. He grabbed us and shook with tears. Ron held him, just as he might have held him thirty years before when this sobbing man was only a kid. He and his brother were supposed to leave Alice together, but the man with the bandages left earlier, not wanting to wait. His brother finished drinking late and then started out toward home. He never made the turn, the car skidded off the road, rolled and crashed. According to tribal custom, this man standing before us, now deep in sorrow, should have been there to protect his brother and not leave him to come home alone. Punishment was swift—three spears to the thigh.

Even widows receive punishment and suffering according to the laws of women's business. A grieving wife will suffer the loss of all her personal belongings after her husband's death. The purging of all remembrances of the couple is part of the mourning, the grieving, the spiritual process of the passage from life to death. Her upper body is covered with white paint and she is brought into a circle of tribal women for physical punishment and humiliation.

Several of the women motioned me to come, cry, shake their hand, pray for them. The men shook hands with Ron, their head down, tears flowing. We watched the sun set and the fires light up. When newcomers to the scene drove up, the wailing started again, handfuls of dirt were thrown to the wind, a few tempers flared. Ron took out the guitar and started to sing. Others joined in and soon we came around the main fire, as relatives talked about 'kuminara'—the deceased—and their own sadness. When someone dies, their name ceases to be said. The word 'kuminara' is a stand-in for that person's name.

There are lots of 'kuminaras' throughout the centre of Australia. The burden of sadness is too great for them to hear that name again. It even disappears from the desert, like dust in the wind. Once in a while there might be a whisper of that name in another's ear, so no one else can hear it. Anyone else who has that name also has to change it. From the time that Ron came out to the desert in the 1960s they never called him by his name, only 'Kurta Kurta', brother to everyone. They will never have to change that name.

Other special items also disappear at the time of death. Photographs of the person, which are usually a cherished highlight of any visit, are burned, along with items of clothing. Even a car might be abandoned and the key thrown into the bush. Memories are too tender to embrace. For the time being anyway.

After a year of proper mourning, the reburial, or memorial, service is held and the family then resumes its business. The houses are occupied again, there is more talk and memories about the one who had died, but the name is still not mentioned. And still no photographs are shown.

Later, when the sorrow had ended, Ron sat in the circle with the elders of the clans. 'This is our history,' he said to them in their language while he spread out the photographs in front of him. 'It belongs to us, not to the whitefellas, the anthropologists, the university teachers. It's ours. People been come and go, take photos and take 'em away to write books, make speeches, get money, and they act like the story is theirs.

But it's ours. We need to hold onto it.' The elders began to nod and picked up the photographs, one by one.

Coming into Warburton, as in most desert communities, there is a sign: 'NO PHOTOGRAPHS to be taken, unless by permission of the community adviser'. One elder once angrily commented, his arms waving for emphasis as he talked, 'We're not monkeys in a zoo, for tourists to drive around our community, taking photos. They take our spirit away.' A photograph was an image, an image that could be used for good or for evil. Young girls did not want their photos ending up in tribal hands, fearing that a 'marbarn' man would stare at the image, sing his songs, and supernaturally call their spirits toward the desert.

On the other hand, they loved to see themselves in photos or on video. For years, wherever we went, we showed slides, shared photographs, ran the video machine of images of themselves, and now recently, the times, they are a-changing.

'Kurta,' someone whispers. 'You bring us photo of my old grandfather. I want my kids to see him, to know who he was.' The people are reclaiming their story, little by little, piecing together what had been taken away.

❂ ❂ ❂

Wherever we travelled throughout the centre, I found a gentle mixture of shadow and light, harshness of history and sacrifice of commitment. Couples like Herbert and Lorraine Howell had lived in the desert for more than thirty years, had raised their own children there, had sat in sorry camps quietly in the background. When the time came, because of health and age, that they finally packed their belongings, it was those they had carried as toddlers, taught as teenagers, celebrated with as adults, whose relatives they had buried, who then covered them with a pool of tears. This couple, and many like them, will live on in the history of the community, as long as it remains. Their place in the desert story will be passed down from generation to generation.

And then there were others who, on the face of it, had been there, even sacrificially, looking after the mission, but, in their own perversion and unmet needs, had used the people for their own ends.

At Blackstone, I pulled up a crate in front of a little mia-mia, fashioned from canvas and tin, of an old lady and her daughter. The young woman with laughing eyes pulled on my arm and spoke, haltingly, asking if I knew where her son was. 'Me and my mum want to see 'im,' she grinned.

I couldn't understand what she meant. Where was her son? What did she mean?

Everyone knew, but no one spoke of it. A son had been born to her. Taken away at birth, away to Perth or somewhere beyond, unknown to the young woman in her teens, or the little hunched grandmother covered by old blankets and surrounded by mangy dogs, who stirred the coals while the chops sizzled on the fire. The father of the little boy was a missionary who, one day years ago, had his way with this young Aboriginal girl. The life he gave, he also took away.

The shadows of light and dark play against each other, dancing for a moment in harmony, and then scattered by a dissonant chord.

✻ ✻ ✻

The centre of Australia is harsh. Maps of the area speak the warnings to travellers: 'Do not venture through unless stocked with extra water, tyres, tools, and food. Make sure that someone knows where you are going and when you plan to get there.' The terrain is full of surprises, at once both dangerous and excitingly beautiful, appearing and disappearing unexpectedly. Growing out from the midst of a bed of scrubby bushes might be a tree trunk with a few branches, almost dead in the dry heat, a few leaves still hanging on in the breeze, on which a lone chicken hawk will rest, surveying the territory. A lone bird, as if to say, survival is possible.

We were driving along a bush track that, for hour after hour, revealed no sign of human life. Suddenly, around a sandhill I spotted a small, handwritten sign on a jagged piece of board, nailed to a spike, with an arrow: Kalka, a small community homeland hidden in the scrub a few kilometres along a barely discernible dirt track. The homelands movement began in the 1970s, in a shift away from the practice during government protection days of gathering tribal people into mission settlements. Dotted across the desert are these small clans of twenty to fifty people in extended family groups squatting in tin sheds, surrounded by a windmill, perhaps a generator, and a few old cars. It was an attempt to reclaim the roots of their history, the place where their ancestors were born, the sacredness of their tribal life. Now that very life is a mixture of old and new: a rifle instead of a spear, a vehicle instead of trekking by foot for miles, a windmill instead of moving from waterhole to waterhole.

We turned in at the sign for Kalka. 'I've never been here before,' Ron said, motioning for me to drive on. We never knew if anyone would be in a community when we arrived. They were often on walkabout to the next clan, to Alice Springs, a funeral, a football carnival, a Social Security visit, or a Lands Council meeting. We slowly drove around the half-a-dozen houses and the small shop and office, and stopped near a small family group cooking a kangaroo leg on a fire. An old tribal man, red band around his forehead, long, thin white beard that came to a point in the middle of his chest, was gently turning the leg with a long stick. Three middle-aged women were sitting cross-legged around the fire, burning designs into wooden hitting sticks, while a few children played around the group, running in and out of the circle. The usual camp dogs were lazily stretched alongside them all. The flies buzzed as we approached.

'Yuwo.' The old man lifted his thin arm and motioned for us to come. We squatted next to him on the dirt, speaking broken English and a bit of Ngaanyatjarra.

'We been expectin' you.' They nodded their heads and looked at us with smiles. 'That cloud in the sky. 'e told us. 'e point to the road, to say someone comin'. And then we knew, 'cause Jesus bin tell us' (and the old man pointed to the sky while he spoke), 'someone comin' to pray for us, to give us blessing.' One of the women interpreted after the old man spoke his lingo quietly in our direction.

This was no surprise. I respected their knowledge of the supernatural, the signs in creation, the language of the land. These people knew that God spoke to them through the contours of the land, the changes in the sky, the whisper to the heart. We did come. We did pray. We gave them tapes of gospel songs in their language. We shared their billy tea and damper. That was what real faith was all about: believing in something you can't see.

I learned more about faith and faith put-to-the-test during my days in the desert communities than in all my previous years. Contentment oozed from the pores of the old people who quietly waited for answers to prayer. The pace of the rest of the world was unknown in these small communities, which appeared as little oases in a seemingly barren land. Their faith said, 'Keep going. Don't give up. It will turn out all right in the end. No need to rush.'

Rush results from the desire to control. In our desire to control time, we find that time controls us. The desert is timeless. The people who live in the desert are timeless. Plans can be made, but that is only a scaffold to life, easily pulled down and put up again at another time or another place.

❃ ❃ ❃

We were headed for an outstation at Walu Bore for a bush Bible study. The sky threatened to open up and pour, but all of us, missionaries, tribal leaders and trucks of women and children, decided to push through anyway. We had driven over a thousand kilometres, so we weren't going to turn back because of a little rain. The roads turned into a slippery mudslide, deep trenches sucking the tyres right into the ground. I gripped the wheel, my knuckles turning white. I feared that the least little slip would take us into the bank, where we would have to remain until the rain stopped. The wipers worked overtime, clogged with the torrents of muddy water slung up over the windshield from the tyres. It's raining red mud, I thought. The crossing of the Red Sea took on new meaning, as the nose of the vehicle plunged through the middle of this desert deluge.

We spent the night in a small hut on the outskirts of a homeland camp. We fell into the swag exhausted, and left our mud-covered jeans and boots at the door. The caravan of vehicles continued at the crack of dawn, the rest of the way, taking turns pulling each other out of bogs. The roads had begun to dry up, but some places could easily fool the driver, coming up so quickly around a bend that the momentary swing of the steering wheel was enough to bring the journey to a stop.

Eventually we reached the designated site for the camp, threw a tarp over the trees, put up a makeshift windbreak, started the generator and settled in for a relaxing weekend. That night, amidst the refrains of the guitar, the muddy roads were a thing of the past. By the time Monday morning came, the water had soaked into the desert floor. The only marks left were rock-hard, sun-baked ruts, which would remain until the next grader came along. That might be six months away.

Rain in the desert brought forth treasures usually hidden in the soil. Pink and white flowers now carpeted the desert floor. The rain formed rivulets and streams that ran across the roads, making it necessary to discern their depth before we attempted to drive through. On one such occasion along the Arnhem Highway, obviously misnamed since it was basically a dirt track through tall grass, Ron convinced me, half teasing, to get out of the car and walk through the swollen river just to make sure our vehicle could make it through.

It was only later that he told me that crocodiles were often seen in the area, migrating from the swamps in the north. In some mischievous way he had enjoyed putting me to the test.

After leaving the last camp in Western Australia, we drove slowly into Ernabella, a community in the northern part of neighbouring South Australia, only five hours south of Alice Springs. It was very late at night because we had taken a wrong turn down an even lonelier bush track that we finally decided was going nowhere. When we eventually got back on the right road and caught sight of the one very tall security lamp gleaming in the centre of the community, it was after midnight. No other lights were on.

We parked underneath a tall shadow of a gum tree at the edge of the dirt oval, and prepared to catch a few hours' sleep in the back of the Landrover. I didn't know which was worse: leaving the window open to let in fresh air and a bit of breeze and fight off the mozzies at the same time; or closing the windows as protection against the buzzing dive-bombers, and consequently suffocating in the warm, still air.

I was finding it hard to rest and harder still to turn over to find a more comfortable position wedged between Ron and Lydia. It was quite a squeeze. From the corner of my eye I caught a glimpse of some movement some fifty metres away. I sat up on one elbow, my eyes adjusting to the lamp's glow. I could just barely discern two figures huddled together covered by blankets, walking slowly toward one of the houses. When they reached the edge of the lamp's range of light, for a few seconds I could see a reflection of metal, what I thought was a gas mask around their heads. It was ghostly, like a scene from a movie filmed on another planet. Two pairs of dark, thin legs glided as one, slowly shuffling across my view. Petrol sniffers, I thought. A modern, walking death scene moving across an ancient, majestic land. The reflection had come from the tin containers of petrol tied around their heads and covering their noses.

So many times we sat with parents and grandparents as they shook their heads in helplessness, not knowing how to handle this dread that had swept their communities. So many papers and studies have been done about the causes, the cures, the prevention. And still it goes on. Some young teenagers told us, 'There's nothin' happenin' here, so why not have fun before we die.' The future of the desert, the generations to come, are being dried up in smoke and fumes before they can even begin. I couldn't shake the sight. It clung to my senses like the smell of dead wool in lonely paddocks.

These words curled through my journal like puffs of smoke:

A thicket of smoke
  a clearing of bush
    the dingo's long, low echoing howl.
      Rhythm-tapping, tapping sound,
        the drone of a didgeridoo.
          An old tribal elder
            his place by the fire
              many years this camp was his home.
                After days of a long, long walkabout
                  he returned to sit alone.
Something inside began to cry
  his spirit: heavy and sad.
Tears were dropping, dropping down,
  for in the smoke of his fire home . . .
he saw the years ahead.
  His people wandering . . .
his people lost
  where once in the dust
their tracks were clear
  now only shuffling, shuffling, blurred.
Beyond the smoke, the many years
  an image began to appear.

A ghostly, ghostly figure
  his heart gripped in a moment of fear.
    A blanket-wrapped figure—
      a face strangely hidden
reached out a dark hand to his.
    Above the familiar smell of the fire . . .
      the fumes curled round his head
    fumes of the future . . . fumes of death . . .
Oh, no, my son . . . my son.
    Across the red desert and years of time
    faces, young faces, shadows, red eyes.
    What was once our dreaming, our legend, ourselves
    has gone with the fumes, a nightmare, and gloom.

Oh, my son, my heart breaks as you breathe in, breathe out,
    moment by moment your life is drained.
    The desert of dreaming, now the desert of death.
    Oh, no, my son, my son.

Two days later cars from all over that desert region formed a circle
around the red-dirt oval for the championship footy game. Tall, slim-
legged young men from each community, all kicking barefoot, shirt and
no shirts, competed against each other as the wind blew the red dust,
completely obliterating the view of the players from the sidelines. In the
middle of the game, several shots were heard from the direction of the
store. Dogs yelped, women screamed, children ran in all directions, as
two police cars screeched to a halt in front of the store. After a few
moments, they half-carried a young man out, holding a rifle, high on
petrol. The desert paddy-wagon took him to Alice Springs that afternoon. As he was driven away from the community, a little naked
four-year-old boy stood in the middle of the road, watching the disappearing vehicle. He raised his little stick, pointed it at the dust and
shouted, 'Bang! Bang!'

One of the police officers had worked in the communities for seventeen years, loved the people, and quietly, sadly, looked on as the years
ticked by, never seeing any hope. He leaned over the bonnet of his
vehicle, staring into our faces. 'I've seen maybe millions of dollars pour

in and out of the centre. I've seen Toyotas come and go. New Toyotas ain't gonna help. It has to come from within. Maybe what they need is their own dream ... their own dream. Not ours, but their own.'

❂ ❂ ❂

The convention in Alice Springs was unique. For seven years Ron and I had encouraged tribal communities from all over Australia, urban Aboriginal churches and members of the general Australian community to share their experience of Christianity in their own special ways. It was in Alice Springs that they all came together, expectant and unashamed. Small circles of people from a dozen or more language groups from all over the centre dotted the green grass of the Alice Springs Showground on the left of the Stuart Highway coming in to town. Makeshift camps, small tents, mattresses and piles of blankets circled each shady tree, staking a claim for the night. Each evening for a week, the electric guitars signalled the time for gathering. Cars, eleven-seater vans, twenty-seater buses, roadbuses carrying a group from Elcho Island, all converged in the parking areas. Barefooted men and women, carrying blankets, naked babies on the back, and a bottle or two of water, made their way leisurely to their chosen spots.

Advertising around town listed the starting times for the meetings, but in fact they started whenever the singers and the guitar players were ready. The Hermannsburg Choir, dark faced, tribal people harmonising German hymns in Pitjantjatjara, led the way, followed by the rhythmic tapping, traditional dance steps, and waving branches from the Elcho Island singers. Dozens of items ranging from country and western, original songs in tribal languages, as well as renditions of popular songs by Johnny Cash, scrambled their way in between.

The spectators spread their blankets a fair way back from the stage, leaving a large space for children to run flat-out, often followed by a few dogs nipping at their heels. A great finale burst through the ranks with young people from Elcho Island dressed in flowing garments waving multi-coloured banners, tapping tambourines in circular formation, with legs pumping and hips swaying in traditional movements to modern drum beats. It was an awesome sight.

Stitched into this tapestry of colour and excitement, with different desert accents flying back and forth, were the threads of temper, domestic violence and youth uproar. In the dark shadows behind the pavilions, in the bushes, along the gravel road, fights broke out, fuelled by alcohol, arguments between a man and his woman, jealous rages, teenage boys throwing rocks. While the band played on, the Night Patrol made regular visits and the police wagon mustered a few into town for an overnight stay, or an ambulance made a run to the hospital.

Ron and I always pitched our tent in the middle of the tribal zone under the trees, so we could see in all directions. For seven years we had organised the event, after its creator, Ben Mason, a pulpit-thumping, articulate, deep-voiced Aboriginal version of Billy Graham, became too ill to continue. Ben had started the annual convention in 1986 primarily to give the desert people a chance to mount the platform, sing, preach, and celebrate in their own cultural style. At its height, the convention drew several thousand people from all backgrounds, from all around Australia, even attracting visitors from overseas.

Ben and Ron were soulmates. They understood each other without saying a word. They were both strong personalities with piercing eyes, big voices and big hearts, capable of anger, bitterness and hate but for their choice to walk the pathway of forgiveness and reconciliation. Ben was the son of a tribal woman and a German camel driver, born deep in the bush during the days when warriors put sand in the mouths of half-caste babies, not wanting to live with the shame in the camp. Ben's step-dad, Old Mulga Joe, had heard the Christian teaching of mercy and love, so he refused to have the little boy killed. Instead, he placed him in the arms of a missionary outside of Laverton.

The tribal elders and the young men of the centre respected both these men. Even one who, full of grog, staggered up to the platform, grabbed Ben by the arm, and slurred, 'Ya gotta let me s-s-speak, bro-o-ther,' with one foot on the step. Ben blocked his way, telling him to sit down.

'I'll hit you, I'll fix you, you know, tribal way, you, you . . .' the man spluttered.

Old Ben just stared him down. 'Now you listen to me. I'm your uncle and I've got a bigger power.' He pointed to the sky and pulled tribal rank on the young man.

After leading the choir in the trademark finale, 'How Great Thou Art', Ben had passed the convention's torch on to us. 'I want you to carry on,

Ron. You've got a good wife and she'll help you. I don't know anyone else I'd rather see here in the desert than you two.' Two years later, Ben's health deteriorated and Ron laid his body to rest at Mount Margaret Community, seventeen kilometres from Laverton. No one ever replaced Ben in Ron's heart.

We would never get a full night's sleep during the whole week of the convention. Each night when the final vehicle left the showground, and we drank our last cup of tea and settled into bed, someone would whisper at our tent door, 'Kurta, Diana, come help, that boy been fight. We can't sleep.' Over the years, we were rained out, suffered from a bout of extra-tough mosquitoes, heard a mob of horses snorting all through the night, made numerous calls to the police, grabbed a rifle from a young man who wanted to 'set his wife straight', settled domestic disputes at three o'clock in the morning.

Once a love triangle erupted between two brothers and one of their wives. For an hour, I paced the perimeter of the showground, my arms wrapped around the woman, trying to calm her down, while Ron mediated with the brothers. In the end she went back to her husband's camp, but a year later she had moved in with the brother.

Along the banks of the Todd River in Alice Springs there was a parallel life to that which moved along the main shopping mall. On the surface, one could see tourists and visitors from all over the world and hear hundreds of different languages as people walked from shop to shop, which overflowed with dot paintings and intricately woven baskets from the Top End of the nation and resonated with the sounds of the didgeridoo. Huge amounts of tourist dollars kept the streets alive.

But the Todd River was mostly a dry riverbed, no dollars flowing except to pay for the grog. Small groups of dislocated people huddled in the patches of shade under gum trees, one or two white drifters attached to them, looking for a feed, knowing that the blackfellas would help. Among the dislocated, colour knows no barrier.

All around Australia we met scores of spiritually and emotionally lost Australians, begging for someone to take notice of them. Story after story confirmed that they always found comfort, acceptance and recognition among the Aboriginal people. 'Them fellas were the only ones who showed interest in me,' was the usual comment. 'If it hadn't been for them, I wouldn't be alive.' From the beginning years of this continent, the days of the 'currency lads and lasses', the custodians of the land also became the custodians of the lives of orphan children, street-wise teenagers and adults who had been kicked in the teeth by life.

During our visits to the Todd, we often witnessed domestic arguments and helped disarm both men and women of beer bottles and iron bars. We would sit with them while the torment subsided, and then encouraged their re-commitment to one another. Sometimes I wondered if Aboriginal men were capable of tender feelings, after seeing so much hurt among the women. My faith was restored and I looked at the men with new eyes when I heard about Rupert.

Rupert's wife had taken sick with a long-term illness, which left her almost an invalid. For months, Rupert carried her from bed to bath, washed and cared for her tenderly, so tenderly, until she passed away. In the middle of a harsh environment, where survival belonged to the fittest for centuries, here was a touch of a gentleness between a man and a woman that transcended all cultures.

'Nah, these Abo women don't take much lookin' after, not like white women do,' I had heard voiced by both black and white men. Was that the opinion of those who took little children away from the arms of crying mothers? Was that the opinion of those who chained a black woman to a tree to be used for sexual gratification? Was that the opinion of government officials who had dictated who an Aboriginal woman could marry? Was it their opinion that Aboriginal women have no feelings or that they don't want the tenderness, commitment and care that every other woman in the world wants, regardless of colour or race?

'Yeah, we'd like to have flowers brought to us. We've always wanted to be treated special. It's just that we never expect it no more,' one white-haired Aboriginal grandmother revealed to me. I've purposefully asked these questions of tribal women, Aboriginal grandmothers in urban homes, young women nursing babies, left alone by their men who are out drinking with mates. I've wanted to shout the answer from the rooftops, from the hills in the desert, from the tent flaps and car bodies that make up the fringe-dwelling camps. Women are the same everywhere, with a desire, deep down, to celebrate their femaleness.

❂ ❂ ❂

After ten years, we decided that it was time for us to step down from the job of organising the convention. It's good to let go of things and allow others to experience new challenges. It's good for the rivers to flow with fresh water from time to time. The final night came. Ron and I knew that we had made the right decision, but the feelings of sadness and loss intermingled with relief. For the past three years we had considered this decision, with each drive into Alice a question as to whether 'that' should be the last year. The roads had taken a toll on many areas of our life together, not the least of which was that we had never been able to have a holiday at Christmas and the New Year. With Lydia growing older and needing to experience more than meetings and heat during her time off from school, the right moment had come.

Our friends farewelled us with gifts and flowers. Out of the shadows and onto the stage came Yuminia, my special tribal sister. She took my hands and whispered into my ear, 'You taught us that we are special.' Groups of singers rushed the small stage and pushed the amplifiers aside, making more room, to debut the desert translation of 'How Great Thou Art', the convention theme song, especially for us. All of us were crying, not so much because we were leaving, but because the translator of the song, our good friend Roderick, who was our faithful supporter and had helped us manage the locked-up pain and hurt that flowed through the middle of the night at the campground, had passed away since the last convention. His spirit lived on through his words.

Many visitors from the city have come to this gathering in Alice Springs in order to experience something of the 'other world' of Aboriginal Australia. Against the backdrop of the many social problems that the tribal people face—the drunkeness, the anger, and the violence—there is this incredible celebration of life, of beauty and patient faith that their world will change for the better. The visitors have embraced these new images, these new stories which seem to contradict the old ones, confronting the stereotypes, challenging their own history. They always went away changed.

CHAPTER 17

'I'm Five Cultures, Mum'

Ron leaned against the doorway of my hideaway room while I sat on the floor in despair. It was one of those moments when I felt a failure in trying to grapple with the cultural differences that we faced every day, not only from the pressures surrounding us, but within our own relationship. Through red, puffy eyes and with blurred vision from the sheer volume of salty tears I had shed I looked in Ron's direction and uttered a groan. 'Well, then, why did you marry a white person, anyway?' Even in our love and commitment to one another over the years, race became an issue from time to time, especially when it threatened Ron's opinions or decisions.

I had just spent several days packing our gear for a trip through the Kimberley then across to the Northern Territory, back through the desert, and finally home to Kalgoorlie—a trip of four weeks. Ron had dumped over a hundred cassette tapes on my desk to be labelled, had stacked boxes of small books to be sorted on the bench by the back door, and had scattered a myriad of microphones, speakers, cords, and tape recorders all through the garage to be organised for the trip. Then he went to visit the hospital.

We had one day left at home and I had many more tasks to complete.

Lydia needed her schoolwork organised and we needed money from the bank. The kangaroo, chickens and galahs required their supplies of feed. Lists lay scattered on the floor. Too many times before we had forgotten important items, the realisation hitting us a few hours down the road, too far away to turn back. This time I had vowed to do better.

Ron often waited until the night before to sort and pack, relying on his memory and his belief that God would provide all things for us as we took off for parts unknown. His approach to life was spontaneous, without much planning, organisation or preparation for contingencies. That worked surprisingly well sometimes, but over the years he had lost precious heirlooms, treasured books and cameras, expensive tools that he could not replace. He caused many a bridal party to panic, while they waited for the preacher—Ron—who would be the last to arrive.

When the pressures of travelling with a wife, a child, all the attendant paraphernalia, and the checklist of car repairs and spares became too much, Ron just went walkabout or watched television. Invariably, I would be packing the back of our Landcruiser well into the midnight hours before our time of departure the next morning.

This time I had snapped. I suggested that we wait another day or two. I wanted more time to prepare.

'We have a daughter to consider,' I reminded him. 'She's not a baby any more. I can't just put her in the back seat with a stuffed animal and expect her to be happy for four weeks. It's not just you and me.' I blurted out all my frustrations.

Long ago we had decided to do our work as a family. Ron had seen so many pastors in the church lose touch with their wives and children because they were away so much. He didn't want that to happen to us. We were to travel and speak together. And Lydia was to come with us. But I needed more time to make all this happen.

Ron interpreted my hesitancy, my suggestion that we couldn't keep up this pace, this way of managing our family and work, as a 'dampening of his spirit', a criticism of his way of doing things.

'That's what the missionaries used to say. Always telling me this thing and that thing.' His tone of voice was derogatory, frustrated, resigned, and certainly meant to wound. And wounded I was. When I had left the shores of America, prepared to leave all behind and live in the outback, under a tree if need be, and definitely in a tent, I had not wanted to follow the traditional 'colonial missionary' attitude of the past. I wanted to be different, to sit on the ground and learn, to walk beside Aboriginals, talking together, not 'talking down'. For an Aboriginal person to call another one a 'whitefella' was the essence of disgust, almost a curse. I didn't want to be in the same boat. Over the years I had continued to fight my own demon of superiority, that would raise its ugly head at times most inappropriately. I constantly struggled to walk between two worlds, and the words that Ron had spoken put a spear into my heart.

It was only after the explosions, when we communicated, explained our own thoughts and motives that we began to understand each other, to trust each other, to realise that we only wanted good for each other. Ron had lived his life not trusting white people, and I had lived my life not trusting men. When he looked at me, he saw 'white', and whatever I said he then filtered through that grid.

Just saying to each other, 'But you can trust me,' was not enough. We had to walk the bumpy road together, to feel each other's pain, to cry together, to dismantle our own barriers long enough to hear, to touch each other's tears in order to know the meaning of the word 'trust'. We had to be committed, especially in the times when we were tempted to walk away or regard it as a bad experiment. The real glue between us was that we believed that our marriage was made in heaven.

We believed the hand of God had plucked me from New York City, set me down in the middle of the goldfields, watched as Ron toured through Kalgoorlie and sang his songs in the Victoria Gardens, and ignited the spark that fired our marriage. But we also knew the difficulties, the pain of our pilgrimage on earth, the dirt roads, the corrugations, the washouts along the way. The journey of trust was the pathway to the horizon, the edge of the hill that meets the sky, where joys and sorrows all begin to make sense.

'Look,' said Ron, kneeling beside me. 'You know I love you, and I'm sorry for what I said. It just slips out sometimes. Something I have to work on, maybe some bitterness still there. I made a conscious choice to marry a non-Aboriginal person. I didn't want to be boxed into my own race. In a way, I wanted to invade the white world. I didn't want to stay on the 'wood heap' any longer, to stay in my place, stay in the background. I knew that I needed someone strong, who wouldn't back off when I said the wrong word, or when the racial hurts came out.

Someone who could put up with me and who could help me do what I couldn't on my own. I know it's been hard because you've probably done seventy-five per cent of the changing. I've come only twenty-five per cent of the way. But you and me, we're mates, struggling together.'

He squeezed my hand. I couldn't help but smile and shake my head as we made one more step along the road of trust. He leaned back and sighed. 'You know, it's like the old father emu . . .' Even in the middle of our disagreements or my tears, Ron had a story to tell. He wove the yarn about the father emu, whose responsibility it was to sit on the eggs in the nest and to turn them twelve times a day so they would hatch properly. Then after more than fifty days, they would hatch and the father emu would still look after them. When they were big enough, he would lead them away from their birthplace, into another area of country.

'The old father doesn't want them to take a mate from his own country, too much inbreeding, which is bad for them. He took them to a new place, to marry into a different tribe. That's the way our people were, long time, during the ceremonies, they would take wives from another place.' In some strange way, that was Ron trying to explain in his sense of culture why it was important for him to marry me.

We had often joked that one way to conquer the white person was to marry one. On one level, I laughed, realising some of the truth in that statement. On another level, I squirmed, because of what it meant in reality. Pride among westerners is very deeply ingrained. When I thought I knew the answer to some social problem, I had to learn to swallow my words, to keep quiet and listen. I tried to curb my need to talk after hearing one Aboriginal friend's evaluation of whitefellas: 'Oh, we just sit back and let them fellas talk. We just nod and agree, because they don't really want to listen, anyway.'

'I think I should start a white wives' club, Ron,' I suggested half-jokingly. I knew a number of white women married to Aboriginal men around Australia and had often thought how much I needed their advice and companionship. Most of the time our moments together were brief, not saying much, but knowing. Women like Shirley, Carol, Sandra, Jenny, Christine, Marilyn, Kathy, Margaret, Sally, Virginia, Nola, and many others.

'Not a bad idea.' He was serious. 'All of you women know enough about us, the "real" us, that you would either get speared by the elders, or have the whitefellas' mouths hangin' open. You should really do it.'

The wives I know personally, have met briefly, or hear about from others, all have a unique story to tell. Their path has not been easy. Some of them quietly endure persecution, rejection and violence from both Aboriginal and white. Some are abandoned when their husbands have thirsted after the grog or hungered after other women. Some have battled with depression for years, and have been found walking down streets not knowing who they are. Others raise the children plus the grandchildren on their own, while others choose to seek their own career, because the problems are just too much. In spite of all this, the choice was hers—each one—to love, honour and live with a man who battles the world for identity, recognition and respect. It then becomes her own battle as well.

In the early hours of the morning, Ron agreed to postpone our trip for a few more days, so the proper preparations could be made.

✪ ✪ ✪

I loved the remote bush. We always camped away from the road, driving over the lumps of clay, around rockholes and into the scrub to make for ourselves a 'million-star' hotel. After picking the spot, Ron would first collect dry wood to start a fire.

Lydia would follow her dad, bringing small sticks, eventually piling them into her own little camp fire. I would busy myself raking away lumps of dirt, old anthills, and small rocks to clear a place for our swags. I would put out the ground sheet and roll out our swags, a double one and a single one right next to it. After much deliberation we had purchased them in Alice Springs. They were rugged, heavy-duty with extra thick foam, made for the bush by bushmen. The red dirt in the crevices of the swag was there to stay, evidence that we really used them in remote places, not in the urban fringes of prepared campgrounds.

I would set out a small folding table under the shade of a nearby tree and open my perfectly packed box of food and utensils, revealing the film of red dirt and jostled tins, cereal boxes, plates and cutlery.

On each trip I would add a touch of my own cultural trappings. The more I felt comfortable in Ron's world, the more I could appreciate the subtle touches of my own. At first Ron took no notice of these 'fineries' of western life. After all, he used to iron his clothes by placing them under his mattress until the next morning. At least, I hadn't thought he took notice of any of these things until one day he asked me for the sour cream to add to the baked potato that was roasting in the coals after the fire had settled down.

Salt and pepper grinders. Mocha Kenya coffee bags. I would always pack in a special china cup, designed from the Old World, a touch of elegance making its place in the middle of a red dirt 'highway'. These were gifts from Glenda, one of my best friends, whose lounge-room window of her three-level home perched on the banks of Sydney Harbour provided a view of the bridge and the Opera House. Glenda had once gone walkabout with us into the desert communities, swatting flies, chasing goannas and smelling like smoke, the same as the rest of us. Our friendship hung on a balance between red dirt and cappuccinos.

Glenda looked on in wonder during that trip to the centre. 'There is really another world out here, isn't there, Diana? A world that the rest of us know nothing about.' Glenda and I, being of the same skin, so many times following the same train of thought, able to finish each other's sentences, were a gulf apart when it came to the realities of tribal life. But I needed her friendship, to be able to meet her on the edge of our worlds from time to time.

In gentle contrast to the blackened billy can, the ever-present favourite tins of sliced peaches and rice cream, a sizzling tail of kangaroo and a few gum leaves thrown into a hot cup of tea, swirling in Ron's favourite stainless steel oversize mug, stood the bone china cup and espresso coffee.

When Lydia had gone to sleep, we would sit near the fire staring into the deep red, blue and golden coals, telling stories, planning our future, chuckling over the 'why' questions that our daughter was constantly asking, thinking about our families scattered across the world.

'We should do this all the time,' I would say to Ron. 'Sell our house, buy a mobile home, good enough for the bush roads, and just travel from place to place, sharing good things with people, encouraging them, listening.' Ron agreed. He always wanted to do that. It was peaceful out there. Life was simple out there. The bush people had it right. This was the way to live, in Australia, the land of 'going bush'. That was our dream, anyway, when we camped under the stars. Only a dream.

When the fire began to die down and the cool breeze of the desert made our skin jump, we retired to the swags, snuggled close in those intimate moments under a heavenly sky, full of twinkling candlelight, shooting stars, satellites circling the earth, the old man emu constellation looking down at us, and the milky way which formed a wide path across the sky. Nights blessed with dreams and visions of a time past, a time present and a time to come.

The buzzing of the flies told us that morning was here. Lydia would wrap herself up in the sheet and jump in the truck to have her breakfast. She never liked sharing her food with the flies. Ron always woke up before me, took a walk into the scrub before coming back with more bits of dry wood, maybe a goanna to cook for breakfast.

Lydia often went with him, trailing behind, looking for signs of lizards, nanny goats, or kangaroos. Over the years, Ron taught her to gut the roos, dig out the goannas, pluck the feathers from the bush turkeys and follow the tracks of the bush animals. She was a willing and eager student.

The first words that she learned were desert lingo. Her favourites were 'yapu' which meant 'rock, or stone'; 'tja' which meant 'mouth' and 'kuka' which meant 'meat'. She would say them over and over again, relishing our reactions of joy and the encouragement from the tribal people, who thought it was marvellous that this young 'relative' of theirs who also claimed the USA as her heritage was speaking their language.

These words eventually made it to America when, at two years old, Lydia had sat at my mother's table in Oklahoma, and, after chewing a piece of meat, kept looking at me, saying, 'Kuka in tja. Kuka in tja.' It was so out of context around that table that, at first, I hadn't caught what she was saying. As Lydia persisted, looking at me like I should know what was going on, it had clicked. My mother asked if all Australian children said that. 'Well, not all,' I answered and laughed. I didn't tell her that Lydia's teething ring as a baby was a bone joint from a kangaroo tail.

Lydia loved the desert tribes, especially the kids. At each community she found friends who would follow our vehicle every time we drove in, coaxing her out to play with them, remembering her from month to month, year to year as we made our rounds. She learned to play barefoot footy with all the others, first rode a bicycle, made spears, drew in the ground with a 'milbindi', a story wire or stick.

When she was small the desert teenagers carried her around and spoke to her in their language, introducing her to their world. As each year went by, she was welcomed into their circle under the trees, their camp fires in the bush.

She brought these adventures back to Kalgoorlie with her, to her other friends who lived in a narrower world. During their play times, she introduced them to hunting for kangaroos with spears, chasing goannas. They built make-believe fires and pretended to huddle around them. As the imaginary animals lay next to them, Lydia would take charge and announce, 'Now that we've killed 'em, we gotta cook 'em on this fire and eat 'em.'

A little boy once looked at her thoughtfully and asked, 'Are you one of those wi-gi-nes?'

Lydia had looked at him just as thoughtfully. 'I'm just a kid,' she stated.

❂ ❂ ❂

'How many cultures am I, Dad?' Lydia had asked when she was six years old. During her first few years, she had learned Aboriginal words, travelled all around the desert communities, attended preschool with an Aboriginal teacher, and played mostly with other Aboriginal kids. But she also knew that she was an American with dual citizenship. I tried to heed my friend Shirley's words, a wife in a cross-cultural Aboriginal marriage, that the children of such a marriage need to honour and respect their Aboriginal heritage first and foremost. That would help to steel their souls for the heartaches of the future, enable them to be proud of that part of them that others were reluctant to appreciate.

'Well, five cultures, I think,' began Ron, as he held up five fingers to Lydia. 'There is Aboriginal, Australian, English, German and American.' He named each one while the fingers on his hand kept count, until they were all spread out in front of her. 'That's a whole handful, sort of like the United Nations.' Ron always spoke proudly to Lydia of her heritage, not only her Aboriginal heritage, but all the other ones as well. He enthusiastically told everyone he met that he was married to an American whose forebears came from Germany. Ron knew white Australian history better than most white Australians, as well as being known as a 'walking encyclopaedia' among his own people. He could also add flavour to the average person's understanding of American history, having read biographies of the presidents and a number of books on the Civil

War. Adding to that mixture was his fondness of reporting that his great grandfather came off a convict ship, had a long white beard and read to his grandmother from a huge family Bible, not to mention the story of his Uncle Ned, the black American who stood up in court for his rights.

Ron energetically recited Aboriginal legends to Lydia every night before she went to bed, interspersing them with Bible stories, Aesop's fables and fairytales.

Some time during her first year at primary school, she began to ask questions about what mixtures were lurking beneath her skin. 'Why don't people like Aborigines, Mum? What did we do wrong?' Her round eyes innocently appealed for some explanation beyond the reality of her own world.

At some level, there is an exotic appeal in becoming immersed in other traditions and even embarking upon a cross-cultural marriage. For those who are adventurous and pride themselves in their tolerance toward different cultures, jobs in foreign countries seem attractive, and sampling new foods and lifestyles is an exciting part of the package. All over the world, there are relationships that develop across the cultural boundaries: German and French, men from India and women from England and vice versa, Chinese and American, Nigerian and Australian. Those who ponder such relationships from the outside are in wonder and awe at the interesting combinations, the gifts of heritage that each brings to the other, noting the beautiful skin colours and the exciting future for an offspring of such a union.

But there is often a different attitude toward the union between an Aboriginal and a non-Aboriginal. There is no exotic appeal. And wasn't the Aboriginal person a member of the 'despised' race, with nothing to offer to civilisation, who should be out of town by sundown? The quickest way to cut conversation short at an office party is to mention that you are married to an Aboriginal.

I once spoke at a series of talks for women along the East Coast. The short biography on the brochure introduced me as 'an American from New York City married to an Aboriginal pastor'. One guest was expecting me to be a black American. She could not understand why a white American, a woman especially, would want to marry an Aboriginal. Not many years ago, a fair-skinned man didn't dare admit that there was Aboriginal blood in his background or jobs would be hard to get, houses would be hard to buy, and communities would be hard to penetrate. This was the world in which our daughter would grow up. In many a quiet moment I pondered her future.

During my liaison work in the Kalgoorlie school system and Department of Community Services, I floated from school to school, helping Aboriginal kids find some meaning in these educational 'systems'. I sat quietly in the staff rooms that bustled with teachers and overheard revealing comments like, 'Those Abos are hopeless. No use wasting our time.' or 'Those kids won't learn anything anyway.' These same teachers appeared at community discussions on juvenile justice development programs or on creating avenues for the disadvantaged, and when confronted by reports of prejudicial treatment of Aboriginal students in schools, looked me in the eyes and said, 'We're doing all we can. We're not racist.' Once, later on, during a revealing moment in the aisle of a supermarket, there was obvious surprise and embarrassment as Ron appeared at my side. 'Oh, by the way, this is my husband, Reverend Ron Williams.'

By the time Lydia turned ten years old she had been to three foreign countries, all around Australia and through the Red Centre a number of times. She knows more about her country than almost any other child, a knowledge that gives her a confidence beyond her years. She has friends in 'every port', so to speak, happily at home in the dust of the desert as well as among the city lights. One afternoon while I watched her play with her best friends at a birthday party, I realised that they were all either Aboriginal or from mixed-race families, combinations of Australian, Filipino, and Maori.

I had to bridle my passion to flood her life with books, teach her the times-tables when she was still in the cot, or expect her to write an essay at five years old. During the times we trekked around Australia, I was her teacher. It was difficult to establish any routine, between driving through the night to get to the next stop, being guests in other people's camps or homes and having to readjust our schedules, preparing for our own work. Lydia happily wrote in her journal, pasted in photographs, read numerous books, and reviewed her maths times-tables, all in a few minutes a day and usually along the bush tracks. Most of her genuine education came from the land and the people.

The idea of setting up a table in the bush for schoolwork failed miserably because of the numbers of flies that wanted to join in. Lydia had smartly packed her things, climbed into the back of the vehicle, made herself a protective 'tent', and that's where she did her work for the remainder of the trip.

'Close the door, Mum, the flies are getting in,' she would call from the inner sanctum of the four-wheel-drive. When I would peer through the window, I would see her busily writing in her workbook, a blanket over her head on a hot day, sheltering herself from the winged insects that buzzed around her head. One hand clutching a pencil would emerge from the blanket, while the other hand would wave the intruders away from their landing pads on her cheek.

'If the education department could only see her now,' I would mutter to myself while I packed the billy can, doused the fire and helped Ron to put the swag on the roof rack.

'I won't be able to help Lydia with her work,' Ron had said. 'It's beyond me now. I only finished year five.' I had assured him that his storytelling and his knowledge of history were more valuable than knowing how to rule up the page. Lydia joined him in school assemblies on reconciliation, participated in the Aboriginal dance team, fully painted in ochre colours and dressed in an Aboriginal-designed lap-lap. It was an education more than equal to that which is found in books, graphs and essays.

Lydia tells a story like a blackfella, starting out with, 'Well . . .' and then launching into her own journey around the waterhole. On the other hand, in the middle of one of my distinguished oratories on the virtues of carrots, she will interrupt, looking at me with an impish grin and will say, 'And your point being . . .' Two cultural outlooks, two parallel journeys woven into her young life.

❂ ❂ ❂

'I'm Dad's helper,' she proudly announced, as I lined up my camera lens with the surface of the road. She sat cross-legged on the side of the desert road with a spanner in her hand, helping Ron put the finishing touches to a tyre change after one of our many blowouts. The photograph made its debut in the book, *Mates*, published as a celebration of multicultural Australia.

❂ ❂ ❂

'Mum,' called Lydia excitedly, bursting into the kitchen, where I was peeling the potatoes. 'What's the Ku Klux Klan?'

I dropped the knife and thought to myself, 'Where did this come from?' as I turned to face her inquisitive but anxious eyes. 'Where did you hear about that?' I asked. She took my hand and pulled me into the lounge room to the television.

'There,' she pointed. 'They said something about these people, dressed in white and they don't like Aborigines.' I dropped into the chair, she sat on my lap and we watched the story unfold. The gathering of groups of Klan members. Their refutation that they were racist. The denial of wrongdoing to Aboriginal people in Queensland and other places. Scenes of violence against black Americans flashed on the screen, the past, and present, racial hatred in the United States. I recalled the descriptions of Klan-type activity that countless Aboriginal people had told us about all over Australia. After the news report, I tried to calmly explain what it was all about, reassuring her that she had nothing to fear.

Lydia promptly got up, locked all the doors to the house, came back to face me and said, 'Where's Dad? Will these bad people come to kill him too? Will they kill me?'

The impact of this incident and the questions asked continued to surface for a number of weeks, until Lydia seemed satisfied that our lives were not in danger. I looked out at the gum trees bending with the wind in our front yard and I wondered how I could ever explain injustice to my daughter.

In the midst of Lydia's confidence in life, in school, in friendships, there has been a tinge of shyness, perhaps even shame. As she grows older, she retreats more often when faced with new situations. When Ron announces his pride in her, she shrinks back even more, even resenting these bursts of encouragement and pleasure. We talked about it. 'Weren't you like that as a kid?' I asked him, remembering what his Uncle Barney had told me.

'Yeh, I was called Spook. Wore baggy clothes so no one would notice me. Hid away when others were around. It was just me and the dogs, wherever I went.'

That is Lydia. So much like him at times. The shyness of her father's early days and the confidence of her mother play themselves out in her young life. As I consider Ron's life and how he has changed since those days of being a 'spook', no one would ever consider him shy now. It was sometime after Lydia was born, that I began to notice a change in Ron. He began to embrace not only his Aboriginal identity but also the other threads in his heritage. He began to speak out with strength. The whitefellas he came to have most respect for were those who were willing to be silent and listen to him for a while. He could respect men who considered seriously his advice about the road ahead for Aboriginal people, and didn't always push their 'answer to the Aboriginal problem'.

'We can talk just as good as the rest of them,' he would often say.

Ron is most in his element when he mounts the platform to give a speech or to preach. It's as if that square metre behind the pulpit is a safe place, a place where he can let loose and say what he wants to say. He can now proclaim what he has been holding back for so long; now he has the freedom to speak, to shout, to whisper, or to cry, with no one to interrupt him. He modulates his voice, pauses to evoke a timely emotion, his long arms flail about to emphasise his point or the expanse of his topic, and he paces the platform while his eyes sweep the audience.

Ron is outspoken, willing to face cultural shifts, eager to travel into new worlds, and quick to enter controversy. But when I observe him in public situations with white people of authority through eyes that only a wife can have, I still see his discomfort, his insecurity and his shyness display themselves in his body language, the tilt of his head, the twisting of his shirt sleeve, the shadow across his face.

'I always have to be ready for an argument from them. These fellas always have something to say, something to correct me on,' explained Ron. 'Most of the time they don't want to listen to me or hear anything from my point of view. It's like they think they are always right. You know, this is why in the old days, the blackfellas always sent their women to talk to the whitefella boss. The women wouldn't get as angry. They were better educated, had learned English, ways to talk. But the men, they lost out, and they knew they couldn't win in an argument.'

In the beginning years, these dynamics had lurked in the background of our marriage. My outspokenness created a barrier until I realised that Ron was backing off. As our journey of trust began to grow stronger, those barriers slipped away. While I followed his lead, supported his ministry and talents, he in turn wanted to see me fulfilled in my own life's work. Coming from a career background, feminist leanings, and a desire to make the most of my life, I had clashed head-on with a world where women were not encouraged to excel, not expected to enter academic pursuits, not allowed to preach in churches, and not given open and honest respect as an equal.

Ron was different. He was not threatened by my desires to learn, to pursue yet another university degree, to push the limits of my abilities. In fact, he encouraged them. While we planted churches, counselled families, visited prisons, travelled Australia and overseas, raised a child, comforted the dying, I completed a second master's degree. Most of the time the research papers and essays were pounded out on the computer at midnight, or on the road, but eventually it was finished.

At the same time, Ron encouraged me to accept invitations to speak in churches, retreats for women, cross-cultural gatherings in Singapore and Hawaii. We share the load. I type, he washes the dishes. We help each other to be complete. We are best friends. Sometimes fighting and crying our way through the maze of survival, coping with the social pressures that surround us, but most times laughing with each other and with Lydia, whose Christmas card to us one year, said, 'I love you, my mental Mum and Dad.'

Ron tells story after story to illustrate his point, drawing not only upon Aboriginal vignettes but personal stories of people he has met from around the world, and the historical background of the very place where we happen to be standing at that very moment. When we drive into a town or a region, he walks around its perimeter, talks to the local people, visits the library, and when he finally speaks to the gathered flock, he can tell them more about its history than they know themselves.

When we approach an area where Aboriginal people would have camped or lived a long time ago, Ron walks around the area and announces into the atmosphere that we are there, where we have come from and who we are. 'This is the Aboriginal way,' he explains. 'Not my territory. Another tribe here, so they need to know who I am, who we are. It's not the normal tribal way—to camp on another man's land, unless you're invited.' And on and on, he connects with history from place to place all around Australia.

When Lydia was seven we spent a few weeks in Sydney speaking in a number of churches about Aboriginal Christianity and reconciliation. Ron researched the Aboriginal occupation of that whole area, re-read the exploits of Pemulwuy, the Sydney warrior, and sat for hours outside a church in Frenchs Forest near a wooden cross that was perched high enough on a slope that he could see the flight path of the birds in the distance. I didn't know what was brewing in his mind. Before the evening gathering he disappeared after giving directions for all of us to 'just keep singing' around the cross. The guitar players plucked song after song, asking for favourites, someone saying a prayer during a quiet moment.

I wondered what had happened to Ron. Why was he always late to everything? All of a sudden I heard the drone of a didgeridoo in the background and the murmur of people who were standing at the outer edge of this group of thirty or forty people pressing ever so closely to the vertical wooden beam of the cross. I craned my neck in that direction. I couldn't believe what I saw! Someone was pushing his way through the crowd. It was Ron dancing, corroboree-style, toward the centre.

I could hardly recognise him as he appeared through the crowd, covered in paint, his chest with white lines crossing each other, his face smudged with white, red and gold paint, and a few red tinges in his dark hair. Around his loins was fastened a kangaroo skin and draped over his arm, and onto his chest was a piece of cloth painted by one of our desert friends. Tied around his ankles were small bushes that jerked from side to side as his feet beat the earth. My eyes and my mind absorbed the scene before me, when Lydia, who had been riding piggyback behind me, began to pound my back excitedly, whispering incredulously, 'Is that Dad?'

That was the beginning of an outward journey that matched the changes taking place within my husband's heart, as he took hold of his own identity with pride and respect. At the same time, I was on a journey as well. It was time for me to acknowledge my own identity, to realise that I could never be Aboriginal. I could never appropriate for myself what it meant to be truly Aboriginal. Oh, yes, I could enter in, take part, appreciate, honour, hang paintings on my wall, line my bookshelves with Aboriginal books, help Ron to paint himself, make him a shirt with Aboriginal-designed textiles.

I could even sing his songs, tell stories the way he did, talk blackfella way out in the bush. But I could never really get inside his skin. I had to be able to rejoice in my own skin, my own tribe, while embracing his. When two people, two communities or two nations celebrate their own cultures and identities, then they are liberated to offer them to each other without fear of losing them.

In many ways, both Ron and I straddle two cultures. Ron astounds people with his knowledge of history that he can recite with thrilling ease, with his willingness to cross cultural boundaries and his genuine interest in other cultures of the world, not just in some general, vague sense, but in real people, hearing their dreams, their past, their present. Many years later he will reach into his memory bank and retell their stories almost word for word.

Our visitors gasp in disbelief to see the thousands of books that line our shelves in each room of our house and are jammed into the garage. Aboriginals are generally thought to be modern-day nomads, jumping into their vehicle with a small bag and a blanket, just enough for the journey. In fact, that had been Ron's life at the beginning of his adult years, but somewhere along the line that had changed. His thirst for the historical journeys of the peoples of the world is endless.

We are both voracious readers and book collectors. After leaving my many volumes behind in America, I had a lot of catching up to do after browsing through Ron's collection. My reading ventures took me into biographies, memoirs, character studies and psychology. Much of our conversation is steeped in sharing our individual journeys into other world views and other lives that are contained within the pages of books.

I am constantly evaluating the years I've spent in Australia. I have made many adjustments, not just the outward ones of fitting into a marriage, living with another person and all that entails, and having a child, which certainly changes one's life. The more important and enduring adjustments have been those in my identity. I have been able to understand Ron within the context of Aboriginality, not by exchanging my own culture for his, or by grasping tightly to my own, but by creating enough distance from my own identity and culture to make room for his. That is how we become one without losing ourselves in the process.

The trip to connect with my own family, Lydia's grandparents and cousins, was such a mammoth and expensive undertaking that we had postponed going for a number of years. Finally, I realised that the time had come and we must go. We were going to stay with my Dad for three weeks, the first time since I had been a child. He met us in Tulsa and we drove several hours into Arkansas, where he had retired near the fishing spots where our family had spent our childhood holidays. What an irony to come back to the place where I hadn't wanted to be some forty-five years before! Dad and Ellie had a beautiful home nestled in the Arkansas hills, neat and spotless, surrounded by evergreens, and visited by a number of inquisitive squirrels. Ron walked the streets of their residential estate and met more of the neighbours, sharing with them their own Arkansas history, than Dad had met since moving there a few years before.

My dad and Ron were the odd couple. Dad was a perfectionist, with everything in its place. Order reigned supreme. Ron was laid-back, no worries about the crumbs under his feet or the rings on the coffee table created by the sweat from the coffee cup. Ellie and I just laughed as we watched the comedy before us. A revealing moment of my own past relationship with Dad came one evening as I was clearing the table of the dinner dishes and scraping the remains into the rubbish bin. Ellie happened to be standing in the kitchen chatting away when she saw my hand slip, the plate fall into the bin along with the food scraps, my eyes go wide, look around to see if my dad saw the incident, my hand fly up to my mouth as I uttered, 'Oh, no!', and reached in to quickly retrieve it. My eyes met hers and we both burst out laughing. As we did, the old fears I had seemed to melt away. The shadows of my childhood disappeared as I sat down next to Dad and, chuckling, told him the whole story.

Dad and Lydia became great mates, especially in fishing. I saw myself in her, standing next to him, taking instruction on casting, waiting, watching the line, reeling in at the right moment. The first time Lydia felt a pull, she gave a squeal and tried to bring it in. Ron, sitting next to her, grabbed the rod and took over. My dad, watching from the corner of his eye, scolded him. 'Lydia won't learn unless she does it herself,' he muttered to Ron.

Lydia beamed. That fish got away, but she reeled in three more. My dad's words to her were, 'You have to be able to do it yourself.' The very words he had spoken to me as a child, which at the time had seemed harsh but had proved to be his greatest gift. Before we left, I stood alone with him. At these moments, I don't know what to say. What do I say to someone I love when I live so far away, when life moves so quickly, when I want to somehow make up for a lifetime of misunderstanding, hurt, separation. It's only then that the words 'I love you', spoken so many times in a flip and trivial manner, become real and contain so much more than any other words could say.

Dad hugged me, looked at the tears in my eyes through his own, and said, 'Diana, I'm proud of you.'

Every day those words echo in my heart. Those words which can produce tears at the mere thought of them. After fifty-three years of pursuit, the words I always wanted to hear. Thank you, Dad.

❂ ❂ ❂

I walked slowly along the concrete path to my mother's crypt. Lydia held my hand tightly, not fully understanding where we were going or why, but sensing some of her mother's disquiet. Pat had been given the crypt next to my mother. Bruce, my mother's husband for over twenty years, had remarried his first wife and had donated the crypt to our family after Pat had committed suicide. Now, six years after the second death, I stood on my home ground, before the two other women in my family, forever side by side, whose lives had ended in pain. In some ways I could never fully comprehend what they had experienced, yet in other ways I had walked the same path.

During those years, it had never been far from me, a deep well of emotion that spilled over when I watched a movie about a mother and a daughter, or heard the mention of suicide, or read a book about broken marriages. The painful parts of our journey in life are always with us, bringing us back to reality, to the truth of the human condition, but it's in how long we dwell in that place again that can either bring us down or push us on to better paths.

I gazed at their names printed in brass on the side of the crypt: Jean—Mother, Patricia—Daughter. My fingers touched the metal and traced their names. My eye caught a piece of paper stuck in the permanently attached flower vase. Inside were the words of a granddaughter, first to Jean to thank her for being strong, for looking after her when she was little and alone, for being there when her mother couldn't be. The other letter was for Patricia, thanking her for being her mother, for caring even when she couldn't do anything about it, for suffering and for the good times that her daughter will remember for the rest of her life.

From the pen of a young woman, the second generation of the bearer of pain in the family relationship, a final gift of hope, thanksgiving and redemption. I held onto my ten-year-old Lydia, a girl of strength beyond her years.

'Why are you crying, Mum?' She put her arm around my waist and we walked in step away from the crypt.

'It's okay, sweetheart. One day you'll understand.' We also walked away from the shadow of the Pioneer Woman that stood not far away, the beacon of my girlhood, arm in arm, to a more hopeful future for a mother and a daughter in the land of Australia.

We have a dreaming. I use the word with a small *d*. In some ways the small *d* dreaming is like the big *D* Dreaming in its retelling of the past, which still participates in the present and continues into the future. I have learned more about my own past, the unconscious reality of my heritage, through learning about Ron's. The storehouse of memory and threads of connection through my great-grandparents from Germany, my father's birth in New York City, the beginnings of my days in a colonial house on a hill in Vermont, my moments of reflection at the foot of the Pioneer Woman, my own days traversing the streets of New York City, are still with me. These memory connections are my dreaming, the tributaries of my life, which flowed together to form the main stream of the river. These have joined to Ron's dreaming. His storehouse of being born in the bush, running from the police, confronting the spirits of the land along with the prejudice of its people, surviving on tea, flour and sugar, living with murder and violence, feeling the dust beneath his feet. These all form the river of his life, which still flows through the present and into the future.

Lydia has these dreamings flowing through her which will eventually merge to be her own. The waters will sparkle in the sun, sometimes growing dark under the clouds that float across the horizon. They will forge new pathways and cut through hard soil. The waters will sometimes reflect the images along the bank, but the strength of the river will overcome, its song splashing up along the shore, echoing the words, 'I'm proud of you.'

CHAPTER 18

Reconciliations of the Heart

Artistic expressions of life create a space through which to embrace the other. Out of the hidden valleys and recesses of memory lunge forth the brushstrokes, the melodies, the muscular movements, the frame of the lens, the nouns and the verbs that grab the viewer, enfolding him into the other's territory. Memorials of expression capture our eye throughout the day, the week and the year, adorning spaces that would otherwise be left empty. We do not want them to be empty. Our desk tops are lined with framed images of smiling faces and happy moments, making visual contact with the past. Our walls are not left bare, but are private galleries and reminders of places we would like to be, persons we once were, or signposts of an almost-forgotten journey. Often, silence is not welcomed, but blocked out with voices and melodies that collude with our daydreams, making them seem more real.

We adorn the walls of our lives with expressions that we have already embraced. Somehow they fit with our concept of who we are, give support to the choices we have made, strengthen our dreams. When we walk into someone else's territory we are faced with new expressions, a world not our own, memories that we cannot fully understand. At that moment, we have a choice, for to move toward the other is a risk. Will I be changed by this experience? Will I be challenged by this moment? Even more importantly, do I want to make space in my world for the other?

On the other side of the embrace is the one who waits. The one whose arms are open. The one who offers an expression of his world. The one who plays a tune, paints a journey, or tells a story. We announce that we are here. We whisper softly in the other's ear, knock gently at their door. We are inviting the other to plunge into our world. Our cry is, 'We want you. We want you to understand. We cannot exist by ourselves. I have a space for you here.'

The crucial moment in any act of reconciliation is the moment of waiting. In the context of our marriage, Ron and I created space within ourselves for each other but, at times, we tried to invade each other's boundaries to take control. True embrace is learning to wait for each other. Together we have also learned to wait for the arms of others to open in the integrity of reconciliation.

Underneath a dark grey tent erected in Gnangara Village outside Perth, five years of waiting had ended with the touch of an arm on my shoulders. The Aboriginal preacher shouted out the words of Jesus about forgiveness. 'We need to forgive these whitefellas,' he said. 'It'll free us to go on and not feel sorry for ourselves any longer. If you have been hurt by anyone, come up here for prayer.'

I had stood in my place watching Lydia stack coloured blocks with two other little Noongar kids on the blanket in front of me. Dozens of white plastic chairs covered the dirt floor under the tent, some pushed over when their occupants walked up to the front, wanting to shed their bitterness. I hung my head. I've been hurt by Aboriginal people, I thought. Should I have someone pray for me? I've had to move toward those who spoke against me, who excluded me from their world, who excluded Ron from their world because of our marriage.

In the midst of that reflection, I had felt an arm gently come around my shoulders and draw me toward its owner. 'I'm sorry,' whispered the voice. 'I've been wrong about you. I want you to know that I respect you and love you.' Too shocked to raise my head, I could only glimpse the woman holding me close as one who had ferociously condemned my marriage to Ron five years previously. The boundaries had melted, allowing us to embrace.

We waited for Coral, too. For years, she roamed throughout the Kimberley, into Darwin, and finally landed in Sydney. Sometimes we tracked her down through relatives, sent letters to the general post office, or received reverse charge distress calls on the phone. Twice she appeared in Kalgoorlie, at odds with herself and the world, seeking her own identity. Just before one of those visits, she heard that her brother, the only other one of her family (out of five) to be adopted out, had committed suicide after he had returned to his home country. It was as if part of her had died along with him.

We talked. We suggested. We organised career opportunities in modelling, mining and health. We listened and we waited. She left to find her way in Sydney with her new boyfriend. In 1995, we arranged to meet her at Hyde Park, in the centre of the city. Coral had matured into a beautiful woman. The large, dark eyes and fine, slightly stringy hair of the teenager I had known had changed into half-closed eyelids bordered by thick lashes, and ringlets of thick, black hair cascaded around her shoulders. She was the picture of a model, tall, slim, with a carriage that invited passersby to take a second look. Everything about her produced an impact.

We met her outside the Police Central Station, where she was working as a clerk. When we walked down the cement path near Hyde Park to a coffee shop for lunch, the atmosphere was tense. She didn't want to talk. Ron was oblivious to her attitude and spoke non-stop about our travels, her childhood and plans for the future. She kept glaring at him to be quiet. She never liked her business to be broadcast beyond her own hearing.

As much as I wanted to help, I couldn't. The topics of conversation I proposed were innocuous and bland. All the while, I desired for her to appreciate her family, her own background, and find a centre to her own story. My personal journey had been so similar, but I couldn't say any of that. It wouldn't have mattered anyway. We said goodbye on the steps of the tall buildings in the middle of Sydney and turned to walk away.

Ron walked ahead of me, but a sudden urge caused me to turn around. She was still standing there. I walked back. I reached out to hug her and, for that moment, we embraced and cried together. No words. Just tears. I placed an opal necklace engraved with the letter C in her hands and closed her long, slim fingers over it. 'Never forget who you are,' I whispered. She moved on, her sadness giving way to a moment of hope.

We lost track of Coral for a few years after that, only hearing about her through friends who caught sight of her from time to time in Sydney. Every day she was on our minds when we prayed for our families and friends. All we could do was wait. One day that moment came. I had just turned the key to the front door, trying to make it to the phone that was at least on its eighth ring. Breathlessly, I said hello and after a few seconds silence, I heard, 'Hi, Mum, it's Coral.'

We talked, we cried, we forgave, we shared our honesty together. More conversations followed, many late night phone calls, until some difficult, but stunning words tumbled from Coral's lips. 'Look, Mum, as far as I'm concerned, you're my birth mother.' Now, after a decade and a half, giant steps of healing have taken place. In our Aboriginal family, Lydia has a big sister, I have two daughters and Coral has a mum.

❂ ❂ ❂

Aboriginal people have spent a lot of time waiting. Waiting for recognition, waiting for the embrace, waiting for their story to be heard and their expressions of art to create a space. On one of our trips to Warburton, our friend Arthur and his wife invited us to sit next to them on the ground. He rolled out a large painting, two metres long and one and a half metres wide. The top and bottom edges were attached to two polished dark wooden poles. As his hand slowly, gently and reverently unrolled the canvas, a magnificent blend of dots, circles, and half moons appeared before us in a mixture of colours ranging from the shades of the red earth to the blues and greys of the sky.

'This is our story, Kurta,' he and his wife nodded as they spoke. 'It gives us a history, for our kids, a way to live. We want others to know this too.' His voice told the story while his finger traced its journey along the canvas. It started in the ranges, when the land was plentiful with fruit, berries and emus, and the waterholes were bursting with fresh, cool water.

In the middle of our people's camp, while they were rubbing their spears with emu fat and cooking the golden yoke of the emu egg, a little starving frilled-neck lizard staggered in, his skeleton showing through the skin.

The little lizard had begged for food, but the people turned on him and told him to get lost. They told him that he didn't belong to their tribe. The lizard turned to run away, but before he did, he grabbed a piece of meat from the fire. The people chased him with spears and threatened to kill him.

When the lizard bumped into his uncles, the kangaroo spirits, he told them the whole story. They were furious. 'They have broken the law of the desert,' they said. With that, they caused the forces of nature to swirl into a willy-willy that blew into the camp of the people.

Bush huts were blown over. The sky darkened and pieces of stick were flying everywhere. The elders suddenly realised that they had broken the law of survival. But it was too late.

The wind picked up the people and then scattered them over the landscape. They became like rocks, and every time our people see these rocks, they are sad. They broke the law of sharing.

Arthur and his wife passed this story onto us and with it came the painting, now hanging on our wall, that speaks its message every time I serve a meal around our dining-room table.

I often squatted with the Aboriginal artists gathered around a large stretch of canvas placed on the ground. There were no easels propped up to eye level; rather, the artists worked from an aerial view. Art is a group effort, sitting in the dust of their land, touching the rocks, talking the story as they work. In traditional times, the artist became a part of the painting, 'feeling' the ochre paint by blowing it onto the rock or paperbark with their mouths. They remember the walkabouts, the dancing, the singing, the deaths, the hardship as the patterns emerge. The final canvas is not just an object to hang on the wall waiting to be chosen because the colours blend with the décor, but rather a community biography.

For a people who did not invent an aeroplane or climb the highest peaks to spy out the land in order to conquer the next territory for themselves, their art shows a view only possible from the eyes of a soaring bird or perhaps from the eyes of God. The patterns that rise from the earth to meet the gaze of an aeroplane passenger reveal an incredible mixture of light and shadow, circles and hues, that mirror the patterns that are seen on the canvas of Aboriginal art.

The artists are not painting an object, but their history. The artistic expression is like a book, its pages turning as the story is told, as the social laws and customs are explained, as the spiritual connections are made and where daily survival takes place and is recorded. Rising time and time again from the ashes of the fire, the stories emerge like the legendary phoenix that offers itself as a sacrifice, born in the flames of life only to return again. A new phoenix arises from its ashes, a symbol of resurrection, a new story born from the pages of an old one.

❂ ❂ ❂

Australia's National War Memorial in Canberra is an impressive sight. It stands on a mound of earth with its entrance looking across Lake Burley Griffin to the white façade of the Old Parliament House behind which rise the spires from Capital Hill, as if the two major arms of power, the body politic and the armed forces, are watching each other. A month before Ron and I were married, we had had our photo taken on the steps of the War Memorial on a dreary November day amidst grey skies and a drizzle of rain. Ron had proudly guided me through the large exhibition halls, stopping at significant paintings, relics and monuments to the Anzac glory. He has always been intrigued by war and stories of war, not because he loves to fight, but because he loves the idea of mateship in the trenches, the do-or-die attitude of heroism and the toughness that war represents. Perhaps this intense desire is an echo of moments from his childhood, when he listened to a crackling radio, its sounds of war reports emanating from a bush tent. Or perhaps he recalls the soldiers that his mother would befriend. Or the German man living near them who was found dead in the bush, shot as a spy. His proposal of marriage to me with the words to 'join him as a fellow soldier', his insistence that we walk the roughest roads of life together, echoed his love of military tactics. His favourite films were those that revealed some aspect of the Great War, Vietnam or World War II.

Personally, I don't like stories of war. There are too many memories of my father dressing in his uniform on weekends, of being an army wife during the Vietnam crisis, of watching the demonstrators throughout the United States waving flags and banners on university campuses and being tear-gassed by the police.

None of Ron's immediate family had gone to war, but his large, extended Aboriginal family boasted of men who had either never returned or who had never been recognised for their efforts. Some years ago, Ron began a personal crusade to see that recognition would be given to those who had not only died in battle but also to those who had survived and had been forgotten. He extended his arms to welcome their memory. 'I want to keep their spirit alive,' Ron was fond of saying. 'All the people of Australia need to know how Aboriginals have stood beside them, fought beside them in the trenches, given their lives in so many ways. But they are not even in the history books.'

As we poured through the archives, read scores of articles, and listened to the bushmen as we travelled, we learned that Aboriginal trackers have taught the army how to survive in harsh land; have used their keen eyes and ears to warn of danger in the jungles of Malaysia and Vietnam; have given their skills to train the horses for the Light Horse Cavalry.

On a subsequent visit to Canberra, Ron drove me again to the War Memorial. 'I have something to show you,' he said. We got out of the car in the parking lot at the rear of the building. Ron wouldn't answer my questions as to what we were doing or where we were going as he led me across the street behind the parking lot and through a narrow gate leading to a dirt path that wound its way into the bush.

'You know, when I asked a guide in the museum if there was any memorial or plaque commemorating the contribution that Aboriginal men and women have made to the war efforts, he just scratched his head as he looked at me and said he didn't know. He then asked around and finally someone said that if I follow this path, I would come to it.'

'What!' I burst out. 'There's not even a sign to say that there is anything here!' We turned off the path and walked another hundred metres until we came to a small clearing with a few overhanging trees and a plaque embedded into a medium-size stone. No place to sit, no honour roll of names, no fountain of water for the weary, no garden of flowers, only a few dried wreaths lying in disarray at the foot of the plaque.

'This is it,' Ron said, as he gestured matter-of-factly. 'This is what they've given us. There have been thousands of my people serve in the military, for a country that still doesn't want us, and this is all they've given us.' Ron walked around the rock a few times, obviously upset. 'No one even knew where it was.'

'But it's actually a very pretty spot,' I ventured. 'You know you love the bush. All your people love the bush.' The face of the plaque had a magnificent view of Parliament House. The elevation of the hill was just at the spot where a visitor could sit for hours overlooking the building that contained the highest authority in the land of Australia. What an ironic idea! The remembrance of those Aboriginal people who, of their own free will and love for this land, had fought and died shoulder to shoulder with the Aussie battlers, was set on a slope where it could symbolically oversee the political governing of the country. Perhaps a higher authority was at work!

'What we'd like now is a garden, a memorial garden, and a proper pathway, so people can find this place and quietly remember their fallen heroes.' Ron echoed the sentiments of many Aboriginal men and women who have walked the path to stand in quiet contemplation of the contribution their relatives have made to the country of Australia. 'We fought in those wars overseas, sure. But we fought in one at home too.'

Tens of thousands of Aboriginal people died defending their land from invasion, the invasion from Britain. They were fallen heroes, too. One of Ron's personal, private acts of remembrance was to take several plants to this 'bush memorial', lovingly place them in the soil and say his own private prayers for those who had sacrificed, shedding tears for his own people. The creation of memorials provides a pathway for the memory to shuffle back and forth between the past and the present. The past then erupts in the middle of the present to serve as a beacon of light that illuminates that which was and amends that which is. He was heartbroken to learn that some months later, all the plants had been pulled up and discarded, leaving no remembrance of honour or embrace.

Reconciliations of the heart occur when the story is revealed and understood. They occur when we enter the space that is created by the other, when the book on the past is opened up and we walk into its pages and allow them to penetrate our thinking. In Aboriginal culture the spirit of the old people is kept alive when we talk about them, when we rehearse the dreaming, when we visit the graves, when we walk among the rocks and along the sandy beaches, when we sit by the fireside and tell our children over and over again of their significance.

Long ago in the history of the rebuilding of Jerusalem during the early days of the fifth century BC, Ezra the teacher dusted the years of accumulated forgetfulness from the covers of the Law and read aloud from its pages. The first response from those gathered around him upon hearing of their ancestors' journeys through the wilderness, enemy attacks, and disagreements among themselves was grief. But the leaders were quick to point out the sacredness of the revelations of that moment, the joy of celebrating their story together. There was feasting for eight days.

In the same generation, in another part of the world, in Susa, the capital of Persia, another story was revealed that caused much rejoicing. In fact, it became an important, and still celebrated, feast of the Jewish tradition. The moment was a turning point in their history, where their destruction or continuance as a people was being decided. The decision came because of a chronicle of history that was revealed in the middle of the night. The King of Persia could not sleep; his thoughts were troubled. He had signed an edict to have all Jews obliterated, convinced by others that they were a threat to his kingdom.

The king's servant read to him from the chronicles of his reign. Perhaps at a moment like this, a nation's leader, disturbed in his spirit, is thinking of what he might leave behind as a record of his achievements. Perhaps he is bothered by his own conscience of passing laws that restricted others, or put artificial boundaries around them, or led to their eventual demise. Perhaps, in the midnight hours, away from all the media, the bright lights of leadership, the newspaper headlines, the advice from every expert, he can reflect more clearly on the meaning of his life's work.

It was at this moment that the king heard of Mordecai, a Jew, a man of a different culture, born in a faraway place, who had saved his life and, even more than that, had saved the life of his nation, an act that had been forgotten. Books, songs, and message sticks record for all time what men can often forget. When the king found out that nothing had been done for this man he was beside himself. It reflected on his own honour, his own sense of justice, it was a discredit to his nation that Mordecai had not been honoured for his heroic act. For the king, it was not just a personal tragedy that this man had not been given due honour, but a national tragedy to neglect to honour those who had sacrificed for others.

While the fingertips of the early morning light shone through the palace windows, Xerxes ordered that Mordecai be honoured with the king's own robe and that he be presented to the kingdom as a man worthy of that honour. The king took from his own storehouse to give to a man who had himself given his life for his king and country. It was an act of embrace.

The pages of our own nation's storybook have told me of mercies received from the hands and the feet of Aboriginal people from the earliest days. If I listen carefully enough I can hear the trickling of water rushing underground as the tracker helps me quench my thirst and leads me over the next hill into the interior. If I listen to the sounds in the country, I can hear the snips of the first shearing handpiece, which was invented by an Aboriginal man. If I listen to the sounds of war and guns firing, I can hear the shouts of Aboriginal men fighting alongside other Aussies in the trenches.

If I look carefully enough, I may be able to observe teenaged girls serving meals in station houses on remote, mulga-studded desert land, and young Aboriginal boys shoeing the horses and cleaning up the bunkhouse. If I take a walk through the farming regions, I may catch a glimpse of dark figures bent over, clearing the stumps from the paddocks, picking up dead wool, herding the sheep wherever the boss wants them to go. If I stand up with the cheering crowd at the stadium, I just might see an Aboriginal cricketer, a footballer, or a runner crossing the finishing line.

When we have opened the book and have acknowledged not just the stories of injustices done to Australia's original lovers of its land, but also the stories of the memorable deeds of those who watched as the boats rowed to this country's shore, and when we have then celebrated these deeds, we can truly embrace each other in acts of reconciliation, and make a space in our hearts.

❂ ❂ ❂

In 1996, doors of opportunity opened for me to speak to and teach groups of women not only around Australia, but in Hawaii and Singapore. These women from around the world were leaders in their own developing countries. My first visit to Singapore confronted my personal space in yet a deeper way.

The jumbo jet touched down on the tarmac and taxied along the runway towards the Singapore airport. I gradually became aware of the knot forming inside my stomach. I had been invited to attend a three-week lecture series on Christian leadership in developing countries. After unpacking my bags in my room on the ninth floor and greeting my room-mate from Indonesia, I lingered at the doorway of the lecture room, reading the list of forty-eight women who represented thirty-four nations. From the hum of conversation taking place around me in a variety of accents I heard, 'Well, I feel relieved that none of us has English as a first language.'

'All except for me,' I thought. Suddenly I felt that knot in my stomach again. I was the only western-born person at the conference. English was my mother tongue, and that fact reduced me to a minority. The days wore on. I heard of the difficulties that were starting to raise their ugly heads throughout Indonesia. I talked with my room-mate until the early hours of the morning, hearing the stories of persecution and ethnic hatred. During our meals together, the women shared their experiences of the colonial attitudes of the English and the Americans when they had come to their respective countries to 'civilise' and 'Christianise' the 'natives'. Each day brought more understanding as I was compelled to enter their world, to get beneath their skin. Each day I felt more ashamed that I was a westerner and that my mere presence created such a dichotomy.

Each of us was required to share our country's background, our experience of Christianity, and our own work among our people. These women were lawyers, principals of schools, medical doctors, pastors, lecturers, businesswomen and politicians. I came face to face with a woman who was a member of parliament in Nigeria and another who had organised crisis counselling for the survivors of the Rwandan genocide, which had left thousands upon thousands of children without adult family leadership.

When it came my turn to stand in front of such a group, I felt totally inadequate. How could I look into the faces of such experiences, of living through such pain and contradiction? Whatever I said would seem so shallow compared to these life stories. The night before I was to speak, I tossed, I turned, I struggled. What right did I have to stand before them? Which country would I speak of? America? Australia? Aboriginal groups? I wanted to ask their forgiveness, I wanted to say sorry to them for all that had happened in the past. The heart of humanity is so capable of inflicting wounds on others, no matter what generation, time or place.

I spoke of my journey, beginning in New York City, walking through Harlem, then sleeping in a tent along the creek bed, climbing mountains with Ron, sitting on the ground with the tribal women, brushing the coals away from the damper as I pulled it out of the ground, the birth of our child, the strength of Aboriginal women, and walking with others through their own pain. 'I guess the compelling desire in my life is to see the music, the song, the meaning of another person's life that is trapped inside of them, be released,' was the final sentence as I sat down.

I wasn't prepared for the response. Women from South America, the African nations, India and Pakistan thanked me, shook my hand, grabbed me around the shoulders and called me 'sister'. A bond formed. A bridge had been constructed upon which we all walked toward each other. The African women whispered to me that they had never met an American who had sat on the ground with their people. During the remaining weeks, the women embraced me. We embraced each other.

One night, there was a knocking on my door. 'Can I share something with you, Diana?' said this mother of three from Nigeria. Through tears, she told me of her son's love for a white woman from Canada. He had left Africa to study and had now fallen in love and wanted to marry this woman. She was a stunning woman and, in all respects, a perfect match for her son. But she was white! This mother could not accept that. The family had never thought that this would happen. She had spoken to her son roughly, hinting at the possibility of disowning him for bringing such disgrace upon their family and community.

As she continued to speak, I could feel her struggle, the reasons for her response to her son.

But then she looked into my face. 'What you have said to us, what you have shared about your own life, has made me realise how narrow I have been. If this is meant to be, I need to accept my son and his choice of partner. I just wanted to tell you this, because I rang my son this morning to ask his forgiveness and give my blessing to whatever choice he makes.'

There we were, the two of us, sitting at the foot of my bed, arms around each other, weeping tears of forgiveness, honouring each other's countries and each other's pain. It could only happen after we understood the story.

I came back from Singapore a changed person, having made another step out of my own boundaries. I understood more than ever that the effects of the exclusion of other people around the world and the exclusion of Aboriginal people are still present today. A stone was thrown into the middle of Australia when the First Fleet landed upon the shores of this country, and the ripples still continue to emanate. The ripples that we see and read about today come in the form of imprisonment, broken families, health problems, lack of education, shame, loss, and it goes on and on.

Not long after Lydia was born, my friend Laurel had told me again how she was stuffed in a sugar bag in Leonora so she wouldn't be discovered by the authorities, and how other children were blackened with a bit of burnt charcoal so they wouldn't be removed to a mission. Even though I had heard those stories many times, they took on new meaning when I saw my own child before me. I thought to myself, 'I would fight to the death for her. I would never let anyone take her from me.' Even as I allowed those thoughts to form in my mind, I knew that the Aboriginal mothers had been powerless, and so would I have been powerless at that moment.

The grieving over the loss of a child never ends in a mother's heart. It is never forgotten, or 'over and done with'. As one desert warrior once said to me, 'You'll always have your mother's birthmark. There's always a connection,' as he pointed to his navel. The voice and the eyes of that child live on in a mother's heart and are passed onto the next generations. I saw that happen during a gathering in Albany, Western Australia, where I had been invited to speak for the weekend at a camp retreat for around a hundred women. There were two Aboriginal women among them. I had spent the morning weaving my way through stories of acts of forgiveness, acceptance of one another, personal examples and the words of Jesus. The morning tea break was upon us, but no one seemed to want to move. A few women formed a line to speak to me, to have a prayer offered, to cry a tear or to just stand in silence, working through an unnamed grief. As I looked up from this group, I realised that all the other women had made their way out for a cup of tea, had returned and were sitting quietly in the room. The leader of the camp leaned over to me, and said, 'Continue. Something is happening here.'

What would I say now? Where would I go from here?

One by one, a half a dozen women got up, waited at the microphone and then began to share their experiences of loss of children. One had had a stillborn child thirty years ago, during a time when hospitals would whisk away the small body and bury it in an unknown grave, leaving no space for the mother's grief. Another's child had committed suicide while yet another mother shared of her struggle with her schizophrenic son, who, for all she could do for him, seemed lost. The memories and the voices of those lost ones poured out into the room. Tears were flowing, women put their arms around each other. I got up to stand behind the women at the microphone and, at my feet, I saw a pool of water. Looking around to find the glass that had spilled, I realised there was none. The pool had been made from the tears falling from these women's eyes.

Gently, I spoke into the microphone. 'These stories tell us that, as women, we all live with the incredible pain of losing a child, by whatever means, for the rest of our lives and into the next generations. This is the spear that Aboriginal women have carried in their hearts since the invasion of this country and the consequent decisions of government regarding removal of their children. As we stand here, we now understand, we now have entered into each other's pain, we now hear each other's voices.'

Without another word, ninety-eight women surrounded the two Aboriginal mothers, touching, kneeling, in a moment of a reconciliation of the heart.

❂ ❂ ❂

Aboriginal people have been made fringe dwellers in their own land. They have sat at the edge and watched as the miners dug up the ground that they used to feel beneath their feet, taking away whatever the earth would give up, all in the name of progress and greed and leaving only a film of dust behind when the earth would give no more. The mining companies will come and go, but it is the Aboriginal people who stay, and will always stay, camping in the shadow of the discarded steel frames, iron fittings and lost tools. They will walk their boundaries for generations to come.

They have seen land ownership defined by tribal stories and then family clans supplanted by land ownership defined by pieces of paper that contained no stories or family relationships. They watched as the newcomers beckoned them to come and join them, to wear their clothes, live in their houses, walk their streets, but when they came too close they were pushed away, in trouble for being disadvantaged, taking up too much of the 'budget'. Then they were in trouble for being too privileged: a few dollars extra for education, a two per cent reduction in mortgage interest rates if they were lucky enough to have saved for a deposit, or grants to start their own businesses so they could break the cycle of dependency that was created by the government in the first place.

They have watched as some of their tribe have been 'assimilated', taking on as much as they could of the 'other' culture, only to find they were still not accepted. As these men and women then turned to come back to their tribe, the differences were sometimes too great to be accepted there either. In trying to live between two worlds, it was like they walked the edge of a cliff every day and one wrong move could mean destruction.

They have watched as the good fortunes of the Australian nation have been built upon their own misfortunes. The land has been cleared with Aboriginal hands, the cattle has been herded by Aboriginal stockmen, the remote regions of the continent have been opened up to the explorer using Aboriginal thirst. But once the land was no longer available to them, was no longer felt beneath their feet, they were discarded and made responsible for what had been done to them, labelled as drunk, lazy, irresponsible.

They have watched as organisations were formed to 'protect' them, then to help them become self-sufficient, and to learn the white man's skills. They watched as some token of land was given back to them, on the edges of the town, in the remote regions, in the arid country. They laboured over feasibility studies and financial plans and then gratefully accepted handouts, grants, seed money to open up cultural centres. All the while, the spectre of the white man was standing by their shoulder, watching to catch their mistakes.

They have watched as others continue to steal from them, beginning with their land and their culture, then their children and now their art, their legends, their spirituality and their bush tucker. Putting someone else's name on them, exporting them, packaging them for sale. All done without embracing the people, the ones who made it possible, the ones who lived the real story. They have watched as academics and politicians have visited their communities for a day, a week, even for a few months, and then have walked away, saying, 'Oh, I know what the Aboriginal life is all about.' But they haven't walked barefoot on the red soil; they haven't felt the prickles and thorns pierce their feet; they haven't seen their blood mix with the red earth. 'They don't really know,' whisper the old people.

They have watched as their people have denied their Aboriginality because it meant no job, no house, no future. Then they watched as those same people had to prove their Aboriginality to get help to attend school, to join a sporting team, to get a housing loan. Ron grew up running from the authorities, ashamed of being Aboriginal, listening to the derogatory names, wondering what he had done wrong. Now, as an adult, during our own marriage together, he has had to prove his existence, that he was born, in order to get a passport, to get a house, to get sports funding for our daughter. 'But you can see that I am Aboriginal,' Ron uttered with slight frustration in his voice, as he stood before the desk in a regional ATSIC office on one occasion. The Aboriginal woman at the desk had sighed as she explained, 'I know this is difficult, but we have to do this. You see, we get people from all other dark races, trying to cash in on Aboriginal benefits. So we have to check everyone.'

❂ ❂ ❂

'I hate you,' cried Lydia from behind the locked door of her bedroom. 'I'll never go with you. I'll stay here and get new parents.' Lydia sobbed for hours. I had just confirmed to her that we would be moving from Kalgoorlie in March 1999. We had never planned to leave Kalgoorlie. Even though we were always travelling and most people thought we were never at home, we couldn't imagine another home base. The house, the garden, the garage were all lived in and organised as if we would be there forever. Every plant was lovingly nurtured. Every nail was carefully placed in the wall to hang the works of art in just the right place.

Friends around Australia were always asking us to move. To Alice Springs. To Sydney. To Melbourne. To the Oombalgarri community in the far north. Crocodile country. None of the options had seemed right. Our dream had always been to pass on the baton of leadership to

Aboriginal men and women who had worked with us, lived with us and endured hardship with us. 'Aboriginal people can do it themselves,' we told everyone we met. Now it was time to prove it. Perhaps even our own presence could be a bottleneck, preventing others from taking on responsibilities. But where would we go?

The answer came as a surprise. Early the previous year I had been elected to the national board of our church denomination headquartered in Canberra. This meant that four times a year I would be meeting with seven others to discuss issues of pastoral leadership, missionary endeavour and biblical education. In June of 1998, the topic under the microscope was theological training, its future direction and creative implementation.

Undetected, the threads of our future were being woven together: our readiness for change, the needs of the college in Canberra, the desire to encourage Aboriginal men and women to take the lead. They all met together at the right moment. Within two days, we knew that we were to move to Canberra, the 'bush' capital. Guided by Scripture and his talk with God as always, Ron was definite that this was the right move. 'All my life, I've put my hand to reconciliation, even before it was a word in the news,' explained Ron on the telephone. From Canberra to Kalgoorlie, we made a long-distance decision that would completely change our lives. Not unlike another phone conversation in 1984, when he confirmed his desire to marry me. Now he was challenged and eager to come to Canberra, the scene of his meeting with government in 1972, when they had refused to help the Aboriginal Christian leaders of Australia.

Exciting it was, but traumatic. Lydia's life as she had known it was under threat. Our church members were stunned, the fringe dwellers cried and the prisoners grieved. Gradually we dismantled our home, repainting and preparing to sell the parcel of red dirt that Ron thought he would never own and then later, thought he would never leave. We gave away furniture and tools and began to say our goodbyes, our thoughts turning to the east.

While Lydia began her sixth school year, Ron and I made a quick trip to Canberra, ostensibly to hunt for a house. We didn't have much time. It was almost too much to ask, to find the right house in a matter of three days.

I was looking for comfort and a location near the school Lydia would attend. Ron was looking for a garage for his radio and tape studio and the thousands of photos that he dreamed would one day be stored on video or printed for the world to see. We found it all, a brick and tile home surrounded by tall trees, a small hill rising to touch the sky not far away, a double-size garage with the beginnings of a recording studio in one corner. Ron saw his name on it immediately. Due to a fire only eighteen months before, the interior of the house had been completely redone. This was a package tied up with an elegant ribbon, perhaps a final stop on a journey that, for me, began in a tent beside a creek bed, travelled to a house that had once been a morgue, and had stopped for a while in a memory-making 75-year-old goldfields home before resting here in the southern suburbs of the nation's capital.

At the same hour that we were roaming through the rooms, a young couple was sitting at our kitchen table in Kalgoorlie signing the papers to buy our house. It was meant to be.

We were farewelled in Kalgoorlie and in the bush. Ron's family, more than eighty of them, gathered at Bremer Bay, alongside Uncle Barney's old cabin. Ron filled a bottle of red dirt from the goldfields. My workmates from the schools and the counselling clinic toasted my future at one of Kalgoorlie's elegant restaurants. Lydia's school friends made a huge card honouring her friendliness and her spirit of reconciliation. Each goodbye made it all the harder to leave.

I moved around the church after the kangaroo stew had been eaten and the cups of tea were being served. It was difficult to look into the faces of my friends. I didn't know how to tell them of the many lessons they had taught me. I sat next to Noelene, her head down, eyes covered with a tissue. She reached out for my hand. The words spilled out along with the tears. 'I'm really gonna miss you. You have always listened. Who's going to listen to us now?'

If I had ever wanted to achieve anything, it was that. To have been able to honour another by listening to them, by sitting with them, even in the creek beds. Michelle, my protégé, leaned across, crying into my shoulder, shaking. 'You've been like a mother to me.'

These were the moments I wanted to capture, full of grief, but so precious, moments of connecting in ways that had never been evident before. It was difficult to absorb. I hadn't known that this was how they felt. I must have look puzzled as my wise friend, elder in the church and co-pastor with Ron, approached me to shake my hand. His eyes twinkled and his mouth took on a slight grin through his white, bushy beard. 'You've learned to read between the lines, Diana.' That's what it's all about, reading between the lines.

Our white Toyota personnel carrier, pulling a loaded trailer, made its way along the Eyre Highway, heading east across the Nullabor Plain. The silence inside was deafening. Each of us was in a different stage of grief over leaving our home, our friends and our work. The atmosphere was full of colliding memories, each competing for a place of prominence. Lydia's brow would knit together in a frown every time I looked at her, while Ron was concentrating on his driving. I slid a pillow behind my back, one elbow leaning against the door, my chin cupped into my left hand, and stared down the grey bitumen toward the horizon, saying my silent goodbyes to ten years of life. I would miss the counselling team, whom I had worked with for almost three years. I worried about the men and women who had allowed me to enter into their memories of pain in order to help through their journey of healing. Who would pick up the journey from here?

Lydia started to cry in the back seat, alternately sniffling and then complaining. No place would ever be like Kalgoorlie, there would never be any friends like those in Kalgoorlie, there would not be any family on the road up ahead. She clung to Soxy, our little furry companion, and eventually fell asleep with him curled up, nestled against her chest. Ron and I then began to talk of the future, of what challenges would await us in Canberra.

Our smooth sailing down the Nullabor came to an abrupt stop somewhere between Norseman and Balladonia. The rain had begun to pelt down, and we found ourselves stuck behind a long line of cars and huge trucks waiting to go through an area of roadworks. The Eyre Highway was being widened at that point and there was a muddy sidetrack for a detour. Because of the rain the traffic was backed up in both directions, graders were moving back and forth, lights flashing, signals beeping as the gear shifts were thrown into reverse. Before we left I had given up the idea that we would camp in swags along the roads from Kalgoorlie to Canberra. Not with a car crammed with our most precious possessions and a trailer fully packed with keyboard, computer, boxes of tools, kitchenware and clothes. No, I had planned to take advantage of the motels, something we rarely did on our travels. As we sat waiting behind this line of cars straining to move ahead, I realised that we might not make Balladonia before the motel manager closed the shop door, flipped the sign to read 'Closed' and sought out his own bed for the night.

We managed to pull in, car and trailer covered in mud, just in time to hear a television still going in the small apartment next to the shop. The manager graciously gave us the key to a room and, as we sank down into the bed and stretched our cramped, tired bodies their full length, Ron whispered as he fell asleep, 'Well, there's no turning back now.'

Three days after turning the key in the lock of our new home in Canberra, a huge moving truck rumbled across our lawn at seven-thirty in the morning, just as I was preparing Lydia's lunch for her first day at her new school. She wasn't very happy, but rather nervous, sad and fearful all at the same time as she approached this new chapter in her life. I finally packed her off to her class and then joined Ron to help supervise the placement of all our possessions.

'Do you have any furniture in here?' asked one of the movers incredulously. For several hours they had been unloading box after box, which was to be stacked into our oversized garage, all labelled for teaching, recording or just 'books'. I chuckled to myself as I realised that most of what we owned had to do with our work. Eventually, some lounge chairs, a table and a bed appeared, and we began to make ourselves a home.

It took Lydia six months to be able to answer the question that was often put to her, 'How do you like Canberra?', with a mumbled, 'It's okay.' The first week she cried when she came home from school because the girls in her class only talked about boys at lunchtime. Lydia wanted to play soccer or football and was desperate to find another tomboy. The year-six camp helped to break the ice, especially since Ron went along and showed the students some bush tucker, played the gum leaf, gave them tapping sticks to paint and told stories during the evening hours. Lydia joined the school band, able to play her favourite instrument, the drums, and entered all the sporting events possible.

Canberra is known as the sporting centre of the nation, home of the Australian Institute of Sports. The club teams, the development squads and the pathway for young future Olympians are fairly well planned out in this community. Ron and I knew that Lydia had some ability in soccer and basketball, as well as in other areas, and we wanted the best opportunities for her. I know that it would be tempting for me to put all my own dreams and visions onto her and, perhaps unconsciously, try to live my own life through her. We both have to guard against that, but at the same time to support in every way possible her own dreams and visions. Ron's desire is for her to be proud of her Aboriginal heritage, to achieve all that she can and to be part of forging the way ahead for other Aboriginal young people. Some years ago, as Lydia shook hands with Cathy Freeman in Kalgoorlie, Ron had whispered in her ear, 'You can be like her one day.'

Lydia tried out for the position of goalie on a first-division girls' soccer team. There she was, with her slim, almost fragile body, and thin legs that drew the description of 'emu legs' from her teachers, diving, catching, sliding, and blocking like an AFL footy player, reminiscent of her days in the desert. The coaches couldn't believe it. She was in.

Trophies and medals line our shelves, accolades Lydia has received for being runner-up player of the tournament for Kanga Cup, best team player, a member of the ACT primary school team, which travelled to Adelaide, a member of the under-14 women's development squad and a member of the state indoor soccer team, which competed in the national tournament in Canberra. Lydia not only represents her school, her team, her community, and her state, she also represents Aboriginal children, who can be the best they can be as long as the opportunities are provided to nurture their talents.

When we had announced our move to Canberra to various friends and family, almost everyone thought that I would handle the change quite well, but Ron would find city life and leaving his people more difficult. Actually, it has been the other way around. It was easier for me to shift from New York City to a tent in the bush than it has been to come from the bush back into a city, even one of only 350,000 people. Ron knows all the neighbours and the shopkeepers, walks to the top of Monash Hill almost every day to look out over the valley and breathe in the bush, and visits the Aboriginal community groups several times a week. His voice comes over the radio every week with his own program, and his call for reconciliation, as lived out in real life, echoes in the speeches he makes in schools, churches and community gatherings.

It's been harder for me to make the shift since I stand with a foot in both cultures, handling the administration part of our marriage and work together. While Ron moves spontaneously through life, I make lists that somehow serve to bring some organisation to it all. Moving from the laid-back attitude in the Aboriginal community and bush living to the more rigorous demands of structured city life, lecturing in a college, travelling on speaking tours and facing Lydia's approaching teenage years at my age has been more of a cultural change for me than for Ron.

'When are you going to stop travelling, Mum?' asks Lydia, when I tell her about the next flight I'm taking to speak at a weekend retreat somewhere in Australia or to give a lecture series in Singapore or Hawaii. 'Where's Dad going now?' she asks again, when Ron packs his bag for a training seminar in Perth, or Kalgoorlie, or a reconciliation gathering at Uluru, the spiritual heart of the nation. 'Where are we driving to now?' her eyes silently ask, as the three of us pack the car for the World Christian Gathering of Indigenous People in Sydney, an exciting opportunity to hear native drum beats, Maori haka, see cultural dances and listen to similar stories of struggle for survival, searching for identity, and walking toward reconciliation from over thirty tribes.

Only the scenery from our front window has changed. There are still many more miles to travel.

✵ ✵ ✵

'There's just one more mountain to climb,' said Ron one day as we sat at the breakfast table together.

'Oh, no,' I retorted. 'I'm not climbing any more mountains. Those days are over.' But somehow I knew that eventually I would give in.

Mount Kosciusko, the highest mountain in Australia, named after a soldier from Poland who fought in the Revolutionary War in America and helped to fortify and defend West Point, which became the foremost military training college in the country. A man who became a United States citizen and a Brigadier-General. That was the mountain we would climb.

'But it won't stop there, Ron,' I kept talking. 'It's like when you preach. You always have just one more story. Several times over.' I chuckled to myself as I thought of the many times a family preparing for a funeral had approached me, or a pastor of a church where Ron would preach whispered in my ear. Both requests were the same. Please tell Ron not to speak so long. Ron had been known to speak for three hours. He had been known to keep people standing at the graveside for over an hour in the sun. The requests were always kind, and he was always invited back, but Ron's name and the length of his sermons were synonymous.

One more mountain, I thought. It's a good thing that there's a chairlift and a walkway to climb the highest peak. The Snowy Mountain area around Thredbo had been home to a variety of Aboriginal tribes who searched out bogong moths for delicate eating at feasts. There were stories of ceremonies and initiations in the mountainous region.

On top of the mountain I could look toward the west and see, in my mind, our footprints coming from that direction. The footprints began with two people, somewhat parallel, one pair sometimes lagging behind the other, one barefoot, the other one with shoes. The whistling of the gentle wind coming from the cave near the top of Mount Margaret in Western Australia blew over the footprints and I could see that they were getting closer together. Somewhere along the track the shoes had been tossed aside while the barefoot pair had suddenly pulled on boots. All along the path, the footprints came closer and closer to each other, sometimes both with bare feet, and other times both with shoes.

The horizon has always held the human gaze. It is defined scientifically as the outer limit of mental perception; I find that the higher I climb, the further I can see. Our footprints have led us toward the horizon, where the sky meets the ground, toward the vanishing point where all parallel lines seem to meet. Our own attitudes and identities have been shaken, strengthened, then shaken again. My love for Ron and his ways has grown incredibly. Ron has had to work through many years of being excluded by white people, even those whom he has respected and worked with. Many times our clashes came from triggers out of the past within our own cultures and ways of relating to the world around us. His love for me has deepened and his understanding that whitefellas have problems too has helped us to journey together, sharing our hurts and cherishing our joys.

During this journey, my understanding of the roots of this country and the dreaming of the land has enriched my life and given me wisdom I would never have achieved otherwise. Many of my family and friends have commented on how much I had given up to become part of a dislocated people, to suffer along with them, to live within the parameters of the social problems and constant pain. But I have never thought of that decision as giving up anything, but rather a privilege. From the first glimpse of the red earth, through the years of travel and living with a man born in the bush by the side of a lake, I have grown to be a part of this land. As Ron and I have struggled to see eye to eye and to understand each other's ways, we have also joined hands with thousands of others around this country who are also struggling to know one another, to learn from one another, and to walk together.

The journey toward the horizon has helped me to appreciate my American homeland and its struggles, to understand the past and accept it with wisdom, to accept and cherish my mother's strength, and my father's dreams. The journey has helped me to identify with my sister's pain, the loss of her children, her final decision to cut her life short. The journey has helped me to love and accept my brother and long for his well-being. The journey has mixed together the soil of the Oklahoma plains, the concrete of New York City, the red dirt of the Australian desert, the sands of the coastline and the jagged rocks of the outback in the heart of this American–Aussie citizen.

Throughout the years of living in Australia, and being married to the Aboriginal community, I have seen many changes. More Aboriginal voices on the wind, more listening ears, more pride in identity. But I have also heard the same stories repeated over and over again, of unresolved anger, violence toward one another, anti-Aboriginal slogans painted on fences, derogatory comments in the media that resonate with Dampier's demeaning description of Aboriginal people from two centuries past. It's still a long way to the horizon, that place of balance.

'It's time,' an artist friend once said to us as we watched him paint his story on a didgeridoo. 'It's time to throw our colours to the sea.' He did just that. A man who had lived a hard life, who almost lost his wife and family, who didn't see any hope for his future. A man who one day heard a voice whisper into his ear: 'Throw your colours to the sea, and see what happens.' Colin 'threw' his colours and now he is an artist, giving his gift to the world, telling others to throw their gifts to the sea and see them return in abundance.

There are no regrets. Only thankfulness. Thankfulness to our God for His sense of humour in bringing us together, for pointing us toward the horizon, the circular horizon which He drew 'on the face of the waters, as the boundary of light and darkness'.

Standing on the top of the highest peak in Australia, Ron nudged me. 'I have this vision,' he said. 'So many of my people think that Jesus is just for the white people. They don't see that he is for everyone. I see him as a desert warrior, with one foot on Uluru, the spiritual heart of the nation, and the other foot on Canberra, its political heart. And the spear is in his side. He has taken the spear for all of us, black and white. He's taken the pain so we can walk on together.' Ron smiled and looked into my eyes. 'If you had it to do over again, would you still marry me?'

I slipped my arm through his and laughed. 'I'm still here, aren't I?'

The footprints that lay behind me walked over rocks, down through gullies, across many corrugations and through thickets of prickles and thorns. My feet have often bled as we walked over the earth. But along the way, we have also experienced times of touching heaven, many joys have unfolded and songs have been sung as we have journeyed toward the balance at the horizon of our marriage. The land we have walked upon is the link between the joy of heaven and the pain of earth. This land is sacred and the song-line is its history. From the edge of Skull Creek to the top of Australia there have been many song-lines to hear, many stories to live.

I turned and grabbed Lydia's hand and Ron's as we started down from Mount Kosciusko, toward another horizon, before we heard 'just one more story'.